Beyond Free and Fair

Beyond Free and Fair

Monitoring Elections and Building Democracy

Eric C. Bjornlund

Woodrow Wilson Center Press
Washington, D.C.

The Johns Hopkins University Press
Baltimore and London

EDITORIAL OFFICES

Woodrow Wilson Center Press
Woodrow Wilson International Center for Scholars
One Woodrow Wilson Plaza
1300 Pennsylvania Avenue, N.W.
Washington, D.C. 20004-3027
Telephone: 202-691-4010
www.wilsoncenter.org

ORDER FROM

The Johns Hopkins University Press
Hampden Station
P.O. Box 50370
Baltimore, Maryland 21211
Telephone: 1-800-537-5487
www.press.jhu.edu/books

2 4 6 8 9 7 5 3 1

Library of Congress Cataloging-in-Publication Data

Bjornlund, Eric C.
    Beyond free and fair : monitoring elections and building democracy / Eric C. Bjornlund
        p.   cm.
    Includes bibliographical references and index.
    ISBN 0-8018-8048-3 (cloth : alk. paper) — ISBN 0-8018-8050-5 (pbk. : alk. paper)
    1. Election monitoring.   I. Title.
    JF1001.B483 2004
    324.6′5—dc22

                                                                                2004011949

ABOUT THE CENTER

The Center is the living memorial of the United States of America to the nation's twenty-eighth president, Woodrow Wilson. Congress established the Woodrow Wilson Center in 1968 as an international institute for advanced study, "symbolizing and strengthening the fruitful relationship between the world of learning and the world of public affairs." The Center opened in 1970 under its own board of trustees.

In all its activities the Woodrow Wilson Center is a nonprofit, nonpartisan organization, supported financially by annual appropriations from the Congress, and by the contributions of foundations, corporations, and individuals. Conclusions or opinions expressed in Center publications and programs are those of the authors and speakers and do not necessarily reflect the views of the Center staff, fellows, trustees, advisory groups, or any individuals or organizations that provide financial support to the Center.

For Gina

Contents

Part II. International Election Monitoring

Part III. Domestic Election Monitoring

Part IV. Toward More Meaningful
International Election Monitoring

Tables

Foreword

"The world must be made safe for democracy." Those were the words of President Woodrow Wilson on the eve of America's involvement in World War I. Indeed, American foreign policy has always favored democracy on both practical and moral reasoning. Practically, it is better to see disputes settled in parliaments or ballot boxes than battlefields. Democracies are not captive to the impulses of a dictator, and are more versed in peaceful debate, commerce, and diplomacy. Morally, Americans have always believed in the political, economic, religious, and artistic freedoms that allow individuals to thrive. It was these rights that Wilson had in mind when he declared: "We shall be satisfied when those rights have been made as secure as the faith and the freedom of nations can make them."

Thus Americans before and after Wilson have cloaked themselves in the rhetoric of democracy. Today, many in Washington herald democratic development as the silver bullet in winning the war on terrorism. But what do we mean when we advocate for democracy abroad? After all, democracies are complex and multifaceted. A mature democracy must include strong political institutions; the rule of law enforced by a judiciary; some form of market economy; a free press; the participation of women and minorities; and the development of civil society. Only these institutions can provide safeguards against abuse, corruption, and repression, while giving people a means to address differences peacefully. Achieving this is difficult work.

Oftentimes the casting of a ballot is the first step down this complicated road. In the last two decades, the international community has embraced elections and election monitoring as a practical means of promoting and advancing democracy. Elections are not the end of the road—indeed, many a tyrannical regime has embraced "elections" to achieve the appearance of popular legitimacy. But free and fair elections can and do present an essential opening for broader change. Indeed, for many societies, a free and fair election provides the bridge from repression to freedom, and election monitoring helps countries succeed in crossing that bridge.

In this important book, Eric Bjornlund traces the evolution of international and domestic election monitoring. He draws on his own broad experience, access to key players, and extensive review of publicly available and unpublished materials to get at key questions about the effectiveness of foreign aid, technical assistance, and the sustainability of democratic reform. And he shows how election monitoring evolved from modest roots in the 1980s to become the international community's most established and high-profile action in support of democracy around the world.

Just as democracy cannot be imposed at the tip of a gun, it cannot be imposed through the monitoring of an election. Ultimately, countries must build and embrace their own systems. But as this book demonstrates, significant lessons can be learned about effective collaboration between established and emerging democracies in holding elections and moving forward. The international community, nongovernmental organizations, and even concerned individuals can bring expertise to bear, and send a message of international concern and solidarity as countries grapple with new freedoms and responsibilities. Often, this assistance can make the critical difference between the success or failure of an emerging democracy.

Making the world safe for democracy has proven to be long and difficult work. But Wilson's message still sounds prophetic some eighty-five years later: "A steadfast concert for peace can never be maintained except by a partnership of democratic nations." It cannot, and the democratic nations of the world have a responsibility and an interest in aiding the spread of peace and freedom. This book sheds light on the patient work of many individuals and institutions in both the developed and the developing world—activists and diplomats, academics and politicians—all of whom struggle out of sight to move the world closer to Wilson's vision. In its own way, this narrative contributes to the ever-growing dialogue of democracy and momentum of freedom.

Lee H. Hamilton
President and Director
Woodrow Wilson International
Center for Scholars

Acknowledgments

This project was a long time coming, and in many ways I have drawn on ideas and insights from literally hundreds of people I have met in a decade and a half of work in more than twenty-five countries. Many of them have been democracy activists from around the world who have inspired me with their own courage, passion, and creativity. Others have been dedicated government officials and politicians. Still others have been policymakers, aid officials, diplomats, and democracy professionals from the United States, Europe, Asia, Canada, Australia, and elsewhere. I have been fortunate to rub elbows with so many important, talented, and creative people, and I could not help but to have gathered at least some good ideas along the way. I cannot begin to name all of the individuals who have influenced my thinking, given me information, and taught me things that have formed the foundation of this book.

The Woodrow Wilson International Center for Scholars provided me a fellowship to support the research and writing of this book. For fifteen months at the Wilson Center, I found a wonderfully supportive, engaging intellectual community, and a perfect environment for figuring out how to approach this self-assigned project, and I am enormously grateful for the opportunity. A grant from the U.S. Institute of Peace provided important additional support. Both the Wilson Center and the U.S. Institute of Peace deserve credit for their willingness to consider supporting essentially scholarly projects conducted by nontraditional scholars. It is important for practitioners, policymakers, and activists to find opportunities to analyze and reflect on the real-world problems they know so well.

I am lucky as well to have had the opportunity to spend more than a decade at the National Democratic Institute for International Affairs, an organization that has always been a magnet for committed and creative people. I am proud to have been a part of the effort to build the institute and of what it has contributed to the fundamentally important cause of democracy in the world.

I am deeply indebted to the many people who helped me realize my goal of writing this book. My sister Lydia Bjornlund, an outstanding professional writer and editor, edited a number of chapters and offered excellent advice from a lay perspective. Glenn Cowan, who has been a wonderful professional colleague, reviewed chapters and offered a number of fundamental insights and invaluable comments. Blair King and Peter Lewis read the entire manuscript and offered many thoughtful, helpful suggestions. Thomas Carothers, David Carroll, Brian Katulis, Eric Kessler, Thomas Melia, Ned McMahon, Peter Manikas, Gerald Mitchell, Robert Pastor, Sophie Richardson, and David Yang all read one or more chapters at various stages and offered perceptive comments. Joel Barkan, Britta Bjornlund, Horacio Boneo, Shari Bryan, Sean Carroll, Chuck Costello, Bob Dahl, Melissa Estok, Jennifer Ganem, the late Mike Jendrzejczyk, Omar Kader, Richard Klein, Lawrence Lachmansingh, Rodd McGibbon, Sarah Mendelson, Vladimir Solinari, David Timberman, Jim Vermillion, Alan Wall, and Jennifer Windsor provided invaluable help with my research. Kostya Churmasov offered fresh perspective and generously helped me through the many technological challenges of research and writing.

I wish as well to thank President Jimmy Carter for taking the time to talk to me about his experiences with election monitoring and for continuing to inspire so many of us all over the world. Others who also readily met with me and offered a great deal of information and insight include Reginald Austin of the International Institute for Democracy and Electoral Assistance, Hrair Balian of the Organization for Security and Cooperation in Europe, Steven Griner of the Organization of American States, Carina Perelli of the United Nations, Mark Stevens of various European Union observation missions, and Dennis Wendel of the U.S. Agency for International Development. Among the many friends and colleagues who shared information or insights with me were Eva Galabru, Hadar Gumay, Rustam Ibrahim, Feroz Hassan, Koul Panha, Lao Mong Hay, Todung Mulya Lubis, Goenawan Mohammad, Smita Notosusanto, Mariano Quesada, and Thun Saray. Others in Indonesia, Cambodia, the Philippines, Bangladesh, the West Bank and Gaza, Zambia, Macedonia, and elsewhere—whose election processes provide material for case studies and examples in the book—are too numerous to name or would prefer it that way.

At the Wilson Center, Bob Hathaway made me part of his Asia team and reviewed an early version of several chapters. Frew Hailu, then a graduate student at Howard University, and Ed Aparis, a student at the University of California, Riverside, provided first-rate research assistance. Lindsay Collins helped me make the most of my time at the Center. Joe Brinley and Millie Kahn of the Wilson Center Press gave me valuable advice and helped steer me through the publishing process.

While my delightful kids, Marit, Elsa, and Tiger, are still a bit young to comment on drafts or help with research, they have supported me unfailingly with their remarkable interest in my subject and my work. I appreciate as well the many other family members, friends, and neighbors who have talked about this project over many months.

My wife, Gina Giere Bjornlund, used her finely honed professional research skills to help me run down all kinds of obscure documents and information and advised me on difficult questions of judgment and interpretation. More important, she cleared a path to make this personal journey possible and, even though she must have wondered at times, never questioned the value of the enterprise. For that alone, the effort has been well worth it.

Acronyms and Abbreviations

ANFREL   Asian Network for Free Elections
BAFE   Bulgarian Association for Free Elections
BMNA   Bangladesh Movement for Free Elections
       (Bangladesh Mukto Nirbachan Andolan)
CCHRB   Coordinating Council for Human Rights in
       Bangladesh
CEPPS   Consortium on Elections and Political Processes
       Support
CeSID   Center for Free Elections and Democracy
       (Yugoslavia)
CETRO   Centre for Electoral Reform (Indonesia)
CIVITAS   Crusade for Democracy (Chile)
COFFEL   Coalition for Free and Fair Elections (Cambodia)
COMFREL   Committee for Free and Fair Elections (Cambodia)
CSCE   Conference on Security and Cooperation in Europe
EAB   Elections Assistance Bureau (Guyana)
EAD   Electoral Assistance Division (UN)
EMO   election monitoring organization
EU   European Union
FEMA   Fair Election Monitoring Alliance (Bangladesh)
FUNCINPEC   National United Front for an Independent, Neutral,
       Peaceful and Cooperative Cambodia
GERDDES   Groupe d'Etudes et de Recherces sur la Democratie
       et le Développement Economique et Social, or
       Study and Research Group on Democracy and
       Economic and Social Development (West Africa)

GONG	Citizens Organized to Monitor Elections (Croatia)
ICCPR	International Covenant on Civil and Political Rights
IFES	International Foundation for Election Systems
International IDEA	International Institute for Democracy and Electoral Assistance
IRI	International Republican Institute
JAMPPI	Community Network of Indonesian Election Monitors (Jaringan Masyarakat Pemantau Pemilu) (Indonesia)
JIOG	Joint International Observer Group
JOMC	Joint Operations and Media Center (Indonesia)
JPPR	People's Network for Political Education (Jaringan Pendidikan Politik untuk Rakyat) (Indonesia)
KIPP	Independent Election Monitoring Committee (Komisi Independen Pemantau Pemilu) (Indonesia)
KPU	General Election Commission (Komisi Pemilihan Umum) (Indonesia)
LADO	League for the Defense of Human Rights (Romania)
MDC	Movement for Democratic Change (Zimbabwe)
NAMFREL	National Citizens' Movement for Free Elections (Philippines)
NCFE	National Committee for Free Elections (Yemen)
NDI	National Democratic Institute for International Affairs
NED	National Endowment for Democracy
NEPAD	New Partnership for Africa's Development
NGO	nongovernmental organization
NGOCC	NGO Coordinating Committee (Cambodia)
NICFEC	Neutral, Impartial Committee for Free Elections (Cambodia)
ODIHR	Office for Democratic Institutions and Human Rights (OSCE)
OAS	Organization of American States
OAU	Organization of African Unity
OSCE	Organization for Security and Cooperation in Europe

Panwas	Election Oversight Committee (Panitia Pengawasan Pemilu) (Indonesia)
PDI	Indonesian Democratic Party
PVT	parallel vote tabulation
SAARC	South Asian Association for Regional Cooperation
SADC	Southern African Development Community
SBSI	Indonesian Prosperous Trade Union (Serikat Buruh Sejahtera Indonesia)
TMG	Transition Monitoring Group (Nigeria)
UNDP	United Nations Development Program
UNFREL	University Network for Free Elections (Indonesia)
UNTAC	UN Transitional Authority in Cambodia
UNTAG	UN Transition Assistance Group (Namibia)
USAID	U.S. Agency for International Development
WAHLI	Indonesian Forum for the Environment (Wahana Lingkungan Hidup Indonesia)
YAPPIKA	Indonesian Foundation for the Strengthening of Indonesian Community Participation, Initiative, and Partnership (Yayasan Penguatan Partisipasi, Inisiatif dan Kemitraan Masyarakat)
ZANU-PF	Zimbabwe African National Union–Patriotic Front
ZEMCC	Zambia Elections Monitoring Coordinating Committee
ZIMT	Zambia Independent Monitoring Team

Part I

Democracy Promotion, Elections, and Election Monitoring

Chapter 1

The Emergence of Election Monitoring

If we were invited to go into a foreign country to monitor the election and they had similar election standards and procedures [as did Florida], we would refuse to participate at all.

—International election observer and former U.S. president Jimmy Carter.[1]

In November 2000, the U.S. presidential election between George W. Bush and Al Gore ended in a virtual tie. Though Gore narrowly won the nationwide popular vote, the outcome of the election turned on which candidate had won the twenty-five electoral votes in Florida, where the initial count had given Bush an edge of a few hundred votes out of 6 million cast. But it quickly became clear that arthritic voting technology, sloppy voter registration, and partisan election officials had seriously damaged the credibility of the process. After five weeks of legal battles and partial recounts, a sharply divided U.S. Supreme Court decided that there could be no further recounts, thus awarding the presidency to Bush. Ironically, during the thirty-five days between election day on November 7, 2000, and the Supreme Court's decision on December 12, 2000, American observers or United States–supported domestic monitors were present for seven other elections around the world.[2]

In light of this kind of American involvement in overseas elections, many around the world found irony, if not evidence of hypocrisy, in the troubled American election. Beijing's semiofficial *China Daily* commented, "It is clear that the U.S. electoral system is not as fair and perfect as the country boasts." Said Theo Sambuaga, of Indonesia's Golkar Party, "The idea of democracy is not discredited. What is discredited is the American political

3

system." Singapore's *Straits Times* charged the American election "made the U.S. look like a banana republic."[3] Under the front-page headline "Forrest Chumps," the British tabloid *Mirror* joked, "This election's like a box of chocolates. You never know what you're going to get."[4]

Many such comments revealed considerable sensitivities to American election monitoring. Cuban foreign minister Felipe Perez Roque commented, for example, "I believe that those in the United States who have always tried to become judges of the elections that take place elsewhere must be receiving a lesson of modesty and humbleness." Roque questioned whether in the future "it would be necessary to have a more rigorous or strict international scrutiny regarding the transparency of elections."[5] Suggested Malaysian trade minister Rafidah Aziz, "Maybe we, all developing countries, should send an election watch every time they have a presidential election."[6]

The U.S. presidential election in 2000, indeed, was a fiasco that plainly failed to meet now widely accepted international norms for democratic elections. Had there been international election observers applying the same standards as in dozens of developing countries in recent years, they would have concluded that the 2000 presidential election in Florida, and perhaps several other U.S. states, was fundamentally flawed.

First, international election observers and advisers in developing countries routinely call for the establishment of independent electoral authorities, separate from the government or political parties, to oversee election administration and the interpretation and implementation of applicable election laws. Former U.S. president Jimmy Carter's statement in the Dominican Republic in 1990 declared, for example, "The consolidation of democracy requires that the institutions that manage the electoral process be independent, competent, and perceived as completely fair by all the candidates and parties participating in the process."[7] In the United States, in contrast, local political officials run elections at the state and local level.

International election observers would also find fault with any election in which the principal election official was active at the same time in the campaign of one candidate, especially if that official had discretion to interpret the election law in a way that would favor that candidate. Yet even though she was state chair of George W. Bush's presidential campaign, Florida secretary of state Katherine Harris was charged with responsibility for making critical judgment calls about how to interpret an ambiguous and internally inconsistent election law. Election officials in Florida's sixty-seven counties who decided whether to conduct recounts and oversaw the review of ballots were themselves local party officials, led by active Democrats in several of the larger counties with the most serious controversies.

After conducting hearings about the election in Florida, the U.S. Civil Rights Commission issued a report not unlike those made by international election observers in countries without a history of democratic elections. The commission charged that "injustice, ineptitude and inefficiency" had disenfranchised a large number of minority voters. The process of voter registration was flawed, for example, as Republican state officials systematically purged voter rolls of individuals suspected of being former convicted felons and therefore ineligible to vote under state law. Many were removed in error, including a large number of blacks. "Florida's overzealous efforts to purge voters from the rolls, under the guise of an antifraud campaign, resulted in the inexcusable and patently unjust removal of disproportionate numbers of African American voters," concluded the commission.[8]

International election observers would also have faulted an election process that failed to count large numbers of ballots, as was the case in some counties in Florida as well as other places in the United States. Precincts with large minority populations were particularly likely to have older, more mistake-prone election equipment. According to the Civil Rights Commission, African American voters were nearly ten times more likely than white voters to have their ballots rejected, and black voters had a higher rejection rate even in counties where the voting systems were the same. Though they constituted just 11 percent of the state's voters, blacks had cast 54 percent of the ballots rejected as improperly marked.[9]

In emerging democracies, international observers often urge changes in election procedures because of the risk of voter confusion. Such a recommendation certainly would have been appropriate in Palm Beach County, where the infamous "butterfly ballot" was designed so poorly that it evidently confused many voters. In addition to being unfair, the ballot arrangement evidently failed to comply with state law, both because it failed as required to list the names of candidates in one column on the left and because it listed third-party candidate Patrick Buchanan before Democratic Party nominee Gore in violation of the requirement that candidates be listed in the order their parties finished in the last state election for governor.[10]

In short, international observers would criticize any system, like the one in Florida, that left election administration, counting standards, and ballot design to local discretion. That the exercise of this discretion evidently disproportionately affected a particular minority group is even more troubling.

Nor were Florida's problems unique. Similar flaws were evident in Illinois, New Mexico, Oregon, and other states.

Lax processes for the administration of elections have survived in the United States because candidates and the public generally have had confidence in the integrity of elections and the impartiality of those administering them. In transitional or postconflict countries, the lack of such confidence often threatens the chances for fair elections and the consolidation of democracy. The bitter partisan disputes about the balloting and counting in Florida in 2000 mean that such confidence can no longer be presumed in the United States either.

The divisive controversies about the process and outcome of the 2000 U.S. presidential election are a stark reminder that, as it preaches to the rest of the world, the United States should not be too arrogant about its own democracy. In addition to election administration, many other American institutional arrangements might not be good models for new and emerging democracies. Many political scientists argue the merits, for example, of parliamentary systems of government and proportional representation elections over the American system of presidential government and first-past-the-post, district-based elections. Moreover, the American system of funding politics and campaigns is highly flawed, as special interests provide the bulk of funds for exceedingly expensive campaigns, particularly for national office.

The flawed American election in 2000 reminds us that there is nothing inherently superior about the American political system that itself justifies extensive American involvement in democracy promotion and election monitoring abroad. Yet while the reminder that U.S. elections are far from perfect provided something of a distraction and a reality check for American democracy builders, it has not had a significant effect on American democracy assistance abroad. American democracy-promotion organizations and aid officials have long recognized idiosyncrasies and shortcomings, as well as the strengths, of the U.S. system and generally look as well to diverse models from democratic countries around the world. American democracy assistance does not depend on a belief in the superiority of American or Western institutions but on the universality of democratic values.

Democracy Promotion and Election Monitoring

The world has witnessed a dramatic expansion of democracy in recent decades. The "third wave" of democratic transitions, as eminent political scientist Samuel Huntington named it, began in the 1970s in Southern Europe and spread in the 1980s to Latin America and parts of Asia.[11] Democracy expanded through Eastern and Central Europe after the fall of the Berlin Wall in 1989 and continued after the breakup of the Soviet Union. The 1990s also saw dramatic political openings in Africa, Asia, and elsewhere. Eighty-one countries have taken significant steps toward democracy since 1980. Fifty-seven percent of the world's population now lives under democratic regimes, up from 38 percent in 1985, and 140 of the world's nearly 200 countries hold multiparty elections.[12]

Along with this expansion of democracy, the past two decades have brought important, practical initiatives in diplomacy, foreign aid, and technical assistance to support the development of democracy and effective governance. Democracy promotion has ridden the Third Wave. Today, throughout the world, American, European, and multilateral organizations advise political parties, aid government agencies, train judges, establish nongovernmental organizations, conduct civic education campaigns, and help develop new election laws and constitutions. High-profile figures, such as Jimmy Carter, monitor transitional elections and report their findings to national and international audiences. Though the growth of international democracy promotion has been perhaps as much an effect as a cause of democratic transitions, such assistance efforts have nonetheless reinforced the global trend. In some cases, the impact of outside democracy assistance has been considerable. For better or worse, democracy-promotion programs are now well entrenched on the international scene.

The dramatic global expansion of democracy and democracy promotion has led to an extraordinary focus on one democratic institution in particular: elections. In dozens of countries around the world, elections have been expected to initiate or consolidate transitions to democracy or to help resolve long-standing conflicts. Elections have played a major role in the democratic transitions of the past two decades, and fair elections have become an increasingly critical requirement for governments to have international legitimacy. The end of the Cold War removed the justification for American support for certain authoritarian regimes and facilitated an international consensus about the importance of genuine elections and international action to help bring them about.

As much as any political institution or event, elections capture international attention. News about elections in far-flung lands—especially transitional elections in which struggling democrats challenge entrenched, autocratic regimes or elections that mark the end of conflicts—captivates international audiences. The international media routinely report the conclusions of election observers, and makers of foreign policy and the public in the United States and Europe react strongly to election fraud or the refusal of losing autocrats to accept election results.

Elections often provide important opportunities to force political change. In 2000, for example, repressive regimes in Yugoslavia and Peru fell under the weight of domestic and international pressure after they attempted to manipulate national elections. Not long ago, such forthright external pressure for fair elections and democratic change was unheard of.

As part of this attention to elections, the extent and influence of election monitoring, by both international and domestic organizations, has exploded. Since the late 1980s, election monitoring has been a growth industry. There has been a dramatic increase in resources available from foreign assistance budgets for monitoring and otherwise supporting important elections in developing countries. Election monitoring has evolved from an ad hoc activity of largely American and European nongovernmental organizations and Western election experts, politicians, and academics into a routine, institutionalized function of multilateral organizations and professionals.

International election monitoring has grown dramatically for a number of reasons. First, the increasing international emphasis on democratic rights in the wake of the Cold War has made democratic elections a precondition for international political legitimacy. This has created a market for credible outside validation of elections in new and emerging democracies. Second, much as the waning of colonialism led to the establishment of new states during the 1960s and 1970s, the 1990s saw new states emerge from the breakup of larger multinational states, including the former Soviet Union and the former Yugoslavia. Emerging out of conflict or authoritarianism, these states typically sought international help with elections to constitute legitimate governments. Third, opposition forces contesting transitional or postconflict elections have often called for international monitoring because they believe that such monitoring will prevent electoral authorities or ruling parties from committing fraud. Because they do not trust that their rights will be protected or that the rules will be fair, opposition forces generally value a disinterested judgment on the legitimacy and fairness of the process. Fourth, many existing regimes have sought international monitoring to reinforce their legitimacy. In short, no longer is election monitoring solely an unofficial response to exceptional circumstances.

As the demand and resources for international election monitoring have grown, so has its influence. Makers of foreign policy, journalists, and scholars rely on the assessments of international observers. Election contestants and domestic political actors often expect international observers to deter fraud, "level the playing field," and guarantee the integrity of the process. It is common for aggrieved parties to take their complaints directly to international observers, who have no formal or legal role in the process, rather than to the proper local authorities.

Beginning with the experience of the Philippines in the mid-1980s, the world has witnessed a related trend: National civic organizations and citizen networks across the globe have mobilized to monitor watershed elections in their own countries. Though the international community has now generally recognized how domestic election monitoring can deter fraud, improve confidence, and increase transparency, some international observers still view domestic monitors warily. More fundamentally, international donors and advisers have yet to appreciate fully how such monitoring can also spur democracy by energizing civic organizations and drawing people into public affairs.

Election monitoring is perhaps the most visible form of the broader phenomenon of democracy promotion. Yet the story of election monitoring—where it came from and how it is practiced today—remains largely unknown or misunderstood, even by many policymakers, foreign aid professionals, and practitioners in the field. This book tells that story in an effort to increase understanding among consumers of election-monitoring reports, improve election-monitoring programs, and provide some broader insight into modern foreign assistance policies and practices.

Why Study Election Monitoring and Democracy Promotion?

Democracy promotion is not the same as democratization. Democratization refers to the process of democratic change or the political transition toward democracy. The study of democracy and democratization has long been an important field of comparative politics and has attracted extensive scholarship. In contrast, the terms "democracy assistance," "democracy promotion," "democratic development assistance," and even "nation building" refer to conscious, practical international efforts to encourage, support, or influence democratic change and political reform in other countries. There has been relatively little study or serious analysis of democracy assistance—the burgeoning field of international efforts to catalyze or encourage democratic change in other societies.[13]

One notable exception is Thomas Carothers's influential study of American democracy-assistance programs: *Aiding Democracy Abroad: The Learning Curve*. On the basis of case studies of four countries that have yet to make a fully successful transition to democracy, Carothers concludes that democracy promotion is moderately worthwhile but rarely makes a critical difference. Carothers expresses skepticism about many of the more grandiose claims made for the accomplishments of programs and criticizes the "often over-bearing, self-congratulatory style of American democracy promoters." But he also concludes that "many democracy promoters are learning as they go along."[14] Though it has made an extremely important contribution, *The Learning Curve* focuses primarily on Washington foreign assistance policymaking rather than on assessing how or whether particular types of democratic development programs work.[15]

This book is an effort to improve the understanding and analysis of democracy promotion among policymakers, program implementers, and scholars by reviewing the experiences of "democracy promoters" in the specific subfield of election monitoring. It analyzes the impetus and evolution of election monitoring and considers the state of the art after the first fifteen years. It is narrower than *The Learning Curve* because it is more focused on detailed, programmatic questions involving just election monitoring; but it is also broader because it incorporates greater consideration of the performance of European and multilateral organizations. Although the ambitious agenda for democracy assistance extends well beyond elections, election monitoring is a crucial component of American and international support for the development of democratic institutions.

The contributions and limitations of international and domestic election monitoring merit this close study for a number of reasons. The international monitoring of elections has become an important phenomenon in the post–Cold War world. As one of the older forms of democracy assistance, election monitoring is now well accepted and extremely common around the world. Since about 1990, as foreign aid for democracy and governance programs has grown significantly, programs to support democratic elections, including international and domestic election monitoring, have claimed a considerable share of that funding. Election monitoring also tends to be high profile; it is the best-known type of international democracy promotion. And election monitoring continues to be influential in the making of American and European foreign policy and the workings of the international system.

Moreover, journalists, diplomats, aid officials, and national political elites often rely on the assessments of election observers without really understanding their methods, interests, or capabilities. A deeper understanding of such issues can help them judge the professionalism and credibility of observer groups and to make better use of their findings.

In this book, I also argue that despite the large amounts of money directed to domestic monitoring groups, there is an unfortunate tendency to ignore—or even hamper—their efforts. Even as the international community begins to recognize the value of domestic monitoring, it needs to make sure its programs do not inadvertently hinder the long-term benefits of empowering civil society in emerging democracies. Because the accomplishments, challenges, and problems of election monitoring are typical of democratic development programs in general, a careful evaluation of foreign support for domestic monitoring can illuminate some broader strategic questions about foreign aid, such as how to ensure that assistance contributes to meaningful, sustainable change.

Although the promotion of the idea of democracy has been a theme of American foreign policy for many decades and the democratic ideal increasingly colored the international system in the second half of the twentieth century, the notion that outsiders can provide specific, technical assistance to encourage democratic development is still relatively new. Even today, for many developed-country governments and intergovernmental organizations, democracy promotion takes place principally through diplomacy and rhetoric. The United Nations Development Program's *Human Development Report 2002,* for example, breaks important new ground in arguing for the intrinsic and instrumental value of democracy to human and economic development, but it says virtually nothing about how international aid providers can help build democratic institutions, practices, or values. The emerging consensus on the legitimacy of democracy promotion and the increasingly widespread practice of democracy assistance have not led to a clearer understanding of how assistance programs can or should work.

The details of democracy-assistance programs are still the sole domain of the experts, and there is surprisingly little effort outside the democracy-assistance community to address how and whether particular programs work. Efforts to assess democratic development programs more systematically or objectively remain poorly conceived. The U.S. Agency for International Development, for example, has spent considerable energy on largely futile efforts to find quantitative "indicators" that would serve as reasonable proxies for democratic progress.[16]

Because aid agencies have yet to develop reliable assessment methodologies and many lessons from experience remain unexamined or unchallenged outside the democracy-assistance field, new entrants to the business must relearn old lessons and poor programs are as likely to be continued as good ones. Practitioners have captured relatively few of their more important insights in writing, and many "lessons learned" documents are more rhetorical than realistic. The American democracy-promotion organizations are almost entirely activist or implementing ones rather than think tanks or research organizations. They generally have an interest in continuing their own foreign-aid-supported programs, which means they have little incentive to critique their own programs or those of their fellow travelers. Those organizations and individuals that have learned from experience as they have invented this new field through trial and error have little opportunity or incentive to reflect on or share lessons learned.

Flaws in Current International Practice

Like other types of democracy aid, election monitoring and other international assistance to elections can make a modest but nevertheless meaningful contribution to democratic transitions. In politically uncertain environments, monitoring by international and national groups can contribute to public confidence in the integrity of elections by encouraging fairer electoral rules, better campaign practices, and a more informed electorate. By increasing transparency, it also deters fraud and helps reduce irregularities in the election administration. Election monitoring also can provide meaningful moral support to democratic activists or opposition political leaders facing authoritarian regimes, and it educates audiences around the world about the struggle for democracy in particular countries. International and domestic election monitoring has, on balance, improved understanding of democratic elections in international relations and foreign assistance policy.

Paradoxically, however, significant problems with the standard international approach to elections and election monitoring threaten long-term democratization, for five basic reasons. First, too much is expected of elections and election monitoring. The international community often expects elections to spur the process of nation building after violent conflict, as in Angola and Bosnia in the 1990s and now in Afghanistan and Iraq. Diplomats and national political leaders sometimes look to elections to resolve political crises, as in Venezuela in 2002. The international community often makes apparently unrelated diplomatic goals—such as the restoration of foreign aid programs after coups, improved bilateral relations with authoritarian governments, or admission to intergovernmental organizations—contingent on the holding of acceptable elections.

Second, although it has improved substantially over time, the current methodology remains flawed. Despite the growing recognition that elections are broad political processes that unfold over time, international actors still place too much emphasis on election mechanics and election day itself. Thus, international observation can be dangerously superficial. The standard methodology has proved unable to cope with well-administered elections that take place with unfair rules or in highly flawed environments, as in Cambodia in 1998.

Third, monitoring organizations and observation missions often reflect interests and objectives other than democratization. The mandates, interests, and constraints of monitoring groups tend to reflect the national interests of sponsoring countries. Diplomats and donor government officials often refrain from forthright criticisms and, consciously or subconsciously, balance economic, trade, security, and other national interests and foreign policy goals against democratization. Intergovernmental organizations, which now routinely organize election-monitoring efforts, also pursue multiple objectives and often find it extremely difficult to publicly criticize member governments. Some nongovernmental monitoring efforts lack professionalism, betray biases, or do not have legitimacy in the eyes of some audiences. Former president Carter himself has expressed concern about "a disparity in the basic philosophy and basic rules and operation procedures of different kinds of monitors."[17]

Fourth, whereas monitoring by domestic groups, rather than by foreigners, has the most potential to make a significant, sustainable contribution to democratic transitions, high-profile international observation teams still attract much of the available funding and news coverage. Foreign assistance to domestic monitoring has increased dramatically, but much of it is misdirected and fails to take full advantage of the opportunities that domestic election monitoring provides to help democratic activists build sustainable civic organizations and political networks.

Fifth, to avoid doing harm to the credibility of election monitoring and the larger cause of democratization, election assessments must be honest and must apply consistent standards. Judging elections in new or emerging democracies in superficial or relative terms emboldens authoritarian governments, betrays courageous local democrats, and breeds cynicism both within and beyond the country involved. In recent years, the international community has developed a reasonably consistent response to governments that come to power through coups (albeit with exceptions, as after the 1999 coup in Pakistan). But the world community has yet to develop an effective approach for dealing with governments that claim or maintain power based on fraudulent or manipulated elections.

To retain their integrity, assessments of election monitors should be kept separate from questions about the international consequences of stolen elections. That an authoritarian leader retains power after a flawed election, as in Belarus in 2001, may disappoint the international community and set back the prospects for a democratic transition, but it is not necessarily a failure of election monitoring, as long as monitors have accurately reported what happened in the elections. Election monitoring is not, and should not be, responsible for bringing about appropriate sanctions or consequences for flawed elections, but only for providing an honest, comprehensive, public assessment, thereby ensuring that political leaders cannot claim political legitimacy from elections that fail to meet international democratic standards.

In short, election monitoring, both domestic and international, can contribute to democratization but can also be counterproductive. Unreasonable expectations burden many transitional or postconflict elections. The standard methodology has had trouble keeping up with the challenges. Inconsistent responses to antidemocratic forces in different countries and parts of the world, especially because of countervailing security or economic interests, raise questions about the motives of democracy-exporting countries and risk provoking nationalist backlashes. The failure to appreciate and appropriately support domestic democratic activists leads to unintended consequences. A focus on form rather than substance and a failure to adhere to universal standards encourage Potemkin village democracies, as authoritarian governments pretend to hold real elections to please donors or others in the international community. Yet, if properly conceived and implemented, comprehensive international and domestic election monitoring not only provides an objective assessment of a given country's electoral process but can also promote the integrity of the elections and related institutions, build public confidence and participation in the electoral process, and complement and encourage domestic engagement in democratic politics.

Plan of the Book

This book draws on the experiences of election-monitoring organizations since the mid-1980s to consider the value and role of international and domestic election monitoring and its contribution to democracy promotion and democratic change. The book provides an overview of the origins, practice, and state of the art of election monitoring. I draw on election-monitoring experience, including case studies that demonstrate the profound challenges that persist, as well as on my own experience in the field. I also build on the few previous efforts to synthesize guidelines and lessons learned. The book proposes normative conclusions and makes practical recommendations about how election monitoring should evolve in the future if it is to continue to contribute to genuine democratization.

To understand election monitoring, it is necessary to understand the larger historical and political movement of which it is part. Therefore, after the broad introduction of this chapter, part I of the book continues with chapter 2, which puts election monitoring in context by providing an overview of the historical roots of democracy promotion and the emergence of the still-new field of democracy assistance. I consider the American democracy-promotion impulse, the modern universal consensus on democratic values, and the complex array of international organizations and efforts involved in democracy assistance. Next, because of the unique U.S. role in the field, the chapter describes the broad variety of democracy-assistance programs supported by the U.S. government and assesses the posture of recent American administrations toward democracy promotion. I consider the emergence of democracy assistance as a distinct form of foreign aid and distinguish this from more traditional democracy promotion through political rhetoric and diplomacy.

Having considered the broader topic of democracy promotion in chapter 2, part I concludes with chapter 3, which discusses the importance of elections and election monitoring and defines important concepts and terms. First, the chapter addresses the subject of elections themselves. Even while acknowledging that emphasis on elections is sometimes misplaced, I argue that international attention to democratic elections is entirely justifiable. The chapter distinguishes categories of elections to narrow the focus to elections most worthy of, and most likely to attract, international interest. Next, I turn to the topic of election observation and election monitoring. I consider the authority and acceptability of international election observers and review broad concepts and types of election monitoring. In addition to reviewing the distinctions among observation, monitoring, and supervision and between international and domestic election monitoring, I attempt to move toward a better definition of international election observation than has previously been proposed. Finally, to justify further the book's attention on election monitoring, the chapter reviews the broad extent of election monitoring around the world since the period 1989–90. I summarize and draw observations from a comprehensive new database I have compiled about election monitoring in ninety-four newly democratic and semiauthoritarian countries.

Part II of the book describes and assesses specifically international (as opposed to domestic) election observation and election monitoring. Chapters 4 through 9 review and offer lessons from the experiences of observer efforts organized in recent years by a diverse set of actors, including governments, intergovernmental organizations, and international or transnational nongovernmental groups.

Specifically, chapters 4 and 5 are about who is involved in election observation. Chapter 4 describes and compares the approach of a diverse range of international actors that support and monitor elections in democratizing countries, from the United Nations to regional multilateral organizations to government-supported international nongovernmental organizations. Though multilateral organizations—which have institutionalized election monitoring—have broad legitimacy, nongovernmental organizations are less burdened by diplomatic constraints and objectives other than democratization. Next, because former U.S. president Jimmy Carter has become an icon of and a principal influence on international election observation, chapter 5 traces the evolution of his involvement in foreign elections since 1989 and considers how his emphases on preelection assessments, "election mediation," and "parallel vote tabulations" to deter or detect vote-count fraud have profoundly influenced the practice of international election monitoring. In addition to published and unpublished accounts of relevant events, I draw on my own experience working with President Carter in three countries over the course of a decade and a recent interview with him. Much like the rest of the book, my objective is both to provide a historical account and to offer lessons for future programs and policy.

Chapters 6 and 7 synthesize norms and best practices. In chapter 6, I consider the exceedingly difficult question of international standards by which to evaluate elections per se, including the difficult question of whether an election can or should be judged "free and fair." I also consider the preconditions for election observation; in some circumstances, international organizations should decline to observe in the first place. Chapter 7 reviews and critiques the state of the art of modern international election monitoring, including standards of conduct for observers, shortcomings and best practices of the current monitoring methodology, and forms and limitations of coordination among disparate international actors. I argue for professional election-monitoring organizations to further revise their approach.

The next two chapters use case studies of recent notorious elections to examine the challenges to modern election monitoring. Chapter 8 uses the unhappy experience of international election monitoring in Cambodia in

1998 and 2002 to consider limitations and unintended consequences of observing elections that take place in flawed political environments. Many commentators and policymakers have the impression that election observation in Cambodia in 1998 was somehow wanting, but the real lessons of the experience remain largely unappreciated; the 2002 experience demonstrates that subsequent practice has scarcely improved. The Cambodian case reveals the shortcomings of standard election-monitoring methodology, including an excessive focus on election day, a lack of postelection monitoring and follow-up, and a failure of election observer delegations to build on preelection findings. I also discuss how the differing agendas and approaches of diverse types of international actors contributed to divisions within the international community about how to approach difficult elections. Drawing in part on my own experience, I reveal new details and offer a fresh analysis about how observers in Cambodia went astray.

Having addressed in the Cambodia chapter the fundamental challenge of manipulation of *elections,* especially before election day, I move in chapter 9 to the separate problem of host-government manipulation of *election observation.* The chapter uses the experience of elections in Zimbabwe in 2000 and 2002 to address how the international community has responded inadequately not only to flawed elections but also to host-government interference in the monitoring process itself. Left unchecked, this kind of interference threatens the fundamental credibility and effectiveness of international election monitoring.

Part III of the book addresses the separate but equally important phenomenon of nonpartisan domestic election monitoring. Chapter 10 describes the historical emergence of domestic election monitoring, beginning with the seminal work of the National Citizens' Movement for Free Elections (NAMFREL) in the Philippines. Building on NAMFREL's experience, nonpartisan domestic election-monitoring organizations emerged in the late 1980s and early 1990s in every other region of the world and succeeded in catalyzing democratic change and providing momentum to the global struggle for democracy. In the course of this discussion, drawing in part on my own experience working with more than a dozen domestic election-monitoring organizations, I explain how domestic election monitors committed to a professional approach can make critical contributions to the important goal of better elections by deterring or exposing fraud and building public confidence. This is the first contribution of domestic election monitoring.

Chapter 11 considers burgeoning foreign assistance to nonpartisan domestic election monitoring, including inherent trade-offs between objectives that are largely unappreciated. Even more important than improving particular elections, I argue, domestic election monitoring can also encourage citizen involvement in politics, empower civic organizations in public affairs, and build new political networks committed to democratic politics. This is a second, more subtle but potentially more profound contribution of domestic election monitoring. Conventional foreign assistance programs generally fail to take account of how this second set of goals should affect strategies for support of elections and election monitoring.

In chapter 12, again drawing on personal experience, I analyze how foreign advisers and donors supported domestic election monitoring for crucial transitional elections in Indonesia in 1999 as a means of further examining issues raised in the previous chapter. International donors and advisers generously and appropriately supported the efforts of national election-monitoring organizations to improve the quality of the election process by, for example, educating voters and mobilizing pollwatchers. At the same time, however, they largely failed to recognize another important purpose of their support for domestic election monitoring: using the elections as a catalyst to the ongoing process of building democratic practices and institutions.

Chapter 13 reviews and assesses vote-count verification techniques, including statistically based parallel vote tabulations, quick counts, exit polls, and comprehensive counts. Using case studies from Macedonia and Indonesia, I argue that quick counts or parallel vote tabulations based on statistically significant samples are generally more reliable and appropriate in transitional and postconflict elections than exit polls or comprehensive tabulations. The complex details of these exercises are important for two reasons. First, they demonstrate the disarray within the democracy-promotion community when it comes to the often critical question of how best to verify the accuracy and integrity of the vote count. Rather than building confidence in critically important transitional elections, donor-supported efforts to collect and report election results quickly or to test the accuracy of the official count sometimes sow additional confusion about the complicated, controversial vote-counting process. Second, as I explain, these experiences raise troubling questions about competition among international donors and advisers working with domestic organizations.

Although international and domestic election monitoring, like democracy assistance more generally, can claim numerous successes, from the Philippines in 1986 to Peru in 2000, this book focuses primarily on several experiences that were less successful. As chapter 14, which constitutes part IV, summarizes, international election monitoring misses its mark when it neglects to provide an honest, complete account of how a broad election process measures up against established international standards. Domestic monitoring fails to contribute to genuine democratization when it focuses, to the exclusion of other objectives, on mobilizing large numbers of poll-watchers and collecting information about election day, especially when such information is largely for the benefit of international audiences. A review of these lessons can help improve future assistance and thus make a more significant contribution to the cause of democracy in the world.

Election monitoring, like other forms of democracy assistance, need not be merely superficial or symbolic. It can contribute to genuine, concrete improvements in elections and meaningful, sustainable political development. But if such efforts are to avoid contributing to cynicism in the international community and among citizens in authoritarian and semiauthoritarian countries, donors, diplomats, and the democracy-building community will have to review their objectives and refine their techniques.

Chapter 2

The Expansion of Democracy and Democracy Promotion

Among the great variety of developments that have occurred in the twentieth century, I did not, ultimately, have any difficulty in choosing one as the preeminent
development of the period: the rise of democracy. . . . In the distant future, when
people look back at what happened in [the twentieth] century, they will find it difficult not to accord primacy to the emergence of democracy as the preeminently
acceptable form of governance.

—Nobel Prize winner Amartya Sen[1]

From the time of President Woodrow Wilson's World War I crusade to
"make the world safe for democracy," Americans have largely shared an ideological commitment to advancing the cause of democracy and freedom in
the world. The United States fought fascism in World War II in the name of
freedom and spent billions after the war to help Japan and Germany build
democratic governments. U.S. leaders defended American resistance to
Soviet communism during the Cold War as a struggle for human rights
abroad. In the 1960s, President John Kennedy's Alliance for Progress
sought to contribute to the democratization as well as the development of
Latin America. In the late 1970s, President Jimmy Carter raised the profile
of human rights in American foreign policy, and in the 1980s President
Ronald Reagan opposed Soviet communism in the name of democracy. One
scholar has aptly called the spread of democracy the "central ambition of
American foreign policy during the twentieth century."[2]

Generations of Americans have seen their democracy as a model for the
world. President Abraham Lincoln said that the Declaration of Independence gave liberty "not alone to the people of this country, but hope to the
world for all future time." In 1977, President Carter declared, "I like to try

20

to make other people realize that our system works." Recalling John Winthrop's hope for the Massachusetts Bay Colony in 1630, President Reagan many times argued that America was a "shining city on a hill."[3]

Although not all American ideals are shared everywhere, the United Nations and other international organizations founded after World War II made a strong commitment to democracy as a universal value. The Universal Declaration of Human Rights, adopted by the UN General Assembly in 1948, calls for a full range of democratic rights, including freedom of expression, association, and assembly and "periodic and genuine elections." It warns that states can limit individual rights and freedoms only in a manner consistent with a "democratic society." The 1948 Charter of the Organization of American States (OAS) declares as one of the organization's essential purposes "to promote and consolidate representative democracy." The 1949 Statute of the Council of Europe makes democracy a central goal and calls individual freedom, political liberty, and the rule of law "principles which form the basis of all genuine democracies." The UN Declaration on the Granting of Independence to Colonial Countries and Peoples in 1960 reaffirmed the right to self-determination.[4]

With the waning of the Cold War, international institutions renewed and expanded their commitments not only to democratic values but also to international engagement to support democracy. Beginning in 1988, the UN General Assembly made its support for democracy promotion increasingly explicit and unqualified in a series of resolutions on "Efforts of Governments to Promote or Consolidate New or Restored Democracies" and "Enhancing the Effectiveness of the Principle of Periodic and Genuine Elections." Meeting in Copenhagen in 1990, the Conference on Security and Cooperation in Europe made far-reaching commitments to democracy in its member countries in Europe, Eurasia, and North America. In 1991 in Santiago, the OAS General Assembly adopted Resolution 1080 on "representative democracy," which calls for an automatic response in the event of an interruption of the democratic process in a member state. In Harare in the same year, the Commonwealth heads of government (mostly from former British colonies) promised to work "with renewed vigor" to promote democracy and human rights. The 1992 Treaty of the European Union establishes an objective to "develop and consolidate democracy." In fact, some scholars see the right to vote in multiparty elections emerging as a "democratic entitlement" in international law. In 1999, the UN Commission on Human Rights unanimously adopted a resolution titled "Promoting the Right to Democracy."[5]

The new millennium has provided further evidence of a democracy as an entitlement. The UN Millennium Declaration strongly reaffirmed the world community's commitment to democracy. The 2001 Inter-American Democratic Charter of the OAS declares, "The peoples of the Americas have a right to democracy and their governments have an obligation to promote and defend it." The new African Union established in 2002 declared its commitment to the "promotion of democracy and its core values."[6]

International practice undeniably has raised democracy above all other political systems. As Amartya Sen argues, "While democracy is not yet universally practiced, nor indeed uniformly accepted, in the general climate of world opinion, democratic governance has now achieved the status of being taken to be generally right."[7]

In addition to recognizing democracy's intrinsic value, world opinion also now views democracy, good governance, and the rule of law as instrumental to economic and human development. The 1993 Vienna Declaration and Program of Action of the World Conference on Human Rights stated, "Democracy, development and respect for human rights and fundamental freedoms are interdependent and mutually reinforcing." Meeting in Warsaw in 2000, 106 countries working toward a world Community of Democracies recognized the "mutually-reinforcing benefits the democratic process offers to achieving sustained economic growth." In its *Human Development Report 2002,* the United Nations Development Program argues, "Effective governance is central to human development, and lasting solutions need to . . . be firmly grounded in democratic politics." As the U.S. State Department summarizes the argument that democracy contributes to other goals, "Democratically governed nations are more likely to secure the peace, deter aggression, expand open markets, promote economic development, protect American citizens, combat international terrorism and crime, uphold human and worker rights, avoid humanitarian crises and refugee flows, improve the global environment, and protect human health."[8]

A consensus has grown as well that considerations of national sovereignty should not shelter a society's political arrangements from outside criticism. Not only is democracy a universal aspiration, but the international community also has a legitimate interest in trying to bring about democracy everywhere. Though there are practical and legal limits on outside intervention where it is unwelcome, universal norms now demand countries to accept considerable engagement in their political arrangements from the outside world.

In the 2000 Warsaw Declaration of the Community of Democracies, the participating countries affirmed not only their common commitment to "core democratic principles" but also, more significantly, their "determination to work together to promote and strengthen democracy." Promising "to promote government-to-government and people-to-people linkages and promote civic education and literacy, including education for democracy," the participants pledged to "strengthen democratic institutions and practices and support the diffusion of democratic norms and values." They pledged as well to "work with relevant institutions and international organizations, civil society and governments to coordinate support for new and emerging democratic societies." They promised also to "collaborate on democracy-related issues" to "help to create an external environment conducive to democratic development." A follow-up conference in February 2001 declared that "[democratic] crises include not only coups but also fraudulent elections and the erosion of rights."[9]

Similarly, in the UN Millennium Declaration in September 2000, the world's political leaders reaffirmed commitments to international standards and pledged to "spare no effort to promote democracy and strengthen the rule of law." They resolved to "strengthen the capacity of all our countries to implement the principles and practices of democracy."[10] This important international declaration, like many others, again endorsed not only the ideal of democracy but also the idea of concrete international action to bring it about.

The Emergence of Democracy Assistance in the United States

Although rhetoric about spreading democracy goes back to Woodrow Wilson and before, since the 1980s the United States has dramatically expanded and institutionalized its efforts to promote democracy around the world. Under both Republican and Democratic administrations, the United States has made democracy promotion an explicit goal of American foreign policy and, more important, a significant and growing part of American foreign assistance.

In the 1980s, the United States began to focus and institutionalize its efforts to promote democracy abroad. To counter communism during the Cold War, President Reagan, supported by organized labor and congressional leaders from both parties, initiated the modern American democracy-promotion movement. In a famous speech to the British House of Commons in 1982, in which he attacked the Soviet Union as an "evil empire," Reagan proposed that the United States "foster the infrastructure of democracy" abroad and endorsed a bipartisan study "to determine how the United States can best contribute as a nation to the global campaign for democracy now gathering force."[11] The following year, Congress established the National Endowment for Democracy (NED), which supports overseas groups and channels funding to democracy-promotion institutes established by the AFL-CIO, the U.S. Chamber of Commerce, and the U.S. Republican and Democratic Parties. Often referred to as the NED's "core grantees," these institutes are currently called, respectively, the American Center for International Labor Solidarity, the Center for International Private Enterprise, the International Republican Institute (IRI), and the National Democratic Institute for International Affairs (NDI).[12]

Since that time, under both Republican and Democratic administrations, the United States has made the promotion of democracy not only a fundamental goal of American foreign policy but also an increasingly important part of American foreign aid. The U.S. Agency for International Development (USAID) initiated the administration of justice and judicial reform projects in El Salvador and elsewhere in Latin American in the mid-1980s, and the agency's 1990 Democracy Initiative established the promotion of democracy as a central objective. In 1989, as the Cold War waned, the U.S. Congress enacted the landmark Support for Eastern Europe Democracy Act to support democratic transitions in the region. In 1992, Congress added the Freedom Support Act, providing funds for similar programs in Russia and the other republics of the former Soviet Union. Democracy promotion became an explicit goal of U.S. assistance, at least in one very important part of the world.

Washington now devotes substantial resources and attention to aiding democratic transitions and building democratic institutions abroad. The U.S. government budget for democracy promotion, broadly defined, in fiscal 2000 was estimated at $700 million.[13] It is a substantial commitment, equal to more than 7 percent of the U.S. foreign aid budget. This does not include the huge cost of nation building in Afghanistan and Iraq, which the U.S. government has since taken on.

The portion of these funds that goes to the NED is comparatively small, just $37 million in 2000.[14] Much of the funding is channeled through USAID, which parcels out some of the money to fund the programs of more than a dozen nongovernmental organizations (NGOs) that focus on various forms of democracy assistance, such as the core grantees of the NED, the Carter Center, the Asia Foundation, the Central European and Eurasian Law Initiative of the American Bar Association, the Eurasia Foundation, the International Human Rights Law Group, and a number of centers affiliated with universities. It spends a much greater amount through contracts with private consulting firms—sometimes called "Beltway bandits"—that provide both management and technical services. As the U.S. government has increased foreign assistance for democracy and governance programs in response to democratic openings around the world, American democracy NGOs, university centers, and consulting firms have largely invented a new industry.

Democracy promotion has been fully institutionalized within the U.S. government as well. USAID, the State Department, the National Security Council, and other U.S. government agencies have created offices and senior-level positions charged with the responsibility for democracy promotion policies and programs. Since the mid-1990s, USAID missions throughout the world have had "democracy officers" to oversee "democracy and governance" programs. The administration of Bill Clinton established a Democracy Center within USAID, and the inevitable reorganization of the agency in 2001 by George W. Bush's administration set up a new Bureau for Democracy, Conflict, and Humanitarian Assistance. This new "democracy bureaucracy" that emerged in the 1990s has both reflected and spurred the increasing emphasis on democracy promotion in U.S. foreign assistance.[15]

Bipartisan U.S. Commitment to Democracy Promotion

Although some have mistakenly associated democracy promotion in the United States with the Democrats, at least before the war in Iraq, administrations of both parties have long supported democracy promotion. From its beginnings as a Reagan initiative, the modern American commitment to democracy assistance abroad accelerated under the President George H. W. Bush, was consolidated under President Clinton, and has continued under President George W. Bush.

From his first presidential campaign, Clinton promised to make democracy promotion a hallmark of his foreign policy. In 1992, he campaigned for office arguing, "The defense of freedom and the promotion of democracy around the world are not merely a reflection of our deepest values; they are vital to our national interests." After his election, his national security adviser Anthony Lake, in a much-noted speech, talked about a "strategy of enlargement of . . . market democracies." In a speech to the United Nations, Clinton himself spoke of the United States's "overriding purpose" to "expand and strengthen the world's community of market-based democracies." The Clinton administration argued that democracy promotion furthered America's interests as well as its ideals.[16]

Meanwhile, during the 1990s, the Republican-controlled Congress was suspicious of U.S. commitments abroad, and the budget for foreign assistance in general remained under pressure. As Thomas Carothers puts it, Congress was "prone to lump democracy promotion together with the humanitarian interventions they so much dislike."[17]

During the 2000 presidential election campaign, George W. Bush expressed skepticism about democracy promotion. Though "the United States . . . must be proud and confident of our values," he said, we should be "humble in how we treat nations that are figuring out how to chart their own course." Bush flatly rejected the idea of nation building. "We can't be all things to all people in the world. . . . I don't think nation-building missions are worthwhile." As Condoleezza Rice, later Bush's national security adviser, put it, "We don't need to have the 82nd Airborne escorting kids to kindergarten."[18]

At the same time, Colin Powell, who subsequently became President Bush's secretary of state, expressed strong support during the campaign for the idea of American democracy as a model: "We must show to the rest of the world, the beauty and potential of democracy. Our greatest strength is the power of our example to be that shining city on the hill that Ronald Reagan spoke of and that the whole world looks up to." Powell argued that Republicans would "put our nation on a course of hope and optimism for this new century," which he prayed, "historians will look back on and record not [as] the American century or the European century or the Asian century . . . [but] the century of democracy."[19]

In addition to establishing a new bureau at USAID with "democracy" in its name, the new administration requested a significant increase, to $964 million, for democracy and governance programs for fiscal 2003. Citing the Bush administration's "clear commitment to democracy," a senior USAID official told a U.S. Senate committee in 2002, "The demands of human dignity and the need to encourage the spread of democracy . . . is what motivates our agency, informs our programs, and guides our policies." In 2002, President Bush proposed to increase U.S. foreign assistance by 50 percent through a Millennium Challenge Account that would reward countries that, among other things, "govern justly," meaning "nations that root out corruption, respect human rights, and adhere to the rule of law."[20]

The U.S. government, of course, has not consistently supported democracy everywhere. Though the United States has strongly supported democratization in Latin America, Eastern Europe, and Russia during the past two decades, democracy has hardly been a priority in American foreign policy toward China, Egypt, Pakistan, Saudi Arabia, or Central Asia. The U.S. government only began to support democracy seriously in Indonesia and Nigeria after the fall of authoritarian governments in 1998. Both Democratic and Republican administrations have balanced their support for democracy against U.S. economic and security interests.

Since the September 11, 2001, terrorist attacks, as the Bush administration has embarked on the war on terrorism, the U.S. government has altered that balance by reducing emphasis on democracy and human rights. The administration has tolerated abuses by autocratic leaders in Central Asian countries critical to U.S. operations in Afghanistan, for example, and the United States has maintained its support for Pakistani leader General Pervez Musharraf, who seized power in 1999 from a corrupt and ineffective—but elected—government and continued to resist moves toward democracy. Because of the fight against terrorism, the administration improved relations with the Indonesian military, even though Indonesia had not yet met legally mandated preconditions, including accountability for those responsible for gross human rights violations.

Even as the broader world community has embraced democratic values long associated with the West, resentment of U.S. economic and military predominance has grown. The Bush administration advocates greater democracy as part of a strategy to contain support for Islamic extremism, but its unilateral foreign policy has exacerbated the perception that its interest in democracy is more tactical than principled. Even before it unilaterally decided to remove the Iraqi regime by force, the administration rejected the international consensus on everything from global warming to the international criminal court to the Israeli–Palestinian conflict. Having only reluctantly asked the UN Security Council in 2002 for support for its policy of confronting Iraq, the administration then went ahead with the invasion of Iraq in 2003 in the absence of Security Council approval and in the face of world public opinion. As a principal justification for war against the regime of Saddam Hussein, President Bush vowed to bring democracy to Iraq.

USAID Democracy and Governance Programs

Although journalists, commentators, and even many policymakers tend to think primarily of democracy assistance as support for elections, in reality the agenda of the U.S. democracy movement is wide ranging. Elections have never been the sole focus, and it is well recognized that while meaningful elections are a necessary condition for real democracy, they are far from sufficient.

USAID has identified four categories of U.S. foreign assistance programs in support of democracy and governance: (1) enhancing respect for the rule of law and human rights; (2) encouraging the development of an "independent and politically active civil society"; (3) fostering transparent and accountable governance; and (4) promoting meaningful political competition through free and fair electoral processes.[21] European aid agencies and multilateral organizations work on a similar range of issues.

The first three USAID categories do not involve elections. In the area of the rule of law, USAID supports programs that address legal reform, the administration of justice, citizens' access to justice, respect for human rights, and constitutional development. To support civil society, U.S. programs support advocacy NGOs, independent trade unions, journalists and media organizations, and civic education efforts. To improve governance, USAID focuses on anticorruption initiatives, decentralization and local capacity building, legislative strengthening, public policy development, and improved civil–military relations.[22]

The range of international interventions to support elections processes, the fourth category of U.S. democracy and governance assistance, is itself broad. American aid provides support and advice on election systems, laws, and regulations; electoral procedures, such as voter registration, balloting, vote counting, and dispute resolution; election administration, including the composition and mandate of electoral authorities, the training of election administrators, and the design and procurement of ballot papers, ballot boxes, and election commodities; voter education and voter information; and domestic nonpartisan election monitoring and party pollwatching. Programs also target the development of political parties, often, but not always, in anticipation of elections.

Beyond the United States

Europe, Japan, and other developed countries likewise have poured resources and diplomatic capital into the global cause of democracy promotion. The United Nations, the Organization of Security and Cooperation in Europe, the OAS, the Commonwealth (of former British colonies), the new African Union, and other multilateral organizations have made the promotion of elections and democracy a priority. Even the World Bank focuses enormous attention on "good governance." These and other multilateral organizations have established new assistance mechanisms. In 1995 in Sweden, fourteen established and newly democratic countries established a new multilateral organization focused exclusively on democracy assistance, the International Institute for Elections and Democracy Assistance.

The NED and the American political party institutes, IRI and NDI, were modeled in part on the publicly funded foundations affiliated with each of the major political parties in the Federal Republic of Germany, including the Friedrich Ebert Stiftung (affiliated with the Social Democrats), the Konrad Adenauer Stiftung (Christian Democrats), and the Friedrich Naumann Stiftung (Free Democrats). These foundations receive German government funding for their efforts to promote democracy abroad. With combined funding in excess of $450 million as of 1996, the foundations remain active in democracy-building projects around the world.[23] Despite their affiliations with German political parties, however, today they work much less with political parties per se in emerging democracies than do their American counterparts.

Other countries have established organizations to promote democracy and provide democracy assistance, such as the Westminster Foundation in Britain, Rights & Democracy (formerly the International Center for Human Rights and Democratic Development) in Canada, the Center for Democratic Institutions in Australia, the Netherlands Institute for Multiparty Democracy, and political party foundations in Austria, France, the Netherlands, and Sweden. Though many of these organizations are still relatively small, they complement large foreign assistance programs in Europe, Japan, Australia, and Canada. In short, there is a complex array of actors that define, fund, and implement interventions and programs to support democracy in countries all over the world.

Together, these American and foreign nongovernmental and quasi-governmental organizations, private firms, governmental agencies, governmental bureaucracies, and multilateral organizations constitute a new global industry. It is an industry in the sense that many of its diverse actors focus more on technical than ideological objectives. They are engaged primarily in targeted foreign assistance programs rather than in broader diplomacy or foreign policy. It is, moreover, a burgeoning industry, and the availability of resources as well as the political prominence of the activities have attracted many to the cause.

At the same time, these groups are part of a broad movement committed to democracy as a set of principles and values. Speaking of Western NGOs involved in democracy promotion in Russia, the activist and analyst Sarah E. Mendelson concludes, "These NGOs . . . are motivated mainly by ideals, not profits." She adds, "Many Western NGOs receive government funding, but their strategies for pursuing their goals, with a few exceptions, are derived and implemented with minimal interference or supervision from government bureaucracies (or market interests)."[24] Although the rapid emergence of this global enterprise has drawn organizations to this new field and has spawned some questionable programs, the international democracy industry has contributed to an important cause.

Chapter 3

Elections and Election Monitoring

While democracy must be more than free elections, it is also true . . . that it cannot be less.

—UN secretary general Kofi Annan[1]

The greater focus on democracy and the growing acceptance of interventions to support democratic reform have led to an extraordinary focus on elections. The remarkable trend that has made election monitoring a common, accepted international activity has both resulted from and contributed to this attention to elections. Since the late 1980s, election monitoring has exploded. Intergovernmental organizations now routinely support and monitor elections around the world. Formal election monitoring is not generally perceived as necessary in established democracies and is not permitted in closed, nondemocratic societies. But in democratizing and semiauthoritarian countries, election monitoring has become the norm and is now effectively a prerequisite in such countries for elections to be viewed as legitimate.

This chapter assesses the growing international importance of both elections and election monitoring and defines important concepts and terms. First, the chapter addresses elections. Even though the international emphasis on elections is sometimes misplaced, I argue that the international promotion of democratic elections is justifiable. The chapter distinguishes categories of elections in order to narrow the focus to those elections that are most worthy of international attention. Next, I consider the important threshold question of the authority and acceptability of international election observers in international practice. Then I explain broad concepts and types of election monitoring, including important distinctions among observation, monitoring, and supervision and between international and domestic election monitoring. Finally, the chapter reviews the extent of election monitoring around the world since 1990. I summarize and draw observations from a novel, detailed database about election monitoring in ninety-four newly democratic and semiauthoritarian countries.

The Growing Importance of Elections in Democratization and International Relations

It has become fashionable to point out the obvious truth that genuine democracy requires substantially more than democratic elections. Inveighing against "illiberal democracy," the noted commentator Fareed Zakaria argues, "Across the globe, democratically elected regimes . . . are routinely ignoring constitutional limits on their power and depriving their citizens of basic rights."[2] He criticizes the international emphasis on elections:

> In some places, such as Central Asia, elections have paved the way for dictatorships. In others, they have exacerbated group conflict and ethnic tensions. Both Yugoslavia and Indonesia, for example, were far more tolerant and secular when they were ruled by strongmen . . . than they are now as democracies. And in many nondemocracies, elections would not improve matters much. Across the Arab world elections held tomorrow would probably bring to power regimes that are more intolerant, reactionary, anti-Western, and anti-Semitic than the dictatorships currently in place.[3]

Jack Snyder of Columbia University argues that elections often sharpen ethnic and national differences. "Naively pressuring ethnically divided authoritarian states to hold instant elections," he suggests, "can lead to disastrous results."[4] Warns Amy Chua of Yale Law School, "For the last twenty years the United States has been vigorously promoting instantaneous democratization—essentially overnight elections with universal suffrage—throughout the non-Western world. In doing so we are asking developing and post-Communist countries to embrace a process of democratization that no Western nation ever went through."[5]

It is true that the international community sometimes has overemphasized elections. In transitional or postconflict societies, Western governments and multilateral organizations expect elections to do too much or push for them to take place too soon. Certainly elections are far from a panacea, and they can fuel political and social divisions. But the idea that donors, diplomats, and democracy promoters organizations unthinkingly advocate elections above all else is mostly a caricature. Sophisticated development agencies and democracy-assistance organizations recognize the essential importance of building democratic culture and the rule of law as well as the danger of early elections in ethnically divided societies.

Moreover, elections do matter. Samuel Huntington explains, "Elections, open, free and fair, are the essence of democracy, the inescapable sine qua non."[6] All societies need political institutions and processes that are capable of addressing and resolving social divisions and competition for political power through democratic means. The five main reasons for this emphasis on elections are both philosophical and practical.

First, international declarations and international norms unambiguously establish elections as the basis of legitimate government. The Universal Declaration of Human Rights provides that the "will of the people shall be the basis of the authority of government" as "expressed in periodic and genuine elections." The International Covenant on Civil and Political Rights (ICCPR) incorporates this principle in a binding international treaty. The ICCPR provides that "Every citizen shall have the right and the opportunity . . . to vote and to be elected at genuine periodic elections which shall be by universal and equal suffrage and shall be held by secret ballot."[7]

Regional and other international instruments reinforce and elaborate upon these rights. International agreements and declarations in Africa, Europe, and the Americas recognize the right to participate in government, directly or through elected representatives. Most of these documents specifically recognize the right to elections. Regional conventions generally follow the language of the Universal Declaration and the ICCPR that elections need be "periodic" and "genuine." Some use the term "free and fair." Some also add adjectives such as "honest" or "transparent." Regardless of these various formulations, international instruments are consistent in their commitment to democratic elections. In 2000, in response to one-party states that claim to hold democratic elections, the UN Commission on Human Rights specifically recognized a right to vote in "a free and fair process . . . open to multiple parties."[8]

Second, elections contribute to respect for other rights. As the former U.S. State Department official Elizabeth Clark argues, "Elections have come to be contrasted with genuine democracy without recognition that elections that meet emerging universal standards, with their insistence and fair play, support democracy."[9] Pointing to an increase in the number of electoral democracies and the decline in the number of illiberal democracies in the world, Adrian Karatnycky of Freedom House argues that "the emergence of electoral democracies has been the best indicator of subsequent progress in the areas of civil liberties and human rights."[10]

Third, elections have practical, political consequences. An election is often a critically important event in a country's transition from authoritarianism. Competitive elections can catalyze profound but peaceful political change. Although elections are more or less routine in democracies, elections in societies in transition or crisis are unusual events that, if successful, not only confer legitimacy on governments but also can profoundly influence institutions, power arrangements, and expectations. The 1986 election in the Philippines, for example, was critical to the unseating of Ferdinand Marcos and the restoration of democracy; subsequent elections in the Philippines helped strengthen the country's democratic foundation. Since then, elections have furthered democracy in countries as diverse as Indonesia, Mexico, Nigeria, Peru, Poland, South Africa, and Yugoslavia.

Fourth, elections—particularly transitional elections—provide significant new opportunities for citizen involvement in public affairs. They are an opportunity to engage civic organizations and citizens in democratic politics through voter education, election monitoring, policy research, and advocacy. Elections provide an opportunity for younger leaders, with new values and perspectives, to become involved in politics. They also can provide an avenue for the participation of social groups that traditionally have had less access to politics and governance, such as women, minorities, poor people, and those who are socially disadvantaged.

Fifth, even though elections can exacerbate social divisions, competitive elections contribute to effective and stable governance. Elections provide a predictable and accepted mechanism for maintaining governmental accountability and determining leadership succession, in contrast to the uncertainty created by authoritarian systems in countries such as China, Cuba, Iraq, North Korea, and Vietnam. Elections are a vehicle for managing political competition. They stimulate interaction and communication between governments and the governed, and they help to educate the public and politicians. Elections can validate existing regimes, leaders, and policies. Fair elections contribute to, and are increasingly required for, not only international legitimacy but also domestic stability.

In sum, democratic elections are required under international law, encourage respect for other rights, and can be significant catalysts to greater democracy (table 3.1). They provide an important opportunity to broaden citizen participation in public life and offer a means of establishing ac-

Table 3.1

Reasons for the International Emphasis on Elections

1. International law and international norms establish the right to "periodic and genuine elections."
2. Elections reinforce respect for human rights.
3. Elections can catalyze political transitions.
4. Election provide opportunities for citizen participation and political involvement.
5. Elections contribute to effective, accountable, and stable governance.

countability and channeling political competition. For these reasons, elections are an entirely appropriate focus of democracy assistance.

Types of Elections

Elections attracting international attention are often national contests for political office, such as president or national parliament, but also significant are elections held for constituent assemblies responsible for promulgating new constitutions as well as referenda, plebiscites, or other electoral exercises on fundamental questions such as independence, peace accords, or constitutional arrangements.[11] It is useful to distinguish four types of elections: regular, transitional, postconflict, and consolidating.

Regular elections are those in which electoral authorities are generally trusted to be impartial and the rules and outcomes are largely accepted. Although no elections are perfect, and the 2000 presidential election in the United States reminds us that elections in established democracies do not always gain full public acceptance, elections in democracies are not discontinuous or exceptional events. In democratic countries, electoral rules or procedures tend not to be a leading source of controversy, and candidates and parties contest elections over policies, parties, and personalities rather than the political system itself.

Transitional elections—sometimes called "first" or "first-generation" elections—mark a move from an authoritarian or controlled political system toward a more open and democratic one. These elections, by definition, are substantially more open and competitive than those that preceded them. They may initiate broader political transitions or they may effectively mark the end of an important transitional phase. Transitional elections often, although not necessarily, involve a shift in political power to a new government. They may be part of a transition process that is managed by existing political elites or one that is demanded by opposition forces or the public, but in any case they are elections that are discontinuous, that mark a sharp break with the past. Whether given elections are truly transitional, however, sometimes cannot be determined until later.

Postconflict elections occur at the end of civil wars or struggles for self-determination or over sovereignty, generally as part of internationally negotiated or supervised settlements. Often the international community plays a prominent role in such exercises, either by supervising or even organizing them. Electoral contests in such circumstances sometimes take the form of referenda on independence or elections for a constituent assembly responsible for adopting new constitutional arrangements. Postconflict elections have played a prominent role in internationally negotiated settlements of civil wars, as in Nicaragua in 1990 and Cambodia in 1993, and conflicts over areas of contested sovereignty, including Bosnia, East Timor, Kosovo, Namibia, and the West Bank and Gaza.

Consolidating elections take place as part of a country's consolidation of new democratic institutions or continuing political transition. Or they occur in quasi-democratic countries. Such elections typically take place after a transitional or postconflict election, and accordingly election observers, policymakers, and academics sometimes refer to them as "second" (or "third") elections. Though less dramatic than transitional elections, consolidating elections in many countries continue to merit and attract international attention.

Transitional and postconflict elections gain particular attention from the international community. International responses to these exceptional circumstances have increasingly influenced international relations in the context of much less exceptional elections as well.

These types of elections are not necessarily mutually exclusive, because, for example, postconflict elections often mark political transitions.[12] But these categories are useful, for few transitional or postconflict elections avoid questions about the impartiality of electoral authorities or a struggle over rules, and most now attract international monitoring and other international assistance.

The Authority of Election Observers

We now turn from the subject of elections per se to the subject of election observers. On what basis do international observers claim the right to judge whether elections meet international standards? Critics often question who appointed the observers as arbiters of legitimacy.

International observers generally have no juridical role. Unless they are really something more than observers, they have no rights or responsibilities under national or international law to referee disputes or intervene in the election process. For most elections in sovereign countries, in the absence of a formal mandate from the United Nations or other intergovernmental organization, the role of observers is limited to reporting on their findings and seeking to persuade national and international decision makers or to influence national or international public opinion.

Multilateral organizations , nonetheless, have recognized the validity of election observation, which has helped to deflect arguments that election observing constitute interference in the internal affairs of sovereign countries. In 1989 in Kuala Lumpur, the Commonwealth's heads of government authorized it to assist member states through a "facility for mounting observer missions." In 1990 in Copenhagen, the Conference on Security and Cooperation in Europe formally endorsed the practice of international election observation:

> The participating States [of the Conference on Security and Cooperation in Europe] consider that the presence of observers, both foreign and domestic, can enhance the electoral process. . . . They therefore invite observers from any other participating States and any appropriate private institutions and organizations who may wish to do so to observe the course of their national election proceedings, to the extent permitted by law.

Similarly, the Interim Agreement between Israel and the Palestinian Liberation Organization in 1995 opened "all stages of the [Palestinian] electoral process . . . from the announcement through registration, campaign, polling, counting, compiling of results and complaints procedures" to observation by invited governments and intergovernmental organizations, foreign nongovernmental organizations (NGOs), and domestic monitoring groups. The European Commission states, "Human rights field missions and election missions are accepted as part of the mandate of the EU" under the Treaty of the European Union.[13]

International election observation has become a nearly universal trend for elections taking place in the context of transitions away from one-party or authoritarian states. Countries in transition generally seek international and domestic recognition for holding more open elections by inviting outside scrutiny. The legitimacy of international election monitoring is now well established.

Types of Election Monitoring

The terms "election observation" and "election monitoring" have come to describe a range of activities focused on either making controversial elections more acceptable or exposing their flaws. There are at least three distinct types of election monitoring: (1) "international observation" or "international monitoring" of transitional or other exceptional elections conducted by missions sent by governments, multilateral organizations, or international NGOs; (2) "domestic monitoring" by national organizations, especially nonpartisan NGOs and civic groups; and (3) "international supervision" by intergovernmental organizations of postconflict elections, referenda, and other self-determination exercises. In support of more democratic elections, domestic and international groups also involve themselves in voter education, election law reform, advising on election administration, media monitoring, and related activities.

International election observation as it is practiced today began as an ad hoc response of a few concerned outsiders to critically important elections in particular countries. In 1980, during an election that played a key role in the transition to independence in Zimbabwe (then Rhodesia), for example, "election observation" meant four individual activists arriving in the capital shortly before election day to talk to a few citizens about the process.[14] Similarly, in 1982 several NGOs from North America and Europe dispatched a few observers to witness an election in El Salvador.[15] Since that time, however, the common conception and expectations of international observation have fundamentally changed.

The presence of international observers at a series of important transitional elections in Eastern and Central Europe in 1990 helped confirm the increasing international acceptance of election monitoring in sovereign countries. In the immediate aftermath of those elections, the Conference on Security and Cooperation in Europe declared that all member-states should accept the presence of international observers for all national elections. Since 1988, the UN General Assembly repeatedly has endorsed United Nations involvement in election observation and election assistance. The Organization of American States and numerous other multilateral organizations likewise have endorsed and conducted international election observation.

Domestic election monitoring began in the Philippines in the mid-1980s with the pioneering experience of the National Citizens' Movement for Free Elections (NAMFREL), which has inspired many similar efforts around the world. Since then, in more than sixty countries and in every region of the world, nonpartisan domestic election-monitoring organizations (EMOs) have provided momentum to the struggle for democracy by working to ensure that elections are competitive and meaningful (see tables 10.1 through 10.4 in this volume).[16] Domestic coalitions of NGOs, human rights groups, professional associations, social service organizations, university students, and others have worked effectively together to monitor important transitional or otherwise controversial elections in places as diverse as Bangladesh, Kenya, Mexico, Ukraine, and Yemen. EMOs have contributed to more genuine election processes by encouraging fairer campaign practices and a more informed electorate, as well as by reducing the possibility of fraud and irregularities on election day.

International supervision of elections typically refers to the more extensive engagement of multilateral organizations in postconflict elections, often in areas of contested sovereignty. It differs considerably from both international and domestic monitoring. Although the United Nations has supervised elections or referenda in non-self-governing territories since the 1940s, it began a new type of role in 1989 by overseeing elections that played a critical part in the transition to independence in Namibia as part of a peacekeeping operation. Four years later, the UN organized elections and administered key governmental functions as part of an internationally supervised peace settlement of the long-standing conflict in Cambodia. Similarly, in East Timor, the United Nations organized a referendum in 1999 and elections in 2001 and 2002. These extensive efforts differ in character from UN election assistance and election observation in member countries, which began in the early 1990s.

Other intergovernmental organizations have also supervised elections. The Organization for Security and Cooperation in Europe (OSCE) has supervised numerous elections, from Bosnia to Kosovo. The Organization of American States has had extensive involvement in various elections in Latin America.

Toward a Better Definition of Election Observation

Even defining what we mean by election observation has proven difficult. The Stockholm-based International Institute for Democracy and Electoral Assistance (International IDEA), a multilateral research and standard-setting organization, has defined election observation as "the purposeful gathering of information regarding an electoral process and the making of informed judgments on the conduct of such a process on the basis of the

information collected by persons who are not inherently authorized to intervene in the process."[17] This definition is unsatisfying, however, because
it distinguishes international observers by who they are not: election authorities or others with an official role in the process. Yet many actors who
are not international election observers in the conventional sense, such as
journalists and diplomats, gather information and make informed judgments about potentially controversial elections in the absence of a mandate
to intervene. Also, though observers may not be "inherently authorized to
intervene," as we have seen, election laws and international norms increasingly recognize a role for both international and domestic observers.

Moreover, International IDEA's definition leaves out several elements
that are key to the modern understanding of international election observation. Therefore, I would amend that definition to add focus on the purpose
of the activity, the identity of the actors, and the use of the judgments, as
follows. *International election observation is the purposeful gathering of
information about an electoral process and public assessment of that
process against universal standards for democratic elections by responsible foreign or international organizations committed to neutrality and to the
democratic process for the purpose of building public and international
confidence about the election's integrity or documenting and exposing the
ways in which the process falls short.*

To be legitimate, international election observation must be intended
solely to support democratic elections and democratic development rather
than to assist particular parties or candidates or to further particular policy
preferences or other interests of external actors. International election observation is an activity conducted by responsible, professional, credible foreign or international organizations focused on such objectives. This emphasis on the goals of the activity and the nature of the actors distinguishes
international election observation from "electoral tourism," from partisan
external intervention in domestic politics, and from efforts to further outside interests in a given country as opposed to that country's own national
interest in having democratic institutions and genuine, periodic elections.

Observation versus Monitoring

International or domestic actors may engage in the "observation," "monitoring," "supervision," or "administration" of elections. The United Nations, rather than observing or monitoring elections, conducts what it calls

"verification." Jimmy Carter and other international actors sometimes involve themselves in the "mediation" of election-related disputes. Terminology is important, in part because foreign involvement in elections in other countries still raises sensitivities about encroaching on national sovereignty.

Accepted practice views the terms "observation" and "monitoring" as referring to different points of a continuum along two different dimensions: (1) the degree of involvement in the process, and (2) the period of time over which the activity takes place. With respect to involvement in the process, "observation" generally refers to something that is relatively passive, whereas "monitoring" connotes an activity that is at least somewhat more engaged. In theory, "observation" is strictly limited to recording and reporting; "monitoring" suggests at least the possibility of some modest interventions to correct imperfections or to make recommendations for action. In practice, though, observers at polling stations often provide advice and guidance or point out problems that can be fixed, at least if they can do so in an unobtrusive way. Likewise, leaders of observation missions often suggest improvements in the process to the authorities.

"Observation," says International IDEA, "involves gathering information and making informed judgements from that information." In contrast, "Monitoring . . . involves the authority to observe an election process and to intervene in that process if relevant laws or standard procedures are being violated or ignored."[18] As used by most election-monitoring organizations, however, "monitoring" does not involve the legal or formal authority to intervene. Monitoring suggests attention to a broad range of issues. These kinds of interventions are entirely appropriate for citizens in their own country. They may or may not be acceptable for international actors. By definition, neither observers nor monitors have a formal role.

With respect to the period of time, "observation" suggests a briefer involvement than does monitoring.[19] The activity of international figures or organizations that focus principally on polling day itself, and thus are not present in the country for very long, is best termed "observation" and the individuals, "observers." When domestic or international groups pay attention to an election process over time, their engagement might better be termed "monitoring," but individuals representing such monitoring groups who witness only the balloting and counting might still be referred to as "observers." Though much international attention to elections is superficial, particularly when it focuses narrowly on election day, the term "observation" should not be considered a pejorative one.

Following the practice of several experienced organizations, in this book, I generally refer to the presence of foreigners for election day, and the days immediately surrounding election day, as "observation." I generally call longer-term or more substantive involvement, whether by domestic or foreign organizations, "monitoring." But because there can be considerable ambiguity and overlap between these terms, this distinction is not rigorous. In addition, as chapter 5 explains with respect to Jimmy Carter, election monitoring can also edge into election mediation, as local actors invite or allow international figures to mediate election-related disputes or defer to what they perceive as more impartial judgments and recommendations offered by international actors.

International organizations, especially intergovernmental organizations, are sometimes called upon to "supervise" or "administer" postconflict elections or other electoral exercises that occur as part of internationally negotiated agreements. Supervision is further along the time and involvement continuums than is monitoring. "Supervision" of elections implies that another authority is responsible for organizing and administering the elections, but that the organization with a mandate to supervise has a defined role in the process. In Namibia in 1989, for example, the South African authorities remained responsible for organizing the elections under the supervision of the United Nations. Typically, that role is to follow the process much more closely than would an outside monitoring organization, to help arrange the legal framework, to advise on administrative and technical preparations, and to make recommendations on changes or reforms. Entities authorized to supervise an election often have an explicit or implicit veto over election procedures or plans. A supervising authority might well have a mandate to certify the process or parts of the process and would generally have larger numbers of personnel than would a monitoring organization. It might also have a funding role.

International organizations only "administer" elections when they have an explicit mandate to do so, either because there is no sovereign government or because the sovereign has for some reason conferred this role on an international or foreign entity. The United Nations, for example, administered 1993 elections in Cambodia during an internationally supervised transition period called for by a peace accord.

This book does not extensively consider case studies that specifically address election supervision and administration. That kind of international involvement in elections, which generally occurs in the context of conflict resolution and peacekeeping, raises considerably different issues and has been the subject of greater study and comment than have election observation and election monitoring.[20]

The Extent of Election Monitoring

Election monitoring has become nearly routine in international relations. Between 1989 and 2002, international election observers were present for 86 percent of the national elections in ninety-five newly democratic or semi-authoritarian countries. These include the sixty-two countries that have held their first multiparty, competitive elections since 1989 and were rated "democratic" by Freedom House as of 2000. They also include the thirty-three countries rated by Freedom House as "authoritarian" or as "restricting democratic practices" that received election observers or external election assistance for at least one national election during that period. (I refer to countries in both of these less-than-democratic categories in this database as "semiauthoritarian." By definition, these are countries that have permitted at least some external engagement in their election.)[21]

As is shown in table 3.2 and the appendix at the end of the book, international election observers witnessed 303 of 352 national elections in the ninety-five countries. This does not count dozens of local elections, constitutional referenda, and other electoral exercises that observers have also witnessed. In the sixty-two Third Wave democracies meeting the criteria for the database, international election observers were present for 211 of 243 national elections (87 percent) that took place between 1989 and 2002. In the thirty-two semiauthoritarian countries, election observers (or, in a few cases, external technical advisers) were present for 92 of 109 national elections (84 percent). (The data do not cover established democracies—meaning, in this case, countries that held competitive, multiparty elections before 1989–or nondemocratic countries; in established democracies and nondemocratic countries, formal election observation is either not common or not permitted.) In addition, nonpartisan domestic EMOs have monitored more than 150 elections in more than two-thirds of the countries (sixty-six of ninety-five) in the survey universe.

International Election Observation by Region

Election observation is especially widespread in Eastern and Central Europe and the former Soviet Union, Latin America, and Africa. Election ob-

Table 3.2

Elections and Election Monitoring in Newly Democratic and Semiauthoritarian Countries

Region and Type of Government	Number of Countries	Number of Elections	International Observers Were Present		International Observers Were Not Present		Observers' Assessments						Countries with EMOs	
							Positive		Negative		Mixed			
			No.	%	No.	%	No.	%	No.	%	No.	%	Subtotal[a]	No.	%
Europe and Former Soviet Union															
Democratic	21	95	84	88	11	12	54	76	10	14	7	10	71	15	71
Semiauthoritarian	7	29	24	83	5	17	3	14	17	81	1	5	21	6	86
Total[b]	28	124	108	87	16	13	57	62	27	29	8	9	92	21	75
Asia and Pacific															
Democratic	10	32	24	75	8	25	20	100	0	0	0	0	20	7	70
Semiauthoritarian	4	12	10	83	2	17	3	38	2	25	3	38	8	4	100
Total	14	44	34	77	10	23	23	82	2	7	3	11	28	11	79
Africa (Sub-Saharan)															
Democratic	15	51	47	92	4	8	8	53	4	27	3	20	15	14	93
Semiauthoritarian	17	51	44	86	7	14	10	38	12	46	4	15	26	9	53
Total	32	102	91	89	11	11	18	43	16	40	7	18	41	23	72

Latin America and Caribbean															
Democratic	16	65	56	86	9	14	12	80	2	13	1	7	15	7	44
Semiauthoritarian	2	7	7	100	0	0	2	50	1	25	1	25	4	2	100
Total	18	72	63	88	9	13	14	74	3	16	2	11	19	9	50
Middle East and North Africa															
Democratic	0	0	0											0	
Semiauthoritarian	3	10	7	70	3	30	3	75	0	0	1	25	4	2	67
Total	3	10	7	70	3	30	3	75	0	0	1	25	4	2	67
Overall															
Democratic	62	243	211	87	32	13	94	78	16	13	11	9	121	43	69
Semiauthoritarian	33	109	92	84	17	16	21	33	32	51	10	16	63	23	70
Total[c]	95	352	303	86	49	14	115	63	48	26	21	11	184	66	69

Note: For detailed data by country, see the appendix table at the end of this volume. EMO = election-monitoring organization.

[a]Subtotal of elections for which it was possible to determine whether the observers' assessments were positive, negative, or mixed.

[b]The actual number of countries in Europe and the Former Soviet Union in the database is 27 because one country (Yugoslavia) is counted in both the democratic and the semiauthoritarian categories.

[c]The actual number of countries in the database is 94 because one country (Yugoslavia) is counted in both the democratic and the semiauthoritarian categories.

Sources: See the appendix at the end of this volume.

servers have been present for more than four-fifths of the elections in newly democratic and semiauthoritarian countries in these regions.

In Eastern and Central Europe and the former Soviet Union, the region covered by the OSCE, twenty-seven countries have accepted international observers from OSCE and elsewhere, covering 87 percent of the national elections (108 of 124) in those countries since 1990. This includes 88 percent of the elections (84 of 95) in the twenty-one newly democratic countries in the region. This experience certainly reflects the 1990 OSCE commitments to election observation. Formal observers were absent only for several elections in semiauthoritarian countries in the region early in the 1990s and for some elections in the unambiguously democratic countries of Central Europe and the Baltic Sea region. In the latter case, observers would presumably have been welcome but were not considered necessary.

Election observation has also been extremely common in Latin America and Africa. In Latin America and the Caribbean, observers from the Organization of American States and other organizations witnessed 88 percent of the national elections (63 of 72) in eighteen countries between 1989 and 2002. In Sub-Saharan Africa, there were observers (or foreign technical advisers) present for 89 percent of the elections (91 of 102) during the period, including 86 percent (44 of 51) in seventeen semiauthoritarian countries. In addition to multilateral organizations based in Africa, observers for elections on the continent typically came from Europe and the United States as well.

Election observers have been somewhat less common in the Asia-Pacific region. About three-quarters of the elections (34 of 44) in the thirteen relevant countries have had observers. Unlike Eurasia, Africa, and Latin America, Asia lacks a regional organization involved in election observing. Democratizing countries in Asia have also been relatively more affluent than in some other regions of the world, making them as a group less dependent on foreign aid.

Because competitive elections remain largely absent in the Middle East and North Africa, only three countries or territories have had formal international election observation: Yemen, Algeria, and Palestine.

Nonpartisan domestic groups have monitored elections in eleven of fourteen countries in the database in (79 percent) in Asia, twenty-one of twenty-eight countries (75 percent) in the OSCE region, two of three countries (67 percent) in the Middle East, twenty-three of thirty-two countries (72 percent) in Africa, and nine of eighteen countries (50 percent) in Latin America. There are no dramatic differences across regions in the experience with nonpartisan domestic election monitoring in countries at comparable stages of democratic development.

International Election Observation in Newly Democratic versus Semiauthoritarian Countries

There is no significant difference in the extent of election observation in new democracies as compared with semiauthoritarian countries in the study overall (87 vs. 84 percent). Observers are slightly more likely to be present for elections in semiauthoritarian countries where elections are more likely to be controversial, as in Azerbaijan, Belarus, Cambodia, Kazakhstan, Kenya, Pakistan, and Zimbabwe. These are countries in which there is at least a possibility of competitive elections to attract the participation of observers. In new but stable democracies, such as Argentina, Chile, the Czech Republic, Hungary, and South Korea, the potential contribution of election observers is considerably less significant. Authoritarian countries that make no real pretense of holding multiparty, competitive elections generally do not invite or attract observers and therefore are not included in the data.

Although there is relatively little difference in the extent of observation between democratic and semiauthoritarian countries, the assessments of observers in semiauthoritarian countries tend to be considerably more negative. For elections for which it can be determined whether the assessments of international observers were essentially positive, negative, or mixed, observers seriously criticized only 13 percent of the elections in new democracies, while they reported favorably on 78 percent. For elections in semiauthoritarian countries, in contrast, international observers issued negative public reports in more than half the cases and made positive statements in only about a third.

There was little difference in this pattern by region. In the OSCE region, observers issued positive reports for elections in democratic countries 76 percent of the time as compared with 14 percent in semiauthoritarian countries. In Asia, observers gave positive assessments for 100 percent of the elections in newly democratic countries as compared with only three of the eight elections they observed in semiauthoritarian countries. In Africa, there were positive reports for about half of the relevant elections in new democracies as compared with just over a third of the rated elections in less democratic countries. In Latin America, the relevant numbers are 80 percent positive in newly democratic countries as compared with two of four elections in semiauthoritarian ones.

It is not surprising that observers would tend to find elections in newly democratic countries more satisfactory than elections semiauthoritarian ones. Indeed, a country presumably must hold reasonably competitive, fair elections to be rated a democracy in the first place. In many instances, less-than-democratic elections took place before the transition to democracy.

Toward Universal Norms

International observation is now an international norm, and established democracies, like emerging ones, must and do welcome international observers. Observers of regular elections in the United States or Western Europe may be less inclined to offer public assessments of the fairness of those elections, but only because the election process itself is generally a good bit less newsworthy. In addressing whether international election observers are necessary in developed democracies, Hrair Balian, the former head of the election section at the OSCE, asks rhetorically whether they "can add anything in terms of building confidence, deterring violations, raising early warning, mitigating conflict, and providing assistance." Civil society organizations, the judiciary, and administrative processes in developed democracies, he suggests, are "better equipped to address the problems than foreign observers."[22] (Elections in Florida may now be an exception; several American and foreign organizations, from the NAACP to the OSCE, monitored and issued public assessments of the 2002 elections in the state.)[23]

Democracy and elections are accepted international norms. The legitimacy and appropriateness of democracy promotion is also now universally agreed. But there is a need for more practical and effective assistance. Election monitoring is the highest-profile democracy-promotion activity and continues to attract much attention and resources. Those interested in supporting global democracy need to better understand the genesis of the phenomenon of election monitoring so they can learn how to improve it. The rest of this book tells the story of the origins of international and domestic election monitoring and uses examples and case studies to show how election monitoring has contributed or failed to contribute to democratization. The lessons from this experience should help policymakers, program managers, donors, and diplomats make better contributions to global democratization in the future.

This first part of the book has explained the emergence of international and national election monitoring during the past fifteen years in the context of three related trends: the democratization of countries around the world, the emergence and growing international acceptance of democracy promotion, and the continuing and justifiable international attention to elections. Election observation and election monitoring, by international or foreign organizations and by nonpartisan domestic groups, have built upon and reinforced these trends. We now turn to the subject of the rest of the book: a close examination of the emergence, contributions, and prospects of the closely related but different phenomena of international and domestic election monitoring.

Part II

International Election Monitoring

Chapter 4

From Nongovernmental to Intergovernmental Organizations: Actors in International Election Monitoring

> For as long as democracy fails to flourish in all countries, it cannot thrive in one alone.
>
> —John F. Kennedy

By the 1990s, a distinct election-monitoring and democracy-promotion industry had emerged, partly in response to the Third Wave of democratization and the rapidly growing international interest in developing-country elections. Organizations involved in election monitoring formed the core of this loose, diverse democracy industry, which extended well beyond the core of American government–supported nongovernmental organizations (NGOs). It also included other NGOs and private organizations from the United States and Europe, bilateral donors, and major multilateral organizations. In particular, in a considerable shift from the early days, when election monitoring was the province of NGOs alone, elections and democracy became a major priority of intergovernmental organizations around the world.

This chapter describes and evaluates the approach of a diverse range of international actors that support and monitor elections in democratizing countries, from the United Nations to regional multilateral organizations to government-supported American NGOs. To understand international election monitoring and election assistance, it is necessary to have a sense of the diverse organizations involved. During the early 1990s, the United Nations and other multilateral organizations became increasingly active in monitoring elections. The chapter first discusses the evolution and current role of the United Nations and UN agencies in establishing democratic norms and encouraging democratic elections. Next, I consider and compare the particular experiences and approaches of other leading intergovernmental organizations, including the Organization for Security and Cooperation in Europe (OSCE), the European Union, the Commonwealth, the Organization of American States (OAS), and the International Institute for Democracy and Electoral Assistance (International IDEA). Finally, the chapter considers the principal United States–based NGOs in the election field, including the National Democratic Institute for International Affairs (NDI), the International Republican Institute (IRI), the Carter Center, and the International Foundation for Electoral Systems (IFES).

The institutionalization of election monitoring at intergovernmental organizations reinforces democratic elections as an international norm and demonstrates the broad acceptability of election monitoring. In monitoring particular elections, multilateral organizations have broad legitimacy. At the same time, NGOs, which are less burdened by diplomatic constraints and objectives other than democratization, still can make an important contribution to democratization through election monitoring.

The United Nations and Elections

The United Nations has played a leading role in developing international democratic standards and providing electoral assistance. UN involvement in elections per se began in the context of decolonization but expanded dramatically during the 1990s. Beginning in 1989 in Namibia, the United Nations began to supervise or administer elections as part of comprehensive peacekeeping operations or internationally sponsored conflict settlements. By 1990, the United Nations had also monitored important transitional elections in sovereign member states, namely Haiti and Nicaragua. These case-by-case interventions evolved into a wholesale effort to advance democracy and political rights in all member countries, and UN verification or technical assistance for elections in member countries has become routine.

Shortly after its founding, the United Nations was called upon to supervise an election in Korea. In the fall of 1947, taking up a dispute between the United States and the Soviet Union, the UN General Assembly called for Korea to be unified under an elected government.[1] The United Nations formed a commission to implement and supervise free elections. Even though the Soviet Union refused to allow elections in the north, the new world body decided to go ahead in the American-controlled south. The elections, which took place on May 10, 1948, led to the establishment in Seoul on August 15, 1948, of the Republic of Korea (South Korea).

In 1956, the UN Trusteeship Council, composed of the permanent members of the Security Council, established a mission to monitor a plebiscite on independence in British Togoland in West Africa. The United Nations appointed a commissioner to supervise the organization and conduct of the electoral process, including the wording of the ballot question put to the voters. The United Nations subsequently supervised referenda in Northern Cameroon (1959 and 1961) and legislative elections in French Togoland (1958) and Ruanda-Urundi (1961). The world body conducted more limited observations of elections and referenda in the Trust Territory of the Pacific Islands (1978–90). From 1956 to 1989, the United Nations supervised or observed thirty plebiscites, referenda, and elections in non-self-governing territories in transition to independence. In each case, the General Assembly, the Security Council, or the Trusteeship Council adopted a resolution that established and defined the mandate of a commissioner or mission. This UN practice represented an important precedent for broader democracy assistance.[2]

The UN supervision of elections in Namibia in 1989, as part of a major peacekeeping operation during the territory's transition to independence, marked the beginning of a second phase of more comprehensive UN election involvement in postconflict, nation-building environments. Although in the tradition of earlier election monitoring in the context of decolonization, the Namibia operation represented a considerable expansion of UN involvement in non-self-governing territories. In 1978, the Security Council had adopted a settlement plan for the conflict over Namibia. The resolution proposed to establish the United Nations Transition Assistance Group (UNTAG) to "ensure the early independence of Namibia through free and fair elections under the supervision and control of the United Nations."[3] South Africa, which controlled Namibia in violation of international law, only agreed to the plan a decade later. Taking up its year-long mandate in April 1989, UNTAG oversaw a process that led to Namibian independence in March 1990. In addition to managing about 8,000 peacekeeping personnel, UNTAG was charged with the responsibility of supervising the constituent assembly elections administered by South Africa and certifying whether those elections were "free and fair." For the first time, UN peacekeeping was associated with a UN role in an election.

The February 1990 UN election-monitoring mission in Nicaragua, in response to a request from the Nicaraguan government, ushered in yet a third type of UN election involvement: verification of an election in a sovereign member state. Secretary General Javier Perez de Cuellar called the request for UN monitoring in an independent country "unprecedented" but concluded that the situation was unique, because the General Assembly had encouraged involvement in the Central American peace process and other Central American states supported the expanded UN role. Former U.S. president Jimmy Carter's engagement may also have been a factor, either because his high-profile involvement was making election monitoring increasingly acceptable internationally or perhaps because multilateral organizations did not want Carter to get all the credit. Although not comparable to Namibia, the UN role was more than passive observation of election day. Arriving six months before the voting, UN personnel attended political rallies and organized a parallel vote tabulation. In addition to observing the balloting, they remained after the elections to monitor the transition.[4]

The secretary general declined a similar request for election observers from Romania in January 1990, on grounds that the United Nations did not monitor elections in sovereign countries unless there was a profound threat to regional security. Nevertheless, the United Nations responded affirmatively the following year to a request for electoral assistance from Haiti, another sovereign member country, even in the absence of a threat to international peace.[5] The initial Haitian request was for technical assistance, but it was later expanded to include verification. The Nicaraguan operation was no longer sui generis. The United Nations had established a precedent for election verification in an independent member state really to promote internal democratization rather than to prevent international conflict.

As part of an effort to end a long-standing, horrific civil war, the United Nations established the UN Transitional Authority in Cambodia (UNTAC) in 1991 to oversee the administration of the country, deploy peacekeeping forces, and conduct elections. The effort built on the experience of Namibia but was even more ambitious. As compared with the UN operations in Nicaragua and Haiti, this was a qualitatively different form of UN engagement in the electoral process of a sovereign country. For the first time, the United Nations took on the responsibility, in effect, for administering a member country, because UNTAC took control of such key ministries as foreign affairs, national defense, finance, public security, and information. Likewise, the United Nations was involved in every phase of the election process, from organization to monitoring to verification.

UN Support for International Standards for Democracy and Elections

The UN Charter reaffirmed the importance of human rights and recognized the principle of self-determination, and the Universal Declaration of Human Rights and the International Covenant on Civil and Political Rights (IC-CPR) call for "periodic and genuine elections." Nevertheless, only the end of the Cold War made it possible for the United Nations to expand its commitment to democracy and freed the world body to offer assistance to elections in all member countries. During the 1990s, the Security Council and General Assembly repeatedly endorsed the importance of elections and a greatly expanded UN role in democracy assistance.

In 1988 the General Assembly, citing the commitments to periodic and genuine elections in the Universal Declaration of Human Rights and the IC-CPR, adopted the first of a series of resolutions on "enhancing the effectiveness of the principle of periodic and genuine elections." The resolution began to lay down specific UN principles on elections by requiring "an electoral process which accommodates distinct alternatives" and "provide[s] an equal opportunity for all citizens to become candidates and put forward their political views, individually and in co-operation with others."[6] Since 1988, the UN secretary general has also reported regularly to the General Assembly on UN electoral assistance and support for the principle of elections.

In 1991, the General Assembly asked member states to consider "ways in which the United Nations can respond to the requests of Member States as they seek to promote and strengthen their electoral institutions and procedures."[7] In accordance with the General Assembly's direction, the secretary general designated the under secretary general for political affairs as the "focal point" for coordination of UN electoral assistance and established the Electoral Assistance Unit to support that function.

At the same time, as it had in earlier resolutions, the General Assembly showed its ambivalence when it reaffirmed by majority vote in 1991 "principles of national sovereignty and non-interference in the internal affairs of States in their electoral processes." Reflecting resistance to the trend toward UN election assistance in more and more countries, the General Assembly cautioned that there was "no universal need for the United Nations to provide electoral assistance to Member States, except in special circumstances such as cases of decolonization, in the context of regional or international peace processes, or at the request of specific sovereign States" and insisted on "resolutions adopted by the Security Council or the General Assembly in each individual case."[8]

Nevertheless, the General Assembly subsequently became increasingly unambiguous in its endorsement of UN involvement in democracy assistance and elections. By 1992, the General Assembly had dropped the language about UN involvement in elections and democracy promotion as an exceptional activity, welcomed the establishment of the UN Electoral Assistance Unit, and called for electoral assistance on a case-by-case basis according to guidelines to be established.[9] Subsequent annual secretary general reports and General Assembly resolutions on enhancing elections have emphasized the conditions necessary for effective UN involvement, such as adequate advance notice and conditions that would permit free and fair elections. As demand for UN election involvement increased, the Electoral Assistance Unit was upgraded in 1994 to become the Electoral Assistance Division (EAD). Since then, the General Assembly has regularly reiterated the importance of UN assistance to elections and commended the work of the EAD.[10]

Supporting Elections within the UN System

Between 1989 and 2001, the United Nations responded to more than 140 requests from member states for electoral assistance. In just three recent years, from 1999 to 2001, the United Nations received 47 requests for electoral assistance from 37 member states, and, including previously received requests, the Electoral Assistance Division undertook 53 projects. Most of these were for relatively small-scale technical assistance projects. The United Nations also continues to supervise self-determination elections, as it did in East Timor in August 1999.[11]

Several different actors within the UN system are now involved in efforts to support democracy, democratic elections, and good governance. These include the EAD, the United Nations Development Program (UNDP), the Office of the High Commissioner for Human Rights, and a number of specific peacekeeping and nation-building operations.

There have been considerable struggles over coordination and division of responsibilities within the UN system. While both the EAD and the UNDP have offered election assistance, they have not always agreed on approach. As separate entities within a huge UN system, the EAD and UNDP, of course, have different interests, comparative advantages, and points of view. The relationship between the organizations also reflects inevitable tensions between the center, where the EAD is situated, and the field, where the UNDP effectively makes its decisions and conducts its programs.

The UNDP became involved in elections because of the incorporation of governance into its mandate. It now devotes more than 50 percent of its resources to assistance for good governance.[12] UNDP country offices provide technical assistance for elections and work on longer-term efforts to build capacity and institutions. This often includes the coordination and channeling of donor funds for electoral assistance.

The Electoral Assistance Division has an explicit mandate to serve as the institutional mechanism of the United Nations to respond to requests for election assistance. The secretary general's appointment of a UN "focal point" for electoral assistance was designed to ensure consistency, channel requests, and develop an institutional memory. The EAD undertakes missions to assess needs and maintains a roster of international experts. It coordinates with other parts of the UN system to provide technical assistance and facilitate international observation. The EAD has a strong position in the UN bureaucracy, for its director is the only official at that level who reports directly to an under secretary general.[13]

The EAD has also established formal and informal partnerships with other regional and intergovernmental organizations. The EAD refers requests for observers and formally shares information with regional organizations, including the European Union, the OAS, and the OSCE. The EAD also has a memorandum of understanding with the International IDEA and works closely with Elections Canada, the Federal Electoral Institute of Mexico, the United States–based IFES, and the Australian Electoral Commission.

In response to bureaucratic struggles within the UN system, the United Nations has reaffirmed the leading role of the EAD. In January 2001, the UN undersecretary for political affairs and the UNDP administrator formally agreed on how field offices should proceed in the electoral area. This "note of guidance" states that before providing any type of electoral assistance, the United Nations "must first carefully assess the pre-election conditions in the requesting country . . . in order to ensure involvement only in settings where legitimate elections are likely." The note of guidance calls for (1) a formal request from the relevant government at least four months before the scheduled election, (2) consultations between the EAD and the UNDP, and (3) a "needs assessment" by the UNDP to evaluate the "political, material and institutional situation" and the "appropriateness, necessity and potential impact" of UN assistance. The requirement for such a needs assessment is intended to "reduce the risk of associating the United Nations with elections whose organization and conduct do not adhere to internationally recognized criteria" and thus to uphold "the reputation of the United Nations as a credible, standard-setting institution in this field."[14] As one senior UN official put it, "No part of the [electoral] process is apolitical." The United Nations should "not play around with electoral assistance without being aware of its implications."

In October 2001, the secretary general endorsed this "binding note of guidance," and in December 2001 the EAD received its strongest mandate to date from the General Assembly, which also "note[d] with satisfaction the comprehensive coordination" between the EAD and the UNDP. On the basis of the EAD's "role as coordinator of United Nations electoral assistance," the resolution encouraged the secretary general, through the EAD, "to continue responding to the evolving nature of requests for assistance" and requested the secretary general to provide the EAD "with adequate human and financial resources."[15]

The Scope of Present UN Involvement in Elections

Before engaging in full-blown "electoral assistance," the United Nations can provide "expert advisory services" or conduct "needs-assessment missions." The EAD provides expert advisory services in response to requests for advice from resident coordinators or special representatives of the secretary general "at a very early stage, in the context of United Nations activities such as conflict prevention, peacekeeping, post-conflict peace-building, development and democratic transitions."[16] In response to a formal governmental request for assistance, the EAD is supposed to send a needs-assessment mission to the country to evaluate plans and conditions for elections and make recommendations. Between 1999 and 2001, the EAD conducted thirty-eight such missions.

The secretary general's October 2001 report on electoral support lists five types of electoral assistance: (1) observation and monitoring of elections, (2) process assistance, (3) capacity building, (4) institution building, and (5) system architecture.[17]

Four of the five types involve technical assistance as opposed to monitoring. Process assistance to electoral authorities includes help with electoral administration and voter registration, election budgeting, review of electoral laws and regulations, training of election officials, logistics, voter and civic education, procurement of election materials, coordination of international donor assistance, electoral dispute resolution, computerization of electoral rolls, and boundary delimitation. Advice in these areas "identifies options, analyses comparative advantage and makes recommendations" about new or updated electoral systems. In Peru in 2001, for example, the United Nations provided assistance on planning, logistics, civic education, and computer software systems. Capacity-building programs for election administrators are typically longer-term, joint projects of the EAD and the UNDP. The United Nations supports institution building by offering expert assistance for "the creation or revision of key institutional components of electoral management," such as election laws and procedures and the structure of election commissions. Again, the EAD and UNDP often work together on such projects, as in Cambodia, Nigeria, Pakistan, and Yemen in 2001–2. Finally, UN advice on system architecture for elections involves comprehensive advice on the design of electoral systems and process, consistent with political and social structures, cultural norms, and traditions. Operating under a broad mandate to help East Timor prepare for independence, for example, the United Nations was responsible for drafting election laws and organizing the conduct of the elections.[18]

The United Nations lists four subtypes of observation and monitoring: (1) coordination and support for international observers, (2) provision of UN observers, (3) expert monitoring, and (4) support for domestic monitoring.[19] First, the United Nations often provides "coordination and support" for international observers from various governments and organizations. The EAD and the UNDP typically help to coordinate and provide logistical support for international observers through a joint international observer group (JIOG) or similar mechanism. The United Nations remains neutral and takes no responsibility for the substance of observers' assessments. Coordination and support can make a contribution but, as in Cambodia in 1998, can also make the United Nations politically responsible for a statement in which it had no substantive role. Member groups of a JIOG typically issue one or more joint statements about the elections and sometimes make their own reports as well.

Between 1999 and 2001, the United Nations provided coordination and support in four African countries (Guinea-Bissau, Niger, Rwanda, and Tanzania) and in Guyana. In all but one those cases, it also provided technical assistance to the election commission. In other cases, the United Nations referred requests for observers to the OAS and OSCE.

Second, the General Assembly authorizes the dispatch of UN observers in special cases. In 2001, for example, the General Assembly authorized the establishment of an observation mission to Fiji.[20] In this way, the United

Nations can "verify" elections by observing the electoral process and then publicly commenting on the nature and quality of those elections.

Verification is less intrusive than supervision. The host government remains responsible for organizing and administering the elections, while the United Nations organizes a traditional election observation exercise, which deploys observers during the whole process and throughout the country. This was the nature of UN engagement in elections in Nicaragua and Haiti. Building on earlier UN efforts to verify the redeployment and withdrawal of Cuban troops from Angola, the United Nations expanded the mandate to include verification of elections there in September 1992. That election failed, however, when the opposition UNITA Party rejected the process and resumed its war. In the OAS and OSCE regions, the United Nations now generally refers requests for observers to those organizations and concentrates on technical assistance (table 4.1).

Third, on occasion the United Nations dispatches experts to report on technical election issues, as it did in cooperation with the OSCE in Tajikistan in 2000. In situations where a request arrives too late for the United Nations to provide other assistance, a local UN representative, such as the resident representative of the UNDP, may "follow and report" on the elections to the EAD, or the United Nations will send a small team of officials to prepare an internal report.

Fourth, upon request from a government, the United Nations offers assistance to civic organizations engaged in nonpartisan election monitoring. It provided technical assistance, for example, to domestic monitors in Mexico in 1994 and 2000. For the 1999 transitional elections in Indonesia, the UNDP oversaw $10 million in donor funds for domestic monitoring. This form of UN involvement demonstrates the increasing acceptability of domestic election monitoring.

Table 4.1

Types of UN Election Observation and Monitoring

1. Coordination and support for international observers (often through a Joint International Observer Group)
2. Provision of UN observers for verification
3. Expert monitoring (or "follow and report")
4. Support for domestic monitoring

Other Multilateral Organizations

In addition to the United Nations, election monitoring has become an important function for a number of other multilateral organizations. Among the more active and influential are the OSCE, the European Union, the Council of Europe, the OAS, and the Commonwealth. Beginning in 1990, each of these multilateral organizations received a mandate to promote democracy and democratic elections.

The OSCE has become one of the leading intergovernmental organizations in democracy and election assistance. The Helsinki Final Act, signed during the Cold War in 1975, established the Conference on Security and Cooperation in Europe (CSCE) as a mechanism for East–West dialogue and committed participating states to respect and promote human rights, the rule of law, and democracy. (It was renamed the Organization for Security and Cooperation in Europe in 1994.) In 1990, soon after the fall of the Berlin Wall and transitional elections throughout Eastern and Central Europe, the CSCE's thirty-five participating countries from throughout Europe, Central Asia, and North America meeting in Copenhagen reaffirmed the fundamental obligation of governments to protect human rights and made extensive commitments regarding elections. The 1990 Copenhagen document also provided the first formal international recognition of the emerging practice of international and domestic election observation.

The OAS has likewise strongly supported democracy in its hemisphere. OAS Resolution 1080, as was noted in chapter 2, calls for an automatic response to a coup against a legitimate, democratically elected government, and the Inter-American Democratic Charter of 2001 requires, among other things, "free and fair elections."

Other multilateral organizations have made similar commitments to democracy and human rights. The European Commission calls "the protection and promotion of human rights as well as support for democratisation . . . corner stones of EU foreign policy and EU development co-operation."[21] Heads of government of the Commonwealth, an association of countries with historical ties to the United Kingdom, in 1991 made a commitment in Harare to promote democracy and human rights. Accession to the Council of Europe— founded after World War II to promote human rights, democracy, and the rule of law throughout Europe—"presupposes that the applicant country has brought its institutions and legal system into line with the basic principles of democracy" including "free and fair elections based on universal suffrage."[22]

The OSCE and OAS established distinct institutional mechanisms, much like the UN Electoral Assistance Division, to oversee their efforts in support of elections and democracy. The 1990 Charter of Paris established the Office for Free Elections within the CSCE to facilitate the exchange of information on elections in member states. In 1992, the CSCE expanded the office's mandate to include human rights and democratization and changed its name to the Office for Democratic Institutions and Human Rights (ODIHR). Based in Warsaw, ODIHR now employs more than eighty staff members and is active throughout Central and Eastern Europe, southeastern Europe, the Caucasus, and Central Asia. ODIHR promotes democratic elections through comprehensive election-monitoring and assistance projects. Like American democracy organizations, ODIHR also conducts programs aimed at improving governance, consolidating democratic institutions, promoting human rights and the rule of law, and strengthening civil society. ODIHR advises OSCE country missions and monitors the implementation of OSCE "human dimension" commitments by participating states.

Similarly, the OAS established a Unit for Promotion of Democracy. The unit oversees OAS electoral missions, provides advice and assistance on election law reform and other issues, and conducts programs to improve democratic institutions and processes in more than a dozen member states.

The Experience of Multilateral Organizations with Monitoring

Each of these intergovernmental organizations plays an active role in advising on and monitoring elections. Each sees elections in the broader context of democracy and human rights, and in recent years the OSCE, European Union, and OAS have developed similar methodologies focused on long-term, comprehensive monitoring. Bilateral European observers for particular elections are typically associated with one of the major multilateral organizations.

In 1989, the Commonwealth heads of government declared that the organization could help member governments through "a facility for mounting observer missions." Between 1990 and May 2001, the Commonwealth organized thirty-three election observation missions in twenty-two countries. Most were in Africa, and nine took place during transitional elections. In most cases, observer missions complemented constitutional, electoral, or legal support.[23]

The Council of Europe used to observe elections in countries that were candidates for membership in the organization, but it increasingly observes elections in member countries as well.

The OAS first conducted a systematic monitoring effort for the Nicaraguan election in 1990, which was also a watershed for the United Nations and for Jimmy Carter. For the OAS, the scope of the effort was unprecedented. The regional multilateral organization established a presence in the country beginning six months before election day and ultimately sent 433 observers. Complementing the efforts of President Carter and the United Nations, the OAS monitoring helped increase confidence and encouraged all parties to accept the final results. Similar efforts have followed. In 2002, for example, the OAS sent election observation missions to Bolivia, Colombia, the Dominican Republic, and Honduras. More than other intergovernmental organizations, the OAS has put considerable emphasis on its ability to conduct statistically based quick counts, which are discussed in chapter 13.

The OSCE's ODIHR sends election observation missions to assess the implementation of OSCE election commitments. ODIHR touts its "extensive and carefully developed methodology" which "provides a unique, in-depth insight into all elements of an electoral process."[24] In its election-related activities, ODIHR cooperates closely with the OSCE Parliamentary Assembly and with other multilateral European institutions, including the Parliamentary Assembly of the Council of Europe and the European Union. It often coordinates bilateral observers as well. In its first ten years, ODIHR monitored 102 elections in OSCE states, more than half of them after 1997. During 2000 alone, ODIHR sent more than 3,000 observers to 15 elections in twelve countries.[25]

Although initially timid at times, ODIHR has established itself as a significant force in the election-monitoring field. After it received a mandate for expanded monitoring in December 1994, ODIHR organized its first substantial long-term monitoring program for the May 1996 elections in Albania. On the basis of its preelection findings, the mission found fault with the redistricting process, the disqualification of many candidates, excessive restrictions on opposition rallies, and police intimidation of opposition supporters.[26] In apparent retaliation for these criticisms from ODIHR, the Albanian government said it would restrict the number of ODIHR observers to the local elections set for October of that year. At the same time, the government invited the Council of Europe to send observers without restrictions. In response, ODIHR withdrew from the process.

Monitoring, funding, and technical assistance for elections have played a considerable role in EU foreign policy and foreign aid since the mid-1990s. "Human rights field missions and election missions are accepted as part of the mandate of the EU," says the European Commission.[27] The European Union sent observers to the first multiparty elections in Russia in December 1993, including 116 members of parliament from the European and national parliaments and 91 "experts." The EU also sent observers to South Africa in April 1994 and provided observers to the UN mission (and much of the funding) for elections in Mozambique in October 1994. In Russia again, for a constitutional referendum in 1995 and presidential elections in 1996, the European Union provided technical assistance to central electoral authorities and logistical support for observers from EU institutions and member states.

The European Union now provides technical assistance and observers primarily for elections outside the OSCE region. As is discussed below, the EU coordinated all international observers to elections in the West Bank and Gaza in January 1996. The EU also provided substantial funding for those 1996 Palestinian elections and, through the OSCE, for elections in Bosnia-Herzegovina in 1996, 1997, and 1998. From 1996 to 2002, the EU provided support and/or observers to elections in nineteen countries, from Albania to Zimbabwe.

International IDEA

In 1995, representatives of fourteen countries founded a new intergovernmental organization, the International Institute for Democracy and Electoral Assistance, as "a forum for exchange of ideas and experiences between scholars, policy-makers and practitioners involved in all aspects of democratic governance."[28] Although it has nongovernmental members as well, International IDEA presents itself as an organization of governments, akin to the United Nations, rather than as an international NGO or research organization. The United States is not one of International IDEA's nineteen member countries. Neither is any of the other countries on the UN Security Council. The organization implicitly positioned itself originally as something of a counterweight to the influence of American organizations in international democracy promotion.

Since its founding, International IDEA has sought to develop internationally accepted standards for democratic development. Rather than organizing election-observation programs, the institute "helps to develop and disseminate rules and guidelines which promote transparency and account-ability, professionalism, efficiency and impartiality in the conduct of elec-tions."[29] As a standard-setting organization, International IDEA offers to convene meetings "to explore the lessons learned" from controversial elec-tions. Through applied research, it has helped identify and codify norms. Its normative work has informed the technical approaches of bilateral and mul-tilateral agencies active in democracy support.[30]

U.S. Democracy Organizations

Since the beginning of the modern era of democracy promotion in the 1980s, the United States has carried out election monitoring and other democracy-assistance programs in part through intermediary NGOs. A handful of such organizations, largely supported by public funds, have been among those in the vanguard of election monitoring around the world. Collectively, these American organizations have been involved in nearly every significant election in an emerging democracy or postconflict envi-ronment since the inception of modern international election monitoring in the mid-1980s. They helped invent and professionalize the election-moni-toring field, which has since attracted so much attention from multilateral organizations.

This vanguard group includes NDI, IRI, the Carter Center, and IFES.[31] Other American organizations, such as the Asia Foundation and the African-American Institute, also conduct election-related programs. In partnership with local activists and groups, these American organizations conduct pro-grams in new democracies, societies in conflict, and nondemocratic coun-tries with strong democratic movements.

Each of the American democracy organizations, although based in the United States, presents itself, to a greater or lesser degree, as an interna-tional organization, drawing considerable support from around the world. To a somewhat greater degree than its Republican counterpart IRI, NDI un-der long-time president Kenneth Wollack and current chair Madeleine Al-bright generally seeks to present a multinational face as the institute mar-shals the talents of political practitioners and experts from around the world for all its programs, including its election-monitoring missions. IRI, chaired by U.S. Senator John McCain, also draws on experts from various countries in addition to those from the United States. The Carter Center has drawn political leaders from many countries into election observation and other

Table 4.2

Intergovernmental Organizations Involved in Election Monitoring

Intergovernmental Organization	Phase	Specialized Office	Key Declarations or Decisions	First Election: Country and Date	Dates	No. of Elections[a]	Current Focus
United Nations	Phase I. Decolonization	UN Temporary Commission on Korea	UN Gen. Assembly Res. 122 (1947)	South Korea, 1948			n.a.
United Nations	Phase I. Decolonization	UN Trusteeship Council, Security Council, General Assembly		British Togoland, 1956	1956–89	30	n.a.
United Nations	Phase II. Postconflict	United Nations Transition Assistance Group (Namibia)	UN Security Council Namibia, Resolution 435 (1978) (regarding Namibia)	1989–present November 1989		4	Case-by-case
United Nations	Phase III. Verification in sovereign member countries		UN Gen. Assembly Res. 43/157 (1988) (first of series regarding "periodic and genuine elections"); UN Gen. Assembly Res. 44/10 (1989) (regarding Nicaragua)	Nicaragua, February 1990	1990–present		Case-by-case
United Nations	Phase IV. Technical assistance as norm	UN Electoral Assistance Division (EAD) (established as Electoral Assistance Unit, 1991; renamed 1994); United Nations Development Program	UN Gen. Assembly Res. 46/130 (1991) (establishing EAU); UN Gen. Assembly Res. 56/159 (2001) (endorsing EAD)		1990–present	140 (electoral assistance)	Needs assessments, technical assistance, & coordination of observers

Organization	Key document / founding	First mission location and date	Activity through 2002	Scope
Organization for Security and Cooperation in Europe (OSCE)	Office of Democracy and International Human Rights (ODIHR) (established as Office for Free Elections, 1990; reconstituted and renamed, 1992)	CSCE Copenhagen Document (1990) Charter of Paris (1990) Council of Ministers Decision, Prague (1992)	1990–present	110 elections	Elections in 55 member countries in Europe, Central Asia and North America
European Union (EU)			Russia, December 1993	1996–present	19 countries	Countries outside OSCE Region
Commonwealth		Harare Declaration (1991)		1990–present	33 missions in 22 countries through 2001)	Member countries
Organization of American States (OAS)	Unit for the Promotion of Democracy	OAS Res. 1080 (Santiago Declaration) (1991) Inter-American Democratic Charter (2001)	Nicaragua, February 1990 (modern phase)	1962–present	69 elections in 20 countries	Member countries
Council of Europe	Parliamentary Assembly		Hungary, March-April 1990	1991–present	elections in 20 countries	Member countries and and candidates for membership
International Institute for Democracy and Electoral Assistance (International IDEA)		Founded February 1995 by 14 countries	n.a.	n.a.	Not a monitoring organization— promotes standards and analysis of "lessons learned"
Organization for African Unity (OAU) African Union		Formed at Durban, South Africa (2002)	Namibia, November 1989	2002–present		
Southern Africa Development Community (SADC)		Declaration on Election Standards (2001)		1999–present	9 elections	

Note: n.a. = not applicable.

[a] Through 2002, unless otherwise indicated.

Table 4.3

Selected Nongovernmental and Bilateral Election-Monitoring Organizations

Organization	Home Country	Principal Funding	First Election: Country and Date	Number of Elections Observed or Assisted[a]
The Asia Foundation	United States	U.S. government (U.S. Agency for International Development, or USAID; congressional appropriation)		Elections in 4 countries
Asian Network for Free Elections (ANFREL)	Thailand (NGO Network in Southeast Asia)	Foreign and Asian Donors	Cambodia, 1998	Elections in 11 countries
Australian Election Commission	Australia	Australian government	Namibia, 1989	Elections in 24 countries
The Carter Center	United States	U.S. government, foreign government, and private sources (American, European and other)	Panama, 1989	45 elections in 23 countries(1989–2002)
Center for Democracy[b]	United States	Private sources	El Salvador, 1985	Elections in 10 countries

Organization	Location	Funding	First mission	Activities[a]
International Foundation for Election Systems (IFES)	United States	U.S. government (USAID)		More than 45 election observation missions; more than 75 technical assistance programs; more than 50 preelection assessments; more than 40 countries in which managed election equipment and commodities procurement
International Republican Institute (IRI)	United States	U.S. government (USAID, State Department, National Endowment for Democracy) and private sources	Philippines, 1986	
National Citizens' Movement for Free Elections (NAMFREL)	Philippines	Philippines and Foreign Donors	Philippines, 1984	All elections in the Philippines since 1986; some in other countries
National Democratic Institute for International Affairs (NDI)	United States	U.S. government (USAID, State Department, National Endowment for Democracy) and private sources		45 comprehensive election observation missions; more than 50 preelection assessments; advised domestic EMOs in 52 countries (1986–2002)
Study and Research Group on Democracy and Economic and Social Development (GERDDES)	Benin (Network in West Africa)	Foreign donors	Benin, 1991	10 countries (1990–1999)

[a]Through 2002, unless otherwise indicated.
[b]Merged into International Foundation for Election Systems in 2003.

democracy-building activities. The Carter Center has also drawn consider-able financial support from private and governmental donors outside the United States. IFES has organized regional associations of election admin-istrators in each major region of the world.

Although they are competitors on some level, the principal American election-monitoring organizations try to complement each other, and each tends to find a role in most high-profile elections. For some elections, these groups have worked separately, as in Azerbaijan in 1998, where IRI and NDI organized separate observer efforts, complementing monitors from the OSCE. In Indonesia in 1999, IRI worked with political parties in provinces around the country, while NDI worked with the same parties at the national level, aided domestic monitoring organizations, set up a facilitation center for observers on behalf of the UNDP, and, together with the Carter Center, carried out a comprehensive international monitoring program. For other elections, American democracy groups have conducted separate, but com-plementary, preelection and postelection monitoring activities and have combined their election-day delegations. In Mexico in 1994, for example, IRI, NDI, and the Carter Center organized a joint election-day mission.

Since 1995, IRI, NDI, and IFES have been partners in a joint coopera-tive agreement with the U.S. Agency for International Development (US-AID) called the Consortium on Elections and Political Processes Support (CEPPS). (The Carter Center nominally has been a junior partner in this venture.) This has been USAID's principal mechanism for funding election-related programs. Because the IRI–NDI–IFES joint venture has twice won competitive bids for this overall program, USAID can fund individual elec-tion-related projects of any of these organizations without further compet-itive bidding. Each generally conducts at least some program in nearly every election receiving USAID support. Between 1995 and 2001, USAID pro-grammed nearly $80 million through the CEPPS mechanism.[32]

On occasion, the U.S. government has also dispatched official bilateral election observer delegations, as it did, for example, for the key 1986 tran-sitional elections in the Philippines, in Haiti in 1995, and in Bosnia in 1996. Such a delegation demonstrates high-level U.S. support for democracy, but it can hardly claim any degree of independence from official U.S. govern-ment policy. In any event, such a delegation by its very nature is present in the country for a short time and inevitably focuses on election day.

American groups have often been out in front of other international ac-tors in promoting democracy, including democratic elections. First, the principal American actors in the field are NGOs. Because of their independence from official government policy, notwithstanding their substantial government funding, such groups can focus solely on their democracy-promotion mandate and are less constrained by other foreign policy considerations. Second, whether because they are NGOs or because they are American, U.S. groups are often considerably more willing to take risks than are intergovernmental or bilateral actors. They tend to be less bureaucratic, for example, than governmental or multilateral organizations. Finally, American organizations and American democracy promoters tend to be especially idealistic.

The organizations involved in international election monitoring are diverse (tables 4.2 and 4.3). After a few U.S. organizations effectively invented the field in the late 1980s, the leading intergovernmental organizations brought broader legitimacy and added their diplomatic muscle. But NGOs retain some comparative advantages. The next chapter tells how one person in particular profoundly influenced this important new area of international relations.

Chapter 5

Jimmy Carter and the Popularization of International Election Observation

I am not here as a public official, but as a citizen of a troubled world . . .

—Jimmy Carter, on receiving the Nobel Peace Prize[1]

Jimmy Carter will probably not go down in American history as the most effective President. But he is certainly the best ex-president the country ever had.

—Gunnar Berge, Chair of the Norwegian Nobel Committee,
upon awarding Carter the Nobel Prize[2]

Former U.S. president Jimmy Carter is the reigning celebrity of international election observation. Indeed, for many people the very mention of international election observation brings Carter to mind. Since the end of his presidency, he has earned a well-deserved reputation for effectiveness and seriousness of purpose that perhaps eclipses his standing as president and even helped him win the 2002 Nobel Peace Prize. His extensive involvement in election monitoring helped solidify that reputation.

Carter has profoundly influenced the evolving state of the art of international election monitoring. His emphasis on preelection assessments, "election mediation," and "parallel vote tabulations" to deter or detect vote count fraud became a model. As his involvement raised the profile of international election monitoring, it made it more acceptable for multilateral organizations to aid and monitor elections as well.

This chapter traces the evolution of Carter's involvement in monitoring foreign elections and considers the impact that he and the Carter Center have had on election monitoring. After a brief foray into election issues in Haiti in 1987, Carter really began to focus on election oversight in Panama in 1989. The following year, he led a major international effort to oversee the elections in Nicaragua, where he helped mediate a peaceful transfer of power and helped launch the Organization of American States (OAS) and the United Nations into election monitoring in member states. By then, he was well established at the pinnacle of the world's election-monitoring and democracy movement.

Carter went on to observe extremely close elections in the Dominican Republic in May 1990, but the observation was too limited for him to resolve fully election controversies. In the fall of 1991, Zambia became his first election-monitoring project beyond the Western Hemisphere. In these and later elections, his engagement was not without controversy. He insisted on certain monitoring techniques even where there was local resistance, and he seemed relatively unconcerned about offending certain local or international actors. Nevertheless, in methodology and philosophy, Carter has set the standard for international election monitoring.

The Carter Center Discovers Election Monitoring

After leaving the White House, the former president and the former first lady, Rosalynn Carter, established the Carter Center, a privately funded institution associated with his federally supported presidential library and with Emory University in Atlanta. The center's initial mission was to promote conflict resolution, human rights, and public health under the slogan "Waging Peace. Fighting Disease. Building Hope." The center would provide a platform for Carter to use his influence and stature as a former president, international public figure, and outspoken supporter of human rights.

The Carter Center's initial mission did not expressly target democracy or elections. Election monitoring became the most prominent activity of the center almost by accident, as an extension of its efforts to promote peace. Speaking in 2003, Carter acknowledged, "At the beginning of our effort . . . we didn't see a wide need for the Carter Center or others to participate as monitors in elections." He went on to explain:

> I was interested in preventing conflict and ending existing conflicts, and the first thoughts I had [were] that this would be one more opportunity to accomplish those goals. If they wouldn't let me mediate between the two antagonists or potential antagonists, then we would offer them a way to decide who would be the leader of the nation by peaceful means. Obviously, elections were the best chance.[3]

In 1986, Carter invited a number of former governmental leaders from Latin America to join him in a new Council of Freely Elected Heads of Government, a forum to resolve conflict, reinforce democracy, and encourage economic cooperation in the region. The council later became the means by which the former U.S. president could monitor elections in the hemisphere.

In October 1987, Carter accepted an invitation to visit Haiti, after the assassination of a presidential candidate, to try to help put the election process back on track. Working with the National Democratic Institute for International Affairs (NDI), Carter went to Haiti with George Price, the former prime minister of Belize, on behalf of the Council of Freely Elected Heads of Government. Price returned in November with a delegation sponsored by NDI to observe on election day. The election process was aborted because of violence, but Carter received praise for his efforts. In a letter to Carter, U.S. assistant secretary of state Elliot Abrams lauded the ex-president's "emphasis on elections" which would "increase the chances of a successful transition to democracy."[4] Carter had established the precedent for his involvement in election monitoring.

Panama: A New Potential Unfurled

It was in Panama in 1989, however, where the Carter Center really recognized the potential of international election monitoring.[5] In early 1989, with the support of U.S. secretary of state James Baker, Carter agreed to join former president Gerald Ford in heading a bipartisan delegation organized by NDI and its Republican counterpart, then called the National Republican Institute for International Affairs. Manuel Noriega, Panama's defense forces commander and strongman, backed a hand-picked candidate, Carlos Duque, in the presidential election scheduled for May 7. Noriega's opponents alleged manipulation of voter registration and police intimidation before the election and feared fraud on election day.

After a team representing NDI and the Council of Freely Elected Heads of Government visited Nicaragua in March 1989, the Noriega government seemed to harden its attitude toward international observers. The government tightened visa requirements for U.S. nationals and initially refused to grant visas for anyone beyond Jimmy and Rosalynn Carter, Gerald Ford, and three personal staffers. Yet Carter and his advisers believed that meaningful observation under the circumstances would require at least twenty international observers, and it was important to establish the principle that the host government could not dictate how the job should be done. Carter demanded that Noriega grant permission for at least this number, plus additional professional staff members, and insisted on determining the composition of the group. Rather than risking international isolation if Carter boycotted, Noriega grudgingly agreed. By refusing to negotiate over the size and composition of his team and making clear his willingness to forgo monitoring if his conditions were not met, Carter established the autonomy of observers as an important principle.[6]

Meanwhile, NDI worked with an ad hoc church laity group, which received the support of the Catholic Church hierarchy, to organize an independent "quick count"—sometimes called a parallel vote tabulation—of the actual election results from a representative, statistically significant sample of the 4,000 stations. They designed this quick count to detect any manipulation of the ballot-counting process.

By the morning after the polls on May 7, 1989, the quick count made clear that the opposition had won a resounding victory. Even though quick-count organizers had received results from only 115 polling sites by that morning (they eventually received 164 of the 497 they targeted), the margin was overwhelming. Statistical tests and review of vote counts collected by opposition parties confirmed the validity of the quick-count results, which showed the opposition winning by a three-to-one margin. Organizers shared the details with President Carter's team and with Panama's archbishop. During the course of the day, Carter sought unsuccessfully to negotiate Noriega's acceptance of the outcome. The bishops' conference, based on the quick count, issued a statement reporting the opposition's victory.[7]

Nevertheless, the national election commission began to announce voting results based on obviously falsified tally sheets. As Carter saw the vote count going awry at the national tabulation center, he pushed on to the stage and shouted at the election authorities, in what he later called his "best high school Spanish," "Are you honest officials or thieves? You are stealing the election from the people of Panama." That evening, Noriega's electoral tribunal abruptly shut down the count, and troops prevented Carter from leaving his hotel to go to the press center across the street. At an impromptu press conference in the hotel lobby, Carter reported the outcome of the church's quick count and denounced the blatant fraud.[8]

Three days after the elections, Panama's electoral tribunal nullified the election results. In addition to claiming that some tally sheets were missing, the tribunal blamed the "obstructionist action of many foreigners . . . whose evident purpose was to endorse the idea of electoral fraud."[9]

Although he had failed to deter cheating or negotiate a satisfactory resolution, Carter's exposure of the fraud and impassioned denunciation of the process carried great weight around the world. The OAS condemned the abuses, and the U.S. government imposed sanctions. The real election winners, however, took office only later, after the United States invaded Panama to arrest Noriega in December 1989.

Carter's courageous, outspoken condemnation of the election fraud earned him public praise. A *New York Times* headline announced, "Carter Begins to Shed Negative Public Image." Declared the *New Republic,* "Carter's return to Panama was a masterpiece of guerrilla diplomacy."[10]

Panama helped rehabilitate Carter's international image and established him as the world's most sought-after election observer. His biographer Douglas Brinkley pointed out how Carter's election efforts captured the popular imagination in a way U.S. democracy promotion organizations never could:

> Although virtually no one grasped what acronym organizations like NDI, IRI [International Republican Institute], and NED [National Endowment for Democracy] could do to foster democracy, everyone understood that humanist Jimmy Carter was an honest observer for hire. Just days after the Panamanian presidential contest, Carter began getting requests from other Third World leaders to monitor elections in their countries: from that point on, poll watching became a Carter Center specialty.[11]

Election monitoring offered Jimmy Carter a new means of contributing to conflict resolution and put him back in the international spotlight.

Nicaragua: Carter Invents "Election Mediation"

Having realized the potential value of international election monitoring, both to democratic forces abroad and to his own international stature, Carter agreed to lead a much larger, more ambitious monitoring effort in Nicaragua. For a decade, conflict between the ruling Sandinista government and United States–backed rebels known as the Contras had ravaged the country. Nicaragua had also become a polarizing, contentious issue in U.S. politics, as the administration of Ronald Reagan provided overt and covert political, financial, and military support for the Contras over the objection of the Democratic Congress.

In June 1989, Carter received an invitation from Nicaraguan president Daniel Ortega to a commemoration of the tenth anniversary of the Sandinista revolution. Sensing an opening, Carter wrote back to encourage "free and fair elections" as a means to "end definitively the conflict and divisions within Nicaragua" and "improved relations between your country and the United States." In August 1989, Carter received invitations to monitor expected elections from President Ortega, opposition leader Violeta Barrios de Chamorro, and the Nicaraguan Electoral Council.[12]

The Sandinistas invited Carter, the United Nations, and the OAS to observe their elections because they evidently saw elections as the means to international legitimacy, which in turn could lead to the end of a U.S. embargo and greater foreign aid. They clearly saw the imprimatur of a Jimmy Carter as critical to that legitimacy. As Carter himself put it later, ruling party leaders "were sure they were going to win."[13]

The Sandinistas may also have agreed to international monitoring because they did not anticipate how engaged and effective that monitoring would become. Longtime Carter aide Robert Pastor later suggested that Ortega might have assumed that observers would be passive and respectful of incumbents, as election missions in the region had been in the past : "[Ortega] could be forgiven for not anticipating the unprecedented: that the Carter mission would become deeply involved in negotiating the terms of a free election." Indeed, the Carter effort in Nicaragua established a new model of hands-on, interventionist election monitoring, which Pastor calls "election mediation."[14]

In September 1989, joined by former Argentine president Raúl Alfonsín, President Carter visited Nicaragua to assess the fairness of the election rules. Carter wanted to mediate election-related issues between the two sides, which had been opponents in a civil war. He also encouraged better relations between the Sandinista government and the Bush administration. He made two more trips before the election, in December and January, and returned for the election itself in February 1990.[15]

In response to pressure from Carter, Ortega ultimately accepted significant changes to the election rules and even acquiesced to $9 million in "overt" U.S. assistance, including support for voter education, get-out-the-vote efforts, and infrastructure for the opposition. (The U.S. congressional appropriation also earmarked funds for the Carter Center program.) Carter promised Ortega that he would seek assurances from President Bush that the United States had stopped covert aid to the opposition. The U.S. government had not, however, disarmed the Contras, as it had promised to do in a 1987 regional peace accord.[16]

Carter faced criticism in both Nicaragua and the United States. Opposition leaders complained that Carter was not pushing the Sandinistas hard enough to end their exploitation of state resources and state media for the benefit of their campaign. The Bush administration and U.S. conservatives were suspicious that Carter had grown too close to Ortega. In response, Carter reassured Bush that he would not ignore Sandinista fraud or manipulation. The former president reported that, while there continued to be serious obstacles to a fair election, he was optimistic that observers would be able to detect any fraud on election day.[17]

The Nicaraguan election on February 25, 1990, also marked a major milestone for the United Nations and the OAS as the first time that either organization sent observers to an election in a sovereign member country. The Carter Center coordinated its involvement with both organizations. Indeed, for the election itself, Carter was just the most prominent of 2,578 accredited foreign observers, including 435 from the OAS (led by OAS secretary general João Baena Soares) and 207 from the United Nations (led by former U.S. attorney general and defense secretary Elliot Richardson). Carter's own delegation numbered sixty-two and included seven former Latin American presidents, five U.S. senators, six members of the U.S. House of Representatives, and three former U.S. governors.[18] The American elected officials came from both U.S. political parties. This extraordinarily high-profile international presence demonstrated not only the intensity of interest in this small country but also the emerging importance of monitoring itself.

In his discussions with the Nicaraguan government, electoral authorities, and political parties as well as with the United Nations, the OAS, and the U.S. State Department, President Carter emphasized, on the basis of his experience in Panama, the importance of an independent verification of the ballot count. No domestic group planned a quick count, however, and Carter's own mission was not large enough to do so. Accordingly, the United Nations and the OAS decided to conduct independent quick counts of the election results, the first time for either organization.[19]

By election night, the United Nations and OAS quick counts indicated that the Sandinistas had been soundly defeated. Around midnight, Carter met with a stunned Ortega. Carter expressed empathy: "Like you, I have won a presidential election, and I have lost one," he said, "but losing the election wasn't the end of the world." Reminding the much younger Ortega that he had plenty of time for a political comeback, Carter encouraged the Sandinista leader to cede power gracefully: "Your greatest accomplishment as president will be if you lead a peaceful transition of power."[20]

Ortega conceded defeat early the next morning. For the next two days, Carter worked to broker a transition of power.

Some Republicans, including Senator Jesse Helms and former Reagan administration official Jeane Kirkpatrick, later criticized Carter for allowing the Sandinistas to remain in control of the Nicaraguan military. Elliott Abrams, the administration official who had praised Carter's earlier work in Haiti, accused the former president of covering up Sandinista fraud and abuses during the election. (Abrams later was convicted—and then pardoned—of withholding information from Congress about the Iran-Contra episode.) Abrams now called the former president either "ill-informed or biased."[21]

The Bush White House, however, had a different assessment. When Carter came to Washington upon his return from Managua to brief President George H. W. Bush, the national security adviser, Brent Scowcroft, observed approvingly, "Carter didn't just observe the election—he ran it."[22] Scowcroft's comment neatly captured the way Carter's deep involvement and focus on details had established a precedent for active outside engagement in transitional elections.

Carter's Election Monitoring Comes of Age

Carter soon received invitations to monitor other elections in the region. Having established in Panama and Nicaragua, respectively, that he would stand up to fraud and that he could mediate election-related disputes, Carter's subsequent involvement in the Dominican Republic convinced him of the need for early involvement and for independent means of verifying the vote count.

Soon after the Nicaraguan election, Carter agreed to observe the May 1990 presidential election in the Dominican Republic. That election turned out to be extremely close and controversial. Election authorities eventually reported that the incumbent president, Joaquin Balaguer, had won by only about 24,000 votes or 1.2 percentage points. Problems with voter registration lists and vote tally sheets and delays in tabulation led the opposition candidate, Juan Bosch, to allege fraud. As Bosch's bitter supporters threatened protests after election day, concern grew that street demonstrations might turn violent.[23]

Unfortunately, because he was invited only two weeks before the election, Carter and his team had arrived too late to assess fully alleged preelection irregularities, such as problems with the voter registration lists, and there was no quick count or parallel vote tabulation to help in assessing the integrity of the vote-counting process. In contrast to his early and sustained involvement in the process in Nicaragua, Carter's presence only for the election itself in the Dominican Republic left him unable to tell whether fraud had determined the election's outcome.

Despite these handicaps, the former president was able to defuse the crisis. He successfully urged all parties to avoid violence and to bring their complaints to the attention of duly constituted authorities. The opposition agreed to not take their grievances "into the streets," and both sides consented to waiting for the Carter Center to investigate their complaints. Carter's team concluded shortly after the election that there was insufficient evidence to sustain allegations of systematic fraud in favor of the incumbent. Carter subsequently wrote to the chairman of the electoral board, "I have not yet seen fraud, by which I mean a pattern of irregularities that favors a particular candidate or party."[24]

Given the difficult position in which he had found himself in the Dominican Republic, Carter committed himself to early and sustained engagement in Haiti for elections later in 1990. In July and October, Carter traveled again to the island to discuss the conditions and rules for elections. In December, he led an observation mission to the Haiti elections, in which the young Catholic priest Jean-Bertrand Aristide was first elected president. Carter's preelection involvement had ensured his input, and his involvement in Haiti provided another example of the emerging, preferred methodology for election monitoring.

Meanwhile, in September 1990, President Desmond Hoyte and opposition leaders in Guyana invited Carter to monitor expected elections in that country. In October, Carter visited Guyana and made a number of increasingly familiar recommendations, including an updated voter list and an independent election commission. Carter also recommended a change in the vote-counting process; rather than moving ballots to more central locations for counting, he urged that election officials count all ballots at the polling places immediately upon the completion of balloting. Carter believed this would greatly reduce the opportunity for stuffing, switching, or tampering with the ballot boxes and would increase the transparency of the count. Significantly, a polling site count also made possible parallel vote tabulation.[25]

So began a long Carter Center association with the democratization process in Guyana. Carter fully implemented the mediation methodology that he had pioneered in Nicaragua. After several delays to address Carter's concerns, especially about voter registration, the election in Guyana was eventually held two years later, on October 5, 1992. But first Carter would take his new model of election mediation to Africa.

Zambia: Bringing Election Mediation and Parallel Counts beyond Latin America

The elections in Zambia in October 1991 saw the first comprehensive effort at election monitoring in independent Africa. For the first time, a sovereign African state with an internationally recognized government invited a high-level foreign election observer presence. But with those observers came controversy. As they pressed for solutions to perceived problems with the electoral process, as they had in Nicaragua and Guyana, Jimmy Carter and other international observers posed an unfamiliar challenge for Zambian authorities and surprised even some locally based diplomats.

As the threat of violent conflict loomed in Zambia, Carter agreed in mid-1991 to lead the international effort to observe that country's first multiparty elections, the first time he monitored an election beyond Latin America. A broad-based opposition movement challenged the increasingly unpopular, long-time autocratic president, Kenneth Kaunda. Expecting an election victory nonetheless, President Kaunda evidently believed that he needed the imprimatur of independent observers to encourage acceptance of that victory and avoid civil unrest. Accordingly, Kaunda invited Carter, already the best-known and most credible international observer. Carter accepted and, as he had in Latin America, invited NDI to work with him.

The Carter Center and NDI conducted a comprehensive monitoring project beginning three months before the elections. For the elections themselves, the two organizations jointly fielded the largest international observer group, composed of more than fifty members and staffers from thirteen countries. Throughout the process, Carter also acted in effect as the spokesperson for all international observers and donors, including those from Europe and Africa, and the Carter Center–NDI team oversaw much of the foreign aid to domestic monitors (as is discussed in chapter 11).[26]

As by then had become his custom, Carter visited before the elections. He arrived in Zambia in September 1991, about five weeks before election day. Again, he sought to remedy problems by assessing the rules, considering issues, and making recommendations before the elections took place. At the end of his visit, he expressed serious reservations about the electoral preparations, bluntly criticized the broadcast media for unfairness, and recommended substantial changes in the election system.[27]

Carter's strong words drew vehement protests from Zambia's ruling party. Despite Kaunda's invitation to Carter and other observers, many ruling-party leaders now viewed international monitoring as an infringement on the nation's sovereignty. In a full-page newspaper advertisement, shortly after the preelection visit, the party rebutted Carter's charge that the government was not ready to conduct legitimate elections and harshly criticized international support for Zambian monitoring groups. Kaunda himself mused publicly that he should have imposed restrictions on international observers. Several weeks later, in another newspaper advertisement, the ruling party dismissed election monitoring as a "big imperialist plot . . . to use the so-called election monitors to influence the outcome to the elections" in favor of the opposition. Citing Nicaragua as "a classic example of this plot," the party charged that, in the "likely" event of a ruling party victory, international observers "will certify that the elections were not free and fair" in order to help the opposition to incite violence. The party singled out Americans, together with domestic monitors, for particular scorn.[28]

More surprisingly, some diplomats in Lusaka worried that observers (meaning Carter) were intervening too aggressively in the country's internal affairs. Although none criticized Carter openly, some distanced themselves privately from his approach and argued for steps to ensure that the monitoring operation would continue to have the ruling party's support. (Some donors, as discussed in chapter 11, also disagreed with the NDI team's strategy for supporting domestic monitors.)

Three weeks later, on behalf of Carter and NDI, Lisbet Palme of Sweden followed up on the former U.S. president's concerns about the process while at the same time trying to mollify critics, both in the Zambian ruling party and the diplomatic community. Palme reassured the government that international observers did not seek to dictate Zambia's electoral rules or to interfere in the process.

The NDI–Carter Center plans for a parallel vote tabulation and President Carter's related demands for changes to the vote counting process proved to be especially contentious. Carter's focus on the potential for fraud in the vote-tabulation process challenged not only Zambian authorities but also his own staff and others involved in monitoring.

Carter's early monitoring experiences had convinced him of the over-whelming importance of effective independent means to assess the honesty of vote counts, known as quick counts or parallel vote tabulations (or PVTs; see chapter 13 for further discussion of PVTs). The PVT in Panama defin-itively revealed the attempt at fraud in the vote count, which Carter later ex-posed and denounced. Likewise, the quick counts in Nicaragua gave Carter and other leaders of the international monitoring effort early, independent information that the Sandinistas had been defeated and allowed him to move quickly to encourage acceptance of the results and to facilitate a peaceful transition of power. The absence of a PVT in the Dominican Republic, in contrast, had made it essentially impossible for Carter and other interna-tional observers to assess the credibility of an extremely close vote count on which the presidency of the country turned. Thus, Carter had come to see a PVT as essential to effective monitoring.

When they took up the challenge of monitoring the transitional election process in Zambia, the Carter Center and NDI were committed to organiz-ing a PVT. Beginning in August 1991, about ten weeks before election day, NDI began working in Zambia with domestic monitoring groups. Because these groups were slow to get started, however, NDI decided to organize a PVT directly under the auspices of the NDI–Carter Center project rather than to advise a domestic group on how to do so. NDI recruited individual Zambians to monitor the polls and collect the necessary election results. Al-though relying on local observers, a private group of international ob-servers—rather than a domestic monitoring group or an intergovernmental organization—for the first time took responsibility for the design of the independent count, the analysis of its results, and the management of its political profile.

As he had in Guyana, Carter pushed for changes in the established vote-counting procedures. As in previous Zambian elections, the authorities planned to count ballots in a relatively small number of district counting centers rather than at thousands of polling places. However, Carter—joined by opposition political parties and domestic monitoring groups—demanded polling site counts because of concerns about tampering with ballot boxes during transportation to district counting centers. District counting also made a PVT impossible, because results on a polling-site basis would not exist. Carter representatives argued that independent verification of the vote count was essential to the credibility of the election results. They also ar-gued that a count by individual polling place had other substantial advan-tages. If a postelection review found serious problems with the balloting process at a given polling station, for example, the commission could disregard the results from that polling site only, rather than having to invalidate the election in an entire constituency.

The Zambian authorities resisted such a significant change in their procedures. They argued that counting the ballots at the polls would substantially increase the need for security to prevent disruption or cheating at the local level. They also argued that the change would increase the perception that there might be reprisals against communities that voted the "wrong way," heighten the risk of inconsistent decisions about invalid ballots, and greatly increase the need for trained, qualified personnel to conduct the count in all of the country's polling stations. These were not unreasonable concerns.

Under pressure from Carter, however, the election commission eventually agreed to a compromise. It would still conduct the count at district centers but would change the procedures to ensure the separate counting of ballots from each polling site. This made the PVT possible, although it did not address the threat of tampering with ballot boxes between the close of the polls and the later counting at district headquarters.

To address concerns about the potential for stuffing or tampering with ballot boxes before they could be counted at the district level, Carter offered a novel solution. Displaying his legendary attention to detail, the former president noted that the Secret Service attached tamper-proof seals to his luggage when he traveled. Such seals, he suggested, could as well be attached to ballot boxes to ensure that any tampering would likewise be detected.

Carter arranged for the delivery of seals from the U.S. Secret Service to the Zambian election commission, which agreed to use them. The seals arrived from the United States sometime before the election in an unmarked box addressed to the Carter Center's temporary office at the Intercontinental Hotel in Lusaka. No one paid attention to the box, which ended up in a corner as a makeshift table with a lamp on top. Only when Carter asked about the seals in a communication from Atlanta a few days before the election did his staff on the ground discover the box and scramble to get the seals to the election commission. But by then, given Zambia's poor transportation infrastructure, it was already too late to distribute them to polling officials in most of the country.[29]

The poor transportation and communications infrastructure also made it difficult to organize the PVT. Although experts in Washington helped to design the PVT, a young NDI staffer in Lusaka worked to recruit, train, and coordinate volunteers around the country to carry it out. She and several

Zambian counterparts traveled around the country, sometimes by chartered private plane. Without working telephones to follow up, however, the PVT coordinator could not be certain as election day approached whether she and her Zambian colleagues had built effective local organizations to collect the necessary information in each of country's sixty-three districts. When Carter inquired about PVT preparations, at a meeting with the Carter Center–NDI staff upon his arrival in Lusaka, the organizer at first was vague. When pressed, she predicted good parallel results from at least "fifty-eight to sixty" of the country's sixty-three counting centers. Confronted in private immediately after the meeting by a more senior colleague about how, given all the uncertainty, she could make such a specific, ambitious claim, she responded "it seemed like he wanted a high number."

Carter and NDI representatives publicized their plans to verify the accuracy of the ballot tabulation, even speaking on television about the PVT's purpose and methodology. The PVT, they argued, would provide reassurance to those that did not trust the electoral authorities, the government, or the ruling party. But just days before the election, senior government officials suddenly objected. Perhaps as plans for the PVT became better known, officials became genuinely worried about confusion if the parallel tabulation and the official numbers did not agree, or perhaps it had dawned on them that the PVT would make significant vote count manipulation effectively impossible. "We find no good cause for this exercise," declared Zambia's foreign minister, who also chaired the ruling party's campaign. "We view it as an exercise which can cause unnecessary disorder especially when the projections erroneously pick a losing candidate or party as a winner."[30] The party demanded that the PVT be aborted and instructed government officials not to cooperate. Calling it a "foreign scheme" to undermine Zambian sovereignty, the government-owned television station expressed fears that the PVT "would produce widely contradictory results" that would leave the country "on a precipice for social disorder."[31]

In a national address on the eve of the election, however, Kaunda disassociated himself from attacks on observers and called on Zambians to support the monitoring effort. Apparently referring to the PVT, Kaunda urged Zambians "to assist the observer groups in every way possible to enable them to carry out their tasks in the best way they know how." Kaunda continued that observers "must freely arrive at their own candid conclusions on the efforts we are making to go through this important transition successfully."[32]

On election night, October 31, 1991, the PVT revealed a clear trend: Opposition candidate Frederick Chiluba and his party were headed for a landslide victory. According to official results released much later, Chiluba received 76 percent of the votes.

Given often-expressed fears about whether Kaunda would ever give up power, Carter sought to facilitate a smooth transfer of power, much as he had in Nicaragua. On the morning after election day, the former U.S. president visited President Kaunda to encourage him to step aside gracefully. The following day, in a nationally televised address, Kaunda humbly accepted defeat, and Chiluba was sworn in as president.

Because of the lopsided victory and the early concession by Kaunda, the PVT was ultimately unnecessary to reveal the winner. But it had likely served as an important deterrent to manipulation and provided the electorate and the opposition with added confidence in the fairness of the process.

Carter made no apologies for pushing the Zambian authorities to make changes. As in Nicaragua, he had helped prevent a breakdown of the process before the election by mediating between opposition and government, and his presence had provided much-needed reassurance that the election results would be respected. As before, he and other international observers helped in a modest way to settle disputes over rules, to cool down an overheated election campaign, and to ease the governmental handover. But the hint of controversy over Carter's tactics within the diplomatic community as well as among Zambian political elites suggested an increasing realization that effective election monitoring had the potential to challenge established interests, including interests of the diplomatic community for smooth bilateral relations.

Guyana: Too Much Focus on PVTs?

Carter's unapologetic interventions and forthright public assessments were bound to leave some political leaders unhappy with him. At the same time, as its later experience in Guyana illustrates, the Carter Center may have put more faith in certain monitoring techniques, even in the face of substantial obstacles and methodological questions, than those techniques might always have merited.

The Carter Center in effect endorsed the legitimacy of Guyana's 1992 elections, which sent the Afro-Guyanese party of President Hoyte into opposition after nearly three decades in office. (Hoyte himself had become president after the death of the long-time authoritarian president Forbes Burnham in 1985.) Hoyte was reportedly unhappy with Carter for validating the party's election loss. He also criticized the Carter Center for its involvement with the new government's "national development strategy," which he reportedly saw as an American-driven document drawn up without his party's input. These perceptions led the Carter Center to sit out Guyanese elections in 1996. In both 1992 and 1996, Hoyte's party did not accept the election results, alleging a number of election irregularities.

Before the elections in March 2001, the Carter Center dispatched a PVT expert to Guyana to assess the prospects for an effective parallel count. The expert recommended against a Carter Center PVT for several reasons. First, and most important, the Carter Center lacked a good local partner. The principal domestic monitoring organization in Guyana, the Elections Assistance Bureau (EAB), had decided against a PVT because its 1996 effort to project the results had ended badly. In that election, because of misgivings about its own methodology and incomplete results, the EAB decided not to report the numbers from its PVT. Nevertheless, without authorization, one international adviser (not affiliated with the Carter Center) announced the EAB's incomplete results at a public forum in Washington a short time later. The EAB wanted to avoid a repeat of such a mishap in 2001. Second, had it wanted to conduct a PVT, the EAB lacked the necessary technical capacity. Since the prior election, it had lost both its executive director and chairman, the two organizational leaders who had designed and implemented the earlier PVT. Third, because some in the opposition did not trust the Carter Center, however unfair this may have been, an independent finding from the center ratifying the official results might not assuage the opposition if it lost.

In an echo of Zambia a decade earlier, Carter Center staffers decided to conduct a PVT even without a viable local partner. The center decided to draw its own sample and have international observers collect election results from particular polling stations on election day. This was unlike the operation in Zambia, though, where the NDI–Carter Center team established its own network of domestic pollwatchers to collect PVT results rather than having the international observers do so. Because of concerns that the small sample size in Guyana made the margin of error too great, staff members and technical advisers agreed that the independent count would be for private purposes only. They would not announce PVT results or use them to project winners or to verify the official count.

On election day, upon the completion of the count, each Carter Center observer was called upon to collect results from several of the ninety stations in the sample. This raised methodological questions. Because the international observers had not been at the polling stations to witness the balloting throughout the day, they could not verify that each of the polling stations in the sample was reporting the results of a process free of ballot stuffing, polling day disruptions or intimidation, voter register problems, or other manipulation. Accordingly, the PVT could at best verify the tabulation process based on the assumption that there had been no fraud at the polling places; there was no way to be sure that the results from the polling stations were themselves legitimate.

Even though Carter mentioned it to the press upon his arrival in Guyana shortly before election day, the PVT attracted little notice. No one even asked about it in the postelection press conference.

Carter's representatives focused too much on conducting a PVT, even when it was not feasible or methodologically sound. Moreover, for peculiar reasons and perhaps through no fault of its own, the Carter Center no longer commanded the trust of the opposition in this small country. Thus, the center was not in a position to mediate disputes or reassure opposition supporters about the integrity of the process. In such a situation, even a former U.S. president renowned for his integrity and sophistication found that there were limits on his means to help bring about democratic elections.

Institutionalizing Election Monitoring and Democracy Promotion at the Carter Center

As the 1990s wore on, election monitoring became a staple activity of the Carter Center. Between 1989 and 2002, former president Carter or Carter Center representatives observed forty-five elections in twenty-three countries (see table 5.1).[33]

For his early election-monitoring efforts, Carter typically headed missions organized by NDI or called on NDI to provide him with professional and logistical support. Because of its ties to the Democratic Party, NDI was a natural partner for Carter. At the time, its chair was Walter Mondale, Carter's former vice president, and its president was the former Carter administration official Brian Atwood (who later served as administrator of the U.S. Agency for International Development, or USAID, under President Bill Clinton). NDI was happy to associate itself with and to take direction from the former Democratic president and offered the services of an increasingly experienced, professional staff in return. Although Carter un-

Table 5.1

Elections Observed by the Carter Center, 1989–2002

Country	Date
Panama	May 1989
Nicaragua	February 1990
Dominican Republic	May 1990
Haiti	December 1990
Zambia	October 1991
Guyana	October 1992
Ghana	November 1992
Paraguay	May 1993
Panama	May 1994
Mexico	August 1994
West Bank and Gaza (Palestine)	January 1996
Dominican Republic	June 1996
Nicaragua	October 1996
China (village elections)	March 1997
China (village elections)	July 1997
Liberia	July 1997
Mexico	July 1997
Jamaica	December 1997
China (village elections)	March 1998
Venezuela	December 1998
Nigeria	December 1998
China (village elections)	January 1999
Nigeria	February 1999
Indonesia	June 1999
Cherokee Nation	July 1999
East Timor	August 1999
China (village elections)	September 1999
Mozambique	December 1999
China (village Elections)	January 2000
Dominican Republic	May 2000
Mexico	July 2000
Venezuela	July 2000
China (village elections)	August 2000
Guyana	March 2001
Peru	June 2001
East Timor	August 2001
China (village elections)	August 2001
Nicaragua	November 2001
Zambia	December 2001
China (village elections)	December 2001
Mali	April 2002
East Timor	April 2002
Sierra Leone	May 2002
Jamaica	October 2002
Kenya	December 2002

Source: Carter Center Web site, www.cartercenter.org

derstandably received virtually all the international attention—and the NDI name typically remained in the background—Carter's participation opened doors for NDI programs in a number of countries. In Zambia in 1991, for example, before USAID was willing to fund democracy-assistance programs anywhere in Africa, Carter's involvement enabled NDI to get funding for domestic monitoring and PVT programs from European donors.

As elections became an increasingly important part of the Carter Center's portfolio, however, the center began to develop its own in-house capacity to provide both logistical support and election-monitoring experience to the former president. In Guyana in 1992, the center for the first time organized an international monitoring program separate from NDI. Thereafter, the center hired additional staff members or short-term consultants with election-monitoring experience, many of whom had worked previously for NDI. Though Carter himself remained its most valuable asset, the center began to assert its institutional identity as well.

Carter himself has derived enormous personal satisfaction from his experiences since 1990 with elections around the world. Asked recently for his favorite or most memorable election-monitoring experience, Carter recalled visiting his first polling site of the day in Lusaka in 1991 with South African Franklin Sonn, then a university rector and senior official of the African National Congress. Upon walking into the school gymnasium that held the polling station, Carter recalled, the South African burst into tears: "I'm fifty-three years old," Carter remembered Sonn telling him. "This is the first time I ever saw anyone vote."[34]

Jimmy Carter also remembers the profound emotions he felt in Liberia in 1997. Before the election, he worked hard to convince the "warlords" to accept a liberal interpretation of eligibility to vote, to ensure that returning refugees were not disenfranchised because of problems proving their citizenship. When they arrived at a polling station outside Monrovia before dawn, well before the opening, he and Rosalynn were moved to find three-quarters of the eligible local voters were already there, lined up "standing in the dark, in [the] rain, drenched, just waiting for a chance for the first time in their lives to cast a ballot."[35]

Former president Carter has also drawn many leaders from the global South into international election monitoring, which has helped make the practice internationally acceptable and has blunted objections of developing-country governments about interference from the West. Former Zambian president Kaunda, for example, served as a Carter Center observer for Kenya's breakthrough election in December 2002. When, after twenty-four years in power, Kenya's autocratic president Daniel arap Moi decided to step down, hold real elections, and abide by the result, Kaunda remarked, "All of those leaders who are in power today by dirty methods—Kenya has given a good lesson which they should emulate."[36]

Carter's election monitoring has necessarily reflected his own interests and idiosyncrasies. He has focused, for example, on the details of certain methodologies, including PVTs. He has emphasized mediation of conflicts about election rules and resolution of disputes about election procedures or results, for which his personal involvement has often been indispensable.

Yet there is only one Jimmy Carter. As a former U.S. president with an incontrovertible reputation for high ethical standards and a well-known commitment to human rights, he is in a unique position to act as mediator between polarized political forces or to insist on procedural reforms. As the sensitivities of political elites and diplomats to his interventions might suggest, mediation or strong intervention may be entirely inappropriate for other international actors.

Carter has become an icon of election monitoring, and his commitment to election monitoring has contributed significantly to its widespread acceptance around the world. Before he became involved, many leaders in developing countries and diplomats in multilateral organizations viewed election monitoring as an inherently inappropriate infringement on national sovereignty. But even though his focus and effectiveness have sometimes drawn opposition, his involvement has changed the issue from whether election monitoring is appropriate to how it can contribute. The questions have become "What issues are amenable to outside mediation?" and "How hard should international observers push their recommendations on national authorities?" rather than whether observers have the right to be involved in the first place. Despite Carter's unique stature, he nevertheless has legitimized a role for other international observers to recommend changes and mediate disputes, even if they must necessarily be more deferential or careful in doing so.

Moreover, in addition to legitimizing a more active role for international election observers, former president Carter has made an invaluable contribution to the professionalization of election monitoring. By focusing on the preelection environment, election preparations, and the vote count in election monitoring's early days, he ensured that international election monitoring would be more than superficial and symbolic. His preelection assessment visits and interest in parallel counts have set high standards for the international promotion of democracy.

Chapter 6

Toward "Free and Fair" Elections?

> It is not possible to have free and fair elections anywhere in the world, but we cannot give up on the term free and fair.
>
> —John Makumbe, professor and election observer, Zimbabwe[1]

In recent years, an international consensus has more or less emerged in principle on what constitutes democratic elections. In addition to fair conduct of the balloting and counting, there must be opportunities for political parties to compete, reasonably equitable access to media, impartial election administration, fair rules, a political environment free of intimidation, and prompt and just resolution of election-related disputes and grievances. Elections that meet these standards are often referred to as being "free and fair."

This broad understanding of an election as a fundamentally political process argues against undue emphasis by monitors on polling day or election administration. Rather, preelection monitoring of the legal and institutional framework, voter registration, candidate and party eligibility, campaign environment, voter education programs, and media access and balance enables elections to be seen in context. Similarly, continued monitoring after election day can reveal whether the vote count is fair and the election results are respected. Observer groups now generally agree that they should monitor all significant parts of the electoral process.

Despite such consensus in theory, however, the standards by which international observers assess elections remain vague, even though a number of international organizations and commentators have proposed particular criteria. Although typically articulated as minimum standards for free and fair elections, such criteria are usually broad aspirations. Assessing whether a given election has met such standards can be extremely difficult, and external considerations often influence such assessments. Judgments about political context often seem subjective or tend to make minimum requirements for democratic elections appear more relative than universal. The phrase "free and fair" has tended to obscure rather than clarify.

In the previous two chapters, I have described the principal organizations and actors in international election monitoring. This chapter is about international standards for elections. The chapter first considers the conundrum of trying to determine whether given elections are free and fair and examines the merits and implications of alternative verbal formulations. I argue that the existing criteria for assessing elections are impractical and inconsistent with actual practice, and that the search for better combinations of words reveals a weakness of international monitoring. Then, the chapter addresses the considerations that inform an international group's determination about whether to observe a given election in the first place. Both of these issues have proven problematic in practice for election observers, and efforts to articulate standards have been largely unrealistic.

Sources of Evaluation Standards

Explicitly or implicitly, election observers judge whether elections are democratic according to standards derived from three sources: (1) national law; (2) international law, including applicable provisions of international human rights documents; and (3) international norms and expectations.

First, elections must be held in accordance with applicable, preexisting national laws and regulations. Although national electoral and legal authorities are responsible for ensuring that their elections fully comply with local law, international observers can and should point out if the conduct of elections diverges from those applicable legal requirements. (International observers, of course, also should point it out if a nation's laws themselves do not comport with international law or international democratic norms.)

Second, international law imposes certain obligations on electoral authorities and the conduct of elections. Such obligations come from applicable provisions of international human rights agreements and from norms that have become "customary international law." The Universal Declaration of Human Rights, the International Covenant on Civil and Political Rights, and other international instruments establish two essential conditions for democratic elections: (1) universal and equal suffrage, and (2) a secret ballot.[2] International conventions banning discrimination based on race or gender further reinforce the right to participate in elections on the basis of "universal and equal suffrage."[3] International law also guarantees other political and human rights that are fundamental to free elections, such as freedom of expression, assembly, and association.[4]

Third, international observers judge whether given elections comply with international norms established by standard practice for democratic elections around the world, even though such norms may not have achieved the status of customary international law. International observers also assess elections by reference to laws and practices in democratic countries. Election systems, rules governing politics, and ways of organizing elections vary substantially, but practices in democratic countries reveal a shared commitment to core principles. Although elections in emerging democracies need not follow exactly all practices of established democracies, they should be expected to adopt procedures consistent with these core principles. As the 2000 U.S. presidential election debacle in Florida reminds us, however, even established democracies sometimes countenance flawed elections that fall short of these principles.

Since the mid-1990s, the Inter-Parliamentary Union, the Bergstraesser Institute in Germany, the Norwegian Helskinki Committee, the Office for Democratic Institutions and Human Rights (ODIHR) of the Organization for Security and Cooperation in Europe (OSCE), the European Union, and others have made declarations about the requirements for free and fair or democratic elections and/or the criteria by which observers should judge elections (see tables 6.1 through 6.5). These declarations explicitly or implicitly synthesize international legal obligations and accepted norms. Scholars and democracy organizations likewise have analyzed and synthesized these criteria. Yet an agreed-upon set of specific practical criteria for judging elections remains elusive.

The "Free and Fair" Standard

International observers, journalists, diplomats, academics, and others often talk about whether elections are free and fair. Indeed, this standard has become the rhetorical touchstone for most assessments of transitional or post-conflict elections, and most people assume that the observers' job is to determine whether an election is free and fair. Yet observation practice has not clearly established what this means.

Measuring elections against a free and fair standard suggests a dichotomy —that elections either pass or fail a test of legitimacy—when elections are actually political processes more realistically judged along a continuum and placed in context. This focus on the free and fair determination has encouraged international election assessments to make categorical, "bottom-line" judgments that fail to take nuances and context into account. Such judgments imply, inaccurately, that elections in democratic countries are beyond reproach.

Despite the long-standing use of the phrase and the great significance attached to it, there has been surprisingly little progress in the development of a practical set of criteria by which to judge whether an election has been free and fair. Efforts to make the standard more precise have been largely unsatisfactory.

References to "free and fair" elections are not new. In 1927, Henry Stimson, as special emissary of U.S. president Calvin Coolidge, "pledged the United States to a fair and free election" in Nicaragua, as part of an early effort at postconflict nation building.[5] In 1956, a United Nations report on a plebiscite on the future of Togoland used the term.[6] But the phrase first achieved salience when the United Nations established the process by which Namibia would gain independence. In 1978, UN Security Council Resolution 435 called for "the early independence of Namibia through free and fair elections under the supervision and control of the United Nations."[7] The secretary general appointed a special representative to carry out this mandate.

As election monitoring took off in the 1990s, a number of international organizations attempted to define better the free and fair standard or to articulate the standard's many components. The 1990 Copenhagen document, for example, sets forth international standards for elections in OSCE member countries. Following the requirements of the Universal Declaration of Human Rights, the OSCE standards require that member countries hold free elections at reasonable intervals, guarantee universal and equal suffrage, and ensure that votes are cast by secret ballot. The Copenhagen document also goes further to make several other requirements explicit. Member states must permit all seats in at least one chamber of the national legislature to be freely contested, ensure that the votes are counted and reported honestly, respect the rights of citizens to seek political office, ensure that law and public policy permit a free campaign environment, provide for unimpeded access to the media, and ensure that the candidates who obtain the necessary number of votes are duly installed in office.[8] In 1994, the Inter-Parliamentary Union (IPU) formally adopted a *Declaration on Criteria for Free and Fair*

Elections, which declared a broad range of rights of citizens, candidates, parties, and states as necessary for free and fair elections.[9] These declarations of the OSCE and the IPU reflect a broad consensus in principle on what constitutes free and fair elections and have served as a model for the development of similar standards by other intergovernmental organizations.

In a 1997 article in the *Journal of Democracy,* the Danish political scientists Jørgen Elklit and Palle Svensson closely analyze the free and fair standard. Elklit and Svensson write that *freedom* refers to "voters' opportunity to participate in the election without coercion or restrictions." They define *fairness* as "impartiality" in the sense both of "regularity (unbiased application of rules) and reasonableness (the not-too-unequal distribution of relevant resources among competitors)."[10] In a German study of election observation, Stefan Mair states an election is fair "if all voters have the same number of votes, no political group is excluded . . . in a discriminatory fashion and all groups involved in the election are able to advertise their stand equally."[11] Many democracy organizations and practitioners talk about the need for a "level playing field" if an election is to be fair.[12] The ODIHR's handbook says, for example, "The principle of fairness should ideally assure a level playing field for all participants in the election process."[13]

Election observers must somehow apply these important but vague conditions for free and fair elections to real situations. The synthesis of Elklit and Svensson, however, like other attempts to examine the concept of free and fair elections, fails to offer much help in developing practical, real-world guidelines. Addressing the role of observers, Elklit and Svensson develop an extensive checklist of criteria for both the "free" and the "fair" dimensions and for each of three phases of the process: before polling day, on polling day, and after polling day. So, for example, to evaluate whether the election process was "free" before polling day, observers should consider whether there has been freedom of movement, assembly, association, and speech (for candidates, media, voters, and others), as well as "freedom from fear in connection with the election and the electoral campaign," "absence of impediments to standing for election," and "equal and universal suffrage." Similarly, for the process before polling day to be "fair," these scholars suggest that there must be an electoral process that is "transparent," a legal framework that grants "no special privileges to any political party or social group," an "independent and impartial election commission," "equal opportunities for political parties and independent candidates to stand," "impartial voter-education programs," "equal access to publicly controlled media," "no misuse of government facilities for campaign purposes," and so on[14] (see tables 6.1 through 6.5).

Alternative formulations, developed expressly to guide observers, seek to establish comprehensive standards for judging elections but typically offer little of real, practical use. A synthesis compiled by the Bergstraesser Institute and funded by the European Commission, titled *Observing Democratic Elections: A European Approach,* suggests that elections must meet four fundamental criteria rather than two: "Elections should be universal, equal, secret and free."[15] The ensuing checklist of this *European Approach* includes questions about both the legal rules and the electoral process for each of these four dimensions. For example, to judge whether elections meet the "universal" test, it would ask whether the laws entitle all citizens to vote and all parties to name candidates, and whether the electoral process provided for fair voter registration and permitted all eligible candidates to run.[16] To the four fundamental criteria of the *European Approach,* the Norwegian Helsinki Committee adds a fifth, namely, whether an election is "transparent." To be transparent, an election must have predictable procedures; have published results, both aggregated and broken down by constituency and polling station; and ensure security against fraud.[17] Few would questions the intentions behind these additional requirements, but they seem only to complicate the analysis.

In proposing standards for consideration by its own election observers, the OSCE's ODIHR lists and elaborates upon seven essential principles for democratic elections: universality, equality, fairness, secrecy, freedom, transparency, and accountability. This adds the requirements of "fairness" and "accountability" to the previous five. By "accountability," the ODIHR handbook means that "those elected [must be] duly installed in office and recognize their accountability to the electorate." The ODIHR principles also provide additional detail to several of the previous five components of democratic elections; for example, the "principle of equality requires that one's vote be given equivalent weight to that of the other voters . . ." and the "principle of freedom should ensure a citizen's ability to cast his/her ballot free from intimidation and secure in the knowledge that his/her rights of freedom of express, freedom of association, and freedom of assembly will be upheld throughout the entire election process."[18] The *Handbook for European Union Election Observation Missions* offers eight principles, derived from the Universal Declaration of Human Rights and the International Covenant on Civil and Political Rights, that are necessary for a "meaning-

Table 6.1

Criteria for Free and Fair Elections—Legal Framework and Equality Constituencies

General Criteria	Specific Criteria	UDHR[a] 1948	ICCPR[b] 1966	OSCE Copenhagen Document[c] 1990	Inter-Parliamentary Union[d] 1994	Bergstraesser Institute European Approach[e] 1995	Norwegian Helsinki Committee[f] 1996, 2000	Elklit and Svensson[g] 1997	European Council Decision 9262/98[h] 1998	OSCE ODIHR Election Observation Handbook[i] 1999	National Democratic Institute[j] 1999	Handbook for European Election Observation[k] 2002
Legal framework: scope and system												
Right to periodic elections		X	X	X								
Transparency	Legislative procedures for establishing ground rules transparent and inclusive						X					X
	Predictable procedures—described in law and regulations, published in advance						X			X		

Parties agree on rules		
Parties agree on legal framework		X
Equality: constituencies and districting		
One person, one vote	X X X	
Right to vote of equivalent value/weight (one person, one vote)	X	X

a *The Universal Declaration of Human Rights*, UN General Assembly Resolution 217A (III) (1948), arts. 19–21, 29. (Note: The Universal Declaration does not explicitly tie fundamental freedoms, such as freedom of expression, association and assembly, to elections.)

b *International Covenant on Civil and Political Rights*, Resolution 2200A (XXI), UN Doc. A/6316 (1966), art. 25.

c Conference on Security and Cooperation in Europe, *The Document of the 1990 Copenhagen Meeting of the Conference on the Human Dimension* (Copenhagen, June 29, 1990).

d Inter-Parliamentary Council, *Declaration on Criteria for Free and Fair Elections*, 154th Session, Paris, March 26, 1994.

e Theodor Hanf, Maria R. Macchiaverna, Bernard Owen, and Julian Santamaria, *Observing Democratic Elections: A European Approach* (Frieburg: Arnold-Bergstraesser-Institut, 1995).

f Norwegian Helsinki Committee, *Election Observation: An Introduction to the Methodology and Organization*, (Olso: Norwegian Helsinki Commitment, 2000).

g Jørgen Elklit and Palle Svensson, "What Makes Elections Free and Fair?" *Journal of Democracy* 8, no. 3 (July 1997).

h Council of the European Union, *Guidelines—EU Policy on Electoral Observation*, Council Decision 9262/98 (1998).

i Organization for Security and Cooperation in Europe, *The ODIHR Election Observation Handbook*, Fourth Edition (Warsaw: OSCE Office for Democratic Institutions and Human Rights, 1999).

j National Democratic Institute for International Affairs (NDI), *Lessons Learned and Challenges Facing International Election Monitoring* (Washington, D.C.: NDI, 1999).

k Anders Erikson, ed., *Handbook for European Union Election Observation Missions* (Stockholm: Swedish International Development Cooperation Agency, 2002) (citing Council of the European Union, *Guidelines—EU Policy on Electoral Observation*).

Table 6.2

Criteria for Free and Fair Elections—Impartiality: Administration and Management; and Universality and Equality: Right to Vote

General Criteria	Specific Criteria	UDHR[a] 1948	ICCPR[b] 1966	OSCE Copenhagen Document[c] 1990	Inter-Parliamentary Union[d] 1994	Bergstraesser Institute European Approach[e] 1995	Norwegian Helsinki Committee[f] 1996, 2000	Eklit and Svensson[g] 1997	European Council Decision 9262/98[h] 1998	OSCE ODIHR Election Observation Handbook[i] 1999	National Democratic Institute[j] 1999	Handbook for European Election Observation[k] 2002
Impartiality: administration and management												
Election authorities	Independent, impartial election authority (neutral, impartial or balanced mechanism for election management)				X		X	X			X	X
Ballots and election materials	Secure ballot design and distribution of election materials (proper precautions)[l]						X	X				X
Procedures and materials	Effective design of ballot papers							X				
	Proper ballot boxes							X				
	Conduct of polling and counting in accordance with electoral law							X				

Universality and equality:
right to vote

Equal and universal suffrage	Equal and universal suffrage	X				X		X	X
	All adult citizens have right to vote on nondiscriminatory basis		X	X	X	X		X	
Voter registration	Effective, impartial, nondiscriminatory voter registration (absence of impediments)			X	X	X	X	X	
	Denial of right to vote only in accordance with objectively verifiable criteria and with international law			X	X	X			
	Right to appeal denial of registration				X				
	Opportunity to check electoral rolls in advance								X
	Fair issuance of voter identification documentation								X
	Fair citizenship process								
	Citizenship for people "who have lived in the country as de facto citizens for a substantial number of years"					X			
	Fair treatment of noncitizen permanent residents								X

(continued)

Table 6.2 Continued

General Criteria	Specific Criteria	UDHR[a] 1948	ICCPR[b] 1966	OSCE Copenhagen Document[c] 1990	Inter-Parliamentary Union[d] 1994	Bergstraesser Institute European Approach[e] 1995	Norwegian Helsinki Committee[f] 1996, 2000	Elklit and Svensson[g] 1997	European Council Decision 9262/98[h] 1998	OSCE ODIHR Election Observation Handbook[i] 1999	National Democratic Institute[j] 1999	Handbook for European Election Observation[k] 2002
Equal treatment	Equal rights regardless of gender, race, religion, national minority status / Absence of special privileges for any political party or social group	X		X			X (with exceptions for disadvantaged geographical areas)					X

[a]The Universal Declaration of Human Rights, arts. 19–21, 29. (Note: The Universal Declaration does not explicitly tie fundamental freedoms, such as freedom of expression, association and assembly, to elections.)

[b]International Covenant on Civil and Political Rights, art. 25.

[c]Conference on Security and Cooperation in Europe, The Document of the 1990 Copenhagen Meeting of the Conference on the Human Dimension.

[d]Inter-Parliamentary Council, Declaration on Criteria for Free and Fair Elections.

[e]Theodor Hanf, Maria R. Macchiaverna, Bernard Owen, and Julian Santamaria, Observing Democratic Elections: A European Approach.

[f]Norwegian Helsinki Committee, Election Observation: An Introduction to the Methodology and Organization, (Olso: Norwegian Helsinki Commitment, 2000).

[g]Jørgen Elklit and Palle Svensson, "What Makes Elections Free and Fair?"

[h]Council of the European Union, Guidelines—EU Policy on Electoral Observation.

[i]Organization for Security and Cooperation in Europe, The ODIHR Election Observation Handbook.

[j]NDI. Lessons Learned and Challenges Facing International Election Monitoring.

[k]Anders Erikson, ed., Handbook for European Union Election Observation Missions (citing Council of the European Union, Guidelines—EU Policy on Electoral Observation).

[l]Elklit and Svensson put under "polling day" category rather than "before polling day."

Table 6.3

Criteria for Free and Fair Elections—Candidacies and Political Parties; and Campaign, Including Media Access and Financing

General Criteria	Specific Criteria	UDHR[a] 1948	ICCPR[b] 1966	OSCE Copenhagen Document[c] 1990	Inter-Parliamentary Union[d] 1994	Bergstraesser Institute European Approach[e] 1995	Norwegian Helsinki Committee[f] 1996, 2000	Elklit and Svensson[g] 1997	European Council Decision 9262/98[h] 1998	OSCE ODIHR Election Observation Handbook[i] 1999	National Democratic Institute[j] 1999	Handbook for European Election Observation[k] 2002
Candidacies and political parties												
Right to become candidate	Equal opportunity to become candidate according to criteria in accordance with national and international law / Absence of impediments to standing for election (parties and independent candidates)		X	X	X	X		X	X		X	X
Nondiscrimination	Impartial treatment of candidates by police, military and courts						X	X	X			X
	Equal opportunities for parties (and independent candidates) to stand for election or nominate candidates			X		X	X		X			

(continued)

Table 6.3 Continued

General Criteria	Specific Criteria	UDHR[a]	ICCPR[b]	OSCE Copenhagen Document[c]	Inter-Parliamentary Union[d]	Bergstraesser Institute European Approach[e]	Norwegian Helsinki Committee[f]	Elklit and Svensson[g]	European Council Decision 9262/98[h]	OSCE ODIHR Election Observation Handbook[i]	National Democratic Institute[j]	Handbook for European Election Observation[k]
		1948	1966	1990	1994	1995	1996, 2000	1997	1998	1999	1999	2002
	Right to appeal denial of candidature, party or campaign rights				X							
Campaign, including media access and financing												
Fundamental freedoms	Freedom of movement		X		X	X	X	X	X		X	X
	Freedom of speech / expression / opinion (for candidates, media, voter, others)	X	X	X	X	X	X	X	X		X	X
	Freedom of assembly	X	X	X	X	X	X	X	X		X	X
	Freedom from fear in connection with the election and campaign							X				
	Freedom of association—right to join or establish political party	X	X	X	X	X	X				X	X
	Freedom of association—right to form NGOs, trade unions and human rights monitoring groups			X								

Category	Criterion	1	2	3	4	5	6
	Freedom to campaign					X	
	Right to protection of law and remedy for violation of political and electoral rights				X	X	X
Security	Orderly election campaign / peaceful conditions			X		X	
	Right to security of lives and property		X		X		
	Absence of intimidation of voters	X		X	X	X	
Media	Equal access (opportunity of access/fairness) to publicly controlled media	X		X	X	X	X
	Reasonable opportunities to present electoral platform (electorate adequately informed)		X	X			
	News media free to gather and impart information about political contestants and issues				X	X	
Voter education	Impartial (effective and timely) voter education				X		X
	Citizen organizations free to conduct voter education					X	
Public confidence	Electorate believes choices will be accurately recorded and respected					X	
Campaign finance	Rules on campaign finance provide all reasonable access to campaign funds						X

(continued)

Table 6.3 *Continued*

General Criteria	Specific Criteria	UDHR[a] 1948	ICCPR[b] 1966	OSCE Copenhagen Document[c] 1990	Inter-Parliamentary Union[d] 1994	Bergstraesser Institute European Approach[e] 1995	Norwegian Helsinki Committee[f] 1996, 2000	Eklit and Svensson[g] 1997	European Council Decision 9262/98[h] 1998	OSCE ODIHR Election Observation Handbook[i] 1999	National Democratic Institute[j] 1999	Handbook for European Election Observation[k] 2002
Campaign finance	Impartial allotment of public funds to political parties (if applicable)							X				
	No misuse of government facilities for campaign purposes							X				
	Separation between parties and state			X								
	No bribery or vote buying											
	Fairness of access to state resources										X	

[a]*The Universal Declaration of Human Rights*, arts. 19–21, 29. (Note: The Universal Declaration does not explicitly tie fundamental freedoms, such as freedom of expression, association and assembly, to elections.)

[b]*International Covenant on Civil and Political Rights*, art. 25.

[c]Conference on Security and Cooperation in Europe, *The Document of the 1990 Copenhagen Meeting of the Conference on the Human Dimension.*

[d]Inter-Parliamentary Council, *Declaration on Criteria for Free and Fair Elections.*

[e]Theodor Hanf, Maria R. Macchiaverna, Bernard Owen, and Julian Santamaria, *Observing Democratic Elections: A European Approach.*

[f]Norwegian Helsinki Committee, *Election Observation: An Introduction to the Methodology and Organization.*

[g]Jørgen Elklit and Palle Svensson, "What Makes Elections Free and Fair?"

[h]Council of the European Union, *Guidelines—EU Policy on Electoral Observation*, Council Decision 9262/98 (1998).

[i]Organization for Security and Cooperation in Europe, *The ODIHR Election Observation Handbook*, Fourth Edition (Warsaw: OSCE Office for Democratic Institutions and Human Rights, 1999).

[j]National Democratic Institute for International Affairs (NDI), *Lessons Learned and Challenges Facing International Election Monitoring* (Washington, D.C.: NDI, 1999).

[k]Anders Erikson, ed., *Handbook for European Union Election Observation Missions* (Stockholm: Swedish International Development Cooperation Agency, 2002) (citing Council of the European Union, *Guidelines—EU Policy on Electoral Observation.*

Table 6.4

Criteria for Free and Fair Elections—Voting Process

General Criteria	Specific Criteria	UDHR[a] 1948	ICCPR[b] 1966	OSCE Copenhagen Document[c] 1990	Inter-Parliamentary Union[d] 1994	Bergstraesser Institute European Approach[e] 1995	Norwegian Helsinki Committee[f] 1996, 2000	Elklit and Svensson[g] 1997	European Council Decision 9262/98[h] 1998	OSCE ODIHR Election Observation Handbook[i] 1999	National Democratic Institute[j] 1999	Handbook for European Election Observation[k] 2002
Secrecy of ballot	Secrecy of ballot	X	X	X	X	X	X	X				X
	Right to cast ballot alone											X
	Right to use secure, private polling booth											X
	Atmosphere free from pressure and intimidation						X					
	Right to "personally and privately" deposit ballot paper in ballot box						X					X
	Impartial assistance to voters (if necessary to address illiteracy or other impediments)						X	X				X
Access to polling stations	Right to "equal and effective access" to polling stations for voters				X							X
No multiple voting	No multiple voting						X					X

(continued)

Table 6.4 Continued

General Criteria	Specific Criteria	UDHR[a] 1948	ICCPR[b] 1966	OSCE Copenhagen Document[c] 1990	Inter-Parliamentary Union[d] 1994	Bergstraesser Institute European Approach[e] 1995	Norwegian Helsinki Committee[f] 1996, 2000	Eiklit and Svensson[g] 1997	European Council Decision 9262/98[h] 1998	OSCE ODIHR Election Observation Handbook[i] 1999	National Democratic Institute[j] 1999	Handbook for European Election Observation[k] 2002
Security	Impartial protection of polling stations							X				
	Opportunity to participate in election							X				
	Peaceful conditions						X					

[a]The Universal Declaration of Human Rights, arts. 19–21, 29. (Note: The Universal Declaration does not explicitly tie fundamental freedoms, such as freedom of expression, association and assembly, to elections.)
[b]International Covenant on Civil and Political Rights, art. 25.
[c]Conference on Security and Cooperation in Europe, The Document of the 1990 Copenhagen Meeting of the Conference on the Human Dimension.
[d]Inter-Parliamentary Council, Declaration on Criteria for Free and Fair Elections.
[e]Theodor Hanf, Maria R. Macchiaverna, Bernard Owen, and Julian Santamaria, Observing Democratic Elections: A European Approach.
[f]Norwegian Helsinki Committee, Election Observation: An Introduction to the Methodology and Organization.
[g]Jørgen Elklit and Palle Svensson, "What Makes Elections Free and Fair?"
[h]Council of the European Union, Guidelines—EU Policy on Electoral Observation.
[i]Organization for Security and Cooperation in Europe, The ODIHR Election Observation Handbook.
[j]NDI, Lessons Learned and Challenges Facing International Election Monitoring.
[k]Anders Erikson, ed., Handbook for European Union Election Observation Missions (citing Council of the European Union, Guidelines—EU Policy on Electoral Observation).

Table 6.5

Criteria for Free and Fair Elections—Results: Determination, Publication, and Implementation; Complaints and Appeals; and Domestic and International Monitoring

General Criteria	Specific Criteria	UDHR[a] 1948	ICCPR[b] 1966	OSCE Copenhagen Document[c] 1990	Inter-Parliamentary Union[d] 1994	Bergstraesser Institute European Approach[e] 1995	Norwegian Helsinki Committee[f] 1996, 2000	Elklit and Svensson[g] 1997	European Council Decision 9262/98[h] 1998	OSCE ODIHR Election Observation Handbook[i] 1999	National Democratic Institute[j] 1999	Handbook for European Election Observation[k] 2002
Results: determination, publication, and implementation												
Accurate, verifiable count and aggregation of results	Proper counting procedures (correct transmission of votes during count, aggregation and verification)						X (method must be "predetermined, visible, and verifiable")	X				X
	Proper treatment of void ballots							X				
Announcement of results	Official, expeditious announcement of election results							X				
	Results published both aggregated and by constituency and polling station						X					

(continued)

Table 6.5 *Continued*

General Criteria	Specific Criteria	UDHR[a] 1948	ICCPR[b] 1966	OSCE Copenhagen Document[c] 1990	Inter-Parliamentary Union[d] 1994	Bergstraesser Institute European Approach[e] 1995	Norwegian Helsinki Committee[f] 1996, 2000	Elklit and Svensson[g] 1997	European Council Decision 9262/98[h] 1998	OSCE ODIHR Election Observation Handbook[i] 1999	National Democratic Institute[j] 1999	Handbook for European Election Observation[k] 2002
	Impartial reports on election result by media							X				
Acceptance of results	Acceptance of election results by all involved							X				
Complaints and appeals												
Dispute resolution	Timely judicial review and accessible dispute resolution (Legal possibilities of complaint)							X			X	X
	Effective means of redress against administrative decisions			X								
	Impartial treatment of election complaints							X				

Domestic and international monitoring

	a	b	c	d	e	f	g	h	i	j	k
Monitoring											
Domestic observers permitted to organize and observe entire electoral process			X					X	X		
International observers invited			X						X		X
Access to polling stations											
Access to polling stations for parties, accredited national and international observers, and media			X		X			X			
Transparency											
Transparency of the entire electoral process including presence of party agents and duly accredited observers			X		X			X			
Vote count visible and verifiable at all levels									X		

[a] *The Universal Declaration of Human Rights*, arts. 19–21, 29 (Note: The Universal Declaration does not explicitly tie fundamental freedoms, such as freedom of expression, association and assembly, to elections.)

[b] *International Covenant on Civil and Political Rights*, art. 25.

[c] Conference on Security and Cooperation in Europe, *The Document of the 1990 Copenhagen Meeting of the Conference on the Human Dimension*.

[d] Inter-Parliamentary Council, *Declaration on Criteria for Free and Fair Elections*.

[e] Theodor Hanf, Maria R. Macchiaverna, Bernard Owen, and Julian Santamaria, *Observing Democratic Elections: A European Approach*.

[f] Norwegian Helsinki Committee, *Election Observation: An Introduction to the Methodology and Organization*.

[g] Jørgen Elklit and Palle Svensson, "What Makes Elections Free and Fair?"

[h] Council of the European Union, *Guidelines—EU Policy on Electoral Observation*.

[i] Organization for Security and Cooperation in Europe, *The ODIHR Election Observation Handbook*, Fourth Edition.

[j] NDI, *Lessons Learned and Challenges Facing International Election Monitoring*.

[k] Anders Erikson, ed., *Handbook for European Union Election Observation Missions* (citing Council of the European Union, *Guidelines—EU Policy on Electoral Observation Missions*).

Table 6.6

Preconditions for Observation

Precondition	Stefan Mair, Stiftung Wissenschaft und Politik (Germany)[a]	Bergstraesser Institute European Approach[b]	Norwegian Helsinki Committee[c]	International IDEA[d]	European Council Decision 9262/98[e]	OSCE ODIHR Election Observation Handbook[f]	ACE Project[g]	European Commission[h]	Handbook for European Election Observation[i]
	1994	1995	1996, 2000	1999	1998	1999	1999	2000	2002
Whether advisable									
Universal franchise	X							X	
Freedom for individuals and parties to participate, freedom of association	X							X	
Freedom of expression	X							X	
Freedom of movement						X	X	X	
Freedom of assembly	X							X	
Reasonable access to media								X	
Respect for basic civil and political rights	X			X					
Commitment to free and fair elections							X		
Legal framework for election meets democratic standards	X	X							
Admissibility of local monitors	X								
Whether viable									
Invitation from host country	X			X	X		X	X	X

Support from principal political parties	X "societal consensus"			X But not "veto power"	X	X
Host government responsive to recommendations for improvements to election preparations	X				X	
Previous EU monitoring of political developments in host country		X			X	X
Capacity of international observers—previous monitoring of political situation					X	X
Enough lead time before election day	X 4 months	X	X 3 months		X	X
Whether useful (cost–benefit analysis)	X				X	
Commitments from host government to observer organization		X				
Formal agreement with host country		X			X	X
Freedom to visit any polling station or counting center (geographical)	X		X		X	X
Freedom to observe entire electoral process (over time)	X					
Freedom of movement for observers		X				

(continued)

Table 6.6 *Continued*

Precondition	Stefan Mair, Stiftung Wissenschaft und Politik (Germany)[a] 1994	Bergstraesser Institute European Approach[b] 1995	Norwegian Helsinki Committee[c] 1996, 2000	International IDEA[d] 1999	European Council Decision 9262/98[e] 1998	OSCE ODIHR Election Observation Handbook[f] 1999	ACE Project[g] 1999	European Commission[h] 2000	Handbook for European Election Observation[i] 2002
Freedom to determine number of observers and to choose observers	X	X				X			X
Official accreditation	X	X				X "Simple nondiscriminatory procedure"	X		X "Clearly defined and nondiscriminatory procedure"
Freedom to meet with any election official	X	X						X	X
Availability of election authorities		X				X		X	X
Access to all necessary information					X				
Freedom to meet with candidates, parties, voters, etc.						X		X	X
Access of observers to media ("both for informational purposes and to send out any message that [observers] may wish to convey")									X

Criteria			
Right to request police protection and emergency medical evacuation	X		
Host government cooperation on logistics and security	X	X	X
Freedom to report independently/ issue public statements	X		
Access to special voting procedures (e.g., mobile ballot boxes, voting in prisons, military voting)	X		X
Other criteria			
Reasonable probability of peaceful circumstances	X		
Credible election authority	X		
Transportation and communication	X		
Distinctive dress for observers	X		
No doubts as to safety	X		

[a]Stefan Mair, "International Election Observation: One Form of Democratization Assistence" (report, Stiftung Wissenschaft und Politik, Research Institute for International Politics and Security, Bonn, April/July 1994).

[b]Theodor Hanf, Maria R. Macchiaverna, Bernard Owen, and Julian Santamaria, *Observing Democratic Elections: A European Approach.*

[c]Norwegian Helsinki Committee, *Election Observation: An Introduction to the Methodology and Organization.*

[d]International Institute for Democracy and Electoral Assistance (International IDEA), *The Future of International Electoral Observation: Lessons Learned and Recommendations* (Stockholm: International IDEA, 1999).

[e]Council of the European Union, *Guidelines—EU Policy on Electoral Observation.*

[f]Organization for Security and Cooperation in Europe, *The ODIHR Election Observation Handbook.*

[g]Sue Nelson, "Integrity in International Observation," *Administration and Cost of Elections (ACE) Project,* International Foundation for Election Systems, United Nations, and International IDEA; www.aceproject.org.

[h]Commission of the European Communities, "Communication from the Commission on EU Election Assistance and Observation" (memorandum, Brussels, April 11, 2000).

[i]Anders Erikson, ed., *Handbook for European Union Election Observation Missions* (citing in part European Union, *Guidelines—EU Policy on Electoral Observation*).

ful and genuine election process."[19] The National Democratic Institute for International Affairs (NDI) lists twelve separate requirements "for an election to be genuine," and even these, it says, are "not exhaustive."[20]

Unfortunately, such lists identify benchmarks that are rarely fully met in elections in the real world. By describing the ideal rather than the minimum elements of an acceptable election, they provide neither a satisfactory theoretical definition of the free and fair standard nor a practical guide for observers. Political science offers some important insights and international guidelines provide worthy aspirations, but few elections—especially in transitional environments—fully meet all the purported requirements for elections to be free and fair. As one expert points out, "International observers are dealing with inherently difficult cases."[21]

The various formulations and criteria provide no help with the task of determining whether a given test has been met, how to deal with criteria that are ambiguous or conditions that have been only partially fulfilled, or what relative weight should be given to various criteria. In other words, they provide no objective means by which to judge. As a result, there are serious practical difficulties in using them to determine whether an election is free and fair. What, then, should the observers do?

To start with, experienced monitoring organizations now generally avoid the "free and fair" formulation because it seems more definitive than observers typically can or should be. It has become a cliché. Until 1993, the Commonwealth expressly directed its observation missions to say whether an election was free and fair. Despite cataloging numerous deficiencies in elections in Kenya in 1992, though, the Commonwealth observer delegation there admitted, "This was an election that proved difficult to evaluate in terms of freeness and fairness."[22] After receiving significant criticism for its failure to condemn those elections, the Commonwealth decided thereafter to avoid judging whether elections were free and fair.[23] For a difficult election in Cambodia in 1998, the European Union's representative expressed a "determination not to be constrained by a vocabulary which is . . . inappropriate in the circumstances we find."[24] Likewise, the European Parliament's Committee on Development and Cooperation concluded in 2001 that "there are inherent difficulties with the use of the words 'free and fair' as a verdict on an election."[25] After 1990, no mission sponsored by NDI appears to have used the phrase in characterizing any of dozens of elections.[26] Nor has the OSCE used the term in its public statements in recent years.

Seeking to avoid the linguistic trap posed by the free and fair standard, some observers and monitoring organizations have suggested that their responsibility is rather to determine whether an election reflects the "will of the people." The leader of an Australian parliamentary delegation to Zimbabwe's troubled elections in 2000 explained this in a postelection press conference:

> We have deliberately chosen not to use or refer to the term "free and fair" for these elections because in a climate of intimidation and violence that occurred in the months prior to polling we don't think it is an appropriate use of the term at any stage; rather, the question that we've asked ourselves is "does the result of the election have the legitimacy of reflecting the democratic *will of the people* of Zimbabwe?"[27]

Similarly, after its unhappy experience in Kenya in 1992, the Commonwealth amended its standard terms of reference to require a mission to "consider the various factors impinging on the credibility of the electoral process as a whole and determine in its own judgement whether the conditions exist for a free expression of will by the electors and if the result of the election reflects the *wishes of the people*."[28] The European Union's observer mission to Nigeria in 1999, though expressing "serious concern" about fraud, said, "We judge that the result of the election . . . reflects the *wishes of the Nigerian people*."[29] The International Republican Institute (IRI) declared that elections in Mongolia in 2000 "clearly reflected the *will of the Mongolian voters*."[30] The 2002 *Handbook for European Election Observation Missions* emphasizes "the concept of 'genuine' elections, to underline the broad criteria that must be taken into account when judging whether an election is to be considered a meaningful reflection of the *will of the electorate*."[31] In his thoughtful study of election observation, Mair questions this trend: "However understandable it is to avoid the apodictic free and fair, it is even more problematic to speculate on voter intentions and election results. How else can the voter's intention be registered than by an election, and how can this take place correctly other than in a free and fair election?"[32]

The election expert Elizabeth Clark agrees that observers should avoid the free and fair label. She suggests that observers "use less loaded terms such as 'acceptable' that would better reflect what observers actually have in mind when they look at the degree to which elections conform to minimum electoral standards."[33] The OSCE often, as in Montenegro in 2002, makes the test whether elections were "conducted generally in accordance with international commitments and standards for democratic elections."[34] The 2002 parliamentary elections in Ukraine, said the OSCE in a typical formulation, "indicated progress over the 1998 parliamentary polls towards meeting international commitments and standards, though important flaws persist."[35] In its controversial preliminary assessment of 1990 parliamentary elections in Pakistan, NDI cited serious flaws but said it did "not believe that [those] problems significantly altered the outcome of the elections."[36] Mair endorses this formulation: "Observers should reflect upon whether the number and extent of irregularities exceeded an acceptable level and could significantly affect the outcome of the election."[37] Yet critics questioned the NDI delegation's statement in Pakistan on the ground that a difference of even a few seats in a parliamentary election, even if it does not change the overall national winner, should be considered a significantly different outcome.

Election observers have adopted other semantic compromises in assessing elections. Often they will call a reasonably flawed transitional election a "step forward" toward democracy. In Kenya in 1992, for example, the Commonwealth called the elections "a giant step on the road to multi-party democracy."[38] The OSCE's preliminary statement in Armenia in 1998 concluded, "Overall, these elections are a step forward from the troubled 1996 elections toward a functioning democracy."[39] In Cambodia in 1998, the International Republican Institute delegation leader James Lilley said, "The process on [election day] appeared to be a step forward for Cambodian democracy."[40]

Elklit and Svensson argue that election observers, in making their evaluation, should make "'political' judgment[s]" such as whether an election will stimulate further democratization, encourage political contestation, involve more people in the political process, or improve the quality of political debate. "If observers are to view an election not as an isolated event but as part of the democratization process, they cannot avoid considering whether and how it contributes to that process."[41]

Unfortunately, these judgments about whether elections reflect the "will of the people," were "acceptable," met "international standards," or represent a "step forward" for democracy seem no less subjective than judgments about whether an election is free and fair. Conversely, these alternatives do at least suggest the importance of a nuanced, careful judgment based on context, rather than an unrealistic "black and white" standard. Though this may be semantics, the alternative wording at least has the advantage of not being burdened by so much baggage. It may suggest a less formulaic, more analytical process of making assessments.

In any event, though observers may avoid the "free and fair" terminology to try to focus attention on nuances and details, national and international journalists still typically look for "thumbs-up or thumbs-down" assessments.

Thus, in practice, even when observers studiously avoid categorical judgments or magic words, journalists almost always translate observers' assessments into judgments about whether elections were free and fair.

Does this mean that there are no universal, specific, minimum standards for elections as opposed to mere hortatory principles? Elklit and Svensson conclude, "The phrase 'free and fair' cannot denote compliance with a fixed, universal standard of electoral competition; no such standard exists, and the complexity of the electoral process makes the notion of any simple formula unrealistic."[42] Krishna Kumar of the U.S. Agency for International Development and Marina Ottaway of the Carnegie Endowment for International Peace suggest that the ambiguity of the free and fair standard is "not a problem that can be solved by more research."

> Rather the problem is one of instilling more professional attitudes among election observers, and of communicating more clearly to the media, and to the public in general, how elections are being judged and what constitutes an acceptable election under the conditions prevailing in the specific country.[43]

Even though substantial consensus on international norms governing the legitimacy of elections has emerged, it has so far proven extremely difficult to develop a practical standard or standards against which to measure transitional elections in the real world. Accordingly, those concerned with encouraging democracy through election monitoring should focus on the methodologies and professionalism of observers and the quality of their analysis rather than merely on whether they endorse or question an election's legitimacy.

Standards in Context

An election is a political process that unfolds over time and must be assessed in accordance with established international standards, including international standards for political freedoms and human rights. At the same time, though international standards are universal, elections must also be judged in their political context. The introduction of context, however, seems to make the analysis more subjective and threatens to unleash it from the moorings of universal standards. Somehow, international observers must take account of context without transforming universal democratic standards into relative ones or "lowering the bar."

Each election takes place in a particular political, historical, and cultural setting. Such factors as whether a country has experience with competitive elections or the extent of its socioeconomic development necessarily affect election quality. Many analysts, government officials, and monitoring organizations argue that elections in developing countries should not be held to the same standards as elections in countries that have well-established democratic practices and experience with genuine, competitive elections. Addressing transitional elections in Paraguay in 1989, NDI said, for example, "Focusing only on the fraud and administrative irregularities would be a disservice to the many Paraguayans who, for the first time, were energized by an election." Leading a delegation from the Organization of African Unity to the troubled 2000 elections in Zimbabwe, former Liberian president Amos Sawyer said, in the same vein, "You cannot compare an election in Zimbabwe with one in Liberia or Ghana, let alone Europe or North America; the circumstances are all different."[44]

Rather than accepting the lowering of the bar in semiauthoritarian environments, NDI in recent years has argued the opposite: that certain authoritarian governments, because they are not trusted, should have to meet higher standards. An NDI official testifying before Congress in 2000, for example, argued that "in countries like Zimbabwe, where violence and fear undermine the credibility of elections, it is necessary to go beyond the minimum requirements of the election law to build sufficient public confidence in the process" and called for "*extraordinary steps* to promote electoral rights and open dialogue among the political contestants."[45] An NDI delegation to Mexico in 2000 made the same argument: "In countries where one party has dominated political life for many years, *extraordinary steps* are often required to build public confidence in elections."[46] Likewise, referring to "recurring problems in Armenia's electoral practice," an NDI delegation to Armenia in 2002 said:

> In the face of such problems, *extraordinary efforts* are required by the government and election authorities to demonstrate that the 2003 elections will be properly conducted. Authorities must take the *extra steps* to eliminate the perception of malfeasance. . . . While this is a difficult task, authorities must demonstrate sufficient action to cause the public to believe that the upcoming elections break with the past.[47]

Although public confidence in these types of elections is understandably lacking, this new argument that bad actors have special obligations seems like a mistake. Like assessments that excuse problems that should be unacceptable, placing special burdens on some governments or countries seems to make international assessments seem unduly relative, opens such observers to charges of bias, and weakens the notion of international standards as universal. That is, just as standards should not be lowered for some, neither should they be raised for others.

Preconditions to Observation

Several international organizations have set out the criteria by which they will judge whether it is appropriate to observe given elections in the first place. Before sending observers, international donors and democracy organizations should always consider the important threshold question of whether to observe at all. For many consolidating elections, monitoring may be unnecessary—and thus wasteful of time, energy, and money. For elections in closed or undemocratic environments, monitoring may simply be inappropriate.

Most important, donors and democracy organizations generally agree that potential observers must consider the possibility that their participation in a flawed process may lend unintended support or legitimacy to that process. The European Union warns, "Care should be taken if a decision to send an EU observation mission could contribute to legitimising an illegitimate process."[48] The EU declined to send observers to flawed elections in Kazakhstan or Togo in 1999, for example, to avoid providing undue legitimacy. Similarly, according to an agreement between the United Nations Development Program and the Electoral Assistance Division endorsed by the secretary general and the General Assembly, before the United Nations can provide any electoral assistance or send observers, it "must first carefully assess the preelection conditions . . . in order to ensure involvement only in settings where legitimate elections are likely."[49]

Reginald Austin, formerly of the International Institute for Democracy and Electoral Assistance (International IDEA), points out that Zimbabwe's 2002 election raised the same question: "Is it worthwhile to observe an election where the context makes it obvious in advance that it can be neither free nor fair? The tendency has been to observe rather than decline." But he worries that "a mission entering such a prejudiced environment risks granting legitimacy to a government which has not been 'elected' through an exercise of free choice."[50] The Dutch scholar Oda van Cranenburgh agrees that if the host government "is not clearly committed to democratic reforms, the sending of observers may end up granting undue legitimation of the elections," and adds the insight that this "implies that the decision on the preconditions is in fact the crucial one."[51]

Conversely, an analysis under the auspices of the Administration and Cost of Elections Project of the United Nations, International IDEA, and the International Foundation for Election Systems suggests that "questionable or bad elections also need to be observed so that illegal or unethical practices are uncovered, evaluated and widely publicized through international reporting. Lessons learned can come from 'what not to do' as well as 'what to do.'"[52] The *ODIHR Handbook* says simply, "The ODIHR does not subscribe to the view that the mere presence of observers adds legitimacy to an election process."[53]

A group of election-monitoring experts convened by International IDEA in 1998 advised that international actors use the leverage offered by the possibility of sending observers to insist on improvements. It is before deciding to send observers that an organization "enjoys the greatest flexibility and 'bargaining power' over the potential host," which enables it to "point out any deficiencies within a country's electoral process" and "help the government recognize these deficiencies and rectify them." International IDEA recommends that international actors try to leverage a country's desire for the legitimacy that comes with international monitoring to secure improvements in the election process. "Maximum moral pressure often can be exerted by the international community at the point of deciding whether or not to get involved in election observation, rather than at the later stage of declaring whether or not the election was free and fair."[54] Mair, the author of the German study, argues long-term monitors, in place well before election day, can provide input into the question of "whether foreign and development pressure should be exerted on the host country in order to create the conditions for sending a larger election observing delegation."[55]

Like existing criteria for assessing elections, discussions of the criteria used in determining whether to mount an observation program, though, tend to be unrealistic. Proposed international guidelines essentially call on international observers to boycott if an election seems unlikely to be reasonably democratic. The European Commission, for example, suggests that EU election observers should participate only when their presence would be "advisable," "viable," and "useful."[56] A decision of the European Council establishing the EU policy on election observation sets out a number of specific preconditions.[57] International IDEA suggests that international observers should not participate in an election unless two conditions are met:

there is "basic agreement with the host country," including "general support from the principal political parties"; and the election process and environment will permit a fair election[58] (see table 6.6).

In determining whether its participation is "advisable," the European Commission lists a number of "minimally acceptable conditions": universal franchise; freedom of participation, expression, movement, and assembly; and "reasonable access to the media."[59] International IDEA proposes that potential observers make an initial assessment of the "likely character" of the elections to assure themselves of the "minimum acceptable credibility" of the electoral authority (which is not specifically mentioned by the European Commission) and that basic civil and political rights and fundamental freedoms respected.[60] Along the same lines, the Norwegian Helsinki Committee and the Bergstraesser Institute's *European Approach* both call for a "reasonable probability [of] peaceful circumstances" and a legal framework that meets "democratic standards" as two of three "strict preconditions" to sending observers.[61]

The requirement that potential observers assure themselves that an election is reasonably likely to be a good one before committing themselves to observe is stated too categorically. On the one hand, if the electoral authority is credible and basic civil and political rights are respected, then the election may not be one that really needs to be observed. On the other hand, few observer groups follow this guideline anyway. Most convince themselves of the need to observe, if they are so inclined and funding is available, even if the conditions clearly impede the possibility of a free and fair election.

With regard to whether observers are "viable," the European Commission would first require a request from the host government, although unlike International IDEA or the German study, the commission would not necessarily require a "formal official invitation" if there was a "clear indication of a government's willingness" to have observers. The commission also would also look for a "host government responsive to EU requests for specific amendments or improvements to electoral preparations," support from the main parties, the existence of previous EU monitoring of political developments, and enough lead time to mount an effective effort. The United Nations requires a formal request from the relevant government at least four months before the scheduled election.[62] The Norwegian Helsinki Committee and the *European Approach* also make having enough lead time, which "as a rule" should be "at least four months," their third "strict condition."[63] The idea of time to prepare and to organize preelection and long-term monitoring is laudable, but the notion that a specified period of time should be a strict requirement is unrealistic, not to mention wholly inconsistent with current practice.

Certainly potential observers must consider the views of political parties and political leaders and cannot participate without at least the acquiescence of the host government. But holding out for "formal official invitations" may, in some cases, put form over substance. Such invitations, even when forthcoming, are generally directed to governments and intergovernmental organizations—and often to former president Jimmy Carter as well!—rather than to nongovernmental organizations. Yet American and other third-country nongovernmental organizations often bring much-needed expertise and impartiality.

In suggesting that observers be "useful," the European Commission essentially calls for consideration of costs and benefits, both financial and political. Along the same lines, in considering the threshold question of whether international monitoring would be important for transitional elections Indonesia in 1999, NDI expressly considered the potential for serious election-related problems, the extent of trust in the process, the risk that election losers would not accept the results, the danger of civil strife, and the likely credibility of foreign observers.[64] Preconditions or criteria for determining whether to observe offered by other organizations do not mention expressly any cost–benefit analysis, but the European Commission's requirement that observers must be useful is a good addition, because the money spent on observation may well be better spent supporting democratization in other ways.

In addition to election-related preconditions for sending observers, the Bergstrasser Institute's *European Approach* goes on to list ten more requirements with respect to the observation process itself, which its authors claim are the responsibility of the host government or inviting authority. Several of these are logistical and unduly detailed (and hardly seem the responsibility of the host government), such as the need for satisfactory transportation, security, and "distinctive form of dress." Others are more important questions of principle regarding observers' autonomy, including, for example, that observer groups must have access to the entire election process, the freedom to choose their own observers, the authority to contact anyone they want, and the "right to report independently and periodically throughout the election process . . . inside and outside the country."[65]

Hence, though existing lists of preconditions suggest useful considerations, they are neither practical nor probably desirable as literal prerequisites. Few transitional elections that merit or receive international observation take place in entirely peaceful circumstances under fully democratic rules. Few international organizations involved in election monitoring insist on such a high threshold, and, were they to do so, they would certainly miss an opportunity to make a contribution in many tense environments. Widely monitored elections in the late 1990s and early 2000s in Albania, Armenia, Azerbaijan, Cambodia, Kazakhstan, Kenya, Macedonia, Pakistan, Peru, Togo, Zambia, and Zimbabwe, to name a few, would likely not have met the preconditions for a peaceful environment, a democratic legal framework, or respect for fundamental political rights proposed by International IDEA, the European Commission, or other international groups. In some of these cases, the dispatch of observers may have been a mistake, because their mere presence provided legitimacy regardless of what they said. But in others, the presence of observers undoubtedly contributed to transparency, helped reduce violence, deterred fraud, and exposed problems that might have otherwise gone unnoticed or unaddressed.

In reality, international organizations have tended to make decisions according to vague political judgments about whether international observers can make a significant contribution balanced against the risk that their presence will confer undeserved legitimacy. In Cambodia, NDI and IRI worried—with good reason, as it turned out—that international observers might provide undue legitimacy or focus too much attention on election day, without enough consideration of the context, including violence, an unfair legal framework, and biased electoral institutions. Despite this risk, they decided to send observers nonetheless in an effort to "deter further violence and intimidation" and provide moral support to candidates and civic activists participating in the process.[66] Reginald Austin, even as he cautions about providing undue legitimacy, admits that parties facing intimidation or fearing fraud "almost invariably . . . prefer observers to be present."[67] Monitoring by impartial outsiders can contribute to public confidence and help create a climate in which successful elections are more likely, although their ability to do so may be more limited than advertised if unscrupulous authorities are determined to do whatever it takes to remain in power.

Thus, international organizations considering whether to send observers to flawed elections face a dilemma. If they decide to do so, they can deter intimidation, support prodemocracy forces, and offer an honest assessment. But even if they try to do otherwise, they also run a real risk of providing undeserved legitimization.

Judging Elections

The question of how observers should judge an election is a difficult one. Though there really is broad international agreement on the nature of democratic elections, there has been great difficulty translating that consensus into practical approaches for international observers. Certainly, international organizations need to think about elections in broad terms. Journalists, diplomats, donors, and others interested in monitoring reports need to understand that the job of observers is to offer informed reports on a broad range of issues rather than to give a passing or failing grade.

All elections must be judged honestly, by the same internationally recognized standards. Many important parts of an election process unfold at other times than election day. Although they should place elections in context, observers should make no excuses for failures to meet international standards. At the same time, as discussed in the next chapter, there is need for broader understanding and the acceptance of a more effective, realistic monitoring methodology.

Chapter 7

The Scope and Methodology of International Election Observation

Elections, while easily manipulated, are the only system that offers any hope of holding leaders accountable. It is progress, moreover, that the manipulators can find themselves outcasts.

—editorial, *New York Times*[1]

There has been much criticism that the typical focus of international observers is too narrow. "Observers generally devote too much energy and attention to the events of election day," asserts Thomas Carothers. "The major American observer organizations have evolved toward more comprehensive approaches," he concedes, "but even they still concentrate too much on the actual voting."[2] One study of the Commonwealth observers said, "Where criticisms of the Commonwealth observers have arisen, it is generally because of their short-term presence in the country."[3] The *New York Times,* in a 1999 editorial, likewise contended that "international election observers are still too narrowly focused on election day itself."[4]

This criticism continues even though the more professional groups recognized the importance of a broader approach in the early days of international monitoring. In 1990, for example, former U.S. president Jimmy Carter's Council of Freely Elected Heads of Government and the National Democratic Institute for International Affairs (NDI) made the point in Haiti: "In observing this election, the delegation was aware that an election process involves not only what happens on election day, but also in the pre-election campaign and the post-election transition."[5] At a summit in Budapest in 1994, the Organization for Security and Cooperation in Europe (OSCE) gave its Office for Democratic Institutions and Human Rights

(ODIHR) a mandate for "an enhanced role in election monitoring, before, during and after elections."[6] After reviewing the experience and literature as of early 1994, Stefan Mair concluded, "Almost all election observation experts call for long-term observing."[7]

Practitioners agree that monitoring should be comprehensive. The guidelines issued by the International Institute for Democracy and Electoral Assistance (International IDEA) call for election observers to be "comprehensive in their review of the election, considering all relevant circumstances."[8] "Elections are not one-day events," agrees the European Union. "It is necessary to observe all stages of the electoral process to have a well-founded and comprehensive assessment."[9] NDI has urged "further steps to monitor other elements of the election process" and has called on observers to "ensure that these elements receive adequate weight, so that impressions gained through short-term observation do not overwhelm the electoral assessment."[10]

Despite this consensus, the critique that observers still tend to overemphasize events on election day remains apt. For one thing, with the increasing acceptance of and funding for international election observation during the past decade or so, a number of less-experienced groups and individuals, from more- and less-established democracies, have involved themselves in such activities. These groups tend to be less sensitive to the problem of disproportionate emphasis on election day. The performance of bilateral and nongovernmental observers in Cambodia in 1999, which is discussed in chapter 8, demonstrates this problem.

More fundamentally, the established methodology of more experienced, established groups—the core of the democracy-promotion community—continues to be inherently, though inadvertently, biased toward balloting and counting on election day. Most international election observers still arrive only days before an election and leave a couple of days after the polls close. The vagaries of international news cycles and the understandably limited attention span of the international community exacerbate this tendency. Media interest in any given election rarely extends much beyond election day. Elements of the process that unfold before or after that time, regardless of how important they are, tend to be much less newsworthy.

In the last chapter, I focused on standards for judging elections. In this chapter, I consider standards and methods for election observers. This chapter is both empirical and normative. It reviews modern international election-observation methodology and proposes best practices. First, I review and comment on standards of conduct for observers. Though there is a reasonable consensus on broad principles for observers' conduct, the codes of conduct articulated by various international organizations tend to veer off into peripheral issues or the personal comportment of individual observers. Second, I describe and advocate comprehensive monitoring, including pre-election and long-term monitoring, observation of polling and counting, and postelection monitoring. Third, I address the timing, content, and owner-ship of postelection statements, the principal product of election-observa-tion missions. In this discussion, I also consider some other troublesome methodological issues, including the design of election-day checklists, "qualitative monitoring," and burdens of proof. Finally, drawing in part on the particular experience of the Palestinian elections in 1996, I address forms and limitations of coordination among disparate international actors and argue for one model of loose coordination. My discussion of these is-sues should provide a good overall sense of the state of the art of and the challenges to international election monitoring.

Standards of Conduct for Observers

It is widely agreed that international observer groups should comply with in-ternationally recognized standards of conduct for observing elections. Al-though these standards have not been authoritatively declared anywhere, there have been a few efforts to synthesize and articulate guidelines. One of the earliest and most influential was Larry Garber's *Guidelines for Interna-tional Election Observing,* published by the International Human Rights Law Group in 1984. As international observation was becoming more com-mon, the *Guidelines* called for a more professional approach to choosing ob-servers, organizing an observation mission, assessing an electoral process, and disseminating a mission's conclusions. More recently, International IDEA reviewed existing practice, consulted with experienced organizations, and compiled a code of conduct for international election observation. The OSCE, the European Union, and other international organizations have adopted similar standards of conduct for election observers.[11] Thus, experi-ence has led to a general consensus on basic standards, which is summarized in table 7.1.

First, international observers must comply with all national laws and reg-ulations.[12] Generally, observers have no special immunities. They should comply with, among other things, legal provisions that govern their access to the electoral process. Most election authorities will accredit legitimate international observers and allow them access to polling places and other

Table 7.1
Codes of Conduct for Election Observers

Standard	Bergstraesser Institute European Approach[a]	International IDEA Code of Conduct[b]	OSCE ODIHR Handbook[c]	European Union Handbook[d]
Compliance with the law	X	(Listed under "respect for host-country sovereignty")		X
Comply with national law	X	X	X	X
"Show respect for people and culture of host country"		X		
Impartiality and neutrality				
Maintain impartiality	X	X	X	X
Avoid partisan symbols, colors or banners	X	X	X	X
Undertake duties in "unobtrusive manner"e; do not disrupt or interfere with election process		X	X	X
No gifts or favors from parties or others involved in election process		X		
No participation in "any function or activity that could lead to perception of sympathy" for any party or candidate		X		
No expression of a "view on any subject that is likely to be an issue in the election"		X		
Noninterference	X	(Listed under "respect for host-country sovereignty")	X	X
Do not give instructions or countermand election officials		X	X	X
No interference with "internal jurisdiction or affairs" of host country		X		

Objectivity, transparency, and accuracy

Objectivity, transparency, and accuracy				
Base conclusions on "well documented, factual and verifiable evidence" and keep recording of places visited			X	X X
Fully disclose "methods, assumptions, data, analyses and ... details" of observations	X			
Follow "principles based on recognized scientific methodology"	X			
Identify "exact information ... used as a basis for [observers'] assessment"	X			
"[W]hen reporting statistical information, identify the basis of sampling they have carried out, and disclose measures of uncertainty associated with those statistics"	X			
Identify objectives	X			
Identify assumptions	X			
Provide evidence and argument to support assumptions and judgments	X			
Ensure information collected, compiled and published in "systematic, clear and unambiguous" way	X			
Ensure information is "received first-hand and verifiable"	X	X		
Seek response from targets of criticism before treating allegations as valid	X			
"[T]reat as confidential all information gathered"	X	X		

(continued)

Table 7.1 *Continued*

Standard	Bergstraesser Institute European Approach[a]	International IDEA Code of Conduct[b]	OSCE ODIHR Handbook[c]	European Union Handbook[d]
No conflicts of interest	X	X (Listed under neutrality)		X
Act entirely in interests of observing organization		X		
No unauthorized or private activity leading to actual or perceived conflict of interest		X		
"Election observation and election assistance should be strictly separated."	X			
"commitment to overall objective of the observation mission"				X
Relationship with election officials				
"Respect the role, status, and authority of election officials"		X		
"Avoid announcing election results without the authority of the election management body"		X		
"Maintain close liaison" with election authorities		X		
Inform election authorities of objectives of observation process		X		
Comply with rules and decisions of election authorities	X	X		
Provide copies of public statements to election authorities		X		
Report problems to election authorities		X		
Public comment				
Refrain from personal or premature comments to media	X	X "Be especially careful when making any public statement that could reflect on the election management body"	X	X

Relationship with observer team and other observers	[a]	[b]	[c]	[d]	[e]
Participate in briefings		X		X	X
Follow direction of leaders, terms of reference and rules of observation organization		X		X	X
Liaise with other observers and monitoring teams		X	X	X	X
Participate in postelection debriefings and contribute reports			X		
Report incidents that "could reflect on the work" of sponsoring organization		X			
Personal comportment of individual observers					
"[B]ehave blamelessly, exercise sound judgement, and observe the highest level of personal discretion"		X		X	
Carry prescribed identification	X	X	X	X	X
Display required notices identifying observer and/or vehicle		X			
Obey rules regarding photography		X			
Avoid weapons		X			

[a] Theodor Hanf, Maria R. Macchiaverna, Bernard Owen, and Julian Santamaria, *Observing Democratic Elections: A European Approach* (Frieburg: Arnold-Bergstraesser-Institut, 1995).

[b] International Institute for Democracy and Electoral Assistance (International IDEA), *Code of Conduct: Ethical and Professional Observation of Elections* (Stockholm: International IDEA, 1997).

[c] Organization for Security and Cooperation in Europe (OSCE), *The ODIHR Election Observation Handbook*, 4th ed. (Warsaw: OSCE Office for Democratic Institutions and Human Rights, 1999).

[d] Anders Erikson, ed., *Handbook for European Union Election Observation Missions* (Stockholm: Swedish International Development Cooperation Agency, 2002), citing Council of the European Union, *Guidelines—EU Policy on Electoral Observation*, Council Decision 9262/98 (1998).

[e] Erikson, *Handbook for European Union Election Observation Missions*, 19; OSCE, *ODIHR Election Observation Handbook*, 6.

parts of the process, both before and after polling. When a government does not permit access of legitimate observers on a nondiscriminatory basis without valid reason, as in Albania in 1996 or Zimbabwe in 2000 and 2002, other observers should consider withdrawing. Similarly, election-monitoring organizations should reconsider their participation if national laws fail to comply with international norms by unreasonably interfering with the observers' work.

Second, observers should remain neutral regarding electoral outcomes. They should not express a preference for any political party or candidates. Their commitment should be solely to the integrity of the process. In accordance with a decision of the European Council, the EU and OSCE guidelines require that observers shall "maintain strict impartiality in the conduct of their duties, and shall at no time express any bias or preference in relation to national authorities, parties, candidates, or with reference to any issues in contention in the election process."[13]

Unfortunately, however, not all observers adhere to this standard. In Cambodia in 1998, for example, some observers sought to support the government's effort to regain international standing after it took over in a coup the year before. Others made clear their preference for a victory of the opposition. In reporting on elections Nicaragua in 2001, the International Republican Institute (IRI) perhaps inadvertently revealed its own preferences: "While the elections' administration was admirable, and there [*sic*] results relieving to many both inside and outside of the country, Nicaragua faces new challenges."[14] Canadian election official Ron Gould, who has advised election authorities and observed elections in dozens of countries, comments that international observers in general "are not necessarily completely objective observers just because they are from elsewhere."[15]

Bias can result from partisan interests in electoral outcomes. It may also come from preconceived notions of who should win a fair contest. Individual observers on occasion may even seek to curry favor with governments for their own private interests. More commonly and more subtly, observers may—wittingly or unwittingly—act as the agents of a broader agenda of their sponsoring countries or organizations. They may, for example, seek to justify foreign assistance or improved relations between a government and other countries, as in Cambodia in 1998 (which is discussed in depth in chapter 8). Or as a commentator on election observers in Ethiopia in 1995 put it,

Diplomatic observers are—bound by diplomatic convention itself— usually not willing to compromise in any serious way their relations to the host-country government. They cannot and will not report in a critical or sometimes even in a balanced manner.[16]

Third, observers should avoid interfering or intervening in the process. International observers must respect local sovereignty. They have no mandate to correct mistakes or resolve local disputes. Recognition of the legitimacy of election observation is not a license for foreigners to supervise or interfere with elections. Thus, while calling on states to invite observers, the Organization on Security and Cooperation in Europe's Copenhagen document continues, "Observers will undertake not to interfere in the electoral proceedings."[17]

Even while inviting observers, governments are sensitive to the perception of outside interference. Indonesia is typical. Although the government of Indonesia welcomed international observers to its transitional elections in June 1999, it made clear it did not want to "internationalize" the elections. As a sovereign country with understandable nationalist sensitivities, Indonesia did not want its elections or political transition to be controlled, supervised, or certified by the international community. At the same time, the country sought international recognition for its new governmental institutions and the government that would emerge from the elections. Similarly, the top immigration official from Mexico's Interior Ministry warned prospective observers in 2000 that Mexico planned to vigorously enforce its laws barring foreigners from taking part in Mexican politics. "We are open to observation, but not to scrutiny, judgment or intervention," he said.[18]

At the same time, leaders of election-monitoring efforts are sometimes welcomed or accepted as mediators or conduits for concerns of election participants. In particular, highly respected foreign leaders, such as former U.S. president Jimmy Carter, have openly played such a mediating role. Democracy organizations more generally tend to do so only in very indirect, discrete ways.

Fourth, observers should always distinguish facts from subjective judgments. They should attempt to make their observations specific and fact-based and to document fully their observations as much as possible. Election observation, as International IDEA puts it, must be "accurate."[19]

The requirement for observers to base conclusions on facts, however, should not be an excuse for limiting judgments to narrow technical issues. Moreover, how observers see the "burden of proof"—the extent to which they believe they should not criticize aspects of the elections in the absence of irrefutable evidence—will often determine the fundamental nature of their assessments.

Fifth, election observer groups should take care to avoid potential conflicts of interest. Accordingly, groups closely associated with the organization or administration of an election process are probably not well placed to make a public assessment of the same process. It is potentially problematic for a group to be judging the performance of a body in which it has invested heavily, in effect to be both player and referee.

Therefore, election observation should generally be kept separate from election assistance. Reflecting the consensus of experts, International IDEA warns that observers should generally avoid involvement in mediation or technical assistance activities.[20] Most organizations and commentators agree that those involved in advising electoral authorities, preparing election laws, or training electoral officials should generally not be involved in subsequently judging the corresponding elections. Nevertheless, the UN Electoral Assistance Division often has advised election authorities and coordinated observers for the same elections, which, according to one analyst, has led to "some uneasiness with this combination of roles" within the division.[21] In Cambodia in 1998, the European Union provided funding and extensive technical assistance to the Cambodian election commission and then led the international observation effort. If such organizations must be involved in observation, they should at least seek ways to build firewalls between their various efforts.

Table 7.1 summarizes codes of conduct of observers offered by International IDEA, the OSCE's ODIHR, the European Union, and the German Bergstraesser Institute. On the basis of a conference in 1995, International IDEA published a code of conduct in 1997 intended to apply to all international observers. The code of conduct set out guidelines for "ethical and professional observation of elections." Subsequently, the OSCE and the European Union set out codes of conduct for their own observers. In the table, I have organized the specific guidelines and admonitions according to the five broad, agreed-upon principles of conduct identified above. In addition to elaborating upon more general principles, other guidelines establish the rules of sponsoring organizations with which individual observers are expected to comply.

A few of the guidelines proposed by some organizations conflict with those established by others. The Bergstraesser Institute's *Observing Democratic Elections: A European Approach* bizarrely directs observers to "treat as confidential all information gathered in the course of their duties." This may be intended to refer to protecting the confidentiality of sources but is not otherwise explained.[22] Even if it is read to apply only to confidentiality of sources, it appears to conflict with International IDEA's code, which directs observers to "identify the exact information they have gathered and used as a basis for their assessment."[23] Both the *European Approach* and the International IDEA direct observers to ensure that all information is "received first-hand," but Garber's *Guidelines for International Election Observing,* which is consistent with the general practice, states, "The observers should consider all evidence presented, even if not based on first-hand observation, so long as its credibility is otherwise assured."[24]

Alone among the organizations proposing codes of conduct, International IDEA urges considerable deference to election authorities. Its code of conduct, for example, would impose specific requirements on observers to "respect the role, status, and authority of election officials, and show a respectful and courteous attitude to election officials"; "maintain close liaison" with election authorities; inform election authorities of the objectives of the observation process; and report problems directly to election authorities. It cautions observers to "be especially careful when making any public statement that could reflect on the election management body."[25] Though well intentioned, these guidelines seem inappropriate in circumstances in which the political opposition, the public, or even the international community mistrust the election authorities, a situation that often prevails in transitional or postconflict elections.

Nevertheless, these codes of conduct are consistent and correct in emphasizing the importance of ethics and professionalism in international election observation. Much more than further elaboration of standards for free and fair elections, it is the degree to which observers are ethical and professional that ultimately will determine whether international election observing can continue to contribute to genuine democratization in the future.

The Scope and Methodology of Observation

Although practical standards for elections have proved elusive, the expansive conception of what makes an election democratic and the recognition that an election is a political process that unfolds over time have led to a consensus in theory about the need for comprehensive election monitoring. Specifically, experts and practitioners agree that election observation must have a broad scope in three separate ways: subject matter, time, and geography.

First, with respect to subject matter, the consensus about the nature of a democratic election suggests that observers should assess a comparably broad range of substantive issues. These issues can be grouped into three categories: (1) the administration or conduct of the election; (2) the legal and institutional framework for the election (the rules); and (3) the political context and environment in which the election takes place, including the extent of compliance with broader human rights standards and the extent to which there is a "level playing field." In other words, professional observers must find facts not only about the administration and conduct of an election but also about the extent of political rights, both in law and in practice.

Second, it is also clear that effective monitoring programs must consider all aspects of an election process over time, from beginning to end. An election process begins at least when an election is called or becomes expected, if not when the legal framework is established and rules are written. The end does not occur until the count is completed and certified, election-related complaints are adjudicated, and a new government is constituted in accordance with the election results (or other appropriate consequences on the basis of the results take place). Thus, professional organizations monitor all phases of the election process: (1) the preelection period, including the formal or informal campaign period; (2) the balloting and initial counting on election day; and (3) the postelection phase, including the aggregation and tabulation of votes, the adjudication of complaints, and the formation of a new government. As the UN secretary general emphasized in the seminal case of Namibia (in which the United Nations supervised the elections), "*At each stage of the entire electoral process* the Special Representative must satisfy himself as to the fairness and appropriateness of *all measures affecting the political process at all levels of the administration.*"[26]

The legitimacy of an election process is often determined well before election day, or it may be compromised by events after election day. Election-monitoring groups must therefore pay attention to preelection and postelection developments in addition to election day itself.

Third, international election monitors also must be able to develop an accurate view of what is taking place throughout the country. This means that preelection, election-day, and postelection monitors must be present in sufficient numbers and be deployed in a manner that gives a sense of the country as a whole. International observers should develop reliable relationships with credible local sources of information, including journalists, political leaders, candidates, party activists, governmental officials, and nonpartisan national election monitors, at both national and subnational levels. What goes on in outlying areas is often very different from what happens in the nation's capital. There need not be an international observer in every village, but there must be enough observers to determine whether and how experiences or impressions differ in various parts of the country.

Accordingly, to complement if not replace the larger delegations that come to witness a process on election day, international monitoring organizations are putting increasing emphasis on long-term, in-country monitors, who follow the process before and after election day. Experienced monitoring groups also organize smaller assessment missions that visit the country for shorter periods of time before, and sometimes after, election day.

Preelection and Long-Term Monitoring

More sophisticated observers appreciate that the quality and acceptability of elections are often determined by factors in place long before election day, such as whether the legal framework is fair, violence or threats intimidate candidates or voters, access to the news media and other essential campaign resources is reasonably equitable, or vote buying or other campaign finance abuses distort the process. Thus, international election monitors must be present in the country for a long enough period of time before the election itself to gauge the entire process and understand the overall election environment.

In recent years, international groups have begun to put much greater emphasis on long-term election monitoring. Long-term monitoring has become standard practice for the European Union and the OSCE. According to Hrair Balian, ODIHR's comprehensive methodology, which was reconsidered and articulated in 1997, "has permitted ODIHR to be more consistent and thorough in its analysis, making its reporting less susceptible to political pressure or double standards, and therefore more credible."[27] Likewise, a UN General Assembly resolution in 2000 recommended that "United Nations electoral assistance be geared towards comprehensive observation of the entire time-span of the electoral process."[28]

Long-term monitoring can promote public confidence and inform the assessments of missions to observe the elections themselves. For most internationally monitored elections, it is important to have long-term international monitors in place in various locations around the country well before the elections, ideally eight weeks or more before election day. This allows them to better understand and report on the political environment in which the election is taking place. To do their job properly, long-term monitors should not focus principally, as they sometimes do, on logistical arrangements and information collection for the benefit of short-term observers.

Preelection assessment missions can complement long-term monitoring, and established election-monitoring organizations increasingly make such missions a significant part of their monitoring methodology. NDI, for one, now often focuses on preelection assessments (and support for domestic monitors) in lieu of election-day observation, especially for elections already drawing considerable international attention. Ideally, such missions are scheduled periodically, beginning as early in the process as possible and continuing until well after the election. Small numbers of relatively high-profile foreign political leaders, activists, or experts draw on the findings of long-term monitors and reports from other credible sources and make direct observations from meetings with political and governmental leaders and other key actors. The missions usually issue statements on their findings and observations and may make recommendations for improving the electoral process.

Both long-term monitors and preelection teams assess the political environment, the legal and regulatory framework, the credibility and neutrality of electoral authorities, the fairness of the media, and the opportunities for the opposition to compete. They also evaluate relevant technical issues such as delimitation of constituency boundaries, the process of voter registration, the number and location of polling places, balloting procedures, ballot design, the production and distribution of election materials, and the like. Monitoring groups have not yet figured out how to effectively assess campaign funding, although campaign and political financing remains a critical challenge to democratic elections and the consolidation of democracy.

Long-term monitors can collect a great deal of information from around the country and discern trends over time. Their presence can also deter intimidation and violence. Smaller, short-term missions can draw considerable attention to shortcomings and catalyze improvements. Thus, both forms of preelection monitoring can improve the quality of elections and build public confidence.

Election-Day Balloting and Counting

The voting and counting of ballots are the central acts of any election process. They are significant, often challenging administrative tasks. Of course, manipulation or mishandling of the processes of balloting and counting can destroy the integrity of an election. Though blatant manipulation on election day seems less and less common, in considerable part because of the success of election monitoring, observation of election-day processes and electoral activities immediately before and after election day remains an important part of assessing the genuineness of elections. So-called short-term observers arrive to witness the end of the campaign and the voting and counting process. They continue to play a role in any comprehensive election assessment.

Typically, there are considerably larger numbers of these short-term observers than there are long-term monitors or participants in preelection and postelection missions. This is in part because—for all the talk about the importance of political environment, legal rules, and campaign issues and the energy devoted to long-term monitoring—much attention remains focused on election day. Prominent foreign observers tend to have limited time to spend in country and naturally are inclined to observe the "main event"— the elections themselves. Short-term observers in general are not difficult to recruit. As the former UN official Horaceo Boneo and his colleagues observed, "Although this is not usually a remunerated activity, it is an interesting and a generally prized experience and it is a contribution to a cause reputed to be useful."[29] International election monitoring almost by definition includes a presence for election day.

In theory, the number of short-term observers should depend upon geographical, demographic, and political factors. Such factors might include the size of the country, the degree of confidence the international community has in domestic sources of information (nonpartisan national monitors, media and parties/candidates), the extent of cooperation between international observers and domestic monitors, the extent of coordination among different international monitoring efforts, and the type of election problems feared. But in reality, the number of international observers is more typically a function of the visibility of, and extent of overseas interest in, a given election, not to mention the availability of funding (which is itself a function of visibility and interest).

The number of observers does not generally depend in practice on a country's size or population or even on the extent of the political challenges to democratic elections. For important, high-profile transitional elections in Indonesia in 1999, for example, only 600 international observers were present even though there were about 300,000 polling stations and more than 100 million eligible voters spread over thousands of islands. Because of the sheer magnitude of those elections, international observers obviously had to take great care, in their methodology and in their public and private comments on the process, to recognize the limits of their information and to avoid superficial assessments. In tiny Macedonia in 2002, in contrast, the OSCE alone sent more than 800 observers to an election with just 3,000 polling stations (1 percent of the number in Indonesia) and only 1.6 million voters. The international community had a considerable stake in maintaining peace after an outbreak of violence the previous year threatened to escalate into another Balkan war.

Opposition activists and others who do not trust authorities often complain that there are too few international observers present for a given election. Yet international observers generally do not have the numbers or the capabilities to detect fraud directly. Without the resources and special mandate to supervise rather than observe an election, international observers invariably move from place to place on polling day. Opposition leaders and critics of the observers object that international observers cannot detect or deter fraud if they do not remain in one place, and accordingly they argue for much larger numbers of observers. An analysis of the 1992 election in Kenya is typical:

> There were far too few international observers. The result was that only a minority of all polling stations could be visited by observation teams, and the time spent at each station was usually very short.[30]

But this type of criticism misconstrues the observers' role. Without a special mandate for election supervision, foreign observers simply cannot watch the polls everywhere. Party agents and domestic nonpartisan poll watchers, in contrast, can and should. A situation such as that in Panama in 1989, where President Carter himself witnessed material fraud, is relatively unusual, especially now that election authorities everywhere expect oversight from outside. Moreover, the very presence of observers affects what they are observing. It is essentially impossible for observers to arrive at a polling station unnoticed, and anything untoward going on there will almost certainly stop during their visit. The job of international observers is to get good information from others, including election officials, party representatives, and domestic monitors, as well as to get a feel for the process themselves.

The Timing and Process of Issuing Postelection Statements

Observer groups typically make an initial public statement soon after the completion of the balloting. The more experienced groups now generally call this a "preliminary" or "interim" statement because they plan to issue a final statement or report sometime later. Sometimes several international organizations jointly offer a common statement shortly after election day.

One problem with such statements is their timing. Often these preliminary statements are made the day after the balloting. The *Handbook for European Union Election Observation Missions* argues that "it is important to issue a statement while the media are still interested."[31] Some groups will even make an initial, public assessment on election night, even before the initial count is complete. This enables their assessments to be reflected in the "news cycle" of reporting on events of election day. The Commonwealth, in fact, defends its practice of issuing an early interim statement "to present a view of the election day before the results [are] announced."[32] Boneo and his colleagues argue that early reports, issued before the process is complete, "might contribute toward the improvement of the quality of discussions or eliminate imaginary issues, sometimes aired without any real basis."[33]

But statements made too soon may be based on limited or incomplete information and may seem inaccurate or inappropriate if there are subsequent problems with the counting process. Early statements are often made without the benefit of thorough debriefing meetings with observers from around the country and in the absence of an opportunity to build consensus among a given delegation of observers. The leaders or spokespersons of such groups, usually based in the capital, typically will base such assessments on written or telephone reports from their observers around the country.

The better alternative is for leaders of monitoring delegations to refrain from public comment on the balloting and initial counting until observers from around the country are able to return to the capital to get together to share their findings and impressions. Much as juries and corporate boards must generally meet in person to share perspectives and try to develop a consensus, the opportunity to get all its observers together allows a monitoring group to develop a fuller national picture of what are often contested versions of reality, because each observer or deployment team can compare and contrast its observations and information with those of others.[34]

Statements based on such thorough debriefings, however, may be issued too late to have much of an impact, because of news cycles and the tendency of journalists and international audiences both to draw quick conclusions based on early impressions and to have limited resources to follow a story. The international attention span for news of a given election is limited and, for all but the most controversial or highest-profile elections, may not extend long enough to allow observer groups to follow the initial consolidation of the vote count in the regions, get together to hash out a common view, prepare a formal preliminary statement, and report their findings.

Yet international observers must speak to many of their audiences through the media. Though other factors, such as the quality of the statement, the reputation and nationality of the sponsoring organization, and the identity of the delegation leaders affect media coverage, the spotlight of the international media, at least, shines on a given election only for a finite—generally short—period of time. That spotlight shines the brightest just after election day. Accordingly, even for elections that have gained considerable international attention, the foreign media will generally only report on the preliminary or interim assessments offered soon after election day. Although monitoring organizations often commit to continue to monitor after the election and "to issue a comprehensive report at a later date," some organizations often fail to do so. Even when issued, such longer reports necessarily reach a much smaller audience and are generally issued weeks or months later, often long after they can have much practical consequence on policy or even on public or international opinion.

Finally, monitoring organizations more and more confront another problem: reconciling differences between the impressions of long-term and short-term observers. They have had to contend with elections, as in Cambodia in 1998, that are well administered and peaceful on election day but yet take place in flawed political environments, under unfair rules, or administered by biased authorities. Even experienced, unbiased democracy organizations have considerable difficulty effectively and responsibly incorporating concerns about the fairness of the political context or rules into traditional postelection assessments.

The problem of integrating election-day observations with preelection findings results only in part from the increasingly well-recognized problem of too much focus on election day. In part, as well, the problem arises inevitably from having a separate group of observers—often a larger, higher-profile group—looking at a discrete part of the process on election day. Because they typically have not been present in the country during the campaign and preelection period, election-day observers have considerably less personal experience with and feel for problems during that time. Consciously or subconsciously, they may simply discount earlier problems. Election-day observers, or the organizations that sponsor them, may in fact see the job of such delegations to report primarily on that part of the process, with the idea that preelection problems have already been reported and that the assessment of election day will be put in the context of the overall process in a more comprehensive report issued at a later date.

The Interests of Observers and the Ownership of Statements

Election-monitoring organizations and observation missions often reflect interests and objectives other than democratization. The mandates, interests, and constraints of monitoring groups tend to reflect the national interests of sponsoring countries or organizations. Diplomats and government officials often refrain from forthright criticisms and, consciously or unconsciously, balance economic, trade, security, and other national interests and foreign policy goals against the promotion of democracy. Even while organizing election-monitoring efforts, intergovernmental organizations also pursue multiple objectives and often find it extremely difficult to publicly criticize member governments. Some nongovernmental monitoring efforts lack professionalism, betray biases, or do not have legitimacy in the eyes of some audiences. Governments and intergovernmental organizations sending observers may influence, or be perceived to influence, election statements. Dutch analysts Wim van Binsbergen and Jon Abbink discern a tendency for Western governments sponsoring observers in Africa to discourage critical statements and suggest that elections, "if in any way possible, . . . be seen in the light of a probably long process of 'building democracy.'" They blame this tendency on "diplomatic convention, UN middle-of-the-road policy, and by *Realpolitik* and rivalry between the larger donor-countries, wishing to keep or extend their local influence."[35] Commenting on observers to 1995 elections in Ethiopia, for example, Abbink argues, "diplomatic observers are—bound by diplomatic convention itself—usually not willing to compromise in any serious way their relations with the host government.[36]

Much like the different perspectives between long-term monitors and short-term observers, it can also be a significant challenge to reconcile differences between observer delegations and their sponsoring organizations. It sometimes matters whether a statement represents the views of a particular delegation (or delegation leader) or the opinion of the organization that sent that delegation. Sometimes missions in the field and their sponsors have somewhat different assessments and perspectives. Discrepancies are increasingly apparent between immediate postelection statements offered by politicians or diplomats leading delegations and later, more detailed reports prepared by professional staff members.

In Armenia in 1998, for example, the OSCE appointed U.S. ambassador Sam Brown as its special representative for the election. Brown—who evidently was interested in addressing broader diplomatic issues, such as the conflict between Armenia and Azerbaijan over Nagorno-Karabak, as much as evaluating the election—insisted on a more positive statement than many of the observers on his team felt was appropriate. "Overall, these elections are a step forward from the troubled 1996 elections toward a functioning democracy," said the OSCE preliminary statement, reflecting Ambassador Brown's own views. Though acknowledging that the elections fell short of OSCE standards, the statement continued, "These shortcomings do not cause us to question their outcome."[37] Subsequently, the ODIHR staff—trying to set the record straight after this unduly forgiving statement of its own special representative—rushed out a final report that stated flatly that the presidential election "does not meet the OSCE standards to which Armenia has committed itself." While conceding "improvement in some respects over the 1996 election," the statement argued that the flawed, earlier election "is not an appropriate standard for assessing a meaningful election process in line with OSCE commitments."[38]

Preliminary postelection statements and later reports about recent elections in Russia have displayed similar discrepancies. In Russia, according to Sarah Mendelson, "Sunny day-after-election reports contrast with detailed reports issued months later that reveal many glaring inconsistencies in the voting process."[39] The day after Russian presidential election on March 26, 2000, the OSCE's election observation mission declared that the election "marks further progress for the consolidation of democratic elections in the Russian Federation." The mission commended the "politically stable environment," praised the new election law as "consistent with internationally recognized democratic principles," and congratulated the election commission for "administer[ing] the process professionally and independently."[40] In response, one journalist lamented that this "most outrageous piece of propaganda emerged not from the bowels of the Kremlin press office, but from the International Election Observation Mission of the Organization for Security and Cooperation in Europe."[41]

The OSCE's final report was, as Mendelson puts it, "much less glowing and more nuanced."[42] Issued several months later, the report pointed out a number of shortcomings, including "the dependence of much of the media on subsidies from the State," "the vulnerability of the opposition and independent media to administrative pressures," "the decline of credible political party pluralism," "the opportunities to exploit the advantages of incumbency," "the blurred distinctions between the roles of regional and local administrations and election commissions," and "complex requirements for the preparation of vote count protocols often inducing circumventions of the law."[43]

The EU *Handbook* expresses worries as well about the reverse situation, in which a later conciliatory and positive final report contradicts an earlier negative preliminary statement: "Pressure from the host government, or agendas unrelated to the election process itself, can lead to inconsistencies between the postelection statement and the final report." The EU *Handbook* implores, "The postelection statement and final report should be similar in their tone and overall assessment."[44]

Although statements issued in the field are generally those of the individuals or groups that made them, sponsoring organizations understandably are concerned about longer-term implications. Election missions are typically semiautonomous, but their statements necessarily reflect on their sponsoring organizations. On the basis of their own experiences and monitoring over time, these organizations often bring their own perspectives as well. Reconciling these kinds of differences can be a delicate balancing act that requires tact and judgment both in the field and at headquarters. Reducing other pressures and interests on short-term observers and enhancing their professionalism and commitment to neutrality will mitigate the problem.

Finding Facts and Making Assessments: Checklists and Standards of Proof

Collecting massive amounts of raw data and information about an election is hardly valuable in and of itself. Analysis is necessary for this information gathering to be of consequence. Observers must be able to distinguish between irregularities and systematic manipulation. The need for analysis raises several technical, methodological questions about the means of examination and the relationship between the information gathered and the conclusions reached. Among these are the nature of election-day checklists and the use of "qualitative monitoring," burdens of proof, and the nature of postelection statements.

Fact Finding and "Qualitative Monitoring"

Election observers need the means and the evidence to assess the quality of an election process in a professional and credible manner. One challenge has been to figure out how to make their findings less anecdotal and impressionistic.

International observers are inherently limited in their ability to directly find facts. Rarely will international observers actually witness electoral manipulation or lawlessness, either on election day or during other parts of the process. Neither do observers typically find documentary or physical evidence of wrongdoing. The numbers and reach of international observers in a typical monitoring exercise make direct fact finding all but impossible.

Most international observer groups spread their observers geographically as much as possible and have those observers collect data in a more or less haphazard manner. Most err on the side of trying to collect as much information as possible in order to be as comprehensive as they can be. Most operate by applying instinct, judgment, and experience to essentially anecdotal evidence. Though this is useful, it does mean that there are limits to the inferences that can be drawn.

Monitoring organizations generally give their observers observation forms or checklists of information to collect and questions to ask at each polling station on election day. These checklists typically call for information about the administration of the process at each polling station, and they may or may not ask observers to make an overall judgment about the quality of the process at each polling station.

Once observers have collected the available information, they must assess the credibility and extent of alleged deficiencies and irregularities. All elections, whether in new, emerging, or developed democracies, have problems. In other words, almost by definition, observers must put the problems they find in context. Simple mistakes or irregularities caused by a lack of technical capacity or experience are certainly less of a reason for concern than a deliberate attempt to manipulate final results. Irregularities threaten freedom and fairness, as Elklit and Svensson put it, only to the extent that they are extensive, systematic, and decisive in a close race.[45]

To make these determinations, organizers must first determine what information to collect. Monitoring organizations often use substantially similar reporting forms from one election to the next. Certainly, there are issues common to most elections in new or emerging democracies. But, concludes International IDEA, such forms "cannot reflect the actual situation in different countries. In fact, they seem to confuse the evaluation of the election." International IDEA's experts recommend only that "checklist forms be tailored to the specific situation of the country holding elections," which seems reasonable but not especially helpful.[46]

In designing observation forms, monitoring organizations should start with the applicable rules from the election law and regulations. Observers should collect information about the extent to which the process in any given location is consistent with the rules. At the same time, what information is worth collecting and evaluating depends largely on what problems there have been in the past and what are the concerns of parties, nongovernmental organizations (NGOs), citizens, and others.

Although any number of things happening on election day might be worth finding out about, effective observation requires choices about what information is genuinely important. Observation forms or checklists cannot be too long or unwieldy. The more data observers seek to collect, the longer it takes to collect and analyze it. "For an observation to maximize its impact," argue quick count experts Melissa Estok, Neil Nevitte, and Glenn Cowan, "observer groups have to be able to gather key pieces of information quickly, analyze the data quickly and interpret and release the data quickly." They advise limiting observation forms to twelve to fifteen questions that meet specific tests of usefulness, validity, reliability, measurement, and efficiency. Analysts can then search for systemic problems and determine whether problems are likely to have had a material impact.[47]

Some organizations have experimented with this kind of "qualitative monitoring" on election day, which enables them to more confidently draw conclusions that are based on the evidence they have collected. Drawing on the principles of statistics (see chapter 13), observation forms can be collected from statistically significant samples of polling stations. This means that observers can generalize reliably from sample data about the quality of the election-day process throughout the country. It gives observers the means to determine the extent to which problems and errors are random or systematic.[48]

Nevertheless, this is far from the norm. Few international organizations currently develop statistically valid means of making qualitative assessments. Until they do, assessments of election day will continue to be largely based on educated guesses about the quality of the process.

Burdens of Proof

As in American law where the burden of proof in a courtroom or the standard of judicial review in considering the constitutionality of legislation is often determinative, presumptions about standards of proof for observers are critically important. If, for example, authorities are presumed to have conducted fair elections in the absence of proof to the contrary, election observers may be unable to criticize flawed elections. If, conversely, observers can effectively call into question the legitimacy of an election without extremely strong evidence, there is a real danger of bias. How much and what kind of proof should international observers have before they call into question the fairness or the legitimacy of an election? Must international observers have direct evidence of problems, or can they rely on what they believe to be credible reports from other sources, such as nonpartisan domestic monitors or even political parties? Is the burden of proof on those alleging fraud?

Garber's 1984 *Guidelines* recommended a "flexible approach toward fact-finding." The *Guidelines* suggested that "observers consider all evidence presented, even if not independently verified or subjected to due process requirements."[49] More modern handbooks on international election observation do not appear to address this issue directly. However, observers' assumptions, which are generally implicit, can greatly affect the tone of their assessments.

A lack of definitive proof sometimes constrains observers who have or wish to raise questions about an election's integrity. Despite its suspicions, for example, President Carter's delegation to the controversial 1990 election in the Dominican Republic, as discussed in chapter 5, was unable to evaluate preelection claims of tampering with voter registration or allegations of manipulation on election day because it arrived only days before election day and could not gather irrefutable evidence. The lack of preelection monitoring or any parallel count to verify an extremely close vote count hampered the team's ability to assess the extent of the problems. Four years later, in contrast, international election observers helped reduce tensions after another extremely close, controversial presidential election in the same country, by, in effect, substantiating opposition claims of fraud, based more on tendencies from available evidence than on conclusive proof. Some diplomats and foreign advisers at the time argued that observers should pull their punches for fear that critical assessments might inflame passions among supporters of the putative losers. An NDI delegation, led by the former member of Congress Stephen Solarz, however, discerned a "pattern of disenfranchisement" that "suggests the real possibility that a deliberate effort was made to tamper with the electoral process." While acknowledging that it was "not possible at this time to determine the number of votes affected," the statement continued, "Nevertheless, the disenfranchisement, given its magnitude and distribution, could affect the outcome of the elections."[50] This forthright assessment contributed to the negotiation of a peaceful resolution of the dispute, including an agreement on holding early new elections.

Assumptions about how much evidence is needed to justify criticisms drive observers' statements. In Nigeria in 1999, the Carter Center and NDI admitted that they had serious concerns but said they could not call an election into question without systematic evidence:

> While we witnessed a number of abuses, the delegation has no systematic evidence indicating that these abuses would have affected the overall outcome of the election. Nevertheless these abuses may have substantially compromised the integrity of the process in the areas in which they occurred.[51]

After noting problems with voter registration in the presidential elections in Senegal in 1993, an NDI delegation said it had received "no evidence" that such problems had "materially affected the election."[52]

In other elections, the lack of evidence can sound like an excuse for a relatively positive assessment in the face of problems. In Pakistan in 1993, NDI noted problems with the process of identifying and verifying eligible voters and other irregularities but said it "did not receive evidence that these problems were systematic or that they affected the outcome of the elections in the constituencies observed."[53] In the Dominican Republic in 1996, despite the problems in 1994, the Carter Center and NDI implied the election was acceptable in the absence of evidence to the contrary: "The delegation has not been presented with evidence of manipulation or irregularities that would materially affect the outcome of the election."[54] In Mongolia in 2000, a delegation from IRI said, "While IRI is concerned with several aspects of the electoral process, the Institute did not observe any instances of systematic electoral fraud or irregularities."[55]

In short, implicit assumptions about what is the appropriate burden of proof are critically important. If election processes are presumed acceptable in the absence of clear and convincing evidence to the contrary, then observers may find it difficult to raise questions. Alternatively, if they believe they are entitled to report based on their instincts, or they believe that authorities can be criticized if there is a reasonable perception of problems, then they are inclined to criticize the process even without clear, concrete evidence that problems were widespread.

Certainly, it is a mistake to give an election a passing grade just because observers cannot prove fraud beyond a reasonable doubt, especially if there is a danger that the mere presence of observers might provide legitimacy to an otherwise flawed process. In addition to good sense, fair judgment, and broad comparative experience, the ultimate solution to this dilemma lies in the development and use of more effective, statistically significant qualitative monitoring methods.

Postelection Monitoring

International election monitoring often falls apart after election day, after the large delegations have departed and the international media have turned their attention elsewhere. The period immediately following an election is often at least as volatile as election day and the preelection period. Postelection factors—such as whether the system of ballot counting and aggregation guards against fraud and whether the electoral complaint processes after an election function well—are critical.

Thus, there is a need for monitors after election day. Long-term monitors can follow postelection processing of election complaints and challenges; verify problems identified by election-day observers; follow the consolidation of results; monitor postelection violence, intimidation and retribution; and evaluate the process leading to winners taking their offices. They can issue subsequent reports.

Generally, in comprehensive monitoring programs, a relatively small number of long-term monitors remain for some time after elections, typically for at least several weeks and sometimes for some number of months. Postelection missions that can call attention to postelection problems, help reduce tensions, and recommend changes for the future may also be valuable. For the controversial elections in Cambodia on July 26, 1998, for instance, disputes about the election process continued into the fall, and a new coalition government on the basis of the election results was not formed until December 1. Although the circumstances were very different, Indonesia's transitional elections in 1999 really unfolded over five months from the national legislative elections on June 7 until the indirect election of the president and vice president on October 20 and 21. It is difficult but sometimes essential for monitoring organizations to maintain their focus on election processes for weeks or months after election day.

The Coordination of International Election Observers

Many transitional and consolidating elections have participation from all leading democratic countries and donors and, increasingly, from countries and organizations from the developing world. In Indonesia in 1999, for example, the more than 500 international observers came from Australia, the European Union, Japan, Southeast Asia, and the United States, among other places. Other foreign organizations that sent delegations included the Asian Network for Free Elections (ANFREL), the National Citizens' Movement for Free Elections from the Philippines (NAMFREL), NDI, the Carter Center, the Solidarity Center (U.S.), and the Australia Council for Overseas Aid. The United Nations Development Program (UNDP) loosely coordinated all these observers. In Nigeria in the same year, NDI and the Carter Center (together), IRI, the International Foundation for Election Systems, the Solidarity Center, the Commonwealth, the European Union, and the Organization of African Unity each organized its own monitoring program.

The considerable number of organizations interested in observing some elections can cause significant problems. The duplication of monitoring efforts can be wasteful. The demands of so many international groups can overwhelm national electoral authorities. Large numbers of observers can saturate some polling locations and distract local authorities. A chorus of monitoring statements can be confusing, and conflicting statements can exacerbate rather than calm tensions. As President Carter observed, "With the plethora of monitoring organizations now, sometimes even competing with each other for funding and prestige, it . . . creates a cacophony in dealing with election monitoring that the local government or the central election commission has to face."[56]

Therefore, international organizations planning international election monitoring invariably come to the issue of coordinating their efforts. Conventional wisdom suggests that coordination is an unadulterated good, the more the better. After a 1998 conference of experts, International IDEA reported "unanimous consensus that co-ordination among international organizations sending electoral observers is an important focus for the future."[57] The EU *Handbook* agrees, "Whenever it is possible for international organizations to arrive at a common opinion and a Joint Statement, the voice of the international community is united."[58]

Experience shows, however, that too much coordination—or more accurately, too much of certain kinds of coordination or in particular circumstances—can be counterproductive. Though donors, diplomats, and practitioners agree on the value of coordination, the dangers of forcing different kinds of groups with differing capabilities, interests, and motives to work too closely together—insisting on a common statement for example—should override the temptation to look for easy solutions. Commenting on

French observers in South Africa and British-led Commonwealth observers in Kenya, the German analyst Stefan Mair suggests, "it must be feared that a pan-European observation delegation from those countries which have strong foreign policy and economic interests in the host country may tend to give a conformist and false judgment of the elections."[59]

There are actually any number of monitoring activities that can be coordinated for a particular election. Groups can coordinate methodology, briefing and interaction with authorities, logistics, communications, security, geographical deployment of observers, information and findings, and public assessments.

Observers may sometimes work together in one operation, often coordinated by the United Nations and, as mentioned above, typically called a "joint international observer group." Because of concerns about duplication of efforts and the danger of conflicting assessments, donors and diplomats often urge all international observers to "speak with one voice" through such a group. Host countries themselves may worry, not entirely without reason, that conflicting assessments might sow confusion or reinforce the chances of unsubstantiated complaints.

This approach has considerable drawbacks, however. Combining all observers into one group can lower the standard of election assessment to that of the least professional group. This undermines consistent and professional application of international standards for election monitoring. Governments not committed to genuine elections may invite observers from "friendly" governments and other groups. If biased observers participate in the process of developing a joint statement, as in Cambodia in 1998 (discussed in chapter 8), they can dilute the impact of more impartial, professional groups. Similarly, also as in Cambodia, broader diplomatic considerations, rather than a clear focus on the quality of the election process, may unduly influence even well-intentioned observers representing intergovernmental organizations, governments, or local embassies. In such circumstances, a common statement constrains the freedom of other observers to assess the election in a way they feel is more honest. Moreover, the effort to agree on a joint postelection statement can exacerbate the already existing tendency to narrow the focus of election monitoring to events immediately surrounding election day, which tends to undervalue preelection developments and restrict postelection activities. In other words, the need to build a consensus among groups with disparate interests and different capabilities may force a watering down of standards or statement clarity.

The danger of confusion from contradictory statements tends anyway to be overstated. "When there is more than one delegation and more than one statement," concludes Pat Merloe of NDI, "experience demonstrates that the impartial, professional election-monitoring organizations almost always make similar findings and reach similar conclusions." Perhaps reflecting wishful thinking, he adds,

> Moreover, biased or unprofessional statements tend not to stand the test of scrutiny, and even though governments or losing parties may quote them to suit their own partisan purposes, respected news media and international institutions tend to pay attention to the statements from election monitoring organizations with established reputations for impartiality and professionalism.[60]

As an alternative to joint observation, observers might agree on some other form of coordination. This means that observer groups work together in substantial ways but maintain distinct identities and offer separate assessments. Often, a multilateral organization, such as the UN Electoral Assistance Division, the UNDP, the European Union, the OSCE, or the Organization of American States, will establish a secretariat with considerable staff and resources to coordinate observers. The United Nations has on occasion arranged for an experienced nongovernmental organization to run such a secretariat, as it did with NDI in Niger in 1993, Benin in 1995, Algeria in 1997, and Indonesia in 1999. The secretariat typically facilitates accreditation and briefings for international observers with national electoral authorities and provides all observers with briefing materials. If different international groups agree to coordinate closely, the secretariat also might provide terms of reference; organize deployments, including transportation, lodging, and translators; develop common forms and checklists; and even arrange observers' press conferences. If the coordination is somewhat looser, there is no central entity to arrange deployments, transportation or accommodation, although there generally is an effort to share information about deployment plans and maybe about local logistics, such as hotels, transportation, interpretation, and contact information.

In Indonesia in 1999, the government placed responsibility for coordination of international observers with the UNDP—on behalf of which NDI established and managed a "facilitation center" for all international observers. The facilitation center provided briefing materials, including copies of election laws and official documents, analysis from long-term monitoring efforts, materials on observation methodology, and news clippings; information about deployment plans of different observer groups; and logistical information, such as customized maps, accreditation forms, and travel information. It set up a mock polling station to demonstrate how the polling process was supposed to work. In the run-up to the election, the center also hosted regular meetings for organizers from different observer groups, and it arranged orientation and briefing sessions for observers when they arrived in the country. In addition to aiding observers, it also provided a service to electoral authorities because it relieved them of responding separately to requests from each observer group. The facilitation center "offered observers a wealth of information, experience, and contacts," later reported the UNDP. "By providing facilities for observers to share information, it helped create a cooperative and even trusting atmosphere conspicuously absent in earlier international observation exercises."[61]

Most well-established election-monitoring organizations communicate directly with one another to try to ensure that their efforts are complementary and mutually reinforcing. This takes place even in the absence of a formal coordination effort.

Coordinating International Observers for the 1996 Palestinian Elections

Elections in 1996 for the Palestinian legislative council present a good case study for examining issues involved in coordinating disparate international election observers. These elections attracted considerable international attention and a large number of observers from different types of organizations, from the Carter Center to the European Union. Taking responsibility for coordinating international observers for the first time, the European Union developed a set of coordination mechanisms that are typical of such efforts and took a step forward in developing its own comprehensive monitoring methodology.

During 1995, the international community planned its efforts to monitor and support elections for the leader and assembly of the Palestinian Authority, the body that would administer the West Bank and Gaza in accordance with the Oslo Agreements between Israel and the Palestine Liberation Organization. The elections were held on January 20, 1996. Because Israel vetoed the United Nations as coordinator of observers, the European Union stepped in to play that role instead.

The Israeli-Palestinian Agreement expressly contemplated a role for election monitoring and was perhaps the first international agreement to demonstrate a sophisticated understanding of monitoring. It thus reflected increasing international acceptability of international election monitoring and established an important precedent for domestic monitoring as well. The agreement established three categories of election observers (in addition to domestic and international media): (1) observer delegations sent under the authority of invited governments or intergovernmental organizations, (2) international nongovernmental organizations, and (3) domestic monitors. The agreement called on the European Union to coordinate observers, although this coordination appeared to apply mainly to observers from the first category, which it referred to as "official observers." The EU did not seek any role in coordinating international NGOs that planned monitoring programs, such as NDI and the Carter Center, or domestic monitors. The EU made clear that it would not take responsibility for administration, management, or logistics of the other observer delegations, official or otherwise.[62]

The European Union itself had 200 long-term observers, who began arriving about eight weeks before election day, and 100 short-term observers, including members of various parliaments, who arrived a few days before the balloting. Other observers to the Palestinian elections came from Canada, Egypt, Japan, Jordan, Norway, Russia, South Africa, and the United States as well as from the Organization of the Islamic Conference and the Organization of African Unity.

To coordinate the European and other official observers, the European Union established a coordination unit several months before election day with five offices throughout the West Bank and Gaza. This unit acted as liaison with the Palestinian authorities and represented the EU at trilateral meetings with Israel and the Palestinian Authority to address such issues as security, customs, accreditation, and logistics. The EU could take up issues about the conduct of the elections on a bilateral basis with the Palestinian Authority. The coordination unit also monitored administrative preparations for the elections, the public information campaign, and other preelection issues.

The European Union established a hierarchical set of mechanisms for coordination: a coordinating committee of the heads of each delegation, a technical task force to address issues related to the technical administration of the elections, and a "joint operations unit" that coordinated the details of deployment, communications, reporting, and security matters and established links with observer delegations of international NGOs. The European Union sought to get all observer delegations to coordinate deployment, logistics, transportation, reporting, communications, accreditation, training, and briefing of international observers as well as their interaction with the Israeli government and the Palestinian authorities. Each delegation was responsible for the security of its own observers.

At the same time, the European Union accepted that coordination would be voluntary. Though representatives of all observation groups agreed to share reports after the election, the principal American group, a joint effort of NDI and the Carter Center, declined to participate in an effort to achieve a joint statement. When the European Union requested advance notice of preelection statements made by other organizations, the American organizations promised only to remain in close contact and to share information throughout the preelection period.

Before the Palestinian elections, there was a fair amount of discussion about whether in-country diplomats could represent their countries at various coordination meetings before the elections. The EU representatives initially opposed this, because of the importance of keeping the monitoring separate from diplomatic representation to either the Palestinian Authority or the Government of Israel, but they later accepted the participation of diplomats from the countries that did not have monitoring representatives in place until later in the process (which was most of them).

The Palestinian elections in 1996 were the first for which the European Union coordinated other international observers as well as the first for which it organized its own comprehensive monitoring program. The issues of concern, while often mundane, are typical. The European Union did well to coordinate observers without being too heavy-handed. Ultimately, international observers essentially agreed on how to evaluate the process and by their presence made a modest contribution to the confidence of the Palestinian citizens in the process. With this constructive international involvement, the Palestinian elections appeared at the time to be a step forward for both the development of democratic institutions in the West Bank and Gaza and for the Israeli-Palestinian peace process.

Developing More Effective Monitoring

During the 1990s, election monitoring evolved from an activity of NGOs into a regular function of the United Nations, OSCE, the Organization of American States, the Commonwealth, and other intergovernmental organizations. With experience, these organizations have considerably improved their methodology. A number of American organizations have also tended to be involved in every significant election in new and emerging democracies.

As more organizations have become involved in elections in developing countries, concern has grown about duplication and contradictory statements. Yet coordination should not generally mean seeking a single, common assessment of the process. Rather international observers should seek to complement each other and to share information. The United Nations has moved in this direction by generally referring requests for observers to regional organizations. The American democracy organizations need not all be involved in monitoring every overseas election. At the same time, as the American organizations have done already, intergovernmental organizations should consider putting less emphasis on elections as such, especially on election administration and election day. Ultimately, the international community will need to rethink its approach to ensure that it takes advantage of opportunities that elections in new and emerging democracies provide for broader democratic consolidation.

Although international observers have no formal role in an election process, the participation of observers is now an accepted international norm. International norms have emerged as well to govern the conduct of international observers. The essence of these norms is that observers must endeavor to be independent and fair and to avoid undue interference in the process that they observe. The increasing professionalization of monitoring groups has led to a greater understanding and broader acceptance of these standards. Nevertheless, there are still problems with bias. Some groups are less professional than others, and even more established organizations fail to pay enough attention to conflicts of interest.

International election observation still has a contribution to make, but to maintain its relevance it must adapt to new challenges. Even though more experienced organizations well appreciate many of those challenges, the standard election-monitoring methodology still could be considerably improved.

Although short-term, high-profile observation of the days surrounding the balloting can demonstrate the support of the international community for democracy and potentially deter election-day fraud, it is no substitute for longer-term monitoring. Effective observation goes beyond what happens at the polls on election day. Threats to the process may be more real in the weeks and months before or after election day. Accordingly, monitoring efforts should begin well before election day and continue through the adjudication of election-related complaints and the formation of a new government, the seating of a new president, or other appropriate consequences of the election results. Smaller, shorter-term missions before and after elections may complement long-term efforts by highlighting particular issues or concerns. Monitoring groups should adjust their focus and develop new techniques to meet new challenges to the integrity of elections, such as illegal campaign financing. In short, a better election observation methodology is broad in scope—including consideration of political context and human rights—and follows an election as a process over time.

At the same time, one thoughtful, comprehensive evaluation of election observation efforts in Nicaragua suggests that the "ideal" of a comprehensive, long-term approach may not always be cost-effective or practical. As a more realistic alternative, Boneo and his colleagues recommend that international actors work together. They suggest "comprehensive coverage [by] means of the division of duties and specialisation, combined with complete exchange and transparency of information, with a modicum of coordination and/or co-operation."[63]

For many consolidating or second-generation elections, short-term international observers may not be necessary at all. Rather, as is discussed later in this book, long-term monitoring and greater focus on the preelection and postelection periods can complement international support for domestic monitoring, both as a more significant check on election manipulation and as a potentially more meaningful long-term contribution to democratization.

If international organizations do organize observers for election day, they should try to increase the professionalism of their efforts through better "qualitative monitoring," including more carefully designed checklists and more scientifically valid techniques. Short-term observers should also take care in the preparation and timing of interim statements after election day. Experienced observers try to describe the electoral process and avoid categorical conclusions. Elections must be seen as part of a political process and not be overemphasized as particular events. Election observation on or around election day should be just one part of the larger, longer-term monitoring process.

Chapter 8

Cambodia: Challenges to International Election Observation

Sometimes I wonder whether there is a national tourism campaign, or a sign at the airport . . . that reads, "Cambodia: It's better than Burma." Or perhaps, a line on the letterhead of Prime Minister Hun Sen, or a sign on his office door . . . saying, "Hun Sen: He's better than Pol Pot."

—Sam Rainsy, Cambodian opposition leader[1]

Since a 1991 peace agreement ended decades of civil war, the international community has again and again made elections the centerpiece of efforts to bring about stability, development, and democracy in Cambodia. But in doing so, the international community has failed to uphold international democratic standards, has exposed serious weaknesses of international election-monitoring methodology, and has enabled, wittingly or unwittingly, extremely flawed elections to provide a veneer of international legitimacy for a violent, authoritarian regime.

This chapter uses Cambodia as a case study of the limitations and unintended consequences of supporting and observing flawed elections. The international community failed to respond effectively or coherently to a political crisis in Cambodia in the period 1997–98 and ultimately split on how to deal with elections there in 1998. Local elections in 2002 showed that the international community had failed to learn from its earlier mistakes.

An examination of the Cambodian experience offers several lessons for international election observation and democracy promotion. First, the experience reveals the shortcomings of international election-monitoring methods, including an excessive focus on election day, a failure of election observer delegations to build on preelection findings, and a lack of postelection monitoring and follow-up. Second, the divisions within the international community reflected differing agendas and approaches of diverse types of international actors: governmental and nongovernmental, impartial and partisan, pragmatic and idealistic, European and American, experienced and inexperienced. Third, the experience of election monitors in Cambodia demonstrates the inadequacies of the "free and fair" standard for judging the acceptability of elections, the tension between universal and relative standards, and the pitfalls of offering election statements and dealing with the media. In short, the international community expected too much from elections in a society plagued by conflict and repression. Though well intentioned, the international response to elections in Cambodia in recent years has ended up providing undeserved legitimacy to election processes that have fallen short of democratic norms.

Elections and Democratization in Cambodia

Perhaps no country suffered more turmoil and unremitting violence during the second half of the twentieth century than Cambodia. During the Vietnam War, Cambodia suffered intense American bombing. In 1975, Pol Pot's Khmer Rouge came to power and embarked on a genocidal program to radically restructure society, including the evacuation of cities and the mass murder of intellectuals. Nearly 2 million of the country's 8 million people died from execution, disease, starvation, and overwork. A Vietnamese invasion in December 1978 removed the Khmer Rouge regime and installed a new regime headed by a cadre of former Khmer Rouge members who had defected to Vietnam to escape Pol Pot's purges, but a protracted civil war continued for more than a decade. Hun Sen became head of the Vietnamese-backed government in 1985.

In 1991 in Paris, Cambodia's warring factions concluded an internationally supervised peace agreement, which called for a "system of liberal democracy on the basis of pluralism" and mandated "periodic and genuine elections . . . with a requirement that electoral procedures provide a full and fair opportunity to organize and participate in the electoral process."[2] A commitment to "free and fair elections" appears throughout the document.

France, the United States, and other countries pledged to help. To organize elections and administer the country during a transition period, the United Nations established the largest, most costly peacekeeping force in its history, the UN Transitional Authority in Cambodia (UNTAC). UNTAC cost the international community about $1.6 billion.[3] Since that time, international donors and their agents, through massive foreign aid and political direction, have played an unusually extensive role in setting Cambodia's priorities.

In 1993, under the supervision of UNTAC, Cambodia held competitive elections. The elections were for a constituent assembly, but after adopting a new constitution the assembly transformed itself into a parliament and ratified the formation of a new national government. The royalist party, the National United Front for an Independent, Neutral, Peaceful and Cooperative Cambodia (FUNCINPEC), won a clear electoral victory, with 46 percent of the vote and 58 of the 120 available seats. The former communist ruling party, the Cambodian People's Party (CPP), won 38 percent of the vote and 51 seats. Despite its earlier agreement in Paris, the Khmer Rouge rejected the process, and violence blamed on both the Khmer Rouge and the CPP marred the election campaign.

Even with the violence, most Cambodians and the international community viewed the elections as an outstanding success. One expert reported, "Cambodia is widely regarded as the brightest jewel currently to be found in the crown of UN peacekeeping."[4] Another study issued not long after the elections reflected the buoyant conventional wisdom of the time: "In Cambodia, the United Nations' electoral efforts were remarkably successful in bringing about national reconciliation and a government dedicated to reform."[5] The UN Security Council itself declared its

> great satisfaction that, with the successful conclusion of the UNTAC mission following the election of 23–28 May 1993, the goal of the Paris Agreements of restoring to the Cambodian people and their democratically elected leaders their primary responsibility for peace, stability, national reconciliation and reconstruction in their country has been achieved.[6]

Despite its perceived success, the United Nations–supervised election in 1993 failed to bring either democracy or political stability to Cambodia. Hun Sen and the other CPP leaders rejected the election results, claiming that the United Nations had "rigged" the process, and threatened insurrection. UNTAC and foreign governments stood by as the CPP forced its way into a power-sharing agreement, with Prince Norodom Ranariddh and Hun Sen as co–prime ministers. The international community also failed to insist on implementation of other requirements of the Paris Peace Accords to disarm and demobilize the former warring factions and to establish an independent judiciary.[7] The CPP retained control of the security forces, including the police and much of the military, as well as the judiciary and the civilian bureaucracy at all levels of government.

Not surprisingly, the coalition of royalists and former communists—former battlefield enemies—proved dysfunctional. Each government ministry had coministers, which gave both parties a full veto on all government action. This was particularly significant for the CPP, as its long-standing, continuing control of the country gave it a strong incentive to maintain the status quo and its role in government enabled it to slow reforms that threatened the interests of party insiders.

With Ranariddh's agreement or acquiescence, the coalition government purged popular FUNCINPEC reformers. In August 1995, the National Assembly expelled the popular finance minister, Sam Rainsy, after he publicly criticized government corruption. In November 1995, Prince Norodom Sirrivudh—who was the foreign minister and FUNCINPEC secretary general as well as a half-brother of King Sihanouk and the uncle of Prince Ranariddh—was removed from the government, expelled from the National Assembly, and forced into exile on the implausible grounds that he was plotting to assassinate Hun Sen.

Political violence reemerged. This was fully evident on March 30, 1997, when assailants threw grenades into a peaceful antigovernment demonstration led by Sam Rainsy. Sam Rainsy himself was unhurt, but sixteen people were killed, and many others were seriously injured, including an American adviser, Ron Abney, who was the country representative of the International Republican Institute (IRI).

The uneasy coalition of Prince Ranariddh's royalist party and the former communist CPP of Hun Sen eventually unraveled. In July 1997, second prime minister Hun Sen violently ousted his putative coalition partner Ranariddh. Dozens of Ranariddh loyalists were killed. For example, a senior official, Ho Sok, was executed just outside his office at the Interior Ministry. The offices of FUNCINPEC and other parties opposed to the CPP were attacked and vandalized. Prince Ranariddh fled to France, while at least twenty members of parliament and other opposition leaders found exile in Bangkok.

The United States and other countries condemned the violence and suspended aid. The United Nations declined to allow Hun Sen's government to take Cambodia's seat in the General Assembly. The Association of Southeast Asian Nations (ASEAN) postponed Cambodia's pending membership. The American democracy organizations, IRI and the National Democratic

Institute for International Affairs (NDI), provided funding and advice for the united opposition in exile to aid its efforts to try to restore the democratically elected government. To avoid triggering a U.S. law that would have automatically cut off all American assistance, however, the State Department declined to call the violent government takeover a "coup," arguing unpersuasively that the term did not encompass the violent overthrow of one part of a government by another.[8]

Elections as Panacea

For lack of any real alternative to end the stalemate, a fresh election came to seem a panacea. Although they deplored Hun Sen's violent takeover of the government, many donors and diplomats appeared to believe that Cambodia could not be stable without him in charge. Many in the international community had also been disappointed in the performance of Ranariddh's democratically elected government. And there was fear that, without some resolution, the situation might evolve as it had in Burma, where a military junta had repressed the democratically elected government of Aung San Suu Kyi for years. Thus, an election—even an imperfect one—that offered Hun Sen legitimacy and preserved a niche for political opposition seemed to many to be the best available option. As one French diplomat said at the time, "Let's be realistic. We get Hun Sen elected, not free and fair like in our countries, but O.K. good enough. Then we can have legitimacy, diplomacy, investment, order, and these poor people can get on with their lives."[9]

Elections thus became the focus of the international community's efforts to move forward after the coup. In late 1997 and early 1998, the "Friends of Cambodia"—comprising Australia, China, France, India, Russia, and the United States—pushed the CPP to allow exiled political leaders to return and made a competitive election a precondition for improved relations. Under this international pressure, Hun Sen eventually agreed to an election. Along with the new, nominal first prime minister Ung Huot, Hun Sen signed a letter to the UN secretary general providing assurances that the Cambodian government was committed to "ensuring a peaceful environment conducive to free and fair elections in 1998." The letter guaranteed "the physical security and safety of those members of the National Assembly and other political leaders who wish to return to Cambodia and resume their political activities in connection with the forthcoming elections." It pledged that the returning politicians would be free from intimidation and promised them freedom of movement, assembly, and speech.[10] Implicitly recognizing that the free and fair standard sounded like empty rhetoric, the donors called repeatedly for national elections that would be "free, fair, and credible."[11]

Having been coaxed back from exile in early 1998, the opposition agreed under international pressure to participate in an election that would certainly fail that test. UN human rights monitors, for example, continued to document violence and intimidation directed against opposition supporters, and the Cambodian authorities failed to investigate or prosecute extrajudicial killings. CPP supporters dominated the election commission, the judiciary, and the security forces, and opposition parties and candidates faced numerous legal and practical obstacles. In these circumstances, it was difficult to conceive of how elections in Cambodia might be considered free, fair, or credible.

Splits within the International Community

Nevertheless, it appeared that judgments about whether the election passed some test of legitimacy would determine the future of foreign aid and diplomatic relations. For those governments that believed it necessary to deal with the Hun Sen government, this created unfortunate incentives to find the election acceptable. An acceptable election, among other things, would allow donors to restore aid programs thought to be in the interest of the Cambodian people.

Australia, the European Union, Japan, and the United Nations offered money, equipment, and technical assistance to the administration of the election, notwithstanding its many shortcomings, in the hope that an election would help end the political crisis. The American response, in contrast, was more ambivalent. Influenced by American human rights and democracy organizations and Hun Sen critics in Congress, the U.S. government worried that support for the process might help an unsatisfactory election to achieve some measure of international legitimacy. Having suspended aid after the 1997 violence, the United States declined to support the election commission or the electoral process. But the U.S. administration nevertheless shared the hope that the elections might help ameliorate an untenable status quo. Asked about Cambodian elections shortly before election day, for example, the State Department spokesperson James Rubin suggested that the election climate "is about as good as it's likely to be for some time."[12]

Accordingly, the United States channeled its assistance to monitoring and voter education efforts by Cambodian nongovernmental organizations

(NGOs). Cambodian press accounts later played up the differences between the European and American observer groups, which they dubbed "pragmatists" and "idealists," respectively. As of the writing of this book, the split in approach to foreign aid in Cambodia continues, because U.S. law still prohibits most American assistance to the Cambodian government.

At least for the American groups, the flawed environment similarly raised the question whether to send international observers, because their participation might provide undue legitimacy and might focus too much attention on election day rather than the shortcomings of what preceded it. In a statement two weeks before election day, representatives from NDI and IRI said that "under the prevailing circumstances, [we] would not normally recommend sending international observers." Nevertheless, the bipartisan American team reasoned, the election merited observers because political parties were participating and the outcome was "not a foregone conclusion." (Cambodian civic organizations and opposition parties also strongly urged the American groups to observe.) The statement argued, among other things, that international monitoring might "deter further violence and intimidation" and would provide moral support to courageous candidates and civil society groups.[13]

Thus, despite splits over whether to aid the process, the international community eventually agreed on the need to monitor it. Given the immense international investment in Cambodian elections earlier in the decade and the shared hope that new elections might help restore peace, if not a genuine democratic transition, many developing and donor countries and international organizations decided to support election monitoring, by organizing preelection monitoring efforts, supporting domestic monitors, or sending observers for elections themselves.

The United Nations had made a huge investment in Cambodia in the period 1992–93, but it lacked the resources and political will to take the lead once again in 1998. Rather than organizing an effort to supervise or assess the elections in the name of the United Nations, the world body decided to coordinate international observers sent by other countries and organizations. Thus, the United Nations established a secretariat to offer logistical, security, and other support for a so-called Joint International Observer Group (JIOG). It did not, however, control or take political responsibility for the JIOG; that is, the United Nations would not be involved in the JIOG's leadership, approach, composition, or statements.

To complement its technical and financial support for the process, the European Union established its own monitoring program to evaluate the process. As they had for several years, the U.S. government, NDI, and the Asia Foundation supported domestic monitoring, and the U.S. Agency for International Development also funded NDI and IRI to jointly organize the principal American monitoring efforts. The governments of Australia, Canada, Japan, France, Germany, the United Kingdom, and other countries in Asia, Europe, and elsewhere also announced substantial plans to observe the process through the JIOG.

Preelection Monitoring and Preelection Problems

On paper, the international community seemed to adopt a model approach to effective, comprehensive preelection monitoring. The United Nations and the donor countries initiated monitoring programs to build confidence and track progress toward acceptable elections, including preelection missions and long-term monitoring. Several UN offices began formal monitoring programs in the country in the months before the elections. First, the Office of the Secretary General's Personal Representative in Cambodia monitored the "safe return" of opposition political figures. A separate UN office, established by the Office of the UN High Commissioner for Human Rights, monitored the human rights environment. Finally, the United Nations sought to support monitoring of the elections themselves. In April, more than three months before election day, the United Nations established an election-monitoring secretariat for the JIOG.

The European Union deployed about fifty-five long-term election observers around the country beginning in May, led by the Swedish diplomat Sven Linder. NDI and IRI also established a monitoring presence in Phnom Penh at about the same time. Separately, working through the Asia Foundation, the U.S. embassy recruited twenty-five expatriates living around the country to serve as "long-term observers," although most of them had no experience with election or human rights monitoring. NDI and IRI, working together, and a coalition of NGO representatives from Southeast Asia called the Asian Network for Free Elections (ANFREL) sent preelection missions to assess and publicly comment on the shortcomings of the process.

Along with complementary efforts by domestic monitoring groups, these international efforts documented serious shortcomings in the political climate. First and foremost was the problem of political violence. Before the elections, the UN Human Rights Office in Cambodia cited "13 killings, 4 alleged killings, 3 attempted killings, 7 illegal arrests and detention, 6 instances of physical abuse, 1 attempted abduction and over 150 credible allegations of harassment and intimidation" that it believed to be directly related to the election campaign.[14] In addition to the more than 100 people killed during the 1997 coup and its aftermath, 22 "political killings" were reported in the four months before the July 26, 1998, elections, according to a UN Human Rights Office analyst.[15] International monitoring groups, diplomats and domestic election-monitoring organizations (EMOs) expressed concern about the climate of impunity that had prevailed since the July 1997 coup and urged the authorities to investigate and prosecute perpetrators of violence and intimidation.

On July 14, 1998, two weeks before election day, NDI and IRI issued a joint statement in Phnom Penh that expressed concern about the preelection environment, including "pervasive political violence" and a "culture of impunity." The American organizations concluded that "the process leading up to the elections . . . is fundamentally flawed."[16] Likewise, two days before the election, ANFREL cited "political killings, disappearances, threats and intimidation."[17] Although a senior UN official, Francesc Vendrell, reported to the UN Security Council before the elections that Cambodia had committed to investigate extra-judicial killings, which he "hoped . . . would lead to concrete results,"[18] no prosecutions for murders that occurred during the political violence of July 1997 or during the months leading up to the elections in 1998 were ever reported.

Foreign and domestic observers also agreed on the fundamental need to establish impartial, independent election authorities, but they found that the selection process and composition of the new National Election Commission failed that test. For one thing, the regime selected members of the commission in January 1998 while opposition leaders were still in exile in fear for their lives. Even though the law provided that each of the four parties represented in parliament would have a representative on the eleven-member commission, the nominal representatives of FUNCINPEC and Sam Rainsy's party were actually from pro-CPP factions rather than genuine representatives of those parties. The law provided that another representative would come from the NGO community, but the two leading Cambodian nongovernmental monitoring coalitions, the Committee for Free and Fair Elections (COMFREL) and the Coalition for Free and Fair Elections (COFFEL), attacked the integrity of the process by which that representative was chosen.[19] A joint NDI-IRI report issued at the time concluded that the selection process "failed to result in a broadly representative commission."[20] In a report released shortly before the elections, COMFREL concluded that "most members of the [National Election Commission] are linked to or aligned with the ruling party."[21]

Observers also noted restrictions on freedom to campaign. Opposition leaders had been in exile when electoral rules were adopted, election bodies constituted, and arrangements with foreign funders agreed upon. When the opposition parties returned, the CPP government denied them access to radio and television and banned political demonstrations in the capital city of Phnom Penh during the campaign.

Although the early and broad array of international preelection monitoring efforts would theoretically appear to be a good example of international best practices, it ultimately failed to deter serious violence or to find appropriate responses to the blatant problems with election preparations and media access. This failure resulted in part because some monitors ignored or downplayed preelection problems. The locally recruited American observers, for example, never made public reports or shared their findings with other observer groups before or after the elections; this called the very purpose of these observers into question. The JIOG, two days before elections, did note "serious concerns" including "unresolved killings," intimidation of voters and party officials, threats to the secrecy of the ballot, and "unequal access to electronic media." But, inexplicably, it still concluded that "reasonable conditions exist for an election . . . that can be broadly representative of the will of the Cambodian people."[22] Many viewed this statement on the eve of the election as an attempt to move the goalposts by choosing a standard for judging the elections that would be easier to meet than whether they were free and fair. The JIOG spokesperson—Ambassador Linder, who was also head of the EU monitoring team—expressly discounted the effect of the preelection problems, but he failed to explain how observers could dismiss the effect of intimidation and violence so categorically.

The Interests and Agendas of Observers

The Joint International Observer Group was not, strictly speaking, a UN effort, even though the United Nations was later criticized for the JIOG's statements. Neither was the JIOG an EU operation, although the EU and JIOG monitoring efforts for a time became essentially indistinguishable because Ambassador Linder served as the coordinator and spokesperson for both.

NDI and IRI declined to participate in the JIOG or its deliberations. Indeed, while they never admitted as much, the two American organizations had decided to send their own election monitors, rather than to sit out what they believed to be a highly flawed process, in part because they worried that the JIOG's postelection assessment was likely to minimize serious problems. Presumably for similar reasons, reinforced by staunch political opposition to the Hun Sen regime in Washington, the U.S. government decided in mid-June that its locally recruited long-term observers would not participate in the JIOG's deliberations or associate themselves with its statements. Although it was little noted at the time, even the European Union itself grew wary of the United Nations–coordinated process, even though the EU's own chief observer also headed the JIOG. Although monitors from its member states participated in the JIOG, the EU ultimately sent a separate observer delegation headed by Glenys Kinnock, a British member of the European Parliament, to publicly offer its own assessment, separate from that of the United Nations–sponsored, European Union–led JIOG.

In other words, despite ostensibly common goals, the major international actors in Cambodia did not trust each other. The Americans, especially the American democracy organizations, worried that the United Nations and the European Union would whitewash very serious problems. The Europeans and others believed that the Americans were biased against the Hun Sen government. The European Union felt it necessary to offer a second opinion to the United Nations–coordinated group that the EU's own monitoring mission controlled and spoke for. Every group seemed suspicious of the motives or methodologies of the others.

The JIOG ultimately encompassed approximately 500 observers representing 34 separate observer missions from Europe, Southeast Asia, and elsewhere, and there were an estimated 800 international observers overall.[23] Though NDI and IRI declined to participate in the United Nations–coordinated group, they did accept substantial UN assistance in providing security for their observers. Working closely with domestic monitoring groups, IRI and NDI together fielded a delegation for election week of about 60 members representing both parties in the United States and 7 other nations.

Both the European and the American monitoring programs could have been criticized as biased: the Europeans (and others) for helping to fund and organize the elections, and the Americans because of their strong support for the opposition in exile. Because the European Union had played such a prominent role in funding and organizing the election, this meant it was, to a considerable extent, evaluating itself. Experienced EU advisers had overseen voter registration, the recruitment and training of election officials, the preparation of balloting materials, and the finalization of electoral rules. The European Union had also provided a substantial part of the budget for the elections. This substantial commitment to organizing the process would seem to give it an incentive to find the process at least reasonably worthwhile. At the same time, the American organizations were arguably tainted by their substantial financial and political support for the opposition political parties in exile. Conversely, both the Europeans and the Americans had the resources, experience, and credibility, both internationally and in Cambodia, to contribute to a successful monitoring effort.

Although the Americans may have been more moralistic than the Europeans and Asians, the differences in approach probably had more to do with the fact that observers who represent governments or intergovernmental organizations typically have different agendas and constraints than do nongovernmental observers. By establishing and funding NGOs that encourage democratic development as intermediaries, the United States has largely separated democracy assistance from decisions about foreign policy, such as decisions about diplomatic relations and foreign aid. As elsewhere, it was these NGOs that actually organized monitoring programs in Cambodia.

European, Asian, and other countries, in contrast, sent diplomats, bureaucrats, and sitting politicians. (ANFREL, made up of nongovernmental observers, was an exception.) Although unstated, and perhaps even subconscious, their principal agenda in Cambodia was diplomatic: to find a rationale for improving relations with the Hun Sen government, which they considered a fait accompli, in order to restore political stability and foreign assistance. They framed their assessment of the election accordingly. They seemed to justify their muted criticisms by saying, in effect, that given the realities of the political situation, this process was not such a bad outcome. That the actual polling appeared fair, as observers later found, made this approach that much harder to criticize.

In other words, though there was some difference in emphasis between American and European governments, the more important distinction was probably between nongovernmental democracy promoters, whose sole focus was to insist on a genuinely democratic election, on the one hand, and governments and multilateral organizations, which essentially sought to paper over election flaws in pursuit of political stability, on the other. Both the governments and the foreign NGOs saw themselves as seeking the best interests of Cambodians.

Whereas "idealists" and "pragmatists" differed on means and emphasis, the mainstream foreign actors agreed on the authoritarian tendencies of the Hun Sen government, and both idealists and pragmatists sought to support greater respect for human rights and democracy in Cambodia. In contrast, there were others who styled themselves international observers but were really apologists for Hun Sen. Thus, the JIOG, which accepted all comers, was burdened by the participation of two types of unqualified observers.

First, the JIOG included observers dispatched by governments of undemocratic countries, including Burma, China, Laos, and Vietnam, which certainly lacked experience with democratic elections or multiparty politics. In some countries, the participation of observers from nondemocratic countries might advance the democratic cause by exposing them to democratic elections and multiparty politics. In Cambodia, however, observers from nondemocratic countries cared little about truthfully assessing the process. During the JIOG's internal deliberations, for example, election observers sent by governments of nondemocratic countries huddled with those from democratic countries in a conference room at the luxurious Cambodiana Hotel. According to one participant, government representatives from Burma, China, and Vietnam urged the JIOG to certify the Cambodian elections as "free and fair" with little regard for the actual findings of observers either before or during the elections. Reflecting later on Cambodia, the European Commission concluded that the European Union "should avoid formal coordination structures where the EU's integrity and freedom of word and action could be impaired by having to accept the lowest common denominator among a disparate group of international [observers]."[24]

The JIOG also welcomed a second type of biased observers: those not affiliated with any government or established international democracy organization, who had clear partisan agendas. In particular, an ad hoc group calling itself the Volunteer Observers for the Cambodian Elections (VOCE) publicly defended Cambodia's electoral environment and blamed criticisms of the elections on "international politics." One organizer of this group, former Australian ambassador to Cambodia Tony Kevin, had seemed sympathetic to Hun Sen in a 1997 cable to Canberra: "Hun Sen is trying to pull off what he has always wanted—a more or less well-governed Cambodia under CPP control, but legitimized by a reasonably free and fair election."[25] The group's other leader, John McAuliff of the U.S.–Indochina Reconciliation Project, admitted in a press release before the election the group's purpose to help "Cambodia quickly regain normal international standing,"[26] a purpose simply not consistent with impartial monitoring.

Postelection Assessments and Preelection Flaws

Although diverse international actors approach elections differently, there is a general consensus that effective monitoring takes account of the rules and extent of respect for political rights in the preelection period as well as the climate and administration of the process on polling day itself. Yet the experience of international observers during the 1998 elections in Cambodia demonstrated how difficult this may be in practice.

The political climate and institutional framework for the controversial elections in Cambodia in 1998 were highly flawed, but the process on election day, observers agreed, was peaceful and free of fraud. This posed a dilemma. Given the opposition's decision to participate, were the elections necessarily entitled to some measure of credibility when election day went relatively well? Or would acceptance of the results mean that the elections had given international legitimacy to a government that had grabbed and maintained power through violent means? How could it be determined whether intimidation affected voting behavior? The methodology for monitoring the Cambodian election in 1998 did not provide observers with the means to resolve these extremely important questions.

Although the international community now agrees on the need to begin monitoring efforts well before election day, the experience in Cambodia in 1998 showed that international observers have yet to determine how to reflect negative preelection findings in traditional postelection assessments. In Cambodia, the United Nations and American, European, and Asian monitoring groups agreed on the shortcomings of the political climate: violence and pervasive intimidation of opposition supporters; impunity for politically motivated killings; ruling party dominance of the election commission, the judiciary, and the security forces; and a legal framework that unreasonably hampered the opposition. Yet the international community nevertheless failed to force any significant improvements in the process before the election, and observers' ambivalence afterward about the ultimate impact of preelection flaws similarly failed to temper the perception that they had blessed the process. One election observer suggested that the decision of foreign groups to send observers meant that "the legitimacy of the election was still an open question on polling day, unless the 'fundamentally flawed' . . . campaign period negated ipso facto the apparently clean voting day performance."[27] Exposure of very troubling preelection problems did not prevent postelection assessments from providing substantial international legitimacy to the process.

The Cambodian authorities later reported that Hun Sen's ruling party won approximately 42 percent of the ballots cast, which translated into 64 seats, a majority of the 122-member assembly. Prince Ranariddh's party won 31 percent of the vote and 43 seats. The opposition party led by the activist Sam Rainsy won 14 percent and 15 seats.

In all elections in which international observers play a significant role, they are under pressure from the media and others to comment quickly. In Cambodia, their pronouncements were expected to have unusual weight in affecting perceptions about the legitimacy of the victors' right to govern. Nevertheless, other than the JIOG, most delegations waited for their observers to return to Phnom Penh so they could meet and share observations before the groups made their assessments public. Some consulted closely with the leading domestic EMOs as well.

All observer groups agreed that election day had gone surprisingly well. They proved unable to reconcile effectively preelection violence and extreme unfairness with a process that was peaceful and acceptably administered on election day. Despite protestations to the contrary, in the end the standard methodology, even with the presence of long-term monitors and preelection engagement, once again simply focused too much on election day, thus diverting attention from the preexisting flaws. Although for different reasons, in the end all the international actors involved in monitoring failed.

Despite its excellent programs to monitor the political and human rights environment in the preceding months, the United Nations had no mandate of its own to assess the elections. It made the mistake of effectively giving the UN imprimatur to a monitoring process it did not control or endorse.

The Joint International Observer Group demonstrated no reluctance to come to categorical judgments. The JIOG waited neither for the initial ballot count nor for its observers to return to share their findings before it gave the election its "thumbs up." Its statement—which was agreed upon by the leaders of the various delegations participating in the JIOG while their observers were still scattered around the country and was issued just one day after polling—went well beyond commending the election administration and turnout to embrace the overall process. Though noting the violence before the election, it summarily dismissed the possibility of intimidation. The

JIOG endorsed the election, calling the process "free and fair to an extent that enables it to reflect, in a credible way, the will of the Cambodian people." The statement also said that "all parties should accept and honour the results of the election."[28]

One diplomat criticized the JIOG statement as "utterly irresponsible" because "it was released at a time of growing confusion about the counting and was a betrayal of their commitment to see the election process through to the end. . . . They've signed off when the process was far from complete."[29]

Ironically, however, it was the American monitoring effort that came to represent for many the shortcomings of international election monitoring in Cambodia. That NDI and IRI, the international organizations most identified with the opposition to Hun Sen, were themselves perceived as certifying an undeniably flawed process says a great deal about the limitations of international election monitoring.

Observers from the NDI-IRI delegation returned to Phnom Penh the day after polling and shared impressions well into the night. All noted the relative calm of election day and commended the courage of Cambodian voters, who turned out in large numbers despite the intimidation. They found the process surprisingly well administered. Cambodian domestic monitoring groups, which monitored virtually all 11,000 polling stations in the country, concurred. A small team worked through the night to prepare a draft of the delegation's statement, which would be issued the next day.

By accurately reporting what they had witnessed on election day, the election observers largely distracted attention from the fundamental flaws of the larger process. The NDI-IRI delegation tried to avoid this result by reiterating after the election its serious concerns about "violence, extensive intimidation, unfair media access, and ruling party control of the administrative machinery that characterized the preelection period."[30] The European Union also pointed out these problems.

But the very methodology of all the election observers obscured their ability to communicate concerns about the political environment. By bringing most of their observers to the country only days before the election and issuing much-anticipated and well-covered statements shortly thereafter, monitoring groups necessarily brought focus to election day. The hunger of the press for immediate, categorical assessments—whether the election should be judged "free and fair"—and their tendency to ignore nuances and qualifications did not help.

An offhand comment at a packed postelection press conference of the NDI-IRI delegation coleader, former member of Congress Stephen Solarz, came to epitomize for many the fundamental weaknesses of the monitoring process. Having been struck by the surprising success of election day, Solarz hypothesized in response to a reporter's question that, if the grievance process and the formation of the government proceeded smoothly, this election might be seen in the future as "the miracle on the Mekong." Many unfortunately interpreted this as an unqualified endorsement, and the phrase found its way into much of the contemporary press coverage and subsequent discourse about the elections.[31]

The head of the EU delegation, Glenys Kinnock, tersely delivered the EU statement a day later, after the initial barrage of criticism of the seemingly positive assessments of Solarz and other international observers. Although the EU statement was similar in tone and substance to the NDI-IRI one the day before, many perceived it as being considerably more critical of the process overall than the JIOG or the Americans had been.

The European Union also sought to justify its earlier financial and technical assistance. In the first paragraph of its statement, even before commenting on the elections, the EU delegation gratuitously defended its own assistance as "both critical and necessary." "The decision to opt in to the process was not an easy one," the statement argued, implicitly criticizing the policy of the American government, "but . . . it was both a correct and appropriate course of action."[32]

Strains in the Bipartisan American Approach to Cambodian Democracy

Representatives of IRI would later distance themselves from Solarz's assessment and implicitly from NDI. Until that point, for nearly a year, the two institutes had collaborated unusually closely on the Cambodia program. In August 1997, shortly after the coup, the institutes sent a joint mission to assess the political situation. The joint mission condemned the ouster and replacement of First Prime Minister Ranariddh as "the product of violence and an unconstitutional attempt to legitimize it" and concluded, "Unless there are extraordinary and fundamental changes in the existing political environment, it will be impossible to hold genuine, democratic elections" in 1998.[33] After a second mission in October 1997, IRI president (and later assistant secretary of state) Lorne Craner and NDI president Kenneth Wollack jointly concluded, "Political conditions in the country make it premature to look to elections as the primary means for resolving the current crisis."[34]

After the 1997 coup, IRI began to provide direct support for parliamentarians and political leaders in exile in Bangkok. At IRI's invitation and the urging of influential figures in Washington, NDI added its support. This bipartisan effort supported the creation and sustenance of the Union of Cambodian Democrats, a coalition of political parties in exile, to push for the restoration of democracy in Cambodia. Though the institutes have generally avoided providing financial or material aid to political parties, they decided to make an exception for Cambodian parties in exile to keep them alive so they could push for a democratic process. Each institute placed a representative in Bangkok to work directly with the exiled parties and to coordinate with the other.

For most of the next year, through election day, July 26, 1998, IRI and NDI continued to work closely together. (The two institutes had also closely coordinated their programs in Cambodia in 1993–94, even sharing an office in Phnom Penh for a while, but joint programs remained unusual.) Between the coup in 1997 and the elections in 1998, they sent several combined teams to Cambodia and issued joint reports in Washington and Phnom Penh. They both continued to support the Union of Cambodian Democrats in exile. They presented a united front with Washington policymakers in the State Department and on Capitol Hill. And they testified side by side in front of congressional committees. Although there were inevitable tensions, the close collaboration on policy and program was remarkable. That the Republican and Democratic democracy-promotion institutes had made common cause on Cambodia undoubtedly contributed to the strong Washington line on the 1998 election process.

As elections looked increasingly likely, the institutes did pursue separate programs in Cambodia as well. NDI renewed its advice and support for Cambodian EMOs, which had been its focus before the previous year's coup. IRI continued its particularly close relationship with the opposition party founded and led by Sam Rainsy. In due course, each put its own representatives back in Phnom Penh to monitor political developments. NDI was somewhat leery of IRI's stronger identification with the Cambodian opposition. IRI may have questioned the depth of NDI's commitment to that same opposition and undoubtedly resented NDI's generally higher profile. But it seemed only natural to work together to organize a joint election-monitoring program.

Just weeks before the elections, as was mentioned above, the two institutes sent another joint preelection mission to assess the political climate and election preparations and make recommendations on whether to observe the elections themselves. For election week, the two groups sent a joint delegation. Each chose half of the delegates. IRI asked James Lilley, former U.S. ambassador to China and South Korea and former U.S. assistant secretary of defense, to serve as its delegation coleader. NDI invited Stephen Solarz.

Solarz—a Democrat from New York who served as a member of Congress for eighteen years—had had a long association with Cambodia, including with FUNCINPEC and other leading anticommunist politicians. As chair of the Asia Subcommittee of the House Foreign Affairs Committee, Solarz played a prominent role in U.S. policy toward Cambodia and helped bring about the Paris Peace Accord in 1991. After his retirement from Congress in 1992, Solarz became a board member of the National Endowment for Democracy, and he served as President Bill Clinton's envoy to Cambodia after the 1997 coup. When Prince Ranariddh returned to Phnom Penh from exile in early 1998, Solarz accepted his invitation to ride on the plane. Solarz could not be dismissed as an apologist for Hun Sen or the CPP. Indeed, NDI believed that Solarz would not be afraid to condemn the process or those in power.

During the evening of July 27, the day after election day, as NDI-IRI delegates compared observations and considered the tenor of their statement, Hun Sen telephoned Solarz. Hun Sen said privately that he planned to step down as CPP leader and prime minister. He promised to make the announcement during the next several days. Solarz thought that this stunning concession would contribute considerably to postelection reconciliation. He promptly shared the news with Ambassador Lilley, Assistant Secretary Roth, and a few others from NDI and IRI. It is unclear whether or how much this surprising promise affected Solarz's and Lilley's public assessment the following day.

In response to a firestorm of criticism after the "miracle on the Mekong" assessment, Solarz argued in the *Washington Post* that the turnout and atmosphere on election day indicated that efforts to intimidate voters had failed, and he hailed the fact that exiled politicians were able to return and "to participate in an election that independent Cambodian observers concluded was entitled to respect." He suggested that "many of those who have condemned the election have done so because they didn't like the results." While acknowledging that the election "may not have been, as I had originally hoped, a 'miracle on the Mekong' leading to a new birth of democracy and reconciliation," he argued that neither was it a "totally illegitimate electoral charade."[35] He did not mention Hun Sen's private promise to resign, which, of course, was not kept.

After the elections, when the negative reaction to the "miracle" statement became clear, IRI leaders and several prominent IRI delegates distanced themselves from Solarz. IRI representatives argued or implied that they had not joined in his relatively benign conclusion about the process. In congressional testimony and in the press, IRI president Craner backed away from the postelection statement, calling Cambodia's 1998 election "among the worst we [at IRI] have observed since 1993."[36] The institutes issued separate final reports on their common project; in its report IRI listed only its own delegates and did not even refer to the participation of NDI. IRI's postelection report called Solarz's remark a "statement of personal opinion [that] did not reflect the views of the entire delegation."[37]

But IRI had been involved in the drafting process from the start. Craner and delegation coleader Lilley were present in the hotel suite during the drafting process late into the early morning hours of July 28, and they reviewed and expressed satisfaction with the proposed statement before it was released later that day. At the press conference, Lilley was at least as upbeat about the process as Solarz.

Moreover, IRI officials drafted a press release and distributed it before the press conference on July 28, even before copies of the longer, official statement were made available. The one-page press release, naming the IRI press secretary who was present in Phnom Penh as the person to contact, omitted many of the caveats and qualifications of the official statement. The release was headlined "Cambodian Elections: Balloting, Counting Observed Thus Far Appear to be Significant Steps in Democratic Direction," and its first sentence said: "The Cambodian people appear to have overcome months of election-related violence and intimidation by using a secret vote to select members of parliament, [NDI and IRI] announced today." Although the release did state that "Mr. Solarz and Ambassador Lilley cautioned that they reserved final judgement" and said they found "the incidences of violence and intimidation leading up to the balloting are unacceptable," its general tenor was more positive than the longer delegation statement it purportedly summarized. "While the ballots are still being counted," the press release quoted Lilley as saying, "the process on Sunday and Monday [election day and the following day] appeared to be a step forward for Cambodian democracy."[38]

Given IRI's full participation in the process of preparing the statement, the comments of its own coleader after the elections, and its own circulation of a largely upbeat press release, IRI was in a weak position to claim later that Solarz had gone considerably beyond the views of the Republican institute or its delegates at the time.

Postelection Monitoring

Election monitors are at their most irresponsible when they issue apparently definitive, final judgments before the process is over and then hop on the next plane out of the country. Recognizing this, NDI and IRI called their postelection statement, issued the second day after polling, "preliminary" and cautioned that a final assessment of the entire election process would have to await the final tabulation of results, the processing of complaints, and the formation of the next government based on the election results.

> That we do not currently have evidence to challenge the legitimacy of the election should not obscure our very real and continuing concerns over the fundamental flaws. . . . We caution that final judgment on the entire process is premature.[39]

That caution went largely unheeded. In the weeks following the election, most observers and monitoring groups left the country, and the JIOG essentially disbanded. Both European and American monitoring groups maintained representatives in the country to continue to monitor these critically important parts of the electoral process, but international attention largely waned. NDI's public statements after the election went relatively unnoticed, and the Europeans made no further public reports. The observers' first mistake—failing to raise enough concern about the fundamental flaws in the election framework and political environment—was compounded by a second: failing to monitor and report effectively on what came next.

Indeed, after the elections, as the world turned its focus elsewhere, things fell apart, making the foreign observers' upbeat assessments of the election seem all the more disconnected from reality. After struggling to complete the vote count, including a perfunctory attempt to conduct a recount in a few token locations, the CPP-dominated election commission and constitutional court summarily dismissed the numerous complaints filed by opposition parties. Though these complaints alleged mostly minor irregularities in the polling and counting (and one observer detected an opposition "strategy of overloading complaints to the election commissions"),[40] the authorities failed to conduct even cursory investigations. Moreover, after election day, the opposition parties and observers were shocked to learn that the election commission had quietly changed the formula for allocating seats, enough to give Hun Sen's party five additional seats and thus a majority in the National Assembly. One international adviser took responsibility, claiming that the election commission had only wanted to correct a technical mistake that he had made in the previously published regulations. But the change was made behind the scenes, and there were no records that the election commission had followed the required procedures. The refusal to consider complaints and the secret change in the rules further called into question the legitimacy of the election.

In Phnom Penh and other Cambodian cities, postelection protests turned violent. One man was killed. The formation of a new government—which, under the Cambodian constitution required the support of two-thirds of the National Assembly—stalled amid finger pointing and threats.

Four weeks after the election, NDI issued a statement decrying the arbitrary rejection of complaints, the utter lack of an appeals process, the secret change in the rules, and the return of violence.[41] But the army of observers and reporters was gone. Both NDI and IRI testified subsequently at congressional hearings and later issued comprehensive reports, but this did little to dispel the perception that the international community had certified Cambodia's election. After their relatively positive assessments immediately following election day, neither the EU observer mission nor the JIOG ever made another public statement on the election process.

Although the United Nations did not provide political direction over the JIOG, its logistical support and secretariat associated it with the JIOG statements nonetheless. Because of the widely held sense that the international community had failed to agree on and implement a coherent approach, the United Nations organized a "lessons learned" meeting in New York in the fall of 1998 for all its agency heads from Phnom Penh and others involved in the JIOG and other monitoring efforts. Largely because of the Cambodian experience, the United Nations changed its criteria for coordinating election monitors in the absence of a UN mandate, and the United Nations and others in the international community made recommendations about how to improve international coordination in future elections around the world.

The 2002 Local Elections: "Déja Vu All Over Again"

In the light of serious controversies that called the legitimacy of the 1998 election process into question and ultimately contributed to postelection violence, a consensus emerged within the international community—which was supported by the views of Cambodian EMOs, political parties, and some election officials—about the need for fundamental changes in subsequent elections. Donors, diplomats, and international and domestic organizations involved in the 1998 elections made a number of recommendations for the future. Most important, they urged an end to the threat of political violence and the climate of impunity. They also recommended reconstituting the electoral authorities, involving all parties and NGOs in the process of election reform, improving parties' access to the media and the fairness of news coverage, making the election rules clear in advance, ensuring the prompt and fair treatment for election-related complaints, and—presuming the absence of fraud—ensuring respect for the election results.

In February 2002, Cambodia held elections for 1,621 commune (local) councils. More than 75,000 candidates from eight parties competed.

The 2002 local elections represented an important step in a long-planned process of decentralization in Cambodia.[42] Even more important, however, they provided a test of whether the international community had learned from its mistakes in 1998. The 2002 election experience also provided the foundation for future political competition in Cambodia and would necessarily provide the point of comparison of plans for, and donor decisions about support for, the new national elections scheduled for 2003. Unfortunately, the international community did not fare well on this test.

As before, these elections took place largely in response to international urging, with mostly donor funding and substantial foreign technical assistance. Even though these were local elections, there was a massive international monitoring presence. The European Union established a full-scale, comprehensive international monitoring program about six weeks before election day, including 30 long-term and 120 short-term (election-week) observers. ANFREL monitored some provinces before the elections and fielded 65 observers for the elections themselves. IRI sent 17 observers for the elections. In all, the National Election Commission accredited 624 international observers from the European Union, foreign NGOs, UN agencies, and embassies.[43] The scale of international monitoring was unusual for a local election.

Despite the well-documented shortcomings and consensus recommendations in 1998, local elections in Cambodia in 2002 suffered many of the same flaws that had marred the earlier process. Notwithstanding a two-year drafting process with considerable international involvement, for example, the legal framework for the 2002 elections failed to establish independent or impartial electoral authorities. Though Cambodian NGOs made reform of the election commission a key part of an extensive advocacy campaign in 2000 and 2001, donors failed to object strongly to new laws that made no changes to the body's structure and acquiesced when the election commission retained essentially the same CPP-dominated membership it had in 1998.[44] During a high-profile meeting with the donor community in Phnom Penh three weeks before the local elections, Prime Minister Hun Sen implicitly acknowledged the election commission's lack of credibility by calling for substantial reform of its composition, but not until after the 2002 elections.

In coordination meetings sponsored by the United Nations Development Program (UNDP), donors raised concerns about the legal framework and political environment surrounding the elections. Yet at the same time, the donors provided most of the funding for the administration of the elections. Few donors asked for even minimal benchmarks, and even fewer tied their funding to any concrete conditions.

International engagement with the election process was largely uninformed by the experience of 1998. International donors initially promised $15 million of an $18 million budget for election administration. (They ultimately contributed just over $10 million, not counting provision of foreign technical advisers and observers and support for domestic NGOs.)[45] One senior Cambodian official admitted privately that the budget was excessive and claimed that there was considerable corruption in procurement of election materials. Yet a UNDP technical mission to Phnom Penh in April 2001 recommended a considerable increase in the initial proposed budget. Evidently the UNDP was unaware of the 1998 debacle over the proportional representation formula; one of the team's two members was actually the same 1998 National Election Commission adviser who had admitted responsibility for that very mistake! Despite the UN efforts to avoid repeating earlier errors in Cambodia, UNDP representatives responsible for coordinating election funding and technical assistance in 2001–2 admitted that they had no familiarity with the experience of funders, technical experts, or observers in 1998.

One of the few bright spots in 1998 had been the courageous work of Cambodian domestic EMOs. Yet though some donors and international democracy organizations supported domestic monitoring organizations again in 2002, others helped the election authorities place obstacles in their way. Most notably, upon the advice of another international adviser provided by the UNDP, the Commune Election Law established a new NGO Coordinating Committee (NGOCC) to coordinate with the National Election Commission in organizing local observers, including overseeing training and accreditation. This appeared to be the proverbial solution searching to find a problem. Because of the NGOCC, the three domestic election-monitoring coalitions—COMFREL; COFFEL; and the Neutral, Impartial Committee for Free Elections (NICFEC)—issued a joint statement attacking the new election law as "calculated to undermine the independence of election monitoring groups." When COMFREL and NICFEC refused to participate in NGOCC-mandated official training, the NGOCC withheld accreditation of the groups' monitors.

A subsequent compromise provided that the NGOCC, despite its utter lack of election-monitoring experience, would provide "master training" for monitoring group leaders. The National Election Commission also imposed an extraordinarily cumbersome process of accreditation on domestic EMOs, which had the effect if not the purpose of discouraging domestic monitoring. Although this idea that the electoral authorities should have such significant control over NGOs was certainly a bad one, and inconsistent with international norms of free association, the new entity nonetheless received funding and a technical adviser from the aid agencies of Australia and the Netherlands. The UNDP later concluded, against all evidence, that the "NGOCC played a critical role as a reliable conduit allowing the [National Election Commission] to register efficiently the best local observers."[46]

As in 1998, violence and intimidation plagued the political environment before elections in 2002. In the thirteen months before the elections, according to the UN Human Rights Office, seventeen political activists were murdered or died in suspicious circumstances, including ten candidates or prospective candidates, five party activists, one domestic election observer, and the child of a candidate. Fifteen of those killed were affiliated with one of the two opposition parties, the Sam Rainsy Party and FUNCINPEC.[47] The government, however, disputed the UN account. Shortly after the elections, the Ministry of the Interior pronounced categorically that "since before the beginning of the electoral campaign until the present, there has been no politically motivated crime."[48]

Instead of condemning the government's failure to investigate or prosecute most of these murders, the UNDP actually praised the government's ineffectual response to international criticism:

> To its credit, the RCG [Royal Cambodian Government] responded. [The] Deputy Prime Minister and [the] Minister of Interior sent directives to provincial and commune authorities. The King and the Prime Minister both released statements encouraging all players to observe the democratic spirit of the elections.[49]

Downplaying the concerns of its sister UN agency, the UN Human Rights Office, the UNDP concluded:

> These killings were isolated. There was no sign of any centralized or systematic campaign of intimidation. With 75,650 candidates spread over 1,621 communes where high levels of crime prevail, some violence toward candidates over a 13-month period was perhaps unavoidable.[50]

In addition to murder, a report of the UN secretary general's special representative for human rights in Cambodia three weeks before the elections also documented numerous incidents of intimidation around the country. The report cited the illegal collection of voter registration cards by local authorities, death threats against candidates, arson attacks, and the destruction of property and party signs. The report said that the victims in two-thirds of the cases were members of the Sam Rainsy Party and that regions that had strongly supported the CPP in 1998 had reported fewer cases of intimidation. The report argued "seemingly minor offences, that also include such practices as the destruction of political party signboards, exert a powerful intimidatory effect in Cambodia's fragile political environment."[51] Even the UNDP criticized the election commission because "serious complaints relating to intimidation were not dealt with according to the requirements of the law." The UNDP said that the "[commission's] reluctance or inability to impose legal sanctions allowed the climate of impunity that exists in Cambodia to prevail during the election process."[52]

Neither did news coverage or media access improve during 1998. The state-owned broadcast media largely ignored the commune election process and the opposition parties. "In the Cambodian context," rationalized the UNDP, "it is understandable that equal access to all parties poses major problems."[53] More disturbing, official aversion to voter education and political debate reached bizarre proportions. Rather than encouraging voter education and public discussion of the elections, the National Election Commission actually blocked the broadcast of foreign-funded voter education roundtables, party campaign messages, and candidate debates. After initially offering airtime for a series of voter education roundtables sponsored by NGOs, featuring representatives from all parties, the election commission refused to allow the state-run television station or other stations to air the programs.

This reversal came after the taping of one such roundtable in which Mu Suchua, the minister of women's affairs who represented FUNCINPEC in the coalition government, credited her party for a ministry program to empower women. Accusing the minister of improper behavior, the responsible election commission member, Prom Nhean Vichet, canceled the entire series. Even though the roundtable had never been broadcast and the claim that there had been some transgression was absurd, the minister was forced to apologize publicly to the prime minister, and the government dropped from an airplane thousands of copies of a news release criticizing the minister on the matter.[54] Later confirming its cancellation of all of the party roundtables, the election official explained only that some parts of the discussions "may incite problems with the people."[55] Similarly, both state-run and private television stations refused to air taped debates among commune candidates in the absence of written permission from the election commission; the commission's hostility to the debates was a matter of public record.

After the elections, the UNDP legal adviser to the National Election Commission prepared a memorandum that provided an ex post facto rationale for these deliberate obstacles to voter education and political debate. He argued that the 2002 election law, as compared to 1998, had reduced the extent of the commission's control over the media for election education:

In all likelihood, the Legislator [*sic*] has decided that the public and private media, unlike the situation in 1998, were not the most appropriate vehicle to carry the message of the political parties for the Commune election. In order to encourage the establishment of a genuine local democracy, it is not surprising that the Legislator [*sic*] has privileged an electoral campaign at the grassroots level.[56]

In its final report, the UNDP again defended the election commission's suppression of political debate:

Access to the media was complicated by the fact that the political campaigns were meant to be carried out at the local, and not at the national, level. Although the [commission] had no formal duty to get involved in the dissemination of political party platforms, the [commission] nevertheless undertook to produce and broadcast political debates. This raised expectations and caused a dilemma when the [commission] decided not to broadcast.[57]

Others in the international community disagreed with the UNDP's analysis. They thought that the election commission's actions actually were inconsistent with the Cambodian election law, which authorized the commission to "tak[e] measures to ensure equal access to the public media" and required state-run media "to publish or broadcast, free of charge, all information at the request of the [commission] in order to disseminate the progress of the election and the management of election education"[58] The commission had consciously interfered with the broadcast of voter education roundtables and candidate debates, means that would have helped bring about more open political debate and a more democratic process. It had also penalized a party leader for talking publicly about a government program. Even though the UNDP defended these actions, international standards for democratic elections require reasonable opportunities for parties and candidates to communicate their messages and certainly do not condone authorities interfering with voter education efforts.

Lao Mong Hay, the executive director of the Khmer Institute for Democracy, pointed out the UNDP's conflict of interest, arguing that: "The UN body . . . overstepped its mandate by trying to protect the [election commission] from criticism over an important electoral issue, particularly when it had an interest in organizing the election and had sponsored the drafting of the commune election law."[59]

International observers once again struggled with how to assess the overall process, in which extremely serious preelection problems were followed by a well-administered and peaceful election day. The UNDP dismissed the preelection problems; in its final report, the UNDP concluded that the National Election Commission "has produced a credible election under difficult circumstances." Likewise, while noting "concerns" raised by others, the Japanese embassy declared it "feels that the general political climate during the election period did not undermine the credibility of the entire election process." IRI, in contrast, dismissed the whole process without even considering election day; three days before the balloting, even before the arrival of its own observers, an IRI representative told the press, "We are beyond calling this a free and fair election." The European Union and Asian Network for Free Elections tried to have it both ways, as they and others had in 1998. The EU mission offered a positive assessment of election day, as in 1998, but found as well that opposition parties did not have "a fully free environment or equal opportunity and aspects of the pre-election period therefore fell short of international standards." ANFREL called the elections a "positive step in strengthening democracy" but said it remained "deeply concerned about the serious cases of violence and intimidation experienced before the election." NDI, which did not field its own observers, also was ambiguous; while harshly criticizing the political environment and "uneven playing field," NDI's postelection report also conceded, "International and domestic observers widely viewed the decentralization of governmental authority and the incorporation of opposition parties into local government as a significant step towards establishing a more democratic political system." None of these approaches appeared fully satisfactory. Moreover, none of these organizations appeared to have any new answers to the now familiar dilemma from 1998.[60]

The CPP won the 2002 local elections in a landslide. Across the nation, the ruling party won 61 percent of the 4.4 million valid votes and 7,703 or 68 percent of the available seats. It won 99 percent of the available commune chair positions (1,598 of 1,621). Since the first elections nine years earlier, the party had clearly consolidated its political support; its share of the vote had risen from 38 percent in 1993 to 42 percent in 1998 to 68 percent in 2002. This means, in other words, the party increased its vote by 62 percent (26 percentage points) from 1998 to 2002 alone. What caused this dramatic improvement in the CPP's electoral fortunes can only be left for speculation. Perhaps Cambodians no longer believe that elections provide a means to alter the power structure in their society.

The opposition leader Sam Rainsy charged that "the world accepts state sponsored intimidation, violence and electoral manipulation [in Cambodia] . . . so long as it is always a little less than the last time." Though conceding that election day was reasonably competently administered," he complained, "The international community stood by silently while the election was stolen long before Election Day."[61]

In response to international criticism of Cambodia's elections in 2002, Hun Sen derided the "long-noses"—a pejorative for foreigners—saying that "international standards exist only in sports."[62] The process of international monitoring of 1998 and 2002 elections in Cambodia has done little to prove otherwise.

Chapter 9

Host-Government Manipulation of Observers: Elections in Zimbabwe

Our common humanity transcends the oceans and all national boundaries. It binds us together in a common cause against tyranny, to act together in defense of our very humanity. Let it never be asked of any one of us—what did we do when we knew that another was oppressed?

—Nelson Mandela[1]

As election observation has emerged as an international norm, all governments seeking international legitimacy are expected to invite observers. Only governments willing to forgo good relationships with the international community in general, and the West in particular, can afford to refuse foreign observers altogether. Moreover, in transitional elections, opposition parties often insist on international observers as a condition for their participation.

It was the desire for international legitimacy that drove the governments of Ferdinand Marcos in the Philippines, Augusto Pinochet in Chile, Manuel Noriega in Panama, and Daniel Ortega in Nicaragua to invite election observers. Although each of these governments undoubtedly would have preferred to conduct elections without international scrutiny, they wanted international recognition for and acceptance of the outcomes. In each of these cases, the parties in power evidently overestimated their own popularity. In two of them—Chile and Nicaragua—the presence and findings of international and domestic observers forced them to accept the unwelcome results. In the other two—Panama and the Philippines—observers' findings provided the basis for international rejection of the government's actions.

A decade or so later, Hun Sen in Cambodia, Daniel arap Moi in Kenya, Robert Mugabe in Zimbabwe, Alexander Lukashenko in Belarus, and Alberto Fujimori in Peru acquiesced to the presence of international observers for similar reasons. Each sought international legitimization for his country's elections. Each probably also thought he would win in any event. In fact, each was able to survive elections criticized by international observers (although Fujimori was later forced out, and Moi stepped aside in 2002). Unlike a decade earlier, in recent years many governments with questionable commitment to democracy have been able to retain their hold on power even while accepting internationally monitored elections.

Despite international and domestic pressures, governments that lack a genuine commitment to full transparency in their elections sometimes attempt to restrict who can observe or how observers can go about their work. Where governments ostensibly have allowed some independent monitoring while effectively manipulating it, the international community has often found it difficult to fashion an appropriate response.

In this chapter, I address the challenges that host-government manipulation of international observation itself, as opposed to manipulation of the election process, poses for election monitoring. Using the experience of Zimbabwe in 2000 and 2002, I consider how various parts of the international community have responded not only to flawed elections but also to host-government interference in the monitoring process. In many ways, this is a more direct and more profound challenge to the monitoring enterprise, and so far observers have not responded consistently or effectively.

Refusing or Manipulating International Observers

Despite the nearly universal international acceptance of election monitoring, some governments nevertheless have refused to allow any foreign observation of their countries' elections. In 1988, for example, the ruling party in Mexico simply refused to allow foreigners to observe the country's presidential election, despite opposition demands and considerable international interest. It is widely believed that the ruling Institutional Revolutionary Party stole that election on behalf of its candidate, Carlos Salinas de Gortari, when computers tabulating results inexplicably "crashed." Unlike in the Philippines, Chile, Panama, and Nicaragua, however, the absence of effective independent monitoring permitted the ruling party to maintain its hold on power.

By the mid-1990s, however, even semiauthoritarian governments—including those that were prepared to cheat or to appeal to xenophobia—generally felt compelled to accept at least some international observers. Election observers were accepted, if not always welcomed, in Belarus, Cambodia, Kenya, and Peru. For its presidential election in 1994, among other reforms, Mexico accepted international observers for the first time, and that election was more transparent and considerably more honest than the previous one.[2]

Indeed, it is increasingly difficult for countries in transition or lacking a strong tradition of democratic elections to explicitly prohibit international and domestic observers. Governments that do so tend to pay a significant price in international legitimacy.

Rather than barring observers in general, some governments have tried— sometimes successfully—to limit the participation of international observers from what they perceive as unfriendly countries or organizations. The government of Albania, for example, insisted on limiting the number of observers from the Organization for Cooperation and Security in Europe to local elections there in 1996 but put no such limitations on the Council of Europe, from which it expected a more favorable assessment. Sometimes, existing regimes can selectively exclude observers from particular organizations or countries without undue fallout. Even autocrats prepared to manipulate not only elections but also the process of election observation in defiance of international criticism are still at times able to attract the participation of international observers. Recent elections in Zimbabwe provide a good example of these problems (table 9.1).

Restricting Observers to Zimbabwe's Elections in 2000

The elections in Zimbabwe in 2000 and 2002 suffered from many of the same serious flaws as did recent elections in Cambodia, including politically motivated intimidation and violence, unfair rules, biased election administration, and unequal media access. Thus, in Zimbabwe as in Cambodia, the international community faced such questions as whether the elections should be judged against relative or universal standards and how to respond appropriately to problems that existed largely in the political environment rather than with the administration of the process on election day.

The elections in Zimbabwe raised a different question as well, because the host government's restrictions on observers and hostility to many foreign actors offered a significant, additional challenge to international monitoring. The lack of a cohesive response from the international community compounded this challenge. Some observers remained silent about the gov-

Table 9.1

Observers' Assessments in Zimbabwe

Monitoring Group	Elections of 2000: Posture of Zimbabwe Authorities	Elections of 2000: Assessment of Election Process	Elections of 2000: Comment on Restrictions on Election Observers	Elections of 2002: Posture of Zimbabwe Authorities	Elections of 2002: Assessment of Election Process
European Union	Refused accreditation to observers from Kenya, Nigeria, and United Kingdom; attempted to limit number of observers	Negative	No comment in immediate postelection statement; criticized restrictions in final postelection report (team leader criticized Commonwealth statement)	Refused accreditation to observers from Finland, Denmark, Germany, Netherlands, Sweden, and United Kingdom; expelled team leader	Negative (from outside)
Commonwealth	Refused accreditation to observers from United Kingdom	Mixed	None	Accredited observers	Negative
Organization of African Unity	Accredited observers	Positive	None	Accredited observers	Positive
SADC Parliamentary Forum	Accredited observers	Positive	None	Accredited observers	Negative
SADC Election Commissions' Forum	Accredited observers	Positive	None	Accredited observers	Negative
SADC Ministerial Task Force				Accredited observers	Positive
South Africa Observer Mission	Accredited observers	Positive	None	Accredited observers	Positive
Australia Parliamentary Observer Mission	Accredited observers	No judgment	None		
Norwegian Observer Mission	Part of EU Election Observer Mission	n.a.	n.a.	Accredited observers	Negative
International Republican Institute	Refused accreditation	Negative	Criticized restrictions		
National Democratic Institute for International Affairs	Refused accreditation	Negative	Criticized restrictions		
World Council of Churches	Refused accreditation			Accredited observers (Africans only)	Negative
International Catholic Justice and Peace Commission	Refused accreditation				
Network of Independent Monitors (South Africa)	Refused accreditation				

Note: n.a. = not available. SADC = South African Development Community.

ernment's attempt to manipulate the monitoring process, while others were willing to bless even an election process that clearly fell short of any appropriate standard.

Background to the 2000 Elections

A December 1979 peace agreement in what was then Rhodesia ended a long guerrilla struggle against a white minority government and led to transitional elections in early 1980 followed shortly by independence for the new nation of Zimbabwe. Twenty of the 100 seats in parliament were reserved for whites. The independence leader Robert Mugabe became the new nation's first prime minister, and his party, the Zimbabwe African National Union–Patriotic Front (ZANU-PF), became the largest party in the parliament. In 1987, the country abolished the reservation of seats for whites and changed the system of government from a parliamentary to a presidential one. In the legislative elections in 1995, which were boycotted by opposition parties, ZANU-PF won 118 of 120 seats, and in 1996 Mugabe was reelected president with 93 percent of the vote.

In October 1997, with the economy deteriorating and the government's public standing eroding, President Mugabe announced plans to accelerate land reform. The following June, displaced blacks, encouraged by Mugabe, occupied white-owned farms across the country. In 1999, the former union leader Morgan Tsvangirai and other critics of Mugabe formed a new opposition political party, the Movement for Democratic Change (MDC). The party quickly began to build support.

In February 2000, the country held a referendum on a new constitution. With the support of the government and the ruling party, the revised constitution would reestablish the office of prime minister and sanction the seizure of commercial farms for redistribution. With the MDC and a coalition of civic groups opposed, 55 percent of the voters rejected the proposed constitution. In just a few months, from a base of zero, the new opposition party had gained a foothold and had demonstrated genuine support.

Within days of the referendum, self-styled "liberation war veterans" and their supporters began again to occupy white-owned commercial farms, more than 1,000 during the next several months. At least thirty people were killed in the ensuing violence. The courts ruled the occupations illegal, but the police and other authorities failed to enforce the rulings.

In April, even though the voters had rejected the government's land-reform program when they voted down the constitutional referendum, the

Zimbabwe parliament enacted it anyway. The president dissolved parliament and called for new elections.

Accrediting Observers to the 2000 Elections

The crisis over the seizure of white-owned farms heightened international attention to the elections, which were scheduled for June 24 and 25, 2000. A number of foreign governments and international organizations made plans to send observers. The Zimbabwe government, however, refused observers from some groups and nations and placed considerable restrictions on the composition and size of other observer teams.

In May 2000, before any process for credentialing international observers had yet been established, the National Democratic Institute for International Affairs (NDI) posted long-term observers from the United States and southern Africa around the country. On May 22, in an echo of Cambodia in 1998, a preelection mission in Harare sponsored by NDI declared, "The conditions for credible democratic elections do not exist at this time," and it said that the opportunities for opposition parties and candidates to campaign "do not meet international standards for fair electoral competition." The statement cited, among other things, "an atmosphere of anxiety and fear" and restrictions on "freedoms of opinion, expression, association, assembly and movement." NDI's preelection statement did not preclude, however, the possibility of a meaningful election. Rather, NDI called for "immediate and concerted efforts . . . to make improvements to the political environment [and] to create or reinforce safeguards for administrative impartiality."[3]

In response, the Zimbabwean authorities launched an aggressive press campaign against the American group and alleged U.S. "sabotage" of democracy in Zimbabwe. Essentially threatening NDI field monitors, government officials warned about individuals "posing" as international observers but operating without credentials. At the same time, the government refused to accredit observers affiliated with NDI.

Despite being a United States–based organization, NDI drew most of its long-term monitors for Zimbabwe from other countries in southern Africa. Because they were from the region, these observers were particularly familiar with the local situation, but they were also especially vulnerable to intimidation. After the threats, some of the African long-term observers went home before election day. Those who stayed remained at risk because they never received credentials.

The reaction from other international organizations to NDI's exclusion was mixed. Because it had been barred from accreditation, NDI was no longer welcome even at coordination meetings among donors and election observers in Harare. Indeed, some in the international community appeared to believe that NDI's public criticisms had been too strident. In this view, Zimbabwe's elections should be understood in context and could not be expected to be held to the same standards as in, say, Europe. Some diplomats also intimated that, by issuing a critical preelection statement just before the elections, NDI had prejudged the process.

In the weeks before the elections, the publicly announced categories of monitors eligible for accreditation kept shifting. They included at various times observers invited by the government, international organizations in which Zimbabwe was a member, and any delegation of elected representatives (which allowed bilateral delegations of members of parliament). At first, the government said it would deny credentials to diplomats in Harare, but it later backed down. The government said it would allow official delegations, which it defined as those backed by a "diplomatic note," but it then reneged when NDI and the International Republican Institute (IRI) obtained such official backing from the U.S. government. Then, a new regulation passed on June 7, just two and a half weeks before election day, transferred authority for accrediting international observers from the electoral supervisory commission, a constitutional oversight body, to the election directorate, a body responsible under the election law for the coordination of government agencies involved in administering elections. (The regulation also gave the power to accredit domestic monitors to a government official, the registrar general.)[4]

The authorities ultimately accredited observers from intergovernmental organizations—including the European Union, the Commonwealth, the Organization of African Unity (OAU), and the Southern African Development Community (SADC)—and from most bilateral delegations. The government eventually announced that it was denying accreditation to observers from foreign nongovernmental organizations, which prevented up to 200 of 500 potential observers from observing the voting on polling day, including representatives from the World Council of Churches, the International Catholic Justice and Peace Commission, and the Network of Independent Monitors from South Africa, in addition to NDI and IRI.[5] The government also declined to issue credentials to any observers from the United Kingdom.

The government of Zimbabwe had assured representatives of the European Union in May that there would be no restrictions on the size or duration of the EU presence and that EU observers would be free to visit any part of the country.[6] But in addition to denying accreditation to a bilateral delegation from the United Kingdom, the government also refused to permit British citizens to participate in the EU delegation. The government later insisted that the EU delegation include members only from countries that were part of the European Union; thus, it banned ten Kenyan and seven Nigerian observers from participating in the EU team because, according to a state-owned newspaper, they "had apparently been planted by Britain in an effort to subvert the ban by government on the former colonial power not to send observers."[7] The government also charged each foreign observer a $100 fee and, shortly before the elections, reduced the number of observers permitted on the EU team from 150 to 120. The EU declared that these restrictions fell "short of internationally accepted standards."[8]

The United Nations initially accepted the role as principal coordinator of election observers, but it failed to work out an acceptable arrangement with the Zimbabwean government. The United Nations was not clear about what role it wanted. It vacillated on whether it wanted to control accreditation or merely to support and loosely coordinate international observers. Eventually, the United Nations decided to withdraw from playing any coordination role at all.[9]

Meanwhile, IRI continued making plans to send its own election observation mission. But just days before the election, with accreditation not forthcoming, IRI also pulled out and blasted the authorities: "The process is so flawed that it cannot adequately reflect the will of the people. Those responsible for elections in Zimbabwe have failed their country."[10]

It is reasonable to question whether international organizations committed to genuine democracy should engage in a process when a host government excludes other serious groups, individuals, or nationalities; limits the number of observers it will allow; or restricts access to some parts of the process. Even if an international organization decides to go ahead with plans to observe in such circumstances, it seems incumbent on it to continue to raise questions about restrictions on observers, both directly with the authorities and in public assessments of the process. Brazen manipulation of the monitoring process cannot go unchallenged if international monitoring is to retain its independence and credibility.

Although the European Union was consistently and appropriately critical of flaws in the process and the number of its observers eventually grew to 190 (more than the government had wanted), the EU evidently acquiesced to the government's restriction on the nationality of participants and failed even to object or criticize it publicly at the time. In his immediate postelection statement, Pierre Schori, the Swedish diplomat who headed the EU's election mission, mentioned vaguely only that "obstructions were placed in the way of international observers." Neither did EU commissioners Chris Patten and Poul Nielson, in postelection speeches to the European Parliament in which they praised the EU observation mission, mention restrictions on EU or other observers. None of the international observer groups before the elections or in their immediate postelection statements criticized the exclusion of British, American, Kenyan, and Nigerian observers. It was not until its final report that the EU criticized the exclusion of NDI, IRI, and the International Commission for Justice and Peace.[11]

It is unclear why the European Union and other international organizations failed to object more strongly to the exclusion of particular nationalities. Perhaps they sought to avoid further controversy before the elections. Perhaps observers from other countries placed some blame for the problems on the Americans and British themselves or were happy to fill the vacuum left by the absence of American and British observers. In any event, they did not appear to recognize how pernicious these exclusions were.

The Zimbabwean authorities also delayed accrediting domestic election monitors and only began distributing accreditation badges the day before the elections. Thus, there were considerable problems in distributing credentials to the estimated 12,000 domestic election monitors. A regulation promulgated on June 20, only four days before election day, restricted the number of monitors to one per polling station and prohibited monitors from accompanying ballot boxes as they were transported from polling stations to district counting centers. Then, only the day before the voters went to the polls, the chair of the election directorate issued a circular that liberalized the rule slightly, but the change was too little and too late to make much practical difference. Many election officials nevertheless enforced the superseded rule allowing only one domestic observer in the polling station at a time, and many domestic monitors never received their credentials at all. Concluded the EU observation mission, "The confusion over the role of domestic monitors was not due to administrative incompetence but to a deliberate attempt to reduce the effectiveness of independent monitoring of the election."[12]

Despite the widespread intimidation and other problems before the elections, the opposition MDC received a great deal of support in the elections, as it had in the constitutional referendum four months earlier. The ruling ZANU-PF won 62 of the 120 seats, and the MDC won 57.

Incredibly, observer groups from African organizations issued generally positive assessments of the process. The mission from the OAU announced a "tentative conclusion that, all things considered, voting was held in a generally peaceful atmosphere, the voting process was smooth and the Zimbabwean people have successfully exercised their franchise." The delegation of members of parliament from the SADC concluded, "The outcome of the elections is a reflection of the will of the people of Zimbabwe." Likewise, a separate SADC body, the Election Commissions' Forum, said the voting process and the results "are legitimate and reflect the will of the people." One South African observer appeared with Mugabe on television and denounced the European Union for "not allowing Africans to express themselves."[13]

The Commonwealth's engagement was ineffectual. In a preelection visit in May, Commonwealth secretary general Don McKinnon met with President Mugabe and government representatives but failed entirely to meet with anyone from the opposition. McKinnon agreed that the Commonwealth would submit its report to President Mugabe before making it public. The Commonwealth also accepted the exclusion of British delegates and staff members. While the Commonwealth delegation's postelection statement noted a number of problems with the process, it also said the election "mark[s] a significant point in the development of democracy in Zimbabwe." Speaking for the organization, Commonwealth chairperson general Abdulsalami Abubakar of Nigeria—ironically, himself a former unelected head of state who came from the military—went on to praise the voter turnout, the fact that voting was "generally calm, orderly and peaceful," the "efficiency and effectiveness" of election and security officials, and the transparency of the counting process.[14] Schori, the head of the EU's observation mission, whose own statement was the most unequivocal about the election's flaws, criticized the Commonwealth's postelection statement as "wishy-washy."[15]

Meanwhile, a delegation of Australian parliamentarians suggested that "the violence and intimidation that had so badly compromised the preelection campaigning and voter education must have influenced the result in some constituencies" but expressly declined to make an overall judgment of the election.[16]

The clear problems with the fairness of the election process and the obstacles placed in front of observers raise questions about whether international organizations should have sent observers at all. Under various proposed international guidelines, as discussed in chapter 7, the Zimbabwe elections did not merit observation. But, much like the Americans in Cambodia, the European Union defended its decision to send observers, in light of reports of violence and intimidation, "as an act of commitment to the people of Zimbabwe and to democracy world-wide." Its dual goals were "to contribute to a more favourable climate" and "to come up with a clear judgement" on the process. According to the EU's own assessment after the fact, the presence of observers "played an important role in reducing political tensions and calming conflict" and "helped build confidence among the electorate in the voting and counting procedures and the secrecy of their vote."[17]

Observing Zimbabwe's Presidential Election in 2002

Twenty months later, from March 9 to 11, 2002, Zimbabwe held a presidential election, pitting President Mugabe against opposition leader Morgan Tsvangirai. The political climate and prospects for democratic elections, however, had not improved in the interim. Having more or less succeeded in picking and choosing observers in 2000, the government of Zimbabwe was emboldened to do more of the same in 2002.

Once again, a considerable number of European, African, and other international organizations made plans to send observers, but a month before the election Zimbabwe's foreign minister announced that the government would not accredit observers from six European countries that had been outspoken critics of ruling party tactics during the previous two years: Denmark, Finland, Germany, the Netherlands, Sweden, and the United Kingdom. The government subsequently expelled EU mission head Schori, accusing him of "political arrogance." In response, on February 18, the EU withdrew its entire monitoring team and imposed sanctions, including a visa ban and a freeze on the overseas assets of President Mugabe and nineteen associates. Explaining the decision to pull out, Schori said, "There was no room for a credible EU election observation."[18]

As in 2000, some African teams defended the process after the election. An observer team from the OAU declared that the election was "transparent, credible, free and fair." Sam Motsuenyane, the head of the official South African Observer Mission, acknowledged flaws in the process but said the election "should be considered legitimate." The South African delegation's statement concluded, "The outcome of the elections represents the legitimate voice of the people of Zimbabwe." A group sent by the Government of Nigeria said it had "recorded no incidence that was sufficient to threaten the integrity and outcome of the election, in areas monitored by the team." Delegations representing the Governments of Kenya, Namibia, and Tanzania and several other

African intergovernmental bodies, including the SADC Ministerial Task Force, likewise endorsed the process, typically citing the high turnout and lack of election-day violence while downplaying preelection problems.[19]

Zimbabwean domestic monitors and Western observers, however, again condemned the process, joined by representatives of African churches. "There is no way these elections could be described as free and fair," declared Reginald Matchaba-Hove, chairman of the Zimbabwe Election Support Network, a coalition of church and civic groups. "Tens of thousands of Zimbabweans were deliberately and systematically disenfranchised." Eleven of twelve other, smaller domestic monitoring groups likewise condemned the process. A delegation from the World Council of Churches and the All-Africa Conference of Churches lamented widespread intimidation and said documentation and their own observations indicated, "the clear majority of cases should be blamed on the ruling party." Kare Vollan, head of a Norwegian observer mission, reported that violence against opposition supporters had marred the campaign and declared that the poll had failed "key, broadly accepted criteria." From outside the country, the European Union's Schori called the election "a violation of the people of Zimbabwe."[20]

Notably, the Commonwealth adopted a markedly different approach than it had two years earlier. Despite finding that "the actual polling and counting processes were peaceful and the secrecy of the ballot was assured," the intergovernmental group, reciting a litany of other problems, concluded, "The conditions in Zimbabwe did not adequately allow for a free expression of will by the electors."[21]

Even more important, delegates from the SADC Parliamentary Forum differed with their colleagues on the ministerial delegation and concluded, "The climate of insecurity obtaining in Zimbabwe since the 2000 parliamentary elections was such that the electoral process could not be said to adequately comply with the norms and standards for elections in the SADC region." Speaking for the seventy-member delegation, Duke Lefhoko, a member of parliament from Botwsana, pointed to violence and intimidation, questions about the impartiality of the police, problems with voter registration, a shortage of polling stations in urban areas, a lack of independence of electoral authorities, and biased media coverage. In March 2001, the SADC had formally adopted specific, regional standards for elections in member countries. Its criticisms in Zimbabwe suggested that "peer review" in Africa now had some real potential.[22]

After the election, the Commonwealth designated South African president Thabo Mbeki, Nigerian president Olusegun Obasanjo, and Australian prime minister John Howard to decide, on behalf of the organization's fifty-four members, how the Commonwealth should respond to the flawed presidential election in Zimbabwe. Even though observers from their own countries had accepted the election's legitimacy, Mbeki and Obasanjo surprised many by deciding, along with Howard, that the Commonwealth should suspend Zimbabwe for twelve months. Along with the critical assessment of the SADC observers, the decision of the two influential African presidents blunted Mugabe's claim that white Europeans were behind all the criticism of him. At the same time, the decision helped the Commonwealth shore up its damaged credibility.[23]

African leaders judged the credibility of the OAU beyond saving, however, albeit for reasons well beyond the experience in Zimbabwe. In July 2002, leaders from more than thirty African countries meeting in Durban, South Africa, dissolved the OAU and formed the African Union. Building on the New Partnership for Africa's Development announced in 2001, which "is, first and foremost, a pledge by African Leaders to the people of Africa to consolidate democracy," the new African Union requires its members to commit to respect democratic principles and human rights, including free elections and the freedom of opposition parties to campaign. At the Durban meeting, the participating heads of state and government reaffirmed their commitment to the Universal Declaration of Human Rights and to the "promotion of democracy and its core values," including "the inalienable right of the individual to participate by means of free, credible and democratic political processes in periodically electing their leaders." To help enforce the commitments of the new declaration, they also established an African Peer Review Mechanism. South African president Thabo Mbeki, the organization's first chair, declared in his opening speech, "Through our actions, let us proclaim to the world that this is a continent of democracy, a continent of good governance, where the people participate and the rule of law is upheld." Jakkie Cilliers, a South African delegate to the OAU, told the *New York Times,* "The nature of the debate has changed completely from 10 years ago. Democracy is now a growth industry in Africa. And if heads of state approve this document, they are obligated to deal with issues [like] Zimbabwe next time around."[24]

Manipulating Observers

The problems with elections in Zimbabwe, and the responses of outside observers to those problems, were hardly unique. As in Cambodia in 1998, at least some international observers in Zimbabwe in 2000 and 2002 gave elections favorable marks because the balloting appeared to be secret, election day was relatively peaceful, and the count seemed honest. Also as in Cambodia, some observers were simply biased—uninterested in the elections' integrity. But unlike Cambodia, the government and the ruling party in Zimbabwe decided to make an issue of the observers themselves.

President Mugabe and Zimbabwe's ruling party acted rationally from their own point of view. They encouraged their supporters to occupy privately owned farms for political ends and then drew election observers into the debate about the propriety of those land seizures. By playing the "race card," or at least the card of anticolonialism, Mugabe portrayed the West as opposed to Zimbabwean independence and the opposition as bought and paid for by the former colonial power. As a result, British, American, and other outside criticism may actually have helped him.

Yet the reactions of several intergovernmental organizations to the flagrant problems in Zimbabwe may mark a turning point for international election monitoring and democracy promotion. By pulling out, the European Union made the point that what was happening in Zimbabwe was not a genuine election and reinforced the principle of protecting observers' autonomy. Similarly, the Commonwealth's adoption of sanctions, albeit mild ones, with the support of two particularly influential African presidents signaled growing international intolerance for election manipulation even beyond balloting and counting. The professionalism and principle of the parliamentarians from the SADC in documenting and commenting on the 2002 election in Zimbabwe was a welcome change from SADC statements two years earlier and from the unfortunate pattern of many regional multilateral organizations in the past, in Africa and elsewhere. Finally, the establishment of the African Union on a solid foundation of democratic principles, though not directly a response to the hijacking of democracy in Zimbabwe, offers new hope. While the early signals are mixed, the African Union has at least the potential to become a stronger force for democracy than was its predecessor organization, but only if the continent's leaders are willing to ensure that all African regimes are held to international democratic standards.

If international election monitoring is to retain its relevance, donors, diplomats, and election-monitoring organizations from both the developed and the developing worlds will have to object vigorously or withdraw in response to unreasonable restrictions on the scope of monitoring or the identity of observers.

Part III

Domestic Election Monitoring

Chapter 10

The Origins of Domestic Election Monitoring: NAMFREL and Its Successors

Election officials in some countries brag that they know the results shortly after the polls have closed. We knew the results a month in advance.

— Mars Quesada, NAMFREL organizer, February 1995,
reflecting upon Marcos-era elections

It's better to light a candle than to curse the darkness.

— NAMFREL slogan, circa 1983

In October 1983, just weeks after the assassination of popular Philippines opposition leader Benigno Aquino, seventeen people gathered at the home of the businessman Mariano (Mars) Quesada in suburban Manila to discuss the political crisis in their country. These concerned citizens, who were worried that violence would become the only alternative to the increasingly repressive martial law regime of Ferdinand Marcos, resolved to organize a volunteer citizen movement dedicated to restoring democracy in the Philippines through free and fair elections. During the Marcos era, rampant vote buying, fraud, and violence had discouraged Filipinos from viewing elections as a way of challenging the regime. Accordingly, the new group came up with the idea of a monitoring organization to try to prevent or expose fraud. In doing so, they embarked on a crusade that would profoundly change their country and eventually the world.

Thus, nonpartisan domestic election monitoring began in the Philippines in the mid-1980s with the pioneering experience of the National Citizens'

209

Movement for Free Elections (NAMFREL). Before NAMFREL exposed electoral fraud in the Philippines' 1986 "snap" presidential election, non-partisan national election monitoring was largely unknown. Even international observation was not yet common, and there was widespread skepticism about whether independent election monitoring was appropriate or could be effective. But NAMFREL's remarkable success at using election monitoring to capitalize on the Philippine public's revulsion at the Marcos regime demonstrated the potential of domestic monitoring and inspired many similar efforts around the world.

Since the mid-1980s, domestic election-monitoring organizations (EMOs) founded on essentially the same ideals as NAMFREL have provided momentum to the global struggle for democracy. New national groups or domestic coalitions of nongovernmental and civil society organizations, human rights groups, professional associations, religious organizations, students, and others have worked effectively together to monitor important transitional or otherwise controversial elections. Although these groups have emerged in diverse political contexts, they have shared a commitment to ensuring that elections are competitive and meaningful.

This chapter surveys the history and successes of domestic monitoring by nonpartisan nongovernmental organizations (NGOs). Print and broadcast journalists, election officials, and political parties and candidates also monitor the election process, including by organizing pollwatchers to collect information on election day. But the dramatic development of the past two decades is the emergence of nonpartisan election monitoring conducted by organizations from civil society rather than from the formal political sector, electoral authorities, or political parties.

From its roots as an idiosyncratic response to a particular set of circumstances in one country, nonpartisan domestic election monitoring has grown into a global norm. Complemented by international observers and often supported by foreign aid, domestic election-monitoring groups have made important contributions to democratic elections in many countries. Their contribution has been particularly important for transitional elections where, typically, substantial parts of the public or political elite do not trust the authorities to be impartial or to organize fair elections. For many such elections, EMOs have encouraged fairer election rules, better campaign practices, and a more informed electorate. They have also sought to deter or expose fraud and intimidation and to help reduce irregularities on election day. By pursuing these goals, domestic monitoring groups have built public confidence, encouraged participation, and increased the acceptability of results when elections are legitimate.

The Invention of Nonpartisan Domestic Election Monitoring in the Philippines

In 1972, unable to run for a third term, President Marcos proclaimed martial law, interrupting a tradition of regular, more-or-less competitive elections in the Philippines since the period of American colonial rule in the early twentieth century. The Marcos government shut down newspapers, took over television and radio stations, and suppressed individual freedoms. In 1973, Marcos changed the constitution to extend his term of office, allow him to serve simultaneously as president and prime minister, and give him control of a newly established National Assembly. In 1978, pro-Marcos forces used fraud to secure victory in the National Assembly elections. A 1981 constitutional amendment allowed Marcos a renewable six-year term and established direct presidential elections. The amendment also set a new age requirement of fifty years for president, which prevented a challenge from rival Benigno Aquino. In June of that year, Marcos won a new term in an election again riddled with fraud and boycotted by the opposition. One expert on the Philippines said the 1981 election "was accepted as a farce by almost everyone, with the notable exception of George H. W. Bush, the then U.S. vice president, who attended Marcos's inauguration and commended him on his 'adherence to democratic principles and the democratic process.'"[1]

On August 21, 1983, Aquino was shot and killed at the Manila airport, as he arrived back in the Philippines on a flight from abroad after a long exile. Soldiers on site immediately killed the apparent gunman. Eyewitness accounts and other evidence, though, called the official account of Aquino's murder into question and implicated the Marcos regime. National outrage and international condemnation followed.

The new citizens' group that emerged after the Aquino assassination called itself the National Citizens' Movement for Free Elections and later adopted the nickname NAMFREL. Their choice of name initially seemed unfortunate because in the 1950s the U.S. Central Intelligence Agency (CIA) allegedly had backed a group in the Philippines with essentially the same name. Concerned about its credibility, the new NAMFREL explicitly denied any association with the CIA in an open letter published throughout the country. The organization eventually overcame this obstacle as it established its professionalism and gained the important support of church, business, and professional leaders.[2]

José Concepción, an influential, wealthy businessman who had been present at the 1983 meeting at Mars Quesada's house, became NAMFREL's chair. As president of the large Republic Flour Mills Corporation, Concepción gave the new organization credibility with some in the Filipino elite. Quesada became the first secretary general.

For the next six months, in anticipation of legislative elections set for May 1984, Concepción and Quesada traveled around the country to promote the pollwatching idea and to recruit local organizers for the effort. The new organization soon attracted invaluable assistance, including volunteers, money, and computers, from some parts of the business community.

Even more important, the Catholic Church provided crucial support and soon became the backbone of the organization. Parish priests throughout the country gave sermons about safeguarding elections and democracy. Church leaders recruited organizers, solicited funds, and provided credibility. Jaime Cardinal Sin provided strong moral support, and a bishop, Antonio Fortich of Negros Occidental, became NAMFREL cochair.[3]

The organization attracted ever-larger numbers of often-courageous volunteers who were committed to democracy in their country. Volunteer organizer Christian Monsod was typical. Monsod took a leave from his job as chief executive of an investment bank and worked with his wife Winnie to organize Metro Manila for NAMFREL. Later, before the snap presidential election in 1986, Monsod became the organization's secretary general. The almost naive idealism of NAMFREL's organizers was apparent from their slogan: "It is better to light a candle than to curse the darkness."

Organizing for the 1984 Congressional Elections

NAMFREL's initial focus was congressional elections in May 1984. The new organization had surprising early successes in pushing electoral reforms, gaining formal accreditation, and expanding its base of volunteers.

NAMFREL urged broad reforms in the electoral process, such as conducting a new registration of voters, printing ballots on watermarked paper to deter fraud, and using indelible ink to prevent individuals from voting more than once (called "flying voters" in the local slang). It also urged changes to make the process more open, such as legal protections for opposition candidates and fairer access to the media. Perhaps seeking greater international legitimacy, the election commission agreed to some proposed reforms, although there were problems with the new voter registration process and fraud on election day persisted.[4]

To gain access to polling places for its volunteers, NAMFREL requested official accreditation from the Philippines election commission, which was appointed by Marcos. NAMFREL emphasized the broad experience and solid reputation of its board. Again, the commission responded, this time granting the accreditation request, which allowed NAMFREL to claim the mantle of being the official "citizen's arm" of the election commission.

From its humble beginnings, NAMFREL quickly grew to become an umbrella organization for dozens of organizations. It mobilized about 200,000 volunteers who observed at about two-thirds of the polling places during the 1984 elections.

NAMFREL also organized a pioneering "quick count" to collect and tabulate results from polling places. This allowed verification of the accuracy of the official ballot count. The quick count indicated, among other things, that opposition candidates had won in 16 of 21 seats in Metro Manila; the official count subsequently confirmed that result. One observer credits NAMFREL's count with preventing the election commission from stealing any of those particular seats, a contribution with echoes in Chile, Nicaragua, and elsewhere in subsequent years. Through apparent manipulation of the vote count, the election commission held the opposition nationally to just 59 of the 183 elected seats.[5]

The government and election commission accused NAMFREL of partisanship and alleged that the organization had received funding from abroad. After the 1984 elections, the election commission withdrew NAMFREL's accreditation, which would have kept its volunteers out of the polling places in future elections. NAMFREL denied receiving foreign funds and lobbied to be accredited again for future elections. It continued holding meetings around the country to mobilize volunteers and soliciting funds from the business community and through the church. In early 1985, several members of the U.S. Congress visited Manila to urge free elections and offer moral support for NAMFREL. Approval for the organization to monitor again eventually came through at the end of 1985, but only after Chairman Concepción swore under oath that the group did not receive money from outside the country.[6]

NAMFREL's Breakthrough: The 1986 "Snap Election"

In late October 1985, speaking live on American television with the journalist David Brinkley, Marcos unexpectedly announced a presidential election. Subsequently set for February 7, 1986, this "snap election" pitted Marcos against Benigno Aquino's widow Corazon.

The 1986 election proved to be a watershed for the worldwide democracy movement and for domestic election monitoring. In the face of significant intimidation and other obstacles, NAMFREL fielded an estimated 500,000 volunteers to watch the polls in virtually all regions of the country. NAMFREL assisted voters at polling places and used a sophisticated communications network to respond to reported problems. It even borrowed a helicopter to rush observers to places where problems were reported on election day.[7]

Because there was considerable interest in the Philippines election in the United States, several American NGOs, encouraged by members of Congress, sent fact-finding teams after the announcement of an early election. In addition, for the first time, the National Democratic Institute for International Affairs (NDI) and the National Republican Institute (now the International Republican Institute) organized an election observation mission. Senator Richard Lugar led a separate U.S. government observation team.

As in 1984, NAMFREL implemented a quick count to verify the accuracy of the official ballot count in 1986. Volunteers throughout the country collected results from individual polling sites and sent them to provincial offices. Provincial offices, in turn, passed them along to NAMFREL's headquarters at Lasalle University in Manila. The election commission insisted that NAMFREL volunteers obtain an official verification of the polling site results from a provincial election official, but many volunteers immediately transmitted the polling station results without waiting for the official tally sheets.[8] Thus, NAMFREL was able to get an early sense of the election results from around the country.

Two days after the election, the quick count had tabulated 7.7 million votes, about one-third of the more than 20 million cast, and showed Aquino ahead by nearly 1 million votes. The election commission had counted only 2.1 million and showed Marcos and Aquino about even.[9]

The official count proceeded so slowly on election night and the following day that NAMFREL suggested it was a "delaying tactic" and that the election commission was "buying time to determine how many more votes are needed to make Marcos win."[10] A later study of the Philippine revolution agreed that the official count "was not only biased in favor of Marcos, but was being intentionally slowed down so that fraudulent tally sheets could be substituted for the genuine ones."[11] During the tabulation process, nearly forty election commission data-entry personnel walked out in protest, they said, of orders to "cook" the returns. Despite indications to the contrary from NAMFREL's quick count, on February 14 the authorities declared Marcos the winner with 10.8 million votes to Aquino's 9.3 million.[12]

The quick count eventually collected results from 70 percent of the 85,000 polling sites. Although the NAMFREL count was not statistically definitive, it showed Aquino leading Marcos by more than a half-million votes (7.9 million to 7.4 million) and thus convinced Filipinos and the international community that Corazon Aquino had really won the election.[13]

After the election, the Catholic Bishops Conference praised "the thousands of NAMFREL workers and volunteers who risked their very lives to ensure free and fair elections."[14] In fact, three NAMFREL volunteers were killed on election day.[15] In the face of very serious obstacles, NAMFREL's overall effort was a remarkable achievement.

After Marcos claimed victory, Defense Minister Juan Ponce Enrile and some military officers plotted a coup. On February 22, when the plot was discovered, Enrile, joined by Lieutenant General Fidel Ramos, retreated to the Defense Ministry complex in Manila. Encouraged by Cardinal Sin and Corazon Aquino, thousands of protestors rushed to the broad avenue outside the camp, Epifanio de los Santos Avenue, or EDSA, where for the next several days they faced down tanks. Enrile and Ramos demanded that Marcos step down and eventually called for Aquino to be sworn in as president. Finally abandoned by Ronald Reagan's administration and his own military, Marcos was forced to resign and fled to exile in Hawaii. Corazon Aquino took office on February 25, 1986. What became known as the EDSA or the "people power" revolution marked a major milestone in the global Third Wave of democracy.

NAMFREL after the 1986 Elections

Although accused of partisanship from its inception, NAMFREL insisted that its purpose was to safeguard the integrity of the electoral process, not to affect the outcome. But preserving a reputation for neutrality was not easy: By working to ensure fair elections in 1984 and 1986, NAMFREL had certainly been working against the Marcos regime, if only because the regime itself opposed genuine democracy. Yet NAMFREL's insight was the recognition that because the regime purported to respect fair elections, there was an opportunity to try to make that commitment more than an empty promise.

After the 1986 election, the appointment of a number of NAMFREL leaders to key positions in the new administration and the subsequent involvement of others in partisan politics provided new ammunition for charges that NAMFREL had been biased. NAMFREL chair Concepción became minister of trade and industry. Vice chair Vincente Jayme was appointed president of the Philippine National Bank and later joined the cabinet. NAMFREL activists Solita Monsod, Vincente Paterno, and Carlos Dominguez also accepted senior government positions. Secretary general Chris Monsod was named to the Constitutional Commission and later became chair of the Election Commission (although these were no longer partisan positions). NAMFREL organizers Edgardo Angaro, Vincente Paterno, and Ernesto Herrera became candidates in congressional elections in May 1986; Aquino endorsed all three. NAMFREL had to replace thirty-five chairs of provincial and city NAMFREL chapters because they opted to become candidates or otherwise engaged in partisan political activity.[16]

Meanwhile, NAMFREL continued to advocate electoral reform, the modernization of the electoral process, and the appointment of independent, professional election commissioners. In 1987, NAMFREL and its affiliated organizations monitored a constitutional plebiscite and congressional elections.

Election monitoring in the Philippines evolved after 1986 to include many newly created organizations as well as preexisting groups operating with greater autonomy under their own, separate identities. Thus, for subsequent elections, NAMFREL became one of many groups rather than the "brand name" of the overall election-monitoring coalition. For the presidential and congressional elections in 1992, organizers affiliated with the Catholic Church created the Pastoral-Parish Council for Responsible Voting, Vote-Care, and other organizations to educate voters and monitor aspects of the election process. NAMFREL, which continued to exist as a free-standing organization, provided technical assistance to other groups and organized quick counts (sometimes called parallel vote tabulations elsewhere). For the 1992 elections, NAMFREL organized the quick count in cooperation with media organizations under the rubric of the Media-Citizens Quick Count.

The successful quick count in 1992 again showed NAMFREL to be a highly effective, credible organization.

Since the mid-1980s, NAMFREL volunteers have served as pollwatchers, election monitors, and voter education trainers for every national election in the Philippines. Organizers have established an ongoing foundation. During the 1990s, NAMFREL continued to lobby for electoral reforms, recommended independent nominees for the Commission on Elections, and involved itself in the modernization and computerization of the electoral process. In cooperation with other groups, it organized monitoring efforts for subsequent elections in 1995, 1998, and 2001.

NAMFREL succeeded for several reasons. Among others, NAMFREL built on a tradition of electoral politics in the Philippines. Unlike many other countries later holding elections after periods of authoritarianism, the Philippines had considerable previous experience with elections and multiparty competition. NAMFREL sought to restore a process that had been distorted and corrupted rather than to create a new one.

In its early incarnations for the elections in 1984 and 1986, NAMFREL was organized as a coalition or umbrella organization that brought together more than 100 religious groups, professional associations, labor groups, and other NGOs. Member organizations recruited volunteers for the larger effort and often provided and paid for NAMFREL organizers. In this way, NAMFREL mobilized resources effectively and strategically.

NAMFREL also had powerful allies. Businesses owned or managed by reformers within the Philippine elite provided the organization with financial resources and managerial expertise. In addition, NAMFREL was able to tap into the moral authority, political influence, organizational structure, and resources of the Catholic Church.[17]

Sharing the NAMFREL Idea

Activists from a number of countries learned from the remarkable success of domestic election monitoring in the Philippines. Beginning soon after the watershed 1986 election, NAMFREL representatives began actively to share their experiences with nascent election-monitoring groups around the world.

One organization that learned from the NAMFREL experience was the still-young NDI in the United States. Many commentators on democracy promotion have incorrectly assumed that NDI helped NAMFREL get started, when the reverse is actually closer to the truth. Indeed, the NDI decision to organize its first international election observation mission for the 1986 Philippines election and its interaction with NAMFREL during that election was probably the most important formative experience for NDI, if not for U.S. democracy assistance more generally. NDI's experience with international and domestic election monitoring in the Philippines in 1986 helped shape the direction of the institute, and of much of international democracy promotion, for the next decade and a half.

In particular, having witnessed NAMFREL in action and realized the tremendous potential for domestic monitoring, NDI set out to share the idea elsewhere. In early 1987, NDI brought activists from nine countries to the Philippines to observe a constitutional referendum and to learn from NAMFREL's experience. During the next decade or so, NDI and NAMFREL collaborated to promote the potential of domestic monitoring and to share the experiences from the Philippines by sending NAMFREL organizers to dozens of other democratizing countries. NDI likewise brought organizers of other early experiences with domestic monitoring to more and more countries. In January 1991, for example, an activist from Bulgaria joined a representative from NAMFREL in Bangladesh to advise poll-watching groups mobilizing for transitional elections there after public protests forced out strongman Hossain Mohammad Ershad. In August 1991, representatives of groups from Chile and Namibia as well as from NAMFREL participated in the initial planning and training sessions for domestic monitoring in Zambia. In the period 1995–96, election-monitoring organizers from Peru aided a similar effort in Nicaragua. As more and more countries held transitional elections monitored by domestic groups, experienced activists from those countries traveled to other places to encourage and advise new monitoring efforts. In this way, new groups, often working in difficult political environments, were able to learn from earlier successes and failures, to adapt materials and methodologies, and to receive key moral support.[18]

Although the political contexts and challenges differed, activists' motivations and commitment in various countries were essentially the same. Years later, Lawrence Lachmansingh, a founder in the early 1990s of a very successful election-monitoring group in Guyana, the Electoral Assistance Bureau, and later an NDI adviser to new EMOs in several countries, told the *New York Times:*

It's about the same anywhere you go. Always in people's mind is hope and a desire for change and democracy, which they associate first with democratic elections. People often have unrealistic expectations, but always there is that basic ingredient of hope which propels concerned citizens to want to make a contribution. Call it patriotism, saintliness, bravery—martyrdom sometimes.[19]

A significant innovation, these mutually supportive interactions among democratic activists across national boundaries became part of a truly global democracy movement.

Domestic Election Monitoring Consolidates Its Role

After the Philippines, the idea of domestic election monitoring found resonance in Latin America in the late 1980s. In 1988, Chile held a plebiscite on whether to extend the rule of President Augusto Pinochet, who had seized power in a 1973 military coup. Rather than boycotting an inherently undemocratic process, Pinochet's opponents came together to beat the strongman at his own game. The civic organization Crusade for Democracy (CIVITAS) carried out civic education programs to encourage participation, and the Committee for Free Elections conducted an innovative independent vote tabulation, the first using a statistically based sampling methodology. In Panama in 1989, business and church leaders worked together to push for free elections, and a church laity group organized its own parallel vote tabulation. Likewise, the Center for Democratic Studies organized poll-watching and parallel counts in Paraguay for local elections in 1991 and national elections in 1993. Domestic election-monitoring groups played important roles in elections in 1990 in the Dominican Republic and Haiti and began organizing that year in Guyana for elections eventually held in 1992.

In Mexico, the serious fraud that plagued the 1988 elections and the example of civic organizations in the Philippines and elsewhere motivated many civic organizations to take up election-monitoring initiatives. Several Mexican NGOs began monitoring state elections in 1991, with support from international groups such as NDI, Jimmy Carter's Council of Freely Elected Heads of Government, and the Canadian International Center for Human Rights and Democratic Development. Their activities included statistically based quick counts. In late 1993, seven diverse NGOs from across the political spectrum began to meet informally about their common interest in fair elections. In 1994, this informal coalition transformed itself into Civic Alliance. For the presidential election in August 1994, Civic Alliance mobilized a significant election-monitoring effort.[20]

With the fall of the Berlin Wall in late 1989, followed by a rapid series of elections in early 1990, domestic monitoring quickly took hold in Eastern and Central Europe as well. In Bulgaria, a group of students formed the Bulgarian Association for Free Elections (BAFE) to monitor that country's first competitive election for president in June 1990. BAFE, like its predecessors in the Philippines and Latin America, organized election-day pollwatchers. In just a few weeks, the group mobilized more than 8,000 volunteers. Building on the work in Chile, BAFE also organized one of the earliest, and most successful, statistically based parallel vote tabulations. In Romania, the Pro-Democracy Association recruited about 6,000 observers for the elections in 1992. In Albania, in the same year, the newly organized Society for Democratic Culture monitored the first competitive parliamentary elections, in which a new, noncommunist government came to office.[21]

Domestic monitoring also emerged in the early 1990s in Africa. For the United Nations–supervised transitional elections in Namibia in 1989, the Namibian Council of Churches documented election-related intimidation and an NGO called Namibia Peace Plan 435 monitored the media. However, the first broadly targeted election-monitoring organizations in Africa, as discussed below, were created in Zambia for its first multiparty elections in 1991. The Zambia Independent Monitoring Team and the Zambia Elections Monitoring Coordinating Committee (later renamed the Foundation for Democratic Process) modeled themselves directly on the monitoring efforts in the Philippines, Chile, and Bulgaria.

In South and Southeast Asia, NGOs also organized important election-monitoring efforts in several countries in the early 1990s. Two separate coalitions monitored critical transitional elections in Bangladesh in February 1991: the Bangladesh Movement for Fair Elections (Bangladesh Mukto Nirbachan Andolan, or BMNA) and the Coordinating Council on Human Rights in Bangladesh (CCHRB). BMNA was the umbrella organization for the election-monitoring efforts of a number of nongovernmental, human rights, professional, and trade organizations. CCHRB was a preexisting coalition of human rights organizations with experience in monitoring the polls for local elections in March 1990. For the national elections in Bangladesh in 1996, the Fair Election Monitoring Alliance, a new coalition of dozens of NGOs and other local groups, emerged as the principal domestic EMO, a status it retained in 2001. In Thailand in 1992, after a military government that had taken over in an earlier coup stepped down, the caretaker government actually funded the formation of an independent organization, Pollwatch, to monitor elections intended to restore democracy. In Pakistan, the Human Rights Commission, a private human rights group, organized a modest network of pollwatchers for parliamentary elections in 1993. In Nepal, for the first multiparty national elections in 1994, ten human rights and civic organizations came together to create the National Election Observation Committee. In Sri Lanka the same year, a number of NGOs formed the Peoples Action for Free and Fair Elections and the Movement for Free and Fair Elections.

In the Middle East, perhaps the first real EMO was the National Committee for Free Elections in Yemen. In the face of considerable obstacles, this group mobilized more than 4,000 volunteers for Yemen's first multiparty elections in 1993, which took place after the formal reintegration of North Yemen and South Yemen.[22]

In the early 1990s, election observation also became a focus for transnational groupings of NGOs from developing countries and emerging democracies within their own geographical regions. For example, one transnational NGO emerged in West Africa to monitor elections in the region. The Study and Research Group on Democracy and Economic and Social Development, known by its French acronym as GERDDES, brought civic leaders from neighboring countries to observe transitional elections in Benin in 1991. Not, strictly speaking, a domestic monitoring organization, GERDDES was really a hybrid—part domestic, part international; part activist, part academic—that represented an evolution and adaptation of nonpartisan monitoring to incorporate NGOs from developing countries into the emerging system of international observation.

Nongovernmental groups in other regions also came together to monitor regional elections under a common umbrella. The South Asian Association for Regional Cooperation (SAARC), organized by the Colombo-based International Center for Ethnic Studies, has sent nongovernmental observers from the region to elections in South Asia since the transitional elections in Bangladesh in 1991. In 1997, a group of human rights and election-monitoring NGOs principally from Southeast Asia formed the Asian Network for Free Elections (ANFREL) to encourage regional collaboration on election monitoring, especially with an eye on the situation in Cambodia. ANFREL sent observers from its member groups to the Cambodian elections in 1998 and subsequently to elections in Indonesia, East Timor, Bangladesh, and Sri Lanka. Many of the constituent NGOs of these coalitions were formed with purposes other than election monitoring in mind, but subsequently they saw the importance of democratic elections in neighboring countries.

A few years later, having established themselves in their own countries, some national monitoring organizations in Eastern and Central Europe similarly turned their attention to elections in other countries in the region, although they retained their organizational identities rather than forming regional groups. After monitoring elections in its own country in January 2000, for example, Croatia's Citizens Organized to Monitor Elections (GONG) turned its attention to the effort to oust Slobodan Milosevic in Yugoslavia. Likewise, NAMFREL, though nominally part of the Asian Network for Free Elections, has increasingly organized its own international monitoring programs in other countries, including Cambodia in 1998 and Indonesia in 1999 (see tables 10.1 through 10.4).

Domestic Monitoring Meets Resistance

NDI and NAMFREL promoted nonpartisan domestic election monitoring in the early days, joined by the growing roster of EMOs from emerging democracies. The Conference on Security and Cooperation in Europe strongly endorsed the practice in its 1990 Copenhagen Document, which declared, "the presence of observers, *both foreign and domestic,* can enhance the electoral process." The document specifically recognized the principle of allowing observers from "appropriate private institutions and organizations."[23] Later, the Organization for Security and Cooperation in Europe's (OSCE's) Office for Democratic Institutions and Human Rights (ODIHR) took up the cause in its assistance programs and election assessments. By the mid-1990s, the OSCE was increasingly emphasizing the rights of domestic monitoring groups in its assessments of elections in member countries. But despite the Copenhagen Document's commitments, even OSCE member states continued to restrict access for national groups.

As domestic election monitoring became more widespread and proved to be effective, incumbent governments in many countries found it more threatening. Election laws became one new battlefront, with extensive debate over such issues as accreditation of observers and access to polling sites. In many countries, such as Yemen in 1993, the authorities argued that their election laws did not permit domestic pollwatching. In other countries, including Romania and Ukraine, international pressure helped establish legal provisions permitting access to duly accredited, neutral monitoring groups, but the authorities continued to resist. In Romania and Yemen, as elsewhere, the authorities also set up alternative monitoring groups to blunt the impact of existing groups. The authorities in a number of countries simply barred domestic monitors, while others, including Azerbaijan, Belarus, Kazakhstan, and Slovakia, imposed burdensome restrictions on access to polling and counting sites and/or on foreign assistance to domestic monitoring groups. In Belarus and Kyrgyzstan, the authorities evidently resorted to the intimidation of domestic monitors. In Egypt, the authorities brought criminal charges against activists intending to organize monitoring efforts.

Official resistance to allowing domestic monitors for Yemen's 1993 transitional election was typical. In the run-up to transitional elections in Yemen, political parties questioned the motives of the National Committee for Free Elections (NCFE) and the human rights group that sponsored it. Five weeks before election day, the election commission reneged on its earlier agreement to accredit domestic monitors. A second monitoring group, the Yemeni Committee for Free and Democratic Elections, was formed, evidently to undermine the first. Even in the absence of accreditation and in the face of considerable threats from the authorities, the NCFE nevertheless went ahead with a plan to have pollwatchers monitor outside the polling stations if they were not permitted inside.[24]

The reaction of Ukrainian officials was similar. Even though the new Ukrainian election law, influenced by advice from the international community, permitted participation by "nonpartisan committees of voters," the Ukrainian election commission in 1994 resisted accrediting or even meeting with the newly formed Nonpartisan Committee of Voters (later renamed the Committee of Voters of Ukraine). The old mentality died hard. When domestic monitoring leaders joined international advisers from NDI at a meeting, one election commissioner berated Ukrainian organizers for printing letterhead before the government had recognized the committee's existence. Yet for the parliamentary elections in March 1994, no government entity was willing to register such an organization at the national level. The election commission only permitted monitoring by committees organized at the polling station level, and the commission chair called the national organization illegal. For Ukraine's next elections in 1999, the OSCE criticized the

Table 10.1
Selected Domestic Election Monitoring Organizations in Europe and the Former Soviet Union

Country or Jurisdiction	Election-Monitoring Organization	Principal Election(s) Monitored	Number of Pollwatchers Reported (approximate)	Comments
Albania	Society for Democratic Culture	March 1992, May–June 1996, June–July 1997, June–August 2001	2,000 (1992) 1,450 (1997)	
Armenia	It's Your Choice	September 1996, March–May 1998, May 1999		EMOs barred (1998)
Azerbaijan	For the Sake of Civil Society	October 1998, November 2000–January 2001		Restrictions
Belarus	Civic Initiative-Independent Observation Network Assembly of Democratic NGOs Central Coordination Council	October 2000	21,887 accredited (September 2001)	
Bosnia and Herzegovina	Center for Civic Initiatives Network of NGOs Center for Civic Initiatives Elections 2002	September 1998, November 2000 October 2002	More than 5,000 (2000) 6,000	
Bulgaria	Bulgarian Association for Fair Elections and Civil Rights (BAFECR)	June 1990, October 1991, January 1992, December 1994, October–November 1996, April 1997, June 2001	10,000 (1991) More than 10,000 (2001)	
Croatia	Citizens Organized to Monitor Elections (GONG)	April 1997, June 1997, January 2000, February 2000	4,000	Not accredited (1997)
Georgia	International Society for Fair Elections and Democracy	November 1995, October–November 1999, April 2000		
Kosovo (Serbia and Montenegro)	Kosova Action for Civic Initiatives, Council for Defense of Human Rights and Freedoms	October 2000 (local elections)		

Country	Organization	Dates		
Kyrgyz Republic	Coalition for Democracy and Civil Society	February–March 2000, October 2000		
Macedonia	MOST	September 2002	3,000	
	Citizens for Citizens	2000 (local elections)	1,500	
Montenegro (Serbia and Montenegro)	The Monitoring Center (CEMI) Center for Democratic Transition	October 1997, May 1998, April 2001, October 2002		
Moldova	League for the Defense of Human Rights in Moldova	March 1998, February 2001		
Romania	Pro-Democracy, LADO	September 1992, October 1992, November 1996, November 2000	LADO: 4,700 (1996)	Restrictions
Russia	Russian Observers Association Voice Coalition (Liberal parties, not independent)	March 2000		
Slovakia	Civic Eye (formerly Association for Fair Elections), Memo 98 (1998)	September 1998, May 1999, September 2002		Restrictions (1998)
Ukraine	Nonpartisan Committee of Voters of Ukraine	March 1994, June 1994, March 1998, October–November 1999, March 2002	24,000 (2002)	Not permitted (1999)
Serbia and Montenegro	Center for Free Elections and Democracy (CeSID) Center for Monitoring (CEMI)	December 2000, September 2002		

Table 10.2

Selected Domestic Election Monitoring Organizations in the Asia-Pacific Region

Country or Jurisdiction	Election-Monitoring Organization	Principal Election(s) Monitored	Number of Pollwatchers Reported (approximate)
Bangladesh	Fair Election Monitoring Alliance	February 1996, June 1996, October 2001	17,000 (June 1996)
	Coordinating Council for Human Rights in Bangladesh	February 1991	
	Bangladesh Movement for Fair Elections		
	Citizens Election Commission		
	Bangladesh Society for the Enforcement of Human Rights		
Cambodia	Committee for Free and Fair Elections	May 1993, July 1998	
	Coalition for Free and Fair Elections		
	Neutral and Impartial Committee for Free Elections in Cambodia		
Hong Kong	Hong Kong Human Rights Monitor	May 1998, September 2000	
Indonesia	Independent Election Monitoring Committee (KIPP)	May 1997, June 1999	
	University Network for Free Elections (UNFREL), Rectors' Forum, People's Network for Political Education (JPPR)	June 1999	300,000
Malaysia	Malaysian Citizens' Election Watch	November 1999	
Nepal	National Election Observation Committee	November 1994, May 1999	
Pakistan	Human Rights Commission of Pakistan	October 1990, October 1993, February 1997, October 2002	
Philippines	National Citizens' Movement for Free Elections (NAMFREL)	May 1984, February 1986, May 1992, May 1995, May 1998, May 2001	500,000 (1986)
South Korea	Citizens' Coalition for Clean and Fair Elections	December 1992	
Sri Lanka	Movement for Free and Fair Elections	November 1994, August 1994, December 1999, October 2000, December 2001	
	People's Alliance for Free and Fair Elections		
	Center for Monitoring Election Violence		
Thailand	Pollwatch	September 1992, November 1996, March–July 2000	

Ukrainian election law for the "regressive step" of removing the right for domestic nonpartisan observers to observe the election process altogether.[25]

The 1996 election law in Romania provided that "internal observers" could be accredited only for a single polling station and that each polling station could have only one observer. Moreover, as in Yemen, new monitoring groups, apparently sanctioned by the authorities, emerged to compete with existing ones. In addition to two experienced EMOs, Pro Democracy and LADO (the League for the Defense of Human Rights), the Ministry of Justice registered as internal observer groups four other organizations with a more questionable commitment to an impartial, democratic process. Recalling a similar situation in 1992, the OSCE/ODIHR monitoring mission in Romania reported that LADO and Pro Democracy "questioned the authenticity of the late comers and were apprehensive about a repeat of 'ghost organizations' putting forward many thousands of names in order to disrupt the activities of legitimate organizations, and, in turn, a reduction in their presence at polling stations." With help from the International Foundation for Election Systems, the central election bureau ran a lottery to determine which potential observers from the six organizations could observe in which polling stations, but many were unable to travel to the stations to which they were assigned. The OSCE expressed regret that these "severe restrictions" on national observer participation were "contrary to the election related commitments in the Copenhagen Document" and "resulted in a reduced presence at polling station level and no presence at constituency level." Between 1996 and 2000, the OSCE recommended express provisions to permit domestic election monitoring in election laws in Albania, Belarus, Montenegro, and Slovakia and urged legal changes to facilitate monitoring in Azerbaijan, the Kyrgyz Republic, and Romania.[26]

As they became increasingly threatened by the potential power of nonpartisan monitoring groups, some governments, even in the OSCE region, barred them. The election authorities in Croatia and Serbia in 1997, Armenia in 1998, and Yugoslavia in 2000 refused outright to accredit nonpartisan domestic monitors, which OSCE election assessments repeatedly called "contrary to the spirit" of the 1990 Copenhagen Document."[27]

The OSCE criticized the authorities in Azerbaijan in 1998 for placing "administrative obstacles that run contrary to the Freedom of Association and to the principles of election observation" on some local organizations. In 2000, the OSCE denounced an election commission rule in Azerbaijan against monitoring by groups receiving foreign funding as a "serious limi-

Table 10.3

Selected Domestic Election Monitoring Organizations in Africa and the Middle East

Country or Jurisdiction	Election-Monitoring Organization	Principal Election(s) Monitored	Number of Pollwatchers Reported (approximate)	Comments
Benin	GERDDES (Groupe d'Etudes et de Recherces sur la Democratie et le Development Economique et Social)	June 1991, March 1995, March 1996, March 1999, March 2001		
Burundi	Ligue Burundaise de Droits de l'Homme (Burundian League for Human Rights) Group of Independent Observers	June 1993		
Chad	GERDDES-Tchad	June-July 1996		
Egypt	Independent Commission for Electoral Review (sponsored by Egyptian Organization for Human Rights, Ibn Khaldoun Center, other NGOs)	November 1995	600	
	Ibn Khaldoun Center for Social and Developmental Studies	October 1999, November-December 2000		Organizers arrested before 2000 election
Ethiopia	A-Bu-Gi-Da (Ethiopian Congress for Democracy)	June 1992, June 1994		
Ghana	Center for Democracy and Development	December 1996		
	Coalition of Domestic Observers	December 2000		
Kenya	National Election Monitoring Unit	December 1992	7,500–10,000	
	Institute for Education in Democracy National Council of Churches of Kenya Catholic Justice and Peace Commission	December 1997	30,000	
	Transition Monitoring Group	December 2002		
Liberia	Liberian Election Observers Network	July 1997		

Country	Organization	Date(s)	Number
Malawi	Public Affairs Committee	May 1994	
Mozambique	Mozambican Association for Democracy (AMODE)	December 1999	
	Civic Education Forum (FECIV)		
Namibia	Namibia Council of Churches	November 1989	
	Namibia Peace Plan		
Niger	GERDDES-Niger	July 1996	
Nigeria	Transition Monitoring Group	February 1999	
Palestine (West Bank and Gaza)	Palestinian Domestic Monitoring Committee	January 1996	2,200
Senegal	GERDDES	February 1993, May 1993, February 2000, March 2000	
Sierra Leone	National Election Watch	May 2002	
South Africa	South African Civil Society Observation Coalition	April 1994	
Tanzania	Tanzania Election Monitoring Committee	October 2000	
Yemen	National Committee for Free Elections	April 1993	
	Arab Democratic Institute, Election Monitoring Committee	April 1997	More than 15,000
Zambia	Foundation for Democratic Process (formerly, Zambia Election Monitoring Coordinating Committee (ZEMCC))	October 1991, November 1996, December 2001	
	Zambia Independent Monitoring Team (ZIMT)		
Zimbabwe	Election Support Network	June 2000, March 2002	

Table 10.4

Selected Domestic Election Monitoring Organizations in Latin America and the Caribbean

Country or Jurisdiction	Election-Monitoring Organization	Principal Election(s) Monitored	Number of Pollwatchers Reported (approximate)	Comments
Chile	Crusade for Democracy (Participa/CIVITAS) Committee for Free Elections	October 1988		
Dominican Republic	Citizen Participation	May–June 1996, May 1998, May 2000	7,000 (1996) 7,500 (2000)	Number restricted (1996)
Guyana	Electoral Assistance Bureau	October 1992, December 1997, March 2001		
Jamaica	Citizens' Action for Free and Fair Elections	December 1997, October 2002		
Mexico	Civic Alliance	August 1994, July 1997, July 2000	20,000 (1994)	
Nicaragua	Ethics and Transparency	October 1996	4,200 (1996)	
Panama	Justice and Peace Commission Volunteer Delegates Corps	May 1994, May 1999		
Paraguay	Transparency (SAKA) Center for Democratic Studies	1991 (local elections) May 1993 May 1993	5,000	
Peru	Transparencia	April 1995, April–May 2000, April–June 2001		

tation, a step back from previous practice and contrary to the spirit of the Copenhagen Document."[28] NDI reported that this restriction "effectively eliminated" nonpartisan domestic monitoring.[29] The OSCE admonished the authorities in Slovakia in 1998 for only allowing domestic monitors into some polling stations and denying them the opportunity to monitor the count.[30] It similarly complained the following year that some local authorities in Kazakhstan prevented domestic observers from witnessing the vote count.[31] The government of Belarus imposed restrictions on foreign assistance to domestic election monitoring of its presidential election in 2001.

Many EMOs faced intimidation. In 2000, the OSCE criticized the election commission, the Ministry of Justice, prosecutors, and the "government-oriented media" in Kyrgyzstan for "what appeared to be a co-ordinated attempt to undermine [the] work and credibility" of an NGO election-monitoring coalition after the group issued a critical report. Someone also physically assaulted the coalition's executive director.[32] Before the 2001 election in Belarus, the head of the Belarusian KGB reportedly charged that "international assistance in training election observers was [akin to] the recruitment of spies," and the authorities accused domestic monitors of including armed guerrillas. Just before the election, the election commission revoked the credentials of two leading NGOs. Throughout the country, domestic observers were required to produce documents not specified in the law or expelled from polling stations. Government officials also attacked the domestic monitoring organization's parallel vote tabulation.[33]

The authorities in Egypt arrested activist Saad Eddin Ibrahim and twenty-seven others in July 2000 after they announced plans to monitor parliamentary elections that fall. Their organization, the nongovernmental Ibn Khaldoun Center for Social and Developmental Studies, had charged that elections in 1995 were rigged. A lower court twice convicted Ibrahim, a dual national of Egypt and the United States, of defaming the country and accepting funds from overseas without authorization, among other charges, and sentenced him to seven years in prison. In December 2002, Egypt's highest court ordered a retrial, and Ibrahim was released from prison.

U.S. political leaders added their voices on behalf of the rights of domestic election-monitoring groups. When the authorities refused to allow domestic monitoring in Yemen in 1993, Representative Lee Hamilton, chair of the House Committee on Foreign Affairs, wrote to the president of Yemen to suggest that the election commission "be urged to consider carefully how the work of the National Committee for Free Elections can be constructive in the elections process." Likewise, five U.S. senators, including Senator Claiborne Pell, chair of the Senate Foreign Relations Committee, and Senator Daniel Patrick Moynihan, chair of the Middle East subcommittee, urged "every appropriate step to ensure that the National Committee for Free Elections is permitted to pursue its activities without hindrance." In response, Yemen's foreign minister argued that nonpartisan pollwatching was not permitted under the country's election law and that "the outcome of such an experiment would most likely be the creation of controversy and confusion."[34] Just before elections in Slovakia in 1998, President Carter and other international leaders admonished the prime minister for the "unwillingness of the Central Election Commission to accredit trained, organized, and nonpartisan domestic election monitors." Commented Carter, "It is not logical that a country should invite foreign election observers while denying the same invitation to its own citizens."[35] Although not based on the monitoring issue per se, in 2002 President George W. Bush threatened to cut off new aid to Egypt to protest the prosecution of Saad Eddin Ibrahim.

At the same time, more and more election laws did recognize a role for nonpartisan domestic monitors. In 1995, the Israeli–Palestinian Agreement governing elections in the West Bank and Gaza recognized domestic observers as a separate, official category of observers, and the Palestinian election law provided, "All stages of the electoral process . . . shall be public and open to international and domestic observation." The Albanian election law in 1996 provided for access by domestic monitors to polling places but was unclear about whether it permitted access to activities at higher levels. In Croatia, the constitutional court ruled in 1998 that domestic observers had the right to be accredited. Election laws in Albania, Armenia, Croatia (for parliamentary elections), Georgia, Indonesia, Macedonia, the Palestinian territories, and Russia, among many other places, now permit access of domestic nonpartisan monitors to the election process.[36]

It took a while for some international organizations to recognize the importance of domestic monitors. For example, the European Union, which was officially responsible for coordinating international observers for Palestinian elections in 1996, declined to coordinate with Palestinian nonpartisan monitors and was reluctant to raise concerns about the rights of domestic observers with the Palestinian or Israeli authorities. The European Union did not want, officials said, to give the appearance that it was coordinating or representing the interests of domestic monitors.[37]

Eventually, domestic election monitoring became so established and so widespread that international organizations could no longer dismiss or ignore it. After the United Nations supported domestic election monitors for the first time in Mexico in 1994, Boutros Boutros-Ghali, the UN secretary general, praised this support for "its emphasis on long-term capacity-building" and "its contribution to the creation of confidence among citizens in their own electoral process." In his 1997 report on UN support for new or restored democracies, Kofi Annan, the secretary general, suggested that "the focus of observation should move from the international to the national level," and called for support for "domestic organizations, both in the performance of their role as electoral observers and in the development of new functions as watchdogs of democracy." He urged that funds "be dedicated to improving the capacity of domestic observers." In 2000, the Administration and Cost of Elections Project of the United Nations, the International Institute for Democracy and Electoral Assistance, and the International Foundation for Election Systems described monitoring by "organized civil society groups" as "one of the key integrity mechanisms" for elections. The European Commission itself subsequently said "the EU should adopt a strategy which . . . emphasises support to local observers, who can play a key role in the development of democratic institutions." A recent assessment of Commonwealth election observation activities similarly encouraged the provision of resources and training for domestic observers because "it is clear that domestic observer groups are the future of election observation."[38]

In 2001, discussion of domestic monitoring dominated a major conference in Warsaw on election monitoring in OSCE countries. "The development of credible, sincere, nonpartisan election-monitoring groups is one of the positive developments [of recent years]," said Ambassador Gerard Stoudmann, then head of ODIHR, in his opening remarks. Calling support for domestic monitoring a "priority in our strategy," Stoudmann advocated an "increased role in the future [for domestic observers] to ensure the credibility of election processes and, more importantly, to ensure that elections are owned by the people of the country."[39] At ODIHR's invitation, twenty-three EMOs from throughout the region participated along with diplomats and representatives of international organizations in the conference to help build a network of mutual support.

These examples illustrate the trend toward greater support from international organizations for nonpartisan domestic monitoring groups. Since the 1990s, there has been substantial international pressure to allow domestic monitoring. International figures from Jimmy Carter to U.S. congressional leaders to the UN secretary general have strongly supported domestic monitoring. Multilateral organizations have sharply criticized restrictions on domestic monitors.

The success of the mutually reinforcing national and international monitoring efforts in the Philippines proved the value of election observing, especially nonpartisan domestic monitoring. As it spread from one region of the world to another and adapted to new challenges, what began in the Philippines became a truly worldwide movement.

Chapter 11

Domestic Election Monitoring
as an End and a Means

There are more of us.

—Slogan of nongovernmental organization movement in Yugoslavia, 2000

In dozens of countries since the National Citizens' Movement for Free Elections (NAMFREL) first demonstrated the value of nonpartisan domestic election monitoring, national nongovernmental organizations (NGOs) and civic groups have mobilized broad movements for fair elections and democratic change in their own countries. By insisting that elections be competitive and meaningful, these nonpartisan domestic election-monitoring organizations (EMOs) have catalyzed democratic change and provided momentum to the global struggle for democracy.

Paradoxically, however, while domestic monitoring, like elections themselves, is extremely important, it is also overemphasized. Even as domestic monitoring groups have gained influence and international support, international democracy-building programs have sometimes inadvertently hindered them by providing funding in inappropriate ways or taking over their agenda. The international community too often views an election only as an end—as a particular event that either passes or fails some test of legitimacy—rather than as a means of building democratic practices and institutions, an ongoing process that does not end when the winner is announced or an autocrat is unseated. Recognition of the broader potential of domestic monitoring to contribute to democratization would lead foreign donors and advisers to different priorities in their support for domestic organizations.

Though in the previous chapter I told the story of how nonpartisan domestic election monitoring emerged and has evolved, this chapter surveys

235

three important issues that arise in the context of nonpartisan domestic election monitoring, with particular consideration of the relationship between national organizations and the international community. First, the chapter considers how EMOs improve particular elections, still the principal focus of most national groups and foreign donors. I address some issues common to the experience of domestic monitoring groups in many countries, including methodology and approach, partisanship, and organizational form, with the goal of discerning lessons for future monitoring. Second, I suggest that the effective monitoring of controversial elections requires better collaboration between international and domestic groups. At the same time, international observers and donors most effectively support long-term democratization by allowing domestic organizations to set the agenda and take the lead. For example, in Zambia in 1991, when external support for domestic election monitoring was still relatively novel, foreign donors failed to coordinate their support effectively as some continued to support an externally established EMO even when another indigenous organization with deeper local roots emerged. In Yugoslavia in 2000, in contrast, foreign donors effectively coordinated their assistance and allowed domestic NGOs to take the lead in the democracy movement. Third, I argue that while foreign donors and advisers can help EMOs in the short run by providing funds, they also can hinder the contributions of such groups to long-term democratization. Though it is often not appreciated in current programs to support domestic EMOs, elections and election monitoring often provide an unusual opportunity to promote long-term democratic development.

Activities of EMOs during Elections: Approaches and Issues

In their first decade, domestic election-monitoring organizations made pivotal contributions, often in tense circumstances, to important transitional elections in a number of countries. As is discussed in chapter 13, early EMOs contributed in particular by focusing on the vote-counting process, which entrenched, undemocratic regimes often tried to manipulate. As election day pollwatching and verification of election results proved able to expose or deter fraud in the balloting and counting processes, effective EMOs began to increase their attention to other, more vulnerable parts of the process. Thus, for example, domestic monitoring groups have pointed out fundamental problems in the political climate or legal framework for elections. In Cambodia in 1998, domestic EMOs bravely criticized the legal framework, the bias of the election administration, and the climate of impunity surrounding politically motivated violence. In Peru in April 2000, domestic monitors exposed the blatant unfairness of the electoral process, depriving President Alberto Fujimori's reelection of international legitimacy.

Effective domestic monitoring organizations conduct a range of activities to improve the quality and transparency of electoral processes in politically uncertain environments, which has deterred or exposed fraud and helped reduce irregularities in election administration. Like their international counterparts, the more effective, professional domestic EMOs seek to monitor the entire electoral process: before, during, and after election day.

Before election day—when electoral rules are established, election preparations are made and the campaign takes place—domestic EMOs can conduct a broad range of activities that contribute to fairer rules, more effective election administration, a better campaign environment, and a more informed electorate. This is akin to long-term monitoring by international observers.

The International Institute for Democracy and Electoral Assistance suggests that domestic groups might have a comparative advantage over international observers in certain long-term monitoring activities, including the verification of voter registration, documenting intimidation and rights violations, monitoring the media, and monitoring the handling of complaints.[1] EMOs can seek to make elections meaningful processes for the selection of leaders and debate about public policy through efforts to promote the participation of citizens as voters and candidates and to encourage a focus on issues and policies.

The most traditional, best-known domestic monitoring activity, of course, is election-day pollwatching, which benefits most from numbers and a knowledge of local circumstances. On election day, EMOs dispatch pollwatchers to monitor balloting at polling places. This enables monitoring organizations to assess the atmosphere and quality of election administration at the local level. Their presence on election day also tends to provide citizens with a greater sense of security and deter more blatant forms of intimidation. Domestic election monitors sometimes provide assistance to voters or local election administrators, such as sharing information about the specified polling process or the locations of polling places. Observers also monitor the initial vote counting—conducted in many countries at polling places immediately after the completion of balloting—and the subsequent process of tabulating the results, including the reconciliation of ballot papers and materials.

After election day, EMOs analyze and report on the conduct of the balloting and counting, track the investigation and adjudication of election-related complaints, and monitor the process of forming a new government in accordance with the election results. On the basis of their findings, domestic monitoring organizations also often advocate electoral and other institutional reforms, after elections as well as before.

Through these activities, EMOs contribute to public confidence in the integrity of transitional elections and increase the chances that elections will be—in the standard formulation—"free and fair." More broadly, the larger goal of these efforts is to build public confidence in the integrity of the process and to legitimize the results of a competitive election.

Partisanship

One of the issues most common to the experience of EMOs across regions and over time is that of partisanship. In transitional elections, domestic election monitors are almost invariably attacked or dismissed as partisan, especially by the authorities and incumbents who find them threatening or irritating. Yet to be effective and credible, election monitors must demonstrate that they are neutral and nonpartisan.

As we have seen, NAMFREL was accused in the early days of bias against Philippine president Ferdinand Marcos, a charge that seemed harder to dismiss when a number of NAMFREL organizers subsequently joined Corazon Aquino's government. NAMFREL had to work hard to dispel the notion that somehow it could not be objective or fair simply because it opposed the regime's manipulation of elections. Virtually every EMO has faced similar charges of partisanship from parties, governments, election officials, and even the international community. Often they are groups that support political change in environments where defenders of existing regimes essentially oppose democratization. The conventional wisdom in every country facing difficult elections holds that there are no impartial, neutral people.

Indeed, some international experts are themselves skeptical about whether domestic monitoring organizations can ever be independent and credible. The long-time Jimmy Carter adviser Robert Pastor, for example, observes, "In 20 electoral processes in 15 countries, I have never seen a nonpartisan domestic observer group that has enjoyed the trust of all the parties. In most cases, the nonpartisan group is suspicious of the incumbent government, and that distrust is reciprocated." Because domestic monitoring groups are always perceived as biased even when they are not, Pastor argues, "no one should have illusions that such groups can play a decisive role, particularly in a pivotal election."[2]

Although common, this criticism is misplaced. Nonpartisan groups have indeed been able to establish their independence and credibility for many pivotal elections. Beginning with the contributions of NAMFREL in the Philippines in 1986 and the Bulgarian Association for Free Elections in 1990 and running right through the activities of NGOs such as Tranparencia in Peru and the Center for Free Elections and Democracy in Yugoslavia in 2000, EMOs have made critical contributions to many transitions. Many others have helped build confidence and deter fraud, not insignificant contributions even if they were not pivotal. Moreover, as this book argues, domestic election monitoring can make profound contributions beyond pivotal elections by empowering civil society, thus deepening democracy.

Domestic monitoring groups are not partisan because they oppose authoritarian systems or undemocratic elections. The real question is whether such organizations are objective.

In response to inevitable accusations of bias, EMOs must endeavor to convince electoral authorities, parties, the public, and the international community of their neutrality. As part of these efforts, domestic monitoring organizations have often asked their volunteers to sign pledges of nonpartisanship and have forbidden them to make any public demonstration of political preferences. In Bangladesh in 1996, for example, the Fair Election Monitoring Alliance asked all observers to promise not to openly support or oppose any candidate or party. Anyone who violated this pledge would be required to resign.[3] Likewise, the Electoral Assistance Bureau in Guyana in 2001 required each of its observers to attend a training session and to swear that he or she is "neither an activist nor a candidate for any party" and "shall execute [his or her] duties impartially and objectively."[4]

Although such promises from individuals and organizations are not sufficient by themselves, they help demonstrate that an EMO is concerned about its reputation. Every successful EMO has had to establish a reputation for objectivity and effectiveness, by focusing only on the election process, avoiding any indication of support for parties or candidates, and emphasizing training and professionalism of its members. Each EMO must demonstrate its competence and emphasize, in both words and actions, its commitment to the democratic process itself. In most democratizing countries, the relationship between EMOs and election authorities improves over time.

The Diversity of EMOs

The domestic election monitoring trend has accompanied dramatic growth in the number and sophistication of NGOs and other civil society groups in many developing countries. A fairly wide variety of nongovernmental and civil society organizations have become involved in domestic election monitoring, including national and local civic groups, citizen networks, human rights groups, advocacy organizations, student and university-affiliated organizations, professional associations, religious groups, social service organizations, "think tanks," and others. Although the goals and motivations of EMOs over time and across the world are largely the same, the form of engagement and organization has varied considerably in response to varied circumstances.

Democratic activists and concerned citizens have either formed new nonpartisan nongovernmental organizations to monitor elections, expanded the mission of existing NGOs to include election monitoring, or built formal coalitions or informal networks of NGOs and other civic organizations. In Eastern and Central Europe and the former Soviet Union, many EMOs in the early 1990s were new, special-purpose NGOs such as the Bulgarian Association for Fair Elections and the Nonpartisan Committee of Voters of Ukraine. In other parts of the world, where local civil society was more established but also largely elite based, as in Indonesia, Mexico, and some countries in Africa, activists attempted to form coalitions drawing on existing organizations and networks, with greater or lesser success. In very poor countries such as Bangladesh, where donor-supported NGOs provide social services and carry out development projects, existing NGOs with large numbers of employees and considerable reach recognized the importance of democracy and elections. Accordingly, these larger, service-oriented NGOs supported and participated in coalitions for election monitoring initiated by smaller, activist-driven organizations. Some coalitions have taken the form of formal "umbrella organizations," as in the case of NAMFREL in the mid-1980s or Mexico in the 1990s. In other coalitions, as in Zambia for its first multiparty elections and in the Philippines in more recent years, membership organizations have retained their own institutional identities.

The management and structure of groups involved in election monitoring has varied considerably as well. Some EMOs, as in Indonesia, Mexico, and the Philippines, have large memberships and decentralized structures. Others, including many in Eastern Europe, are much smaller and more centralized. Some are permanent organizations with ongoing activities. After its initial incarnation as a coalition, for example, NAMFREL became a permanent organization to work on election reform and civic education. Similarly, Indonesia's Independent Election Monitoring Committee (Komisi Independen Pemantau Pemilu, or KIPP) has continued as an active organization since its founding during the Suharto era in 1996. Others, such as Thailand's Pollwatch, mobilize only for elections. Indonesia's University Network for Free Elections (UNFREL) came together for the transitional elections in 1999 and dissolved itself soon thereafter, although its national secretariat transformed itself into the Center for Electoral Reform (CETRO) and has remained active in issues of electoral, constitutional, and political reform.

Religious networks have provided volunteers and moral support for election monitoring in the Philippines, Latin America, and Africa. In the Philippines, as we have seen, NAMFREL drew on the existing networks and structure, in particular those of the Catholic Church. In Indonesia, the People's Network for Political Education (Jaringan Pendidikan Politik untuk Rakyat, or JPPR) drew on a network of organizations affiliated with leading Islamic organizations. Particularly in predominantly Christian countries, religious leaders have involved themselves in democratic activism, and domestic election monitoring has often had an explicit religious connection. Commitment to values derived from religion and commitment to participatory democracy have been closely related motivations for many election-monitoring volunteers. In some other countries, such as South Korea and Bangladesh, members of the Christian minority (a tiny minority in Bangladesh) were especially active in spurring election monitoring early on.

Election monitoring in Bangladesh, Indonesia, Palestine, and Yemen, like other Muslim societies, has been largely a secular effort, even though some religious organizations have been involved and most leaders of the election-monitoring movement have been Muslims. Though activists in such countries certainly believe that democracy and Islamic religious values are fully consistent, they have did not appealed explicitly to religion. Indeed, some have seen religious fundamentalism as a threat to tolerance and democracy.[5]

Coordination between International and Domestic Observers

Although high-profile international observation teams still attract much of the funding and news coverage for transitional elections, domestic monitors have obvious advantages. Domestic organizations can organize more mean-ingful monitoring because they are present and involved in the process from beginning to end, can mobilize in much larger numbers, speak local lan-guages, and naturally have a deeper knowledge of their own society's po-litical culture and context. Nevertheless, many international observers still fail to build on the findings of domestic monitors or to share the limelight with them. International observers often fail to give voice to national groups' assessments—particularly to international audiences.

The effective monitoring of controversial elections requires collabora-tion between international and domestic groups, often including financial support for domestic organizations. Although, as was discussed in chapter 7, there has been much emphasis on coordination among international groups, coordination between international observers and domestic moni-tors is at least as important.

Both international and domestic monitors benefit from effective coordi-nation between them, for four main reasons. First, international and do-mestic observers bring complementary strengths to the formidable logisti-cal exercise of organizing and deploying pollwatchers. International observers often have expertise on the technical aspects of election observ-ing, such as knowledge of electoral safeguards in other countries, experi-ence with training and deploying pollwatchers, and familiarity with paral-lel vote tabulations. Domestic monitoring groups can mobilize large numbers of volunteers for pollwatching and possess the invaluable local knowledge necessary to adapt observer operations to local conditions. An-alysts increasingly recognize these benefits. An analyst of 1994 elections in Malawi, for example, explained how international observers benefited from learning from domestic monitors about local means of intimidation and cheating:

> In [the] contacts [of international observers] with local monitors, sur-reptitious acts of intimidation could be presented and openly discussed, information on the various means of "rigging" the election procedures could be shared and questions on some of the technical aspects of these procedures could be answered. . . . In this way, both the international ob-servers and the local monitors would feel that their status, efficacy and safety were enhanced by mutual close contact and collaboration. . . . Close partnership will prove to be beneficial to a deeper empirical un-derstanding of local political culture and thereby of the effectiveness of international observing.[6]

Stefan Mair observes likewise, "Local monitors are especially able to note subtle societal processes, register the political mood of the people, pass on rumors and . . . act as mediators between international observers and voters, as the latter often avoid contact with foreigners, or at least avoid telling them too much."[7]

Second, international observers can draw directly on information from the much broader, more geographically disbursed network of domestic monitors. International observers can generally make a more significant contribution if they integrate their fact-finding processes with the work of domestic EMOs. Public assessments of the process—whether in the preelection period, in the immediate aftermath of the balloting, or some time later in the postelection period—necessarily rely on local sources of information, including especially the findings of national election monitoring groups.

Third, by standing in solidarity with local observers, international observers can help legitimize domestic efforts and can provide considerable political protection. In many countries, as Hrair Balian, formerly of the Organization for Security and Cooperation in Europe argues, "domestic observers would not have been able to function as effectively or at all without the presence of international observers."[8] Beyond using domestic monitors as a source of information, the international monitoring groups should consciously seek to help domestic groups to find international media attention. For the February 1999 elections in Nigeria, for example, the Nigerian Transition Monitoring Group (TMG) and international observers

Table 11.1

Preelection Issues Monitored by Domestic Groups

Domestic monitors are well placed to conduct comprehensive preelection monitoring, including monitoring of
- the electoral framework, including election laws regulations and institutional arrangements for election administration;
- the fairness and accuracy of the voter registration process;
- the eligibility and registration of election candidates and parties;
- the campaign environment, including the opportunity for all candidates and parties to campaign, the extent of intimidation, the role of security forces, and the degree of respect for freedom of assembly and speech;
- the media, including both the opportunities for all parties to have access to public airwaves and the fairness of news coverage of candidates and campaigns; and
- official voter information and voter education efforts.[a]

---

[a]In addition to monitoring official voter education programs, many domestic election-monitoring organizations conduct voter education campaigns of their own—though voter education is not technically a monitoring activity.

from the joint delegation of the Carter Center and the National Democratic Institute for International Affairs (NDI) not only shared information but also coordinated news conferences. International news media provided extensive coverage of the findings of the TMG as well as those of international delegations.

The *Handbook for European Union Election Observation Missions,* in contrast, reveals a more traditional wariness of domestic monitors. Though encouraging international observers to "[meet] regularly with credible nonpartisan domestic observer organizations, which can have a broad presence throughout the country and bring a wealth of information to the attention of an international observer mission," the *Handbook* cautions, "It is important to ensure that [European Union observer missions] do not deploy with domestic observers, and organize their activities fully independently from domestic observer groups." The *Handbook* argues this protects the "absolute objectivity and first-hand reporting" of the international observers and "also protects the integrity of the international missions against the possibility or perception of infiltration by partisan domestic actors."[9] Similarly, Mair suggests, "If the local monitors are provided by a non-party organization, it will be difficult for the international observers to gauge whether this organization is truly independent or if it is dominated by one political force. . . . The danger exists that the local monitors act as agents of their organization and attempt to manipulate their colleagues [the international observers] or even to sabotage their work."[10]

Fourth, international observers can extend the benefits of their involvement by making reinforcement of domestic monitoring groups an explicit goal. "If the international community some day expects to put an end to international election observation missions and technical assistance," argues Balian, "domestic observation efforts must be provided with more effective political support and resources."[11] Support for domestic monitoring should include advocacy of the right to monitor, usually including legal recognition and accreditation to the process. The EU *Handbook* says, "International observers can best support the activities of domestic observers by supporting their access to the entire election process . . . [including] unrestricted and unhindered possibilities to carry out their duties on the Election Day/s."[12]

At the same time, when domestic and international groups do work together, there is always the danger that the international groups will come to rely on the national ones primarily for logistical support. If domestic and international organizations deploy joint teams of observers, the foreigners must take care to treat their local counterparts as genuine partners, rather than as local agents who simply provide needed services, such as making appointments, arranging logistics, and providing interpretation.

In short, international observers and the international community provide moral, political, technical, and financial support to help create political space for domestic monitoring and improve the effectiveness and professionalism of that monitoring. In addition to providing a more substantial basis for assessments of the process, domestic monitoring also reinforces the importance of broader civic participation in politics and public life.

Funding and International Support

Organizers of nonpartisan domestic election monitoring efforts generally have looked to foreign aid agencies and organizations for funding. This contrasts markedly with NAMFREL in the first few years, which refused funding from outside the country and relied instead on volunteers, local corporate contributions, donations solicited through the church, and in-kind contributions. Thailand's Pollwatch, organized initially for critical elections in 1992, was also unusual because it received considerable government funding even though its leaders were academics and activists strongly opposed to military rule and it had a genuinely nongovernmental feel. Nevertheless, most nonpartisan EMOs in emerging democracies have received foreign support, and, as the Indonesian experience discussed in chapter 12 suggests, the providers and the amounts of that support have increased considerably in recent years. Though support for domestic monitoring is, overall, a good thing, the increasingly large sums involved, and the sometimes careless way in which they are programmed and disbursed, have at times proved counterproductive.

As domestic election monitoring has become increasingly accepted, foreign funders have often supported organizations with little demonstrated commitment or professionalism. Effective monitoring requires the systematic recruitment and training of volunteers, communication and reporting systems, objective and impartial fact finding, and knowledge of the electoral law and administrative procedures. As Feroz Hassan, the founder and leader of the Fair Election Monitoring Alliance in Bangladesh, puts it in a monitoring manual, "Quality is better than quantity."[13] Yet it is quantity that foreign donors often push.

Foreign funding also runs the risk of detracting from local "ownership" of monitoring efforts. The relationship between EMOs and foreign organizations can be complex, as domestic groups try to accept funding without ceding control and foreign advisers attempt to offer advice without supplanting local leadership. Sometimes, domestic groups feel compelled to accept direction from particular donors in order to receive funding. As experiences in Zambia, Yugoslavia, Indonesia, and elsewhere show, funding and technical assistance from international organizations to domestic EMOs can be extremely valuable or it can be itself the cause of problems.

Foreign Support for Domestic Election Monitoring in Zambia

International support helped mobilize the first comprehensive domestic monitoring effort in Africa for transitional elections in Zambia in 1991 after eighteen years of one-party rule. When the longtime president, Kenneth Kaunda, accepted opposition demands for multiparty elections, he initially refused to countenance the presence of election observers. But the newly formed opposition, with at least tacit support from international donors, insisted on independent election observers as a condition for its participation. Eventually Kaunda acceded to that demand.[14]

In 1988, the prominent Zambian human rights lawyer Roger Chongwe had traveled as part of an NDI program to Chile, where he had witnessed the extremely important contribution made by domestic monitors there. Chongwe subsequently conceived the idea for the Zambia Independent Monitoring Team (ZIMT) in his own country. With encouragement, advice, and funding promises from the international community, ZIMT was constituted as a self-selected board of prominent, respected citizens, including businesspeople, professionals, students and—later—members of the clergy.

Under the overall leadership of former U.S. president Carter, NDI representatives began working with ZIMT in mid-1991 to recruit and train Zambians and to sell the idea of nonpartisan domestic monitoring to donors. NDI also joined forces with the Carter Center to organize a comprehensive international monitoring program. The first training program for Zambian pollwatchers took place in August, about ten weeks before election day, October 31. The program featured experienced organizers of election-monitoring groups from Chile and the Philippines and an activist from the Namibian Council of Churches. They advised Zambian civic activists on how to recruit volunteers, organize and train a nationwide network of pollwatchers, investigate preelection complaints, carry out a nationwide civic education campaign, and monitor the balloting process. Given the stature and involvement of President Carter, a number of donors agreed to provide funding for domestic election monitoring and entrusted the NDI–Carter Center team with oversight of funds for the effort.

As the election approached, however, ZIMT was unable to shake criticisms that it was sympathetic to, if not controlled by, the ruling party. When the founder, Chongwe, decided to run as an opposition candidate for a parliamentary seat, he recruited a well-known former diplomat and central bank governor known to be close to Kaunda to become ZIMT's chair. Though this may have made domestic election monitoring more palatable to the ruling party, it hurt the organization's credibility with opposition activists. Critics from Zambian civil society complained that the organization's board members did not really represent civic, religious, and professional organizations because they served as individuals and had not been chosen by their organizations.

Moreover, the NDI–Carter Center team and some foreign donors grew dissatisfied with ZIMT's lack of progress on organizational and budgetary issues. ZIMT's leaders rejected outside advice on a number of issues, from reaching out more to civil society to declining to pay "sitting fees" for board members to hiring an executive director. Foreign advisers struggled with the dilemma of balancing the importance of local control with the challenge of putting in place an effective, credible effort in a short time.

In mid-September 1991, just six weeks before the election, all three church representatives resigned from the ZIMT board and joined with civic leaders from the NGO community, the legal profession, the journalists' association, and the university to form a new domestic monitoring coalition, the Zambia Elections Monitoring Coordinating Committee (ZEMCC). ZEMCC was set up consciously as a coalition of groups rather than as a new, distinct NGO. It elected a prominent member of the clergy as its leader. ZIMT declined an invitation to join the new umbrella group.

NDI and the Carter Center remained ready and willing to work with both monitoring organizations. They also concluded, however, that ZEMCC had particular potential and credibility as a genuinely grassroots organization because it had elected its leaders and could draw upon organized support from the major institutions of civil society. The NDI–Carter Center team quickly established an effective partnership with ZEMCC.

The tactical disagreements between ZIMT and the American groups were becoming an issue at the same time that ruling-party elites, as was discussed in chapter 5, were stepping up their attacks on President Carter. Concerned about controversy, several European donors decided to fund ZIMT directly rather than through the American-led structure that had been established. The NDI–Carter Center representatives welcomed this decision, because it removed a contentious issue from their relationship with ZIMT and freed them to focus on substantive, technical advice and assistance. At the same time, many donors were worried about fragmented or redundant monitoring programs and either were reluctant to fund the new group or lacked the flexibility to quickly adjust their assistance programs.[15]

Beginning with only local, in-kind support, ZEMCC published training manuals and sent teams to train volunteers around the country. NDI–Carter Center professionals participated in these training programs, which were organized by student and religious groups, and assisted with the production of training manuals. With the additional support it eventually received from other foreign donors, ZEMCC delivered voter education messages through the media and the pulpit and mobilized a considerable election-day poll-watching effort. Meanwhile, ZIMT also broadcast public education messages, provided legal advice about election-related complaints, and raised concerns with the Election Commission.

Both groups proposed and promoted changes in the rules of the game that helped to "level the playing field." Despite delays in the issuance of credentials to pollwatchers, which created particular problems in rural areas, pollwatchers from the two EMOs covered a majority of polling stations on election day, including almost all in urban areas. Notwithstanding donor concerns about duplication, the competition between the two Zambian monitoring groups probably helped to stimulate the recruitment and training of volunteers, the conduct of voter education campaigns, and the deployment of pollwatchers throughout the country. It likely also contributed to the professionalism of both groups.

Foreign engagement made domestic monitoring possible in Zambia, which in turn helped bring about successful elections and became the foundation of civil society in the country. But the interorganizational conflicts among Zambian groups diverted energies away from preparations for election monitoring until late in the process. Moreover, foreign advisers and donors made the mistake of identifying the principle of domestic election monitoring with just one particular organization. Differences of opinion among donors, diplomats, and democratic organizations complicated foreign assistance efforts and were a harbinger of greater disagreements in other countries in later years.

Serbia's Electoral Revolution

Nearly a decade later, civil society groups, backed by foreign assistance, used the elections in Yugoslavia on September 24, 2000, to bring about an "electoral revolution" that removed long-standing autocrat Slobodan Milosevic from power. Supported by experienced monitoring groups, private foundations, and foreign aid programs from Europe, North America, and other parts of the former Yugoslavia, a unified democracy movement organized an extraordinary campaign for democratic elections. In the face of enormous obstacles, this coordinated, well-planned movement, together with a unified political opposition, helped create an environment in which Milosevic was forced to step aside. The depth and breadth of this foreign support shows how far domestic monitoring has come since Zambia in 1991. This success, however, also raises important issues about the nature of foreign support for nongovernmental democracy movements.

Refusing to be intimidated, such citizen groups as Otpor (Resistance) and the Center for Free Elections and Democracy (CeSID) emerged as strong challengers to a repressive government. The politically adept Otpor student movement grew to more than 70,000 members. "Through marches and mockery, physical courage and mental agility, Otpor grew into the mass underground movement that stood at the disciplined core of the hidden revolution that really changed Serbia," wrote Roger Cohen in the *New York Times.* "No other opposition force was as unsettling to the regime or as critical to its overthrow."[16] Meanwhile, CeSID mobilized more than 5,000 volunteers to monitor the 3,500 polling places. At polling stations around the country, these volunteers documented voter intimidation, multiple voting, interference by election authorities, and lack of ballot secrecy. They also collected election results, which complemented results tabulated by the opposition. These efforts helped expose Milosevic's attempted electoral fraud.

Thomas Carothers argues that American democracy promoters have claimed undue credit for this success: "U.S. and European support made a real contribution in broadening and deepening [the] opposition [to Milosevic], but the aid campaign was a facilitator of change, not the engine of it."[17] In any event, early, well-coordinated Western aid and advice and moral support from democracy organizations and EMOs in the region helped.

Western and regional efforts to aid Serbian NGOs began early. Building on a decade-long Serbian effort to get rid of Milosevic, programs to help build capacity for election monitoring and prodemocracy political action began three years before elections were called. Young Serbian activists spent many months learning how to organize, planning their campaign, and building coalitions. At conferences in Budapest and Szeged in Hungary in the spring of 2000, civic activists from the region advised Serbian counterparts on election monitoring, youth mobilization, media monitoring, and organizational capacity building. Civic organizations from Bulgaria, Croatia, Romania, Slovakia, and Ukraine—countries that shared many experiences with Serbia—offered advice and assistance. This enormously effective cooperation of NGOs from the region, itself supported by Western groups and assistance, made a considerable contribution to the planning and mobilization of an election-monitoring movement in Yugoslavia.

Upon the announcement of elections in the summer of 2000, about twenty major NGOs announced a common program they called "Exit 2000." A united opposition and a huge NGO movement worked together toward their common goal of forcing Milosevic from office. They came up with consistent messages of unity and change. They worked to turn fear into distrust of authorities. They campaigned under such slogans as "There are more of us" and "The time is here." Theirs was a nonpartisan campaign for democracy, rather than a campaign for the opposition. In other words, they did not campaign in favor of any parties or candidates but rather opposed Milosevic's authoritarianism. Of particular importance, the politicians from the democratic camp understood and respected the distinction between partisan politics and nonpartisan efforts to support democratic elections.

Western donors, including private foundations, coordinated their efforts effectively and engaged strategically. They provided grants and helped with building capacity. The donors met in the spring in Europe, where they developed a common understanding of their strategies. Donors able to operate in Belgrade, such as the Canadian government and the Open Society Institute, worked to assist civic organizations inside the country. Others, including the U.S. Agency for International Development, Freedom House, the Charles Stewart Mott Foundation, the German Marshall Fund, the National Endowment for Democracy, the International Republican Institute, and NDI, provided funding and organized programs in the region to offer technical assistance and moral support. Meanwhile, the American democracy organizations and donors met regularly in Washington. This allowed them to avoid duplication, ensured the sharing of experiences, and provided opportunities for cofinancing. This coordination was unusually effective and flexible.

The coordination of Western assistance also diluted the perception of heavy U.S. involvement. Rather than just an American effort, this was also a European one. Rather than just an effort of established democracies, this was also an effort of groups from the newer democracies of the former Yugoslavia and Eastern Europe. Rather than being just an effort of governments, the assistance to the Yugoslavian democracy movement also came from outside foundations and NGOs. For all these reasons, though outsiders may be inclined to overstate their role, that contribution was nonetheless real.

Elections and Election Monitoring as Ends or Means

Monitoring the preparation of electoral laws and regulations, voter registration, campaigning, voting, vote counting, and the resolution of election disputes helps to ensure that elections are competitive and meaningful. This, in turn, enhances the confidence of the public and contestants and increases the chances that all sides will accept the results of a reasonably acceptable process.

But transitional elections are not only ends; they are also means—catalysts for the longer-term process of building democratic practices, values, and institutions. Beyond deterring fraud or helping to push out autocrats, election monitoring has empowered civic organizations in public affairs and transformed the way that many citizens view national politics. Organizers of election-monitoring programs can learn how to build coalitions and advocate public policy reforms in a more democratic political system. Organizations, networks, and relationships established to monitor elections prove invaluable in subsequent efforts to press for democracy in other ways, such as monitoring government performance, fighting corruption, advocating legal reform, lobbying public officials, and educating the public about democracy.

In short, nonpartisan domestic election monitoring in new and emerging democracies has two separate purposes. First, monitoring can contribute to better elections, which is especially important where the process or the authorities lack the confidence of significant political parties or parts of the public. This is often true in transitional environments. Second, and perhaps more important, election monitoring can spur the development of civil society and democratization.

These distinct purposes for organizing monitoring efforts may find themselves, at times, in tension. To the extent that the purpose is to improve or report on a particular election, election monitors are likely, for example, to emphasize maximizing the number of pollwatchers on election day. A short-term focus also tends to make foreign donors and advisers want to play a relatively greater role in designing and implementing the monitoring project. But to the extent that the purpose is to build networks and learn lessons for the future, there should be somewhat less focus on collecting information, especially on election day, and more willingness to allow groups to set their own agendas and even to make their own mistakes. Sponsors of monitoring focused primarily on the election process might, for example, pay pollwatchers for their services, whereas monitors seeking primarily to build new civil society organizations and democratic habits might place a higher priority on recruiting and motivating volunteers, even if there were fewer of them.

Elections as Means: Domestic Election Monitoring as an Opportunity for Political Organizing

It is easy to appreciate the goal of domestic election monitoring when it is to improve the quality and transparency of an election set to play an important role in a democratic transition. This worthy goal generally underlies most foreign attempts to support election monitoring. But the separate goal of building civil society is less obvious and less understood. Foreign donors often fail to fully understand the potential of domestic election monitoring. This is representative, perhaps, of a larger problem in foreign assistance: the understandable but unfortunate tendency to focus on short-term outcomes rather than longer-term processes.

International donors and advisers typically focus too much on a given election as an event, as opposed to elections as part of the democratization process. The idea of domestic monitoring has itself become almost too successful. Domestic election monitoring—and its close relation, voter education—have become "motherhood and apple pie" and thus safe for donors. Domestic election monitoring has attracted too much money and too much well-intentioned but inappropriate advice focused on short-term outcomes. Outside help often has unintended consequences. In short, foreign donors sometimes do not appear to appreciate the broader purposes of organizing monitoring efforts and the opportunities presented by transitional elections.

Rather, those interested in promoting democracy in a country that plans elections, including those who seek to support domestic monitoring, should seek to support the democratization process rather than particular short-term outcomes. Election monitoring provides civil society organizations with the opportunity to build networks and relationships that will enable them to continue to press for democracy after elections. It gives them a chance to learn how to build coalitions and advocate public policy reforms in a more democratic political system.

In addition to contributing to the quality and credibility of important transitional elections, domestic monitoring can also develop and strengthen institutions essential to the survival and success of a democratic political system. Whether elections catalyze rapid political change or merely mark incremental steps, they provide an opportunity for existing political and civic groups to expand their missions and memberships and for the creation of new groups. Monitoring efforts help citizens learn the organizational skills necessary to participate actively and effectively in the political life of a country between elections. In country after country, election monitoring has given citizens an opportunity to become involved in public affairs, which has transformed attitudes about participation in politics and governance.

Activities and Opportunities for EMOs after Elections

A transitional election is not only a critically important event in a country's move away from authoritarianism; it is also an opportunity to engage citizens in democratic politics and begin the long-term, ongoing process of building democratic practices and institutions, including civil society and political organizations. Organizations and networks developed to monitor elections often continue subsequently to promote democracy in other ways, including monitoring government performance, fighting corruption, advocating election law reform, and conducting civic education.

Groups that have been formed to monitor elections have often developed into more broadly based organizations, contributing to the development of civil society and the political process. Many of the domestic monitoring groups formed in recent years have also conceived of election monitoring as a means of mobilizing support for other democratic reforms and encouraging continuing civic participation after elections. Zambia's ZEMCC, for example, reconstituted itself after the 1991 election as the Foundation for Democratic Process. As Wimal Fernando, a leader of the Movement for Free and Fair Elections in Sri Lanka, put it, "Monitoring elections is a means to a larger end, namely, to build a broad network of people and organizations to address issues of national importance after elections."[18]

Having animated civil society and engaged many citizens in the political life of their countries for the first time, EMOs seek to build upon this momentum. Accordingly, they have undertaken efforts to advocate political reforms, to conduct public policy research, to promote accountability in government, to provide civic education, and to monitor the government and the legislature. This, in turn, has enhanced political discourse, increased citizen involvement in governance, and heightened public confidence in the political process. It is ultimately the most profound contribution that the monitoring movement can make.

Although election monitoring provides an important opportunity for civic organizing, citizen participation, and public education, elections are only periodic events. To deepen democracy and build democratic institutions beyond elections, citizens must continue to engage in public affairs. Ongoing participation reinforces an essential tenet of democracy: that the political process belongs to the public rather than to the elites.

Accordingly, groups formed to promote and monitor transitional elections have often redefined their role after the elections. First, they can engage in advocacy and activities to influence public policy and promote the public interest. These can be activities designed to shape the political process itself, such as reforming the constitution or governing institutions, or they may be activities dealing with particular public policy issues, such as human rights and civil liberties, corruption, land reform, or the environment. Sometimes, such groups have become research organizations capable of providing government officials and legislators with technical information and advice, such as the Center for Electoral Reform in Indonesia.

Second, EMOs may decide to actively monitor the activities of the government, elected officials, or the legislature. Such efforts can increase accountability by holding the actions of public officials up to public scrutiny. Davorin Popovic of Otpor said after the election in Serbia that his organization must "act as a watchdog of all powers." His colleague Srjda Popovic agreed. "Don't forget, democracy starts here," he warned the new government. "You are responsible to the people."[19]

Third, in seeking to encourage broad citizen participation in politics, election-monitoring groups may after the elections become vehicles to voice opinions, build coalitions, or educate the public about democracy or particular issues.

Unfortunately, foreign assistance for democracy and governance is often "eaten by elections," and foreign donors are unable to sustain significant funding and programs after elections. In a meeting in Croatia after the 2000 elections that replaced Franjo Tudjman, the leader of a domestic monitoring group challenged U.S. secretary of state Madeleine Albright about whether the United States had really only been interested in a change of government, rather than building civil society and democracy, because assistance had all but dried up after the elections.

Toward More Effective Support for Nonpartisan Domestic Political Engagement

Since the late 1990s, foreign support has helped domestic election monitoring to become an increasingly significant international phenomenon. Moral, technical, and financial support from foreign NGOs, foundations, and governments has helped domestic election monitoring to spread throughout the world. As these efforts have spread, they have become increasingly sophisticated, organized, and influential.

Although the international community increasingly recognizes how domestic monitoring can deter fraud, improve confidence, and increase transparency, it has yet to appreciate fully how such monitoring can also spur democracy through energizing civic organizations and drawing people more broadly into public affairs. Indonesia is a case in point, as is discussed in the next chapter. Transitional elections are only one part of the ongoing process of building democratic practices, values, and institutions.

The international community must more effectively support domestic election monitoring not only to report on transitional elections but also to help build sustainable organizations and encourage democratic participation. Indeed, there are lessons for foreign assistance more generally. Foreign aid that reinforces genuinely indigenous efforts and agendas, rather than attracting local people to agendas established elsewhere, is more likely to have significant impact. Those programs and activities that people in the country have developed and become committed to are more likely to be sustained.

Chapter 12

Foreign Support for Domestic Election Monitoring in Indonesia: Missed Opportunities and Unintended Consequences

Suharto pretends to hold elections and we will pretend to monitor them.

—Goenawan Mohamad, chair, Independent Election
Monitoring Committee (KIPP), 1997

For crucial transitional elections in Indonesia in 1999, nongovernmental groups organized the most extensive nonpartisan domestic election-monitoring effort in the world to date. Working with substantial international support, civic organizations, university-based networks, and religious groups collectively mobilized more than a half-million pollwatchers on election day. But the effort was also deeply flawed, as a large number of inadequately prepared groups came to the effort at the last minute, money was poorly spent, and domestic groups and their international supporters largely wasted the opportunity to build a foundation for further democratic reform.

After the longtime autocrat Suharto was forced from office in May 1998, Indonesia moved to organize competitive elections as a critical step away from authoritarianism. The international community—recognizing the profound importance of an opportunity to establish genuine democracy in the world's most populous Islamic country, a nation of more than 200 million people—moved to support Indonesia's political transition with technical assistance and substantial funding. In early 1999, the United Nations Development Program (UNDP) and the government of Indonesia developed a budget

256

that called for $90 million in international contributions for the elections, including support for election administration, voter education, and election monitoring.[1] Dozens of international advisers descended upon Jakarta from Australia, Europe, Japan, North America, and elsewhere. The elections eventually took place on June 7, 1999, under the watch of the Indonesian nonpartisan monitors and nearly 600 international election observers from about thirty countries, including election-monitoring icon Jimmy Carter.

International donors generously and appropriately supported the efforts of national election-monitoring organizations (EMOs) to improve the quality of the election process, for example by educating voters and mobilizing pollwatchers. The broad-based international support for these worthy purposes marked a considerable improvement from the past, in which foreign aid had been largely restricted to government recipients, even aid for transitional elections involving governments with a questionable commitment to democracy. In Indonesia, with government approval, donors channeled a large portion of available funds for the elections to nongovernmental groups.

While international support was appropriate in principle and generous in practice, it was also largely misguided. Foreign donors and advisers focused too much on the elections themselves—particularly on mobilizing pollwatchers—while largely failing to recognize an even more fundamental purpose of their support for domestic election monitoring: using the elections as a catalyst to the ongoing process of building democratic practices and institutions. Because donors were so concerned about how to get information about the quality of the process on election day, they largely failed to support longer-term democratization. In fact, donor obsession with election day inadvertently hampered the new civic organizations and the momentum for reform. Foreign assistance to domestic monitoring had unintended consequences, such as spurring the establishment of dozens of new monitoring groups, discouraging monitoring organizations from joining forces, downplaying the importance of professionalism, and encouraging an inordinate focus on money issues rather than substance. In short, the funding that poured into domestic election monitoring in Indonesia before the election was a mixed blessing at best.

The experience of domestic election monitoring in Indonesia is simultaneously a success story and a cautionary tale. In just three years, domestic election monitoring in the country grew from an activity viewed with suspicion, not only by Indonesian authorities but also by many in the international community, to one that became so popular that it lost its edge. This story highlights some paradoxes and pitfalls raised by foreign assistance for democracy promotion and development. Even well-intentioned programs supporting worthy ends and decent partner organizations may fail to lead to sustainable development if they are not well thought out.

Before the Transition: KIPP and the Precedent for Independent Monitoring in Indonesia

Before the transition to democracy had begun in 1998, the Independent Election Monitoring Committee (Komisi Independen Pemantau Pemilu, or KIPP) had already established a beachhead for domestic election monitoring. Founded in early 1996, KIPP set a precedent for independent election monitoring in Indonesia by organizing pollwatchers and other monitoring activities for national elections in May 1997, the last elections under Suharto.

During the Suharto regime, allegations of fraud plagued elections, and there was a close relationship between the ruling party and the government-controlled election administration. In response, a handful of civic activists, journalists, intellectuals, lawyers, and former government officials formed KIPP to promote fair, competitive elections as a critical step toward genuine democracy.

KIPP was modeled on similar monitoring organizations elsewhere in Asia, including the National Citizens' Movement for Free Elections (NAMFREL) in the Philippines, the Fair Election Monitoring Alliance in Bangladesh, and PollWatch in Thailand. In February 1995, Rustam Ibrahim, then the director of a well-regarded nongovernmental research organization, LP3ES (Lembaga Penelitian, Pendidikan dan Penerangan Ekonomi dan Sosial, or Institute for Social and Economic Research, Education, and Information) participated in a conference of domestic election-monitoring activists from throughout Asia that was held in Manila and organized by NAMFREL and the National Democratic Institute for International Affairs (NDI). Ibrahim took back to Jakarta the idea of organizing a domestic monitoring group in Indonesia, which ultimately led to the formation of KIPP.

NAMFREL served as a particularly important model, given similarities between the neighboring archipelagic countries and between the political situations in the Philippines in the 1980s and Indonesia in the 1990s. In April 1996, shortly after KIPP was established, its leaders invited a representative from NAMFREL to advise them. At the last minute, however, the NAMFREL representative canceled his trip, ostensibly because he lost his passport. There was speculation that the Indonesian government had some-how brought pressure to prevent the visit.

Nongovernmental organizations (NGOs) had criticized certain aspects of previous elections, such as media coverage, intimidation of voters, and ir-regularities in the vote count, but KIPP was the first organization created solely to monitor elections. Although KIPP was originally contemplated as a coalition of journalist, student, youth, professional, religious, and labor groups, it became more of a new NGO than such a coalition.

After being approached by student leaders, Goenawan Mohamad, a widely respected intellectual and journalist, agreed to chair KIPP. Mo-hamad had been the editor of the news weekly *Tempo,* which the govern-ment had closed down in 1994. The human rights lawyer and veteran ac-tivist Mulyana Kusumah was KIPP's secretary general.

In June 1996, threatened by the increasing popularity of Megawati Sukarnoputri, the Indonesian government maneuvered to oust her as head of the Indonesian Democracy Party (PDI), one of two parties permitted to exist as a kind of docile "opposition." Megawati, daughter of Sukarno, In-donesia's founding father and first president, had been elected as PDI chair in 1993, the first time a party leader had not been hand-picked by Suharto. Claiming that her ouster was illegal, Megawati's supporters denounced the government and refused to vacate the PDI headquarters in Jakarta. On July 27, 1996, after a standoff of more than a month, troops stormed the build-ing. Riots erupted, and buildings were set on fire. At least five people were killed, and many more were injured.

Thereafter, as the government cracked down on perceived opposition in the second half of 1996, the political space for KIPP appeared to close. At that point, only students and a few veteran activists were willing to continue organizing KIPP and to identify themselves with it. The Indonesian gov-ernment viewed KIPP warily and declined to recognize the new organiza-tion. KIPP's leaders appeared to risk arrest.

To avoid as much scrutiny from authorities as possible, in October 1996 KIPP conducted a major national organizing meeting and training program in Bangkok, beyond the government's reach. On at least one occasion, in Ujung Pandang (now Makassar), the local police closed down a regional re-cruiting and training session even though organizers had followed govern-ment requirements for notifying the police.[2]

Acknowledging the difficulty of conducting a meaningful monitoring program of a largely staged election in the face of strong opposition from the Suharto government, KIPP's chair, Goenawan Mohamad, quipped, "Suharto pretends to hold elections and we will pretend to monitor them." As in the Philippines in 1983, there was clear recognition in Indonesia in 1996 that democracy activists would have to begin the difficult process of building networks. They had to start somewhere and be prepared for changes when they came. At the time of the elections in May 1997, few Indonesians or foreign observers expected that Suharto would be gone within a year. But, as in the Philippines at the time of the congressional elections of 1984, a nonviolent democracy movement could look to elections as an opportunity to gain some political traction and build its capabilities. As Goenawan Mohamad explained:

> The idea was not to legitimize the election, which was not fair anyway. The idea was to invite citizens to participate in organizing themselves to protect their rights. Over the last 30 years we have lost the capacity to organize ourselves at the grass roots. The other thing was to generate a framework for joint effort for organizations committed to democratic change. We didn't want to follow the Chinese debacle after Tiananmen, when democratic forces were scattered to nothing.[3]

Ultimately, the official reaction to KIPP was relatively muted, perhaps because the government did not see the organization as more than a minor annoyance. In early 1997, apparently seeking to preempt KIPP, the government itself established an official monitoring body, the Committee for the Supervision of the Implementation of Elections (Panitia Pengawasan Pelaksanaan Pemilu), which included government-appointed representatives from the three official parties.

NDI began working with KIPP soon after the organization was formed in 1996. NDI provided ongoing consultations and organized study missions to Bangladesh, the Philippines, and Thailand. Meanwhile, the U.S. Agency for International Development (USAID) arranged for the translation into the Indonesian language of NDI's well-regarded handbook on election monitoring, *How Domestic Organizations Monitor Elections.* NDI also sponsored and helped organize KIPP's first national meeting and workshop on domestic election monitoring in Bangkok in October 1996 and arranged for the participation at that meeting of advisers from Bangladesh, Egypt, the Philippines, Thailand, and the United States to share their experiences and offer advice to Indonesians seeking to organize an election movement. In the first months of 1997, an NDI representative worked in Jakarta with KIPP organizers, and NDI dispatched a small team for elections in May of that year to offer advice and moral support.

NDI also provided financial support for KIPP's pollwatcher training and election-day deployment around the country. Much of that money was never satisfactorily accounted for. Because KIPP indeed carried out the activities the funds were intended to support, however, sloppy record keeping rather than misappropriation seemed largely to blame. The experience nevertheless made NDI leery about funding KIPP in the period 1998–99.

Before the 1997 elections, KIPP monitored media coverage of the campaign and election-related intimidation and violence. On election day, May 29, more than 9,000 KIPP volunteers monitored the polls in various locations across the country, a remarkable achievement given the obstacles the organization confronted. KIPP focused its efforts on certain geographic areas, particularly where it had strong local chapters or where there was a history of election-related conflict. Where possible, KIPP volunteers also monitored the counting of ballots on election day. They were not able to observe the tabulation of votes at the provincial and national levels and did not cover polling places systematically enough to check the results.

Although in 1997 KIPP was unable to affect the electoral system's inherent bias toward the ruling Golkar Party, its public, independent assessment of the electoral process called attention to the process's flaws and advanced the debate on political reform. KIPP's courageous determination to organize a monitoring effort was an important development in its own right. Its modest success established a precedent and began to popularize the idea of domestic monitoring. Although limited, these efforts made possible the later acceptance of citizen participation in the electoral process.

Planning for the 1999 Elections: University-Based Monitoring and More

After the Asian financial crisis of 1997–98, popular protest in Indonesia erupted into violence in May 1998 and forced longtime president Suharto to resign. He had come to power after presiding over a bloody purge of communists in 1965 and forcing aside Sukarno, the country's founding father. Suharto's regime, known as the New Order, suppressed political dissent but also presided over three decades of rapid economic growth. His vice president, B. J. Habibie, became president in 1998 and presided over substantial political reforms and, in 1999, the first open elections in more than four decades before losing a bid to stay in office.

After Suharto's removal in 1998, as plans proceeded for new, more democratic elections, KIPP sought to take the lead in organizing a broader domestic monitoring effort. In September 1998, with support from NDI, KIPP and LP3ES, the NGO involved in founding KIPP, organized a national conference on election monitoring in Indonesia. The objective was to generate and broaden support for citizen involvement in election monitoring and voter education and to begin the planning process for these activities well in advance of the elections. The conference brought together participants in the 1997 KIPP monitoring effort from around the country with representatives of other interested organizations. At NDI's invitation, Chris Monsod, the NAMFREL cofounder and former chair of the election commission in the Philippines, and a representative of Thailand's Pollwatch participated in the conference to share their experiences.

KIPP was conceived originally as a coalition, much like NAMFREL had been. But government resistance in 1996–97 made many organizations and individuals reluctant to be too open in their support of KIPP, and the effort never took the form of a coalition that could mobilize existing organizations for a new purpose. In Mulyana Kusumah, KIPP had a charismatic leader with a significant following, especially among young activists. But many of the other civic leaders involved in originally forming KIPP had since distanced themselves and sought to reconstitute it with a broader base of support. Moreover, in the vastly different political climate of 1998–99, many other civic leaders wanted to be involved in election monitoring and did not want to simply fall in behind Mulyana's leadership. For their part, Mulyana and KIPP's other leaders may be forgiven for seeing many of the new converts to election monitoring as latecomers, less courageous or committed than those involved in KIPP in 1997 had been.

Because of concerns about KIPP's closely held management, and perhaps taking account of concerns with the organization's past accountability problems, a number of civic leaders—some of whom had been KIPP founders or past supporters—decided to move beyond that organization. In addition, faculty members at a number of leading universities sought means to build on the student activism that had contributed so substantially to Suharto's ouster. In late 1998, building on KIPP's experience, two university-based networks were formed to mobilize students and universities in the election-monitoring effort.

Faculty members at one of the nation's premier universities, the University of Indonesia, initiated a new election-monitoring group in October 1998. Building on this initiative, on December 5, 1998, representatives of fourteen universities from across the country formed the University Network for Free Elections (UNFREL), which was expressly intended as an umbrella organization for a university-based network to monitor the elections across the country. The noted human rights lawyer and lecturer in law Todung Mulya Lubis was one of the prime movers and became the national coordinator of UNFREL.

Meanwhile, on November 7, 1998, a conference of 174 university rectors from across the country declared its support for political reform and called for the formation of a national, university-based organization to monitor the upcoming elections. In December 1998, a subcommittee established the Rectors' Forum for Democracy (the Rectors' Forum) as an independent EMO, based at the prestigious Bandung Institute of Technology. Sudjana Sapi'ie, former rector of that university, was appointed executive director of the group.

Thus, by the end of 1998, there were at least three organizations—KIPP, UNFREL, and the Rectors' Forum—with aspirations to build on recent activism, organize national networks, and help bring about democratic elections in Indonesia. Nevertheless, these coalitions failed to provide avenues for all groups and individuals interested in monitoring the elections. In the months leading up to elections, other Indonesian NGOs also established their own monitoring networks. These included a prominent environmental group, an NGO forum, and an independent labor organization, among other groups.[4] Shortly before the elections, the People's Network for Political Education (Jaringan Pendidikan Politik untuk Rakyat, or JPPR) transformed itself from a network of Islamic organizations conducting voter education programs into an EMO. By election day, the Indonesian election commission had accredited more than 100 separate EMOs, including a substantial number of groups organized in particular geographical locations.

Ultimately, many of these groups received substantial funding from international donors, especially the UNDP (with funds from the European Union and from Australia, Japan, and fourteen other countries), and USAID. The British Department for International Development, the Canadian International Development Agency, the German Friedrich Naumann Stiftung, the Stockholm-based International Institute for Democracy and Electoral Assistance, and several United States–based groups operating with USAID funds (including the Asia Foundation, NDI, and the American Center for International Labor Solidarity) also provided funding, encouragement, and advice to particular Indonesian monitoring organizations.

In the months leading up to elections, NDI continued to support the leading domestic monitoring groups. In February 1999, NDI sponsored consultations in Jakarta between the leaders of several Asian domestic monitoring groups and the three national monitoring organizations. Leaders of election-monitoring organizations from Bangladesh, Cambodia, Nepal, the Philippines, and Thailand participated, including several who had advised KIPP since 1996. For the next several months leading up to election day, NDI continued to advise all three groups on technical monitoring issues, including sponsoring a joint public education and recruiting effort, placing the Bangladeshi monitoring expert and longtime KIPP adviser Feroz Hassan in KIPP's offices, and working closely with the Rectors' Forum on a parallel vote tabulation. In early May, about a month before election day, the European Union and the British government likewise provided technical advisers to UNFREL, the Rectors' Forum, and KIPP.[5]

The new election law established an official monitoring body, similar to the body the government had established in 1997, known as the Election Oversight Committee (Panitia Pengawasan Pemilu, or Panwas). Although a subsequent supreme court decree expanded Panwas's mandate to oversee the entire election process and the investigation of disputes, this body was neither an independent monitoring group nor a real electoral body, and its exact role and powers were never satisfactorily defined. Nevertheless, demonstrating how much more acceptable independent monitoring had become, the government invited the leaders of KIPP and UNFREL, Mulyana Kusumah and Mulya Lubis, respectively, to serve as the two vice chairs of Panwas. (A supreme court justice, Sudarko, served as chair.) In 2001, Mulyana was appointed to the reconstituted election commission.

The Performance of Principal EMOs

Although a coalition would undoubtedly have been preferable, many of the Indonesian groups had their own constituencies, objectives, strengths, and methodologies. By itself, the participation of diverse groups was a strength, and collectively the Indonesian EMOs performed admirably on election day. Each of the three largest groups ultimately organized genuinely national networks and mobilized more than 100,000 pollwatchers.

Before the elections, KIPP advocated a fair election framework and monitored voter registration and the campaign environment. It organized a nationwide pollwatching effort of about125,000 for polling day.[6] Throughout the process, KIPP maintained a high profile in the media and a commitment to political action.

The Rectors' Forum conducted long-term monitoring and education programs and reportedly mobilized more than 200,000 students, alumni, teachers, members of NGOs, and other citizens as pollwatchers on election day.[7] As is discussed in chapter 13, the Rectors' Forum also carried out a highly successful parallel vote tabulation (PVT) to independently verify the vote count. This PVT, based on statistically valid samples of actual polling site results from each province, allowed domestic and international observers to assess the accuracy of the official tabulation of election results.

UNFREL also monitored voter registration and the campaign and mobilized an estimated 105,000 university students and faculty members as election observers in twenty-two of the twenty-seven provinces.[8] It sought to constructively engage students, who had led the call for change, in the political process. Of all the EMOs, UNFREL was perhaps the best organized and most professional in its pollwatching effort.

Unintended Consequences of Foreign Funding and Advice

Nevertheless, the Indonesian EMOs ultimately were not as effective as they might have been. Though they proved that they could mobilize large numbers of pollwatchers, many of these volunteers were deployed with little training or direction. The collection and reporting of information about balloting and counting at polling places was not always systematic. Parallel counts were either incomplete or poorly explained. And, in general, the domestic groups never fully earned the confidence of the election authorities or the donor community.

Many Indonesians involved in domestic monitoring suggested that the large number of groups and the failure to gain the confidence of the authorities was partly a legacy of the Suharto era. In the words of one, people "don't trust each other." Egos and personal ambitions certainly played a role as well. At the same time, inadvertent, but perverse, incentives from donors exacerbated the problem.

Foreign donors and advisers were themselves largely responsible for the more fundamental failure of the Indonesian domestic monitoring effort to serve broader democratization goals. By focusing excessively on election day, the international community inadvertently hampered the development of indigenous civic organizations with genuine roots in the society. Foreign assistance to domestic monitoring led to too many groups, diverted attention from important issues, and hampered the evolution of EMOs into sustainable grassroots organizations. Foreign organizations competed with each other and gave often conflicting advice, both to Indonesian EMOs and to foreign donors. Some foreign advisers offered advice that was simply inappropriate or misguided, often because they themselves lacked enough real experience.

Donors understandably wanted Indonesian monitoring groups to work together, in order to avoid duplication and to ensure broad, national coverage on election day. Paradoxically, however, the availability of significant funding and the plethora of international advisers tended in practice to discourage coordinated monitoring efforts.

There was considerable press coverage of donor contributions to the UNDP trust fund for the elections, which would support election monitoring and voter education as well as election administration, which left the impression for many of the availability of virtually unlimited sums. In early March, for example, the UNDP adviser (later government minister) Erna Witoelar told the *Jakarta Post* that the UNDP had received $30 million for the election commission and "the monitoring programs run by civil society before, during and after the election."[9] Two weeks later, the *Jakarta Post* reported that Japan would provide an additional $31 million to the UNDP to support the elections, including "various poll monitoring activities."[10] The paper reported on March 25 that the UNDP had already collected "more than $40 million" of an expected $100 million from seven countries, and a UNDP press release in early April reported that $9 million had been earmarked for monitoring.[11] The UNDP ultimately received $59 million from sixteen countries and the European Union for its election program, and the United States provided another $30 million in parallel funding to the process.[12]

The well-known availability of donor funding created incentives for new groups to be formed. By dangling the possibility of funding, aid donors seeking to support monitoring groups unwittingly created incentives that balkanized existing monitoring groups and encouraged the proliferation of new ones. Mulyana Kusumah of KIPP charged, "With the current phenomenon of so many NGOs suddenly emerging and striving to get grants for the election process, poll monitoring activities have become a kind of commodity."[13] Speaking privately some time later, other national election-monitoring leaders questioned the motives of many of the people who put themselves forward as local EMO organizers, even within their own groups. Many seemed to have organized local election-monitoring chapters because there was money involved. In the first half of 1999, establishing an election-monitoring organization in Indonesia became an entrepreneurial activity akin to starting a "dot-com" business during the Internet stock boom in the United States.

The perception that significant funding was available also distorted the plans of the larger, more established EMOs. In the months leading up to the elections, despite advice to the contrary, each of the major groups planned overly ambitious, unrealistic monitoring efforts, and each requested significant—arguably excessive—financial support. Many apparently sought to use the opportunity to build their own infrastructures of computers and communications equipment.

The amount of money available specifically for domestic monitoring was indeed considerable. Monitoring was the second largest component of the UNDP program (after election administration). The UNDP provided nearly $10 million to five national EMOs, including $2.9 million to the Rectors' Forum, $2.5 million to KIPP, $2.4 million to UNFREL, $1.4 million to JAMPPI (the Community Network of Election Monitors), and $245,000 to the trade union SBSI. It also funded technical advisers, including the British firm Electoral Reform International Services, and set aside 5 percent of available funds for monitoring efforts of provincial voter education groups.[14] Meanwhile, USAID and American organizations with USAID money provided funding for a number of EMOs. KIPP, for example, received 3.3 billion rupiah (approximately $381,000) directly from USAID and another 556 million rupiah (approximately $63,000) from the Asia Foundation.[15]

Although the amount of funding was great, much of it was programmed very late in the process, which complicated coordination among foreign donors and advisers. For example, a lone representative of the European Commission visited Jakarta for about a week in February 1999, six months after the national planning meeting on election monitoring and only four months before election day, to determine how EU funds for the election should be spent. On the basis of this cursory assessment, the European Commission decided to provide €7 million (about $7.2 million as of election day) to support NGOs engaged in voter education, election monitoring, and similar activities through the UNDP trust fund.[16] Such projects were politically safe, but by then they were or should have been well under way, not to mention sufficiently well funded. The European Commission itself later concluded, "the technical assistance team arrived too late to have the expected input."[17]

Most donors failed to make funds available to the UNDP until shortly before or even after the elections. Indeed, four countries contributed a total of $4.6 million within five days of election day, the European Union deposited $5.0 million actually on election day, and an additional $8.2 million was not received until after election day.[18] In other words, 43 percent of the pledged funds were not received by election week; and 32 percent were not transferred until election day or later. Moreover, the UNDP reports, "there was often uncertainty about what financial resources were available at times when disbursements had to proceed quickly."[19]

Accordingly, the UNDP and other donors disbursed much of the funding for election monitoring just days before the polling, which impeded planning, caused considerable logistical difficulties, and made it difficult for the funds to be well used. This also meant, of course, that such funds did not support preelection monitoring or pollwatcher training.

Concerns about financial controls and accountability also contributed to the delay in the availability of funding. There were legitimate reasons for concern about the financial accountability of the Indonesian groups. Because KIPP had failed to fully account for the grant it had received in 1997, NDI advised USAID and UNDP to carefully review the organization's accounting capabilities and financial controls before providing funds. Being new, many other EMOs had no track record or experience at all with handling foreign funds. To their credit, USAID and UNDP invested heavily in assessing and trying to improve the financial management and reporting capabilities of their grantees. The UNDP assigned financial professionals to most EMOs to oversee financial reporting,[20] and USAID conducted capacity audits and provided training on accounting systems to its grantees. But because the amounts involved were so great, the groups were so new, and the time was so short, the problem was significant.

The availability of substantial funds also distracted EMO organizers from important issues. Leaders of EMOs spent enormous energy on funding proposals, budgets, and other money issues rather than on election-monitoring strategies and tactics. Just three weeks before election day, for example, provincial and national leaders of UNFREL met for three days at the University of Indonesia in Depok, outside Jakarta. Yet in this final national planning meeting, they found themselves mired in debates over budgets and money. Rather than discussing such pressing organizational and substantive issues as volunteer recruitment and training, communications systems, election-day deployment plans, or local political conditions, the young leaders from around the country spent much of the time complaining about inadequate budgets for provincial chapters, criticizing the headquarters for hoarding the available money, and even, in a few cases, making apparently specious allegations that funds had been diverted. The university faculty members who had founded this national monitoring network out of idealistic notions of building a more democratic political system and providing a vehicle for university students to constructively channel their political energies admitted their frustration.

The availability of foreign funding for the remuneration of pollwatchers sometimes had anomalous consequences. In North Sumatra, for example, "volunteers" for the Rectors' Forum, who were generally university students, received not insignificant "per diem" allowances of 20,000 rupiah a day (about $2.50), double the amount provided to regular polling station officials, who were typically much older teachers or other civil servants.[21] Even given that polling officials were often already government employees and pollwatcher per diems had to cover transportation costs, it was odd that the student observers—who were supposed to be volunteer activists for democracy—were better compensated for their polling day efforts than the officials.

In these ways, the considerable funds available actually hampered the development of networks of politically active citizens. "If you hire one hundred thousand people," reflected one Indonesian activist sometime later, "they don't really volunteer in a real sense." Although acknowledging that some EMOs were well organized and made an important contribution, this unaffiliated observer argued that "without money to Rectors' Forum or to UNFREL from USAID and UNDP, nothing would have happened." (He dismissed KIPP altogether because it "didn't really do good monitoring.")

After the elections, in part because of their frustration with managing financial relationships with provincial chapters, the principal national leaders of UNFREL decided to disband the network and found a new, Jakarta-based policy research and advocacy organization called the Center for Electoral Reform (CETRO). Though CETRO has been extremely influential and effective in advancing the agenda for electoral and constitutional reform in the ongoing political debate since 1999, it is unfortunate that its leaders found it untenable to manage a national political organization committed to democratic elections and reform. UNFREL did not lead, as it might have, to a sustainable, grassroots political movement for democratic reform.

The foreign money subtly changed the whole purpose of monitoring. Instead of building a stronger Indonesian constituency for democracy, the domestic monitoring effort became all about getting information specified by representatives of the international community, particularly about election day.

Ineffective Coordination among International Organizations and Donors

Although UNDP provided a vehicle for bilateral donors to coordinate their substantial funding, the coordination of policy on NGO support was less effective. Moreover, although bilateral and multilateral donors did attempt to coordinate their programs with each other, nongovernmental democracy organizations from abroad were not initially part of these efforts. The UNDP did not convene broad coordination meetings until about March 1999, long after many international organizations had set their plans and begun their programs. Moreover, even though USAID convened regular coordination meetings among its American and Indonesian partners and grantees, even organizations funded by USAID failed to communicate their plans effectively to each other.

The donors were surprisingly reluctant to listen to experts. Funders, for example, considered large budget requests from EMOs, without asking the opinion of foreign EMO advisers, who often believed that the budgets were excessive. Donors also supported new monitoring groups, regardless whether those new groups had committed themselves to professionalism. Against the advice of at least some foreign experts, donors funded groups that had no plans to train their pollwatchers and demonstrated no commitment to political neutrality.

In part, this failure to seek or heed advice was because donor officials without much experience in political development found it tough to sift through conflicting advice from ostensible experts, and international democracy organizations sometimes promoted competing programs. For example, as is discussed in chapter 13, though USAID agreed to fund the Rectors' Forum PVT, based on advice from NDI, it also decided to fund a separate parallel tabulation advocated by a media adviser from the International Foundation for Election Systems. (USAID funds also supported attempts by other EMOs to collect comprehensive results.) The decision to support competing parallel counts reflected, among other things, an apparent lack of confidence in statistics experts from NDI and the Rectors' Forum. UNDP was even more reluctant to accept the statistically based PVT.

Some smaller donors played favorites, which helped some latecomers and others without much demonstrated commitment or professionalism to get a share of the available funding. Shortly before election day, for example, without any effort to join or coordinate with existing monitoring groups or to train its members as election monitors, the JPPR network of religious organizations that had been conducting voter education programs received funding for election monitoring. Despite prior assurances that the JPPR was an education network only and would not become a monitoring organization, its foreign sponsor agreed to fund monitoring activities. This meant that there was no meaningful opportunity to try to integrate the JPPR with existing monitoring networks or to ensure that its volunteers were well trained and committed to neutrality.

Worse, one international organization inexplicably sided with a dissident faction of UNFREL, led by University of Indonesia faculty member M. Fakhri, which proclaimed that it was the real UNFREL. The faction, which became known as UNFREL-Depok (after the location of its headquarters), sought to gain control, in effect, of the UNFREL name and all the presumptive funding and credibility that came with it. The new faction circulated unsubstantiated, apparently baseless allegations of corruption against principal UNFREL organizers, while proclaiming its "good intention—a pure student's movement—which will monitor the election in Indonesia."[22] For a time, this one donor organization offered advice and encouragement to UNFREL-Depok. Neither the international organization's representative nor the self-proclaimed leaders of UNFREL-Depok had any previous experience with election monitoring.

Although any of the major EMOs might have been accused of bias against the previously established political order, the newer EMOs seemed to have especially close ties to particular political parties. The JPPR emerged from Islamic organizations that also supported particular political parties. JAMPPI drew on an Islamic students' organization. SBSI spawned a political party as well as a monitoring network. Though each publicly committed itself to neutrality,[23] these close ties to political parties made them less than ideal as nonpartisan monitoring groups. But the pull of money gave them an incentive to fit that bill.

Several smaller donors funded newly established election-monitoring groups in the provinces with little demonstrated monitoring expertise. The availability of funding for groups formed outside Jakarta, on the well-intentioned idea that political activity outside the nation's capital was worthy of support, encouraged the creation of autonomous regional groups. By having their own separate identity, these regional groups could attract funds and international attention and thus had no incentive to join existing national networks.

Nor can indiscriminate funding of new groups, regardless of their motivations or professionalism, be justified on grounds of encouraging participation. If election monitoring is worth doing, it is worth doing well. Participation motivated by availability of funding without any expectation of professionalism in return is not sustainable, and thus ultimately not a significant step toward greater democracy.

Poor Advice from International Organizations and Donors

Even as they inadvertently encouraged separate efforts around the country, some donors tried to force the national-level domestic monitoring groups to join forces in ways that were neither effective nor sensitive to local institutional prerogatives and personalities. Donors insisted, for example, that EMOs divide responsibilities for election-day pollwatching along geographical lines before they could receive funding. This unfortunately forced the EMOs to negotiate which organization's pollwatchers would be dispatched to various locations. This was really a waste of time because there was no obvious or logical way to divide responsibilities by province, for all major groups had potential volunteers in virtually all the country's then 27 provinces if not in most of the 327 districts. Dividing responsibility for which organization's pollwatchers would go to which of the country's more than 300,000 polling stations was exceedingly time consuming, not to mention almost impossible to do much in advance of election day. As one EMO leader put it later, the coordination of deployment on election day proved "impossible," because the organizations involved were "very different." This meant that, despite donor efforts, there was duplication in many polling places and no coverage in others.

The EMOs would have been better served by dividing the constituencies that they sought to mobilize or the specific monitoring activities they planned to carry out. Thus, for example, some groups planned to recruit students while others drew on NGO, professional, or religious networks. One group might concentrate on verifying the accuracy of the vote tabulation process, while another might monitor preelection complaints or the adequacy of the legal framework.

In any event, beginning in January, long before donors introduced a focus on dividing election-day responsibilities, the three principal national monitoring organizations were already working together on a common effort, using the media and the Internet, to recruit volunteers and to educate the broader public about the importance of election monitoring. They also had already agreed to develop common monitoring materials, such as training materials and polling day checklists, and had committed to coordinate their election-day deployments.

The joint volunteer recruitment effort included a national media campaign to encourage citizens to join election-monitoring efforts in their regions and to raise awareness about the election and the role of monitors. NDI sponsored the production of advertisements for television, radio, newspapers, and the Internet. The ads included information on how to volunteer to be a pollwatcher and included the names, addresses, and logos of the three national monitoring groups.

Other advice from international sources similarly diverted Indonesian groups from the task of building their own political movement. Rather than allowing the Indonesian groups to set their own priorities and make their own mistakes, some donors pushed much too hard to expand the numbers of pollwatchers and to standardize the election-monitoring methodology without regard to inherent trade-offs. Supported by other donors, the UNDP expressly and more or less arbitrarily set a goal of two pollwatchers at every polling place, which motivated it late in the game to fund several new EMOs.[24] The excessive focus on how many polling stations would be covered on election day tended to overshadow concerns about the training, quality, or motivations of observers and overemphasized the administration of the process on election day to the detriment of efforts to monitor other parts of the process.

International actors also pushed to standardize the information to be collected on polling day. Although it was a good idea in theory to have all pollwatchers collect the same information, donor insistence on the use of a common reporting form to gather comparable information ended up forcing each group to use a lowest-common-denominator checklist. Even as seven leading EMOs sought to develop a common form, one foreign adviser developed his own and proposed that all EMOs use it. The pollwatching questionnaire was unwieldy, for it contained forty-nine separate questions and also called for observers to record, among other things, the results for forty-eight political parties in elections at three separate levels. This made it somewhat difficult for less-than-fully-trained volunteers to fill out quickly and generated an unworkable amount of data to be processed at EMO head-quarters. Given the foreign expert's association with donors, many organizations, themselves dependent on donor funds, felt compelled to use the form. An Indonesian EMO leader later complained that this international organization "came at the last minute and forced us to use their book."

KIPP nevertheless decided not to use the donor-backed checklist, which meant the information it collected could not be compared easily to information from other groups. UNFREL chose to have its volunteers also fill out a separate, shorter form in addition to the common form, which greatly complicated its monitoring program. Thus, the effort to get all groups to use a common election-day form was ultimately unsuccessful, and information collected by different groups was not comparable.

All this further hampered efforts to knit together one or more national networks that could both develop a national picture of the elections and sustain future nationwide advocacy of democracy and good government.

The use of this donor-imposed fact-finding process hampered other goals, such as the rapid communication and analysis of observations and organizational innovation. Such donor requirements failed to take proper account of trade-offs between values and goals that were sometimes in tension. A somewhat smaller, better trained, and more focused domestic election-monitoring effort might have been a more sustainable expression of Indonesian commitment to the principle of democratic elections and thus a more meaningful contribution to Indonesian democracy in the long run.

Collaboration between International and Domestic Observers

In addition to Indonesian pollwatchers, a number of countries, intergovernmental organizations, and international NGOs collectively sent 579 accredited international observers to the Indonesian elections. Former president Carter and the Carter Center joined NDI in organizing a comprehensive international monitoring program beginning with a preelection assessment of the election framework in January. As part of that program, the NDI–Carter Center election mission comprised approximately 100 observers. The European Union fielded 30 long-term observers and 64 short-term observers along with 31 bilateral observers sent by European countries. NAMFREL (100 observers) and the Asian Network for Free Elections (69 observers) also sent large groups for election day.[25]

Although international observers in many countries have tended to discount domestic monitors or have stolen the limelight from them, international observers in Indonesia largely developed constructive relationships with domestic monitoring groups. Building on the relationships between domestic EMOs and their foreign donors and advisers, international election observers from Australia, the Asian Network for Free Elections, the European Union, NDI and the Carter Center, and elsewhere worked closely with, and relied on, domestic partners.

Such collaboration is essential for well-informed international observation because of the difficulty of observing an election in a country of Indonesia's size and geography. Even a group of 100 observers can witness directly only a tiny fraction of the polling places. Domestic organizations obviously can organize more meaningful monitoring of events on election day because they can mobilize in large numbers, speak local languages, and are familiar with the political culture and context. Though international observers cannot effectively cover the country, they can rely upon domestic monitors for perspective and information.

NDI and the Carter Center developed a particularly close working relationship with the Rectors' Forum, NDI's partner in conducting a statistically based parallel vote tabulation. In the weeks before the election, NDI–Carter Center staff members visited the Rectors' Forum offices in many parts of the country to discuss election-day activities and assess preparations for the PVT. The Rectors' Forum volunteers also served as advisers and interpreters for NDI–Carter Center observers around the country before and during the elections, and NDI–Carter Center international observers teamed on election day with local Rectors' Forum representatives to visit polling stations, including polling stations included in the PVT sample. President Carter and other delegation leaders also visited the Rectors' Forum PVT Center in Jakarta before, on, and after election day to discuss the PVT and collect information on the election results. In this way, the PVT results and information from the Rectors' Forum from around the country helped to inform Carter's election assessment.

The NDI–Carter Center mission reinforced the critical role of domestic election-monitoring organizations in the transition to democracy in Indonesia, both by working closely with leading EMOs and by publicly highlighting in its statements and meetings the role and findings of EMOs. In their preliminary statement, the two American democracy groups urged attention to the statements of domestic EMOs in the weeks after the election. In their partnership with the Rectors' Forum, NDI and the Carter Center consciously attempted to establish a precedent for more profound and meaningful collaboration with domestic EMOs. Among other things, NDI and the Carter Center called attention to the existence of the Rectors' Forum PVT, which provided some reassurance that any potential manipulation of the vote tabulation process would be detected and thus may have deterred manipulation of the vote count. This became increasingly important over subsequent weeks as the vote count was delayed.

Calibrating International Assessments in Response to Domestic Concerns

Upon the close of polling, well before the process was completed, international observers and foreign leaders hailed the elections. On election night, the chief EU observer, the British diplomat John Gwyn Morgan, announced the EU team's conclusion that "the conduct of the election in Indonesia was sufficiently free and transparent to guarantee a voting result which will reflect the democratic will of the Indonesian people."[26] New Zealand foreign affairs minister Don McKinnon said the elections were "free, fair and peaceful." Australian prime minister John Howard called the poll "remarkable" and "a real celebration of democracy" and added, "instead of people whingeing [complaining] about it being slow, why don't they applaud the fact that after 40 years of a pretty authoritarian government, a very authoritarian government, we now have democracy, or the beginnings of democracy, in Indonesia."[27]

Former U.S. president Carter likewise appeared ready to declare that democracy had come to Indonesia. Carter sought to tell the world how much Indonesia had changed. Even before the elections, he emphasized how open and competitive the process was. After visiting polling stations on election day and spending a number of hours the following day listening to the reports of other international observers who had returned from all over the country, he was enthusiastic and was prepared to offer a considerably upbeat assessment. "So far, this has been an excellent election," he told reporters.[28]

The leaders of several domestic monitoring groups, however, found Carter's early press statements too positive. They worried that the ballot count might still be manipulated or that forces opposed to reform might yet otherwise interfere or refuse to respect the results. UNFREL's Smita Noto-susanto appealed publicly to Carter and other observers not to come to final conclusions too hastily:

> The actual voting process . . . is only the beginning of the whole election process. The vote counting [is] not finished yet, and we still have to determine whether the counting process is totally transparent, totally monitored, and free from intimidation. . . . We still have no report on that level of the election yet, and I might want to ask foreign observers to also refrain from making such an evaluation.[29]

In an open letter, UNFREL coordinator Mulya Lubis appealed to Carter to "refrain from making a general evaluation that the entire process has been free and fair, due to the fact that the process is still in progress." The letter pointed out that the "counting and tabulation process [which] is still being undertaken . . . is the part of the election that most Indonesians are most concerned about." The letter closed with the admonition that "as you depart from our country we would like to ask you to bear in mind that what will happen in the next few weeks will have an enormous impact on the lives of the Indonesian people who will have to live with the consequences."[30]

Only hours before he would address a huge press conference, Carter agreed to a last-minute meeting with leaders of Indonesian monitoring groups. UNFREL and Rectors' Forum representatives told the former U.S. president frankly that they believed that a premature certification of the election might make Indonesians somewhat less able to expose any subsequent manipulation. Impressed by their directness and professionalism, Carter listened. He went before the television cameras shortly thereafter with a somewhat different message than he had previously planned. Though he praised the process to that point and expressed optimism that it would turn out well, he emphasized the need to pay attention in the days ahead as the votes were counted, the president was selected, and the new government took power. "Until some allegations have been made that have some foundation I think we need to believe that the process is orderly," he said. But he added, "Election monitors will have to be vigilant from now on. I don't think we'll know until November, when a final choice for President is made, whether democracy has indeed come to Indonesia in its fullest form."[31]

The approach of foreign donors and advisers in Indonesia was not unusual. Assistance to domestic election monitoring and other foreign support for civil society in developing countries often suffers these kinds of weaknesses, and in many countries the consequences of a narrow focus on elections as ends rather than means has been much more serious. Until they better understand the trade-offs and tensions involved, aid providers and democracy experts will continue to miss opportunities to have a more profound impact.

Ironically, for all its problems, the international effort to support domestic election monitoring in Indonesia could—and did—reasonably claim success. Indonesian EMOs achieved their political goals by gaining broad international support, establishing an undeniable role for civil society organizations in the election process, helping to build trust in the process, and involving hundreds of thousands of people in political activity. But at the same time, mistakes were made and opportunities were missed. Such mistakes and missed opportunities over time, in Indonesia and other emerging democracies, threaten real, if subtle, harm to the cause of democratization and the effectiveness of democracy promotion. To make genuine contributions to sustainable democratic development, the democracy-promotion community must look more critically even at its ostensible success stories.

Chapter 13

Verifying the Vote Count: Quick Counts, Parallel Tabulations, and Exit Polls in Macedonia and Indonesia

It's not the voting that's democracy; it's the counting.

—Tom Stoppard[1]

Concern about possible manipulation of election results is a classic characteristic of transitional or postconflict environments. This kind of fraud previously was common, as in the Philippines in 1986, Mexico in 1988, and Panama in 1989, but today the sophistication of vote-count verification techniques makes it possible for monitors to detect any significant cheating in the aggregation of election results. After monitoring the actual ballot count at the polling stations, election-monitoring groups routinely verify independently the official aggregation of these results on the basis of a comprehensive assessment or by analyzing random samples of observed ballot counts.

Yet, despite more than fifteen years of experience with vote-count verification methods, international organizations and election experts sometimes still sharply disagree about which techniques are appropriate in a given set of circumstances. Duplication and conflicting expert opinions have beset some verification efforts. These disputes waste resources and, worse, can cause confusion in tense political situations. Conflicting programs and professional differences of opinion risk doing serious damage to the ability of international and domestic monitors to verify the vote count effectively in transitional and postconflict environments.

This chapter reviews and assesses vote-count verification techniques, including statistically based parallel vote tabulations (PVTs), quick counts, exit polls, and comprehensive counts. Using case studies from Macedonia and Indonesia, I argue that quick counts or PVTs based on statistically significant samples are generally more reliable and appropriate in transitional and postconflict elections. Exit polls or comprehensive tabulations, although they may serve very particular objectives in carefully chosen situations, are generally a bad idea for such elections. Beyond these important but somewhat technical questions, the unresolved debate about vote-count verification reveals troubling competition among election-monitoring organizations and disagreement among experts that has confused donors and hampered the larger cause of supporting democratic elections and democratization.

Quick Counts and PVTs

Effective means to verify election results are essential to successful election monitoring. Without such means, as Jimmy Carter explains,

> there's no way to ascertain the accuracy of the vote count. You can detect fraud [at polling places], and you can see if people have actually gone to the polls or if they've been intimidated. You can examine the voting list in advance, . . . see if the laws are accurate and that sort of thing. But there's no way to tell the results of an election, whether they're honest or they're manipulated by the ruling party without some sort of [parallel] vote tabulation or PVT.[2]

A PVT or quick count can deter or detect fraud in the aggregation (adding up or "tabulation") of local election results after the ballots are counted at polling stations. Like opinion research or exit polls, PVTs can use statistical sampling to project results or to assess the accuracy of reported results, within statistically significant margins of error. Thus, its organizers can verify the integrity of the tabulation of results. A PVT differs from opinion research or an exit poll in that it is based on actual results, as counted by election officials and witnessed by monitors, rather than on what individual voters report to interviewers about how they voted. In addition, because they are designed to project results as quickly as possible, exit polls are generally conducted based on historical experience using much smaller sample sizes than do PVTs.

Quick counts and PVTs have their roots in the pioneering work of the National Citizens' Movement for Free Elections (NAMFREL) in the Philippines in the mid-1980s. Though not definitive, NAMFREL's quick count, as we have seen, exposed the Ferdinand Marcos regime's vote tabulation fraud in the critical 1986 presidential election.

For the 1988 plebiscite in Chile on President Augusto Pinochet's continued tenure, the nongovernmental Committee for Free Elections added an important innovation to the quick-count methodology. With advice from Glenn Cowan and Larry Garber of the National Democratic Institute for International Affairs (NDI), the Chilean group decided that, rather than trying to obtain comprehensive results from the entire country, it would instead use random sampling. An independent count drawn from a statistically significant sample would be both faster and more accurate than an attempt to obtain the results from all 22,000 polling places in the country. An analysis of a representative sample of 10 percent of those polling stations revealed well in advance of the official results that the "No" vote had won handily. This preempted the regime from attempting to declare victory on the basis of a doctored vote count.

Garber and Cowan coined the term "parallel vote tabulation" in lieu of "quick count," which they thought better reserved for an independent verification designed to project results quickly rather than to verify the results later. (A quick count, in this lexicon, could be either comprehensive or based on samples.) They chose the term "parallel" to distinguish the operation from the official vote tabulation conducted by relevant authorities. They settled on the word "tabulation" to refer to the aggregation or summing of ballots rather than "count" to avoid any connotation of reviewing and recording individual ballots.[3] Nevertheless, many donors, advisers, and observers continue to use the term "quick count" regardless whether the objective of the exercise is to project results quickly or verify them later and regardless whether the analysis is based on comprehensive or sample-based data.[4]

After the pioneering quick counts or PVTs in the Philippines and Chile, election monitors in other countries recognized the importance of having effective means to deter or detect ballot count fraud in transitional elections by independently collecting election results to compare them with official results. PVTs based on sampling made pivotal contributions, often in tense circumstances, to important transitional elections in several different ways.

Some PVTs exposed vote-count fraud. In Panama in 1989, for example, a church laity group conducted a PVT, based on a representative, statistically significant sample of polling stations, that definitively revealed the regime's attempt at fraud in the vote count. As was discussed in chapter 5, Carter drew on the results of this PVT to expose and denounce the vote-count fraud. In Serbia in 2000, "Without a massive monitoring operation, and an equally massive parallel vote count," concluded one journalist, "[the] effort to unseat Milosevic would almost certainly have failed."[5] Agreed another analyst, "The parallel vote count may have been far more effective than NATO's air campaign in toppling the Serbian strongman."[6]

In other countries, rather than exposing attempted fraud as in the Philippines, Panama, and Serbia, the findings of domestic monitors deterred it by convincing authoritarian incumbents to accept electoral defeats. This in turn facilitated peaceful transitions of power. The results of PVTs in Nicaragua in 1990, as in Chile two years before, provided early, independent information that the ruling party had been defeated. This allowed Carter to move quickly to facilitate a peaceful transition of power. Likewise, in Zambia in 1991, although the election was not close, a PVT provided a basis for Carter to urge President Kenneth Kaunda to accept the verdict of the electorate when Kaunda lost after twenty-seven years in office.

PVTs also served to verify legitimate victories by incumbent governments in polarized political environments, which helped convince opposition forces in several countries to accept bitterly disappointing election results and defuse the possibility of violence. For Bulgaria's first postcommunist, multiparty elections in 1990, the Bulgarian Association for Free Elections conducted a parallel tabulation that confirmed the victory by the incumbent former communist party. This convinced many urban supporters of the opposition that the victory was not the result of vote-count fraud. A PVT in Paraguay in 1989 similarly confirmed an incumbent victory in the face of opposition suspicions of electoral fraud.

International and multilateral organizations have joined domestic monitoring groups in conducting PVTs. For Nicaragua's transitional election, the United Nations and the Organization of American States conducted independent quick counts of the election results, the first time for either organization.[7] In Zambia in 1991, the Carter Center and NDI conducted the PVT themselves for the first time.

Domestic and international observers, working together, have had so much success detecting vote tabulation fraud that the problem has been substantially reduced, even in countries with regimes willing to do almost anything to remain in power. Where effective monitoring is permitted, rulers willing to cheat have learned to focus on other parts of the process, particularly in the preelection period, that can be more easily manipulated and for which domestic and international monitors have yet to develop effective deterrents. At the same time, to continue to deter or be able to detect manipulation of the vote-counting process, election-monitoring organizations must maintain the discipline of rigorous, robust verification of election results.

Statistically Based and Comprehensive Tabulations

Despite their success in dozens of countries since 1988, statistically based PVTs have in recent years drawn fire from some in the international community. Foreign aid officials and technical advisers in some countries have questioned the feasibility and accuracy of a vote-count verification exercise based on statistical sampling. They also have expressed concern that a separate, unofficial vote projection that diverges from the official count might foment postelection unrest (a concern that would apply equally to comprehensive counts and exit polls).

Suspicion among national election authorities and political elites about the purposes and methodology of PVTs is hardly surprising. Even if they have good intentions, the election authorities rarely like the idea of independent organizations, whether domestic or foreign, threatening to second guess the official results or offering their own reports of the election outcome, and the authorities often oppose the release of early results as a challenge to their authority. Moreover, foreign involvement in such exercises can hurt national pride because it implies that the national authorities require international oversight.

For their part, international donors or advisers might object that an independent vote tabulation is a waste of time because they believe fraud (or at least the type of fraud that PVTs can detect, namely, fraud in the process of aggregating results) is unlikely. Alternatively, they might lack confidence in the organizations conducting the PVT exercise, because of doubts about either the group's administrative capabilities or judgment as to how and when to report the results. These concerns may be reasonable but are rarely sufficient to outweigh the arguments in favor of a PVT.

On occasion, national authorities and international actors have objected to sample-based PVTs because they do not understand or accept the validity of the underlying statistics, even though the use of statistical sampling in polling and research is widely accepted among social scientists, media organizations, public opinion researchers, and politicians around the world.

Skepticism about statistics occasionally even has motivated foreign donors and advisers to prefer the vastly more expensive and daunting task of attempting to conduct a comprehensive parallel canvass of results.

A comprehensive independent tabulation can serve constructive purposes, such as providing an organizational focus for volunteers, deterring vote-count fraud, and providing a basis for later investigation of claims of cheating in particular localities. But it generally cannot provide a basis for an assessment of the accuracy of the official vote count, for two important reasons.

First, monitors can never collect results from all the polling stations in a country, even under the best of circumstances. It is generally more difficult to obtain results from more rural or harder-to-reach areas, which might have different voting patterns than other parts of the country. Because the missing data are not random, it is not possible, if the election is close, for a comprehensive tabulation to assess whether the reported vote count is accurate. Even collection of a large percentage of the results will be statistically skewed and potentially misleading.

Second, civic groups using a comprehensive methodology generally cannot process and interpret such an enormous amount of data in a reasonable time after the elections. This is enough of a challenge for the government and the election authorities, with all the resources and authority they command. It is generally impossible for a civil society network of volunteers organized shortly before election day.

Thus, effective vote-count verification necessarily must rely on methods that use statistical sampling. Both sample-based PVTs and exit polls rely on such sampling. Yet in most internationally monitored elections, as the experience in Macedonia in 2002 demonstrates, exit polls are not the answer either.

Limitations of Exit Polls in Transitional or Postconflict Elections: The Experience of Macedonia

Although some donors and foreign advisers have criticized sample-based PVTs for drawing conclusions from too little data, a few others apparently believe, in contrast, that it is possible to draw conclusions from even smaller samples based on voter interviews as opposed to actual results. Yet exit polls can be problematic and controversial even in the United States, where they have a long history. First, they may not be reliable in extremely close contests. In Florida in 2000, for example, television networks relying on exit polls first forecast an Al Gore victory and then reversed this judgment a few hours later, only to conclude finally that they did not actually know the results. There also continues to be concern in U.S. elections that the early release of exit polls will influence those yet to vote.

The experience of an exit poll in Macedonia in 2002 suggests even greater reasons for caution about this technique in transitional or postconflict elections. On September 15, 2002, Macedonia held parliamentary elections in the uncertain political climate lingering from brief but violent ethnic clashes the year before. Sixteen hours after the polls closed, before the national election authorities or other Macedonian organizations could release even preliminary election results, the International Republican Institute (IRI) announced the results of its own exit poll, which it touted as "an important step forward in the country's democratic development."[8] Yet the exit poll was inappropriate and almost certainly flawed.

First, the validity of any exit poll relies on the willingness of voters to tell a stranger how they voted. In Macedonia, violence, intimidation, and extreme nationalist rhetoric had plagued the preelection environment. In the three weeks before election day, two police officers were murdered, security forces physically blocked opposition supporters from entering the capital of Skopje, and party rallies had to be canceled for fear of violence. The interior minister publicly threatened to arrest the leader of the most popular ethnic Albanian party, and many politicians and voters expressed fears about special security forces and paramilitaries. In part because of pervasive intimidation, despite the country's population of only 2 million, the international community mobilized the largest traditional international election observation effort ever, including about 800 observers from the Organization for Security and Cooperation in Europe.

Even the Macedonian election law reflected concerns about intimidation and protecting the secrecy of the ballot. It provided, "Nobody is allowed to call the voter to account for his voting, or ask him to say for whom he has voted or why he has not voted."[9] Though this provision seemed to prohibit the exit poll unambiguously, organizers nevertheless requested and received a ruling from the election commission that allowed them to go ahead.

In an effort to encourage voters to respond to the exit survey and to mitigate the effect of intimidation, pollsters asked voters to fill out a facsimile ballot and deposit it in something resembling a ballot box. This provided no real guarantee of anonymity, however, and could not be expected to reassure anxious citizens who might be reluctant to participate. Ironically, in an oth-

erwise glowing postelection statement, the IRI observer delegation's principal negative finding about the election was interference with the organization's own researchers. "There were a number of incidents of harassment of
interviewers for IRI's exit poll," the observers reported. "In several cases par-
tisans physically attacked exit poll workers or otherwise disrupted proceedings."[10] A domestic Macedonian monitoring organization reported that
many of the complaints it received were actually about the exit poll.

Second, the exit poll's methodology was unsound. Even had the voters
felt safe to express their political preferences, a valid exit poll relies statistically on analysis of past voting patterns that identify key predictive
precincts. Researchers in Macedonia, however, did not have previous
polling station-level results to guide their choice of representative polling
stations. Rather than accept that this made the exercise problematic, they
based the exit poll, instead, on the highly dubious statistical assumption that
polling stations with average *turnout* rates in a previous election would be
predictive of current choices. There was no basis for this assumption.

The sponsors of the exit poll also erred in announcing their results on a
nationwide basis—results dutifully reported in the local and international
media. These results were essentially meaningless, as the only outcomes
that mattered were party results from each of the six parliamentary districts.

Researchers made other judgments not consistent with sound statistics.
At a press conference on September 16 in Skopje, researchers reported they
had conducted approximately 9,400 interviews (later reported as 9,321) and
that the poll's margin of error was 6 percentage points. But because there is
no statistical theory that would generate such a high margin of error on such
a large sample size, this implied that the pollsters had made a subjective assessment of the quality of their own data. Researchers later defended the
methodology on the ground that the exit poll's results matched the official
ones reasonably closely. In an analysis of exit poll results published later,
the polling firm that oversaw the project argued, "There are some elements
of the survey that are somewhat deficient, but can be overlooked because of
the poll's performance and the general lack of 'reliable' census and electoral history data." The polling firm admitted that results projected by the
exit poll varied from actual reported results within electoral districts by up
to 9 percentage points but argued, "Considering that on average exit polls
in the United States have a variance of 4% to 6% the performance of this
exit poll is exceptionally good."[11] Yet a margin of error of 9 percentage
points is very large; it would not allow an assessment of the integrity of reported results if the margin of victory for one candidate or party were less

than 18 percentage points. This usually would be insufficient to the purpose of checking the validity of the reported results.

The exit poll in Macedonia was unnecessary and detracted from a more legitimate parallel tabulation. Citizens Organization MOST, a nonpartisan Macedonian monitoring group, conducted a sample-based PVT and reported these findings for all six of the country's electoral districts. Their data provided a genuine basis by which to assess the credibility of the official count. Nevertheless, the media and international community initially ignored these valid data because a foreign group had provided the first public numbers.

Well-conceived exit polls can be a valuable tool for projecting election results in developed societies with a history of fair elections and where citizens have reasonable confidence in their own safety and security. Assuming that they are accurate, polls in any society—whether conducted on election day or at other times—can provide valuable information about voter motivations and preferences. Exit polls, however, are generally not a good idea in typical transitional or postconflict environments. Referring to elections in developing countries, former president Carter stated recently,

> In general, I think exit polls are worthless because if there is a dominant or abusive ruling party then the people are intimidated. . . . Even if they can give a private interview with an exit poller, they're reluctant to give their true feelings. "I voted against the ruling party." That would be very difficult for some people to make, particularly if it's the first election they've had, and they don't have a sense a sense of security.[12]

Concludes Carter, "An independent tabulation of the votes actually cast in a relatively small number of a representative polling places or mesas, which is a PVT, that's the best way to do it."[13]

As they design vote-count verification strategies, international election observers must also keep in mind their overriding purpose: to support democratization. The interest of international observers, diplomats, and others in early information about the results of transitional elections is not unreasonable. In polarized situations, international observers may be able to use such information to verify official results, preempt fraud, or encourage acceptance of the results. As we have seen, Carter and other observers have used results of parallel counts for these purposes in a number of elections. This was a valid reason why observers were interested in Macedonia in the results of exit polls, assuming those polls were accurate.

At the same time, international actors should resist the temptation to scoop local actors and gain publicity by making unofficial or polling results public. Even if the results of an exit poll or PVT are accurate, this does not require international observers to go public even before election authorities or domestic organizations do so. Public preemption of national actors generally is unnecessary to deter or expose vote-count fraud and does little to build local capacity.

Having compared comprehensive counts, PVTs, quick counts, and exit polls, and considered the problems with an exit poll in Macedonia, I now will examine conflicting efforts to verify the election results in Indonesia in 1999. Though the transitional election was in many ways successful, foreign donors and advisers failed to build confidence in the vote aggregation process. Collectively, they advocated and supported both comprehensive and sample-based vote-count verification, neither of which prevented the ballot tabulation process from becoming the most contentious part of the whole election process. And, apparently for the first time, some donors and technical advisers actually questioned the intellectual basis of a statistically based PVT.

Monitoring the Vote Count in Indonesia:
Too Much of a Good Thing

On election night, Monday, June 7, 1999, hundreds of journalists, diplomats, international election observers, and Indonesian political elites jammed into the marble lobby and large, ornate ballrooms of the five-star Aryaduta Hotel in central Jakarta. They came to watch the unofficial election returns collected by the Joint Operations and Media Center (JOMC). But the JOMC had virtually no election results to report. As of 7:45 the next morning, the JOMC was reporting the results of just 226,906 votes out of more than 100 million cast, or less than ¼ of 1 percent.[14] This number was meaningless. Over the next few days, election results trickled in. Even by Thursday, three days after the elections, the JOMC could report only 7.8 percent of the vote count,[15] still too small to support any conclusions about the outcome of the elections.

Milling about the lobby of the Aryaduta Hotel on election night and in the following days, hundreds of journalists and observers, politicians and diplomats, Indonesians and foreigners waited in frustration, trading rumors and sharing suspicions about why the election results were taking so long. "Two days after the national election," reported the *New York Times,* "the talk of the town [Jakarta] Wednesday was not about who won or lost but about the fact that nobody had any idea of the outcome."[16]

The Joint Operations and Media Center

Ironically, although international funders and advisers had anticipated the problems with the vote count, they actually contributed to the confusion. One of several internationally supported schemes to build confidence in the vote count, the JOMC raised expectations that it failed to meet and ended up competing with other unofficial and quasi-official vote tabulations.

The JOMC was a parallel process to collect and report comprehensive election results in real time. It was established before the elections on behalf of the Indonesian election commission with funding and technical assistance from American, Australian, and Japanese organizations and the UN Development Program (UNDP). With great fanfares of publicity in the last weeks before election day, the JOMC's organizers had promised to provide "early/indicative results for the election" by quickly collecting actual results from each of Indonesia's 3,800 subdistricts, spread across the country's 6,000 inhabited islands. At a grand, ceremonial unveiling of the JOMC three weeks before election day, one of the international organizers had invited journalists and observers to come to the JOMC on election night, promising a "facility . . . capable of reporting reliable results of the elections at the earliest practical moment."[17] The UNDP resident representative lauded plans for the JOMC because it would bring "together modern technology and cross-country expertise to enhance the transparency and openness of the electoral process." In remarks that unfortunately would prove prescient, he added "I cannot underline enough the importance of swift and transparent reporting of results for enhancing the credibility of the process."[18] A series of international experts, diplomats, and Indonesian officials spoke enthusiastically of the large numbers of fax machines, computers, cell phones, data entry operators, and other elements of the elaborate infrastructure being built to rapidly collect the results.

Organizers of the JOMC promised that, thanks to the $2 million operation, Indonesians would start getting results within hours after the close of polls. The results would be continuously updated, fed directly to the national television networks, and released immediately via the Internet. The JOMC's spokesperson told the media he hoped that 50 percent of the results would be known by Tuesday evening, the day after polling. The aim, he said, was "to try to get reliable information as early as possible to the people so they will know what's going on, because in the past there has been so much suspicion about results being changed."[19]

Nevertheless, on election night and even over the next several days, only a small fraction of the country's subdistricts reported information to the JOMC. To make matters worse, election officials were simultaneously reporting separate unofficial results—collected at the village level rather than from the subdistricts and reported through a nationwide computer system made available by Bank Negara Indonesia and Bank Rakyat Indonesia (which became known as the "bank system"). This meant that the Indonesian election authorities were in effect competing with the JOMC, ostensibly their own unofficial reporting mechanism. Not only were the data extremely sparse, but there were actually two different quasi-official systems reporting inconsistent numbers.

The incomplete and inconsistent information caused increasing anxiety. When television stations aired returns the day after the elections showing the former ruling party, Golkar, with the lead, telephoned calls demanding details poured in.[20] While Indonesians waited, many worried that the slow process provided an opportunity for fraud. "If it is taking so much time," said Laksamana Sukardi, a key adviser to opposition leader Megawati, "I am worried about some kind of manipulation."[21]

At packed press conferences several times a day for the few days after the polls closed, Election Commission Chair Rudini offered little explanation. "The election commission is opting for accuracy rather than speed," he said, and blamed "the delay in the process of the vote counting at the village level." The JOMC spokesperson found "nothing sinister"; contradicting his earlier public statements about rapid results, he claimed, "We didn't anticipate any meaningful result for at least 10 days, and we're within that schedule."[22]

The incredibly drawn-out count, the lack of meaningful results, the competing sets of numbers (both ostensibly from the election authorities), the failure to provide any real explanation for the delay, and the widespread mistrust combined to heighten suspicions and concerns. Rather than reassuring Indonesians and the international community about the integrity of the vote count, the expensive JOMC operation had actually undermined confidence by raising expectations that it could not meet.

The Controversy over the Rectors' Forum PVT

It appears that the idea for the JOMC emerged, at least in part, from the competition between international advisers in Jakarta. One group of international advisers and funders—principally the United States–based International Foundation for Election Systems (IFES) and the Australian Election Commission, with funding from the UNDP and the U.S. Agency for International Development (USAID)—probably conceived the JOMC initially in part to counter the PVT recommended by another, the United States–based NDI. In the months before the elections, NDI worked with the Rectors' Forum, a university-based, Indonesian election-monitoring network, to develop and implement a PVT. Skepticism about the PVT's validity and feasibility initially held sway within important parts of the diplomatic and foreign assistance community.

When the PVT was proposed for Indonesia in early 1999, several international experts in Jakarta questioned the feasibility and accuracy of a vote-count verification exercise based on statistical sampling. Many Indonesian election and government officials, a number of American and Australian technical advisers, visiting representatives from NAMFREL, and some at USAID lined up against the PVT. An advisory committee of prominent Indonesian civic leaders—who had little or no experience with technical election-monitoring issues—advised the UNDP not to fund it. On the basis of this advice, the UNDP initially opposed any PVT based on statistical samples.

NDI and the Rectors' Forum representatives in Jakarta argued, however, that objections to an independent verification of the vote tabulation in Indonesia failed to take into account that there was already substantial mistrust of the official vote count and that the parties unhappy with the election results were likely to attack the fairness of the process after the fact. It was inevitable that losing parties would claim that the process had been unfair or that cheating had been permitted. Moreover, the complex, hybrid election system that Indonesia had invented for the 1999 election—the details of which remained unclear even on election day—was, predictably, a source of confusion and dissatisfaction. For Indonesian authorities, with the assistance of the international community, to conduct well-organized, honest elections would not have been enough. Given concerns about manipulation of the vote count in previous Indonesian elections, not to mention elections in other transition environments, verification of the vote count would be an essential part of an effective domestic election-monitoring effort. Assuming an honest count, independent vote tabulation could help satisfy all parties that the results were accurate.

There was no good reason to oppose an independent vote tabulation in Indonesia. Certainly, past experience provided reason for worry about the possibility of vote-count fraud. Indeed, PVT advocates ultimately were proved correct about the potential for problems in 1999, as many smaller parties alleged tabulation fraud in the weeks following election day. These (largely unsupported) allegations delayed certification of the results for weeks and seriously threatened the credibility and acceptability of the entire process.

In addition, even though Indonesian election authorities and their international advisers doubted the capacity of an Indonesian civic network to organize such a complex project or to handle the information responsibly, they would have ample opportunities to influence and check the PVT. The organizers from the Rectors' Forum clearly brought professionalism and seriousness of purpose to the task, and, in NDI, the Rectors' Forum had the assistance of an experienced international organization. Moreover, though election officials might oppose the release of early results as a challenge to their authority, the Rectors' Forum was eager to cooperate and willing to consult with the authorities before announcing its results after the elections.

Many of the PVT's critics lacked a sound understanding of statistics. Some claimed, for example, that random statistical sampling would not work in the absence of extensive baseline demographic data or could not be used for proportional representation elections. These claims were incorrect.

The UNDP's international experts and Indonesian advisers recommended that donors support only verification programs that did not rely on statistics. Instead, they insisted that any independent vote tabulation be comprehensive.

Representatives of NAMFREL sought to work with Indonesian partners to conduct a comprehensive quick count. NAMFREL's founder, José Concepción, traveled to Jakarta twice in the first few months of 1999. NAMFREL—justifiably proud of its many accomplishments, even though its pivotal 1986 quick count in the Philippines had collected results from only about 70 percent of the polling stations—did not acknowledge the methodological limitations of comprehensive parallel tabulations.[23]

But Indonesia's size and geography and the complexity of its election system made collection by civic groups of results from the entire country essentially impossible. In Indonesia, as in the Philippines, it was more difficult to get results from rural communities and from smaller, outlying islands, which might have different voting patterns than other parts of the country. A comprehensive quick count would be even more difficult in Indonesia's 1999 elections, because there were forty-eight parties vying for seats in separate elections in twenty-seven different provinces rather than one national race with just two competitors.[24] Significant gaps in the results that could be collected were inevitable.

Moreover, monitors would not be able to process and interpret the enormous amount of data in a reasonable time after the elections. The quick count would need to add up and tabulate results from 300 polling stations for each of forty-eight parties.[25] In addition, this was not just one national race; each province was a separate electoral district. Even with a large number of computers and data-entry operators, the volume of data that would be generated would take more than a few days to process.

By early 1999, Jimmy Carter also was planning to monitor the Indonesian elections. When he learned of the opposition to a statistically based PVT, he fired off a letter of complaint to Gus Speth, then administrator of the UNDP, in New York. Though UNDP officials in Jakarta were initially annoyed that Carter and Speth back in the United States had been drawn into a technical disagreement in the field, NDI subsequently persuaded them of the importance of the statistically based PVT. By spring, the substantial opposition of the UNDP and others in the diplomatic community had largely waned.

Meanwhile, USAID agreed to fund the sample-based PVT planned by the Rectors' Forum. The UNDP agreed not to oppose the PVT, and UNDP representatives began to run interference for the PVT organizers with Indonesian government and election officials. Nevertheless, while the Rectors' Forum PVT went ahead as planned, other donors and democracy organizations planned and funded their own parallel tabulation of election results: the JOMC.

Ultimately, there were at least five independent tabulations in Indonesia, each of which used a different method: the JOMC, which collected and added up results from subdistricts; the Rectors' Forum, which analyzed random samples of results from polling stations (as further explained below); the election commission's separate, unofficial "bank system," which collected and added up results from village election authorities; a comprehensive tabulation of polling station results in selected locations conducted by the nonpartisan election-monitoring organization Komisi Independen Pemantau Pemilu (KIPP); and a tabulation by the state news agency Antara of unofficial results reported at the provincial level.

The Project Design and Implementation of the Rectors' Forum PVT

With only a few months to prepare, the organizers of any unofficial vote count in Indonesia confronted enormous obstacles. There were more than

117 million registered voters and forty-eight political parties (as compared with the three permitted in previous elections). The election system was new and extremely complex, and reliable information was lacking about the number and location of polling stations, spread across thousands of islands. Most important, there was not one election but many; there were actually distinct elections for the national legislature in each of Indonesia's twenty-seven provinces. Each required a separate, statistically significant parallel tabulation. Indeed, the PVT for Indonesia's elections would be the largest, most complex independent vote tabulation yet undertaken anywhere in the world.

The Rectors' Forum drew on its strong base at the prestigious Bandung Institute of Technology, a national network of statisticians and mathematicians, and a force of about 9,000 student volunteers. Several faculty members led the effort. Sudjana Sapi'ie, the former rector of the Bandung Institute of Technology, served as the group's executive director. Dumaria Tampubolon, a young female mathematics professor at the institute, directed the PVT project. Robert Sembiring, another faculty member, served as the lead statistician.

An international team of parallel tabulation experts assembled by NDI advised the Rectors' Forum on the PVT. They included Glenn Cowan, an NDI senior adviser who had helped pioneer sample-based PVTs; Neil Nevitte, a professor of political science from the University of Toronto who had also worked on the design and analysis of PVTs throughout the world; and Lawrence Lachmansingh, NDI's resident adviser on domestic election monitoring in Jakarta and a former executive director of the Electoral Assistance Bureau, an extremely successful election-monitoring group in his native Guyana.

Because they lacked sufficient baseline demographic and electoral data, the Rectors' Forum team of experts adopted straight random sampling rather than attempting to stratify the sample. Stratification allows statistically significant results to be determined from relatively small samples, which generally can be collected more quickly than random ones. Given a big enough sample, the randomness provides information within given margins of error and with given levels of confidence. The absence of previous meaningful election results, the huge number of parties competing, and the complicated election process made stratification complicated at best.

For each province, the organizers drew a sample of approximately 300 polling stations, for a total of approximately 9,000 polling stations across the country.[26] With polling stations averaging about 300 voters, the total sample size in each province would number approximately 90,000 voters. This would allow the analysis in each province, according to the science of statistics, to have a margin of error of 1.5 percentage points.[27]

The Rectors' Forum recruited and trained approximately 600 volunteers in each province to witness the ballot count and collect the results. After monitoring the balloting and ballot count at the polling site, the volunteers sent the results by telephone or facsimile to a central data-processing center in Jakarta and to "node" universities in each province.[28] Each team was assigned a security code, which permitted verification that the data belonged in the sample.

Before the election, the organizers considered when and how they would announce the results of the PVT. Once they had definitive results, they could decide to make those results public, which would preempt the official count. Alternatively, they might share their findings first with election authorities and other selected audiences, such as diplomats, aid officials, international advisers, and election observers, such as Jimmy Carter. They tentatively decided to wait until the election commission announced its own results, but they also agreed to remain flexible so they could assess and respond most effectively to the situation after election day.

The Rectors' Forum tried to publicize its work in order to inform the public, the parties, and the international community. Preelection media coverage of a PVT is particularly important for deterring fraud and building confidence. A PVT can only deter vote manipulation if anyone tempted to cheat is aware of it, and it can build confidence only to the extent parties and the public know about it. Despite some press coverage, in retrospect it was clear that this coverage was wholly inadequate.

The Rectors' Forum PVT: Technical Success, Political Failure

The PVT plan worked extremely well. In the first few days after the elections, even as the JOMC and the election authorities were reporting essentially meaningless results, the Rectors' Forum had obtained meaningful election results for most of the country. Ultimately, the PVT organizers successfully obtained reliable data from twenty-three of the twenty-seven provinces. As is discussed below, the parallel tabulation was remarkably consistent with the official count, which was not released until weeks later.

The reporting of the results, however, worked less well. Although the Rectors' Forum had the information everyone wanted—how well each party had done in the elections—few took note when the group made this information public. The organization's inadequate public relations and media strategy prevented the PVT from achieving its larger political goal, that of reassuring the parties and the public (not to mention the international community) that any fraud in the tabulation process would be detected. The Indonesian and international press reported the PVT results, but these results failed to reassure those worried about the integrity of the vote count.

After election day, the agonizingly slow official count and brewing controversy prompted the Rectors' Forum to announce its findings. On Thursday, June 10, three days after election day, a Rectors' Forum team of experts, including executive director Sapi'ie and project director Tampubolon, addressed a crowded press conference (held, ironically, at the JOMC at the Aryaduta Hotel). They spoke initially in Indonesian but, dissatisfied with the interpretation of this complicated subject, switched to English to explain their results more clearly to the foreign press and other representatives of the international community. These Indonesian academics-turned-political-organizers announced the definitive PVT results for the eleven provinces for which they had accumulated enough data by that point to allow a high degree of statistical confidence.[29]

Together, these eleven provinces encompassed about 152 million of the country's 209 million people, or about 73 percent of the population. At this point, the JOMC and unofficial election commission counts were still only able to report results from less than 10 percent of the electorate, still too small a sample from which to draw any conclusions.[30] The Rectors' Forum reported that its results had a 1.5 percent margin of error. The PVT showed the results for the largest fifteen parties.

At this point, four days after polling day, the JOMC was still reporting data for the country as a whole, not by province, even though the national numbers revealed relatively little about the election's outcome. There was no direct election for president. Only data reported by province had any real meaning, and the national aggregate numbers reported by the JOMC and the election commission, even if they had been complete, actually had little value.[31] The Rectors' Forum, in contrast, was reporting results by province. This made it possible to project how many seats each party had won in those provinces.

A week later, on June 18, 1999, the Rectors' Forum reported the results of nine more provinces, which together with results reported on June 10, made a total of twenty of the twenty-seven total provinces. Together, these twenty provinces encompassed about 193 million of the country's 209 million people, or 92 percent of the population.

The Rectors' Forum announced the completion of its projections from the PVT on July 2, 1999, still three weeks before the election commission finally released its own complete results. At that time, the Rectors' Forum was able to report statistically significant results for twenty-three provinces, representing 199 million people or 95 percent of the population.[32] This was an extraordinary accomplishment.

The Rectors' Forum was never able to obtain reliable results for four provinces—Aceh, East Timor, Irian Jaya (later called Papua), and East Kalimantan. In Aceh and East Timor, social and political unrest prevented collection of sufficient data to reach a statistically supportable PVT analysis. (East Timor voted less than three months later for independence from Indonesia in a United Nations–supervised referendum.) East Kalimantan and Irian Jaya had an unusually large number of virtually inaccessible polling stations, making it impossible for the volunteers to obtain enough information on local results. Together, these four provinces represented less than 5 percent of the Indonesian population. Given the time, resource, geographical, and other constraints, the inability to obtain statistically reliable results in these provinces was understandable and did not detract from the significance of the overall effort.

The results of the PVT in Indonesia provided strong statistical support for the provisional election results, which many small-party representatives on the election commission refused to certify, and thus discounted the possibility that any significant manipulation of the results occurred during aggregation and tabulation of vote tallies at the local, district, and provincial levels. The PVT had answered the key political questions of the immediate postelection period: how well each party had done and whether any fraud was possible during the drawn out tabulation process. Yet the PVT had failed to assuage concerns, perhaps because it was lost in the cacophony of reported numbers.

Controversy over Slow Tabulation of Ballots after the Election

In the days immediately following the election, while confusion reigned about what was happening with the vote count, the PVT organizers failed to explain the project well enough. At the postelection press conference to explain and report the results of the PVT, for example, the Rectors' Forum executive director Sapi'ie distracted attention from the PVT itself by promising that the group would dispatch monitors to districts all over the country to oversee the data entry process. The PVT, however, was a much more significant check on fraud in the tabulation process and thus actually made monitoring data entry unnecessary (although perhaps of symbolic value). And the Rectors' Forum statistician Sembiring seemed to express doubts about the project: "We've used relatively sophisticated equipment to conduct the monitoring and tabulation," he said. "Yet there have been some obstacles encountered in the process. I must say that I sympathize with the KPU [the election commission] for its slow tallying of poll results."[33]

The Rectors' Forum's international sponsors did not help much either. Asked at their postelection press conference about the possibility of vote-count fraud, NDI and Carter Center representatives offered assurances that such fraud could not go undetected but failed to mention the PVT.

As the process of completing the vote count dragged on for an incredible five weeks after election day, the slow pace continued to be a significant cause for concern. Internal conflicts within the election commission compounded the problem and began to erode that body's credibility.

Although it was important for the election commission to take the time necessary to produce credible results, the delay was not caused by an effort to increase the transparency and legitimacy of the results but rather by the dissatisfaction of certain parties with those results. A number of smaller parties, which did not stand to win seats according to the election results, made specious allegations of election problems and refused to certify the results. They treated the assessment and approval of the results as a bargaining chip to be traded for a future role in the political process.

The NDI–Carter Center monitoring team subsequently analyzed the provisional results and compared them with the PVT and other unofficial election results. On the basis of this analysis, on July 15–more than five weeks after the election but while the controversy dragged on—the NDI–Carter Center team endorsed the credibility of the results: "Fortunately, despite [some] problems, the delays do not appear to have been caused by nor have they created the opportunity for significant manipulation of the election results."[34]

The NDI analysis compared the preliminary results of the election committee for each of the country's provinces—which would become official upon certification by the election commission—with up to five independent, unofficial tabulations of results.[35] Because these data originated in various levels of the election administration, any material attempt to manipulate the tabulation as it progressed up the hierarchy after the elections would have been apparent. NDI concluded, "Significantly, the results of these various unofficial tabulations do not provide any evidence to support allegations of widespread or significant fraud or tampering designed to benefit any particular party or parties."[36]

The operational success of the PVT for Indonesia's 1999 elections sets an important precedent. It proved that a PVT based on statistical sampling for a legislative election in a large, diverse country could provide reliable, meaningful results. It also demonstrated the value of using university networks, with their ready source of statisticians, mathematicians, and social scientists with relevant expertise, as well as a large and accessible pool of potential volunteers.

The unofficial tabulation of results of the JOMC, the comprehensive tabulation attempted by KIPP and NAMFREL, and the PVT of the Rectors' Forum all failed to achieve their principal goal of reassuring the public and the parties about the integrity of the election results. In part, this was because each of these efforts was flawed: The organizers of the JOMC did not anticipate how slow, incomplete, and, thus, disconcerting their reporting would be; the advocates of a comprehensive parallel tabulation failed to realize that such a task was essentially impossible; and the PVT's designers failed to adequately explain their methodology, either before or after the elections. Even more troubling, the competition among the international groups undercut the contributions of all of them.

Choosing Appropriate Tools

Through their disagreements in Indonesia and Macedonia, and perhaps elsewhere, international experts have joined an important debate about the appropriateness and effectiveness of different kinds of vote-count verification techniques. Comprehensive tabulations, which attempt to aggregate 100 percent of the locally counted results, and exit polls, which draw inferences from very small, targeted samples of voter responses, both can provide reliable, valuable information in appropriate circumstances. Statistically based PVTs—which draw on much larger sample sizes than exit polls but, like comprehensive counts, are based on actual results—are generally more reliable in transitional societies lacking a history of successful polling or a fully stable, secure political environment.

International organizations, donors, and advisers share the same goals for elections in new and emerging democracies, but yet they sometimes, as in Indonesia and Macedonia, work at cross purposes. It is critically important for the relevant international organizations and experts to carefully consider the issues involved in designing, implementing, and interpreting vote-count verification exercises and to attempt to agree on which vote-count verification techniques are appropriate in which circumstances. Only such agreement will prevent duplication and a waste of resources, fundamentally conflicting advice, and the potential for confusion that might add to uncertainty in tense political situations.

Since the late 1980s, international and domestic election monitors have developed effective techniques to detect manipulation of election results after the initial count. But to make a real contribution to combating election fraud, PVTs and similar verification efforts must be publicly explained and well understood by authorities and international advisers. Legitimate concerns must be better addressed, and international actors in the democracy field have to try to learn from and cooperate with each other.

Part IV

Toward More Meaningful International Election Monitoring

Chapter 14

Toward More Meaningful International Election Monitoring

Even as democratic legitimacy has been established or restored in many countries over the last two decades, it is threatened today by a new danger, which I call "fig-leaf democracy."

—UN secretary general Kofi Annan[1]

Even as the Third Wave of democracy and the end of the Cold War led at first to a kind of euphoria about the prospects for further democratization, many now worry that the global wave of democracy has lost momentum and that democratic advances could be reversed. Just forty-seven of the eighty-one countries that have embarked on democratic transitions since 1980 have become full democracies.[2] Democratic transitions in many countries have stalled, authoritarian regimes in other countries seem to have successfully dug in, and democratic gains seem ever harder to achieve. These profound challenges provide the context for democracy promotion at the beginning of the new millennium.

Since the end of the Cold War, in dozens of countries around the world, the international community has expected elections to initiate or consolidate transitions to democracy or to play a key role under internationally negotiated peace agreements in resolving major conflicts. Elections have played a major role in the Third Wave of democratization, as multiparty elections have helped usher in political transitions, accountable government, and more open politics. Democratic elections have become an increasingly critical requirement for international legitimacy.

At the same time, the extent and influence of election monitoring, as part of a broader democracy-promotion industry, has exploded. Governments and intergovernmental organizations have provided increasingly significant resources from foreign assistance budgets to election monitoring. Multilateral organizations and Western nongovernmental organizations alike engage deeply in transitional and postconflict elections across the globe. At the same time, national civic organizations and citizen networks all over the world have mobilized to monitor watershed elections in their own countries, often with substantial foreign support.

International election monitoring has gained a role in international relations and a foothold in the international consciousness. International news reports on elections in developing countries, for example, invariably cite the comments and assessments of election observers. Makers of foreign policy and aid officials from developed countries and multilateral organizations put great stock in assessments of election monitors. International aid programs often provide generous support for domestic election monitoring.

Certainly, election monitoring has contributed significantly to the democratic cause in the world. Not least, it has reinforced universal aspirations for democracy and has helped ensure better elections in dozens of countries. Sophisticated election-monitoring techniques have made it considerably more difficult for antidemocratic governments to manipulate election rules, electoral administration, or vote counts. The broad and growing international commitment to democratic elections, the existence and sophistication of domestic monitoring groups, the involvement of international observers, and the use of more sophisticated monitoring methodologies and techniques (e.g., statistically valid parallel vote tabulations) have combined to make blatant fraud on election day almost obsolete in internationally monitored elections. A comprehensive international election-monitoring methodology seeks to promote the integrity of the elections, to build public confidence and participation in electoral processes, and to complement and encourage domestic observation efforts.

The emergence of domestic and international election observation as an international norm has also raised the diplomatic and other costs for governments who refuse to allow genuine, multiparty elections. Wide acceptance of the practice of international election observation has contributed to revised conceptions of national sovereignty and has helped to overcome nationalistic objections to outside efforts in support of human rights and democracy. The involvement of multilateral organizations in election monitoring has helped them to strengthen their commitment to promoting genuine democracy among member states. Meanwhile, nonpartisan domestic election-monitoring groups in developing countries have not only deterred fraud and improved public confidence in important elections but have also encouraged citizen involvement in political life more generally.

Despite these meaningful accomplishments, international election monitoring has created its own problems, unintended consequences, and missed opportunities. Many in the international community are unfamiliar with the origins or considerable evolution of election monitoring, even as they accord it considerable respect and influence. Though its emergence of as an international norm is welcome and positive, election monitoring has grown in part because it is understandable and visible. Multilateral organizations and nongovernmental organizations based in developed countries have sometimes jumped on the bandwagon of international election observation rather than search for newer, potentially more effective ways to help. Election-monitoring programs can be dangerously superficial, which sometimes leads the international community to accept the legitimacy of highly flawed processes and hinders the search for enforceable, universal standards. Bilateral and multilateral donors have sometimes made funds available for domestic election monitoring without due consideration of goals or consequences, even as they often fail to sustain support for civil society programs after transition elections. Election monitoring and other election-related support can also divert funds from other democratic development programs.

Improving the Methodologies and Professionalism of International Election Observers

Policymakers, journalists, scholars, and others often support or rely on the assessments of election observers without really understanding their methodologies, interests, capabilities, and limitations. As this book has discussed, many international observation efforts neglect past experience, and those funding and relying on election assessments have difficulty determining which programs to support and which assessments to trust. Some observers base conclusions on the startlingly cursory fact-finding efforts, as observers offer public assessments even before ballots are counted based on the personal observations of a few outsiders who make brief visits to a handful of polling places. National and international media, the international community, and election observers themselves put inordinate focus on "bottom-line" judgments about whether elections can be judged "free and fair." A narrow focus—on election administration or election day, for example—allows autocratic regimes to manipulate other parts of the process.

Unfortunately, many international observers still put undue emphasis on election administration on polling day, while political context and post-election developments are largely ignored.

Likewise, motivations and potential conflicts of interest are little noted. Some outside groups have partisan interests in electoral outcomes or pre-conceived notions of who would win a fair contest. Observers from inter-governmental organizations and diplomatic missions often have mandates, constraints, and interests that differ substantially from those of nongovern-mental organizations. In Cambodia, for example, international observers split on how to assess the 1998 elections in part because they saw their own roles differently and had different interests and motivations. The experience of Cambodia has also demonstrated the challenges posed by well-administered elections in highly flawed environments.

Donors, multilateral organizations, and international democracy groups can and should improve their election-monitoring programs. As the cases and discussions of policy in this book illustrate, six basic types of im-provements and reforms must be undertaken if election monitoring is to re-tain its value.

First, donors and democracy organizations should continue to review their criteria for whether to support or monitor potentially flawed elections, as in Cambodia, Peru, and Zimbabwe in recent years. International organi-zations seeking to set standards have rightly worried that the mere presence of international observers can appear as an endorsement, and they should worry as well about how foreign technical assistance or funding for elec-tions can also provide unearned legitimacy. Yet suggestions that foreign groups sit out elections that seem unlikely to meet all international norms are naive and fail to take account of legitimate purposes served by engage-ment even in flawed processes. Such support may help make concrete, meaningful improvements, or it might help protect the safety or political op-portunities of courageous opposition politicians or civic activists. It is per-haps more realistic to encourage a broader focus and more comprehensive methodology, which might reduce the tendency of election-day observers and the media to draw unduly positive conclusions.

Second, brazen manipulation of the monitoring process itself cannot go unchallenged if international monitoring is to retain its independence and credibility. When authorities such as those in Zimbabwe decide to exclude serious observers from certain countries or to limit the access of observers to parts of the process, the credibility of the monitoring itself is called into question. Host governments should provide or deny accreditation to foreign observers according to a clearly defined and nondiscriminatory set of standards. International monitoring groups must be able to determine the size, composition, and time frame of their own monitoring teams. They must also have access to all parts of the process and all levels of the election administration.

Third, experience has offered lessons about how international groups can avoid duplication and mitigate the adverse effects of competition among them. A greater emphasis on long-term monitoring and support for domestic observers in lieu of election-day observers would help reduce these problems. Several Western democracy organizations have recognized they no longer add value by organizing observers for most elections, and the United Nations and European Union have appropriately decided to refer requests for observers to other multilateral organizations in many circumstances. In any event, the international community should recognize the difficulties and drawbacks of joint international observation, whether organized under the auspices of the United Nations or another intergovernmental organization. Though coordination among international observer groups, as with donor programs in general, is essential, such coordination should not become an excuse for downplaying serious concerns or "least-common-denominator" assessments. A centralized approach to the promotion of pluralism has its own serious shortcomings.

Fourth, international organizations should continue to seek a more effective, consistent methodology for observation. Election observers should continue to review and improve their methodologies, and they should embrace better techniques, such as enhanced long-term monitoring and statistically based qualitative monitoring. They should move their focus toward endemic problems, such as vote buying and other serious violations of campaign finance rules.

Fifth, donors, diplomats, and democracy organizations must also continue efforts to increase the professionalism of election-monitoring efforts. Among other things, they should reexamine and rearticulate guidelines and a code of conduct for international observers.

Sixth, to be effective in their quest to expand democracy throughout the world, advocates must continue to shore up the international consensus on universal democratic principles and on the importance of democracy promotion. All elections must be judged honestly, by the same internationally recognized standards. In addition to fair balloting and counting, there must be opportunities for political parties to compete, reasonably equitable access to the news media, an impartial election administration, freedom from political intimidation, and prompt and just resolution of election-related grievances. The democracy industry needs to translate the emerging international consensus on these standards for democratic elections into a more effective, realistic monitoring methodology.

Improving International Support for Nonpartisan Domestic Monitoring

As the pioneering domestic election-monitoring effort in the Philippines in the mid-1980s demonstrates, domestic election-monitoring groups can improve the quality of election processes, deter or expose fraud, and increase the chances that losers will accept election results. Perhaps more important, however, domestic election monitoring can energize citizen involvement, empower nongovernmental organizations, and transform public attitudes toward national politics. The local organizations and networks that are created to monitor elections often go on to promote democracy in other ways, by fighting corruption, monitoring government performance, or engaging in civic education.

The international community's newfound support for national election monitoring is encouraging, but it has had its own unintended consequences. External support for domestic organizations runs the risk that foreigners will set the agenda, which may leave organizations and networks created for elections unsustainable thereafter. An excessive focus on election-day pollwatching and too much foreign money can actually hurt efforts to promote voluntary public participation and sustainable political action.

The June 1999 elections in Indonesia, which marked a critically important test for the political transition in that country, demonstrated some of the pitfalls for foreign donors that seek to support domestic monitoring. International funding and technical assistance for national election-monitoring organizations helped to ensure that election-day pollwatching was extraordinarily extensive, but the large sums of money and excessive focus on election day meant that the opportunity to build sustainable networks and democratic habits was largely missed.

It is critically important for supporters of democratic development to increase awareness of these opportunities to establish new democratic norms and empower citizens through domestic election monitoring. Moral support is at least as important as material support, and donors and international democracy promoters should consider the longer-term implications of their programs. Donors should ask themselves whether their support for domestic monitoring contributes domestic political development or is solely designed to acquire information for the diplomatic community.

Toward Best Practices

Former U.S. president Jimmy Carter has set the standard for other international election observers. During the past fifteen years, since he discovered the potential of international election monitoring, Carter has mediated election rules, focused on preelection issues, studied verification techniques, and supported domestic monitoring. He has focused attention where it belongs: on the long-term process of building democracy and the local groups that make it work.

The Organization for Security and Cooperation in Europe and the European Union have articulated and largely implemented an improved long-term monitoring methodology. All the leading intergovernmental organizations have also acknowledged the importance of domestic monitoring. Some American nongovernmental democracy organizations have moved beyond international election observation in favor of broader international monitoring, assistance to domestic monitoring, and other democratic development programs.

With attention to the lessons from experience, donors, diplomats, and democracy-assistance organizations together can overcome many of the ills that beset international support for democratic elections. Shifting attention from election day to the months before and after voters go to the polls already has broad acceptance within the democracy-promotion community. The challenge now is to make that shift a practical reality. Such a shift would underscore the broader point that genuine democratization takes time and that those who are sincere in their efforts to help must make a long-term commitment.

To continue to make a contribution, election monitoring will have to adjust to new challenges. Qualitative monitoring and statistical methods can make election-day monitoring and vote-count verification more effective and definitive, which can mitigate the problem that many monitoring organizations face in addressing ambiguous situations. As other problems transcend the significance of election administration and counting in many elections, resources and attention should move toward the more effective monitoring of the broader election environment, including the rules, the media, the composition of the election authorities, and the extent of intimidation of candidates, parties, and citizens. There is a great need for more information, for example, about why voters make the choices they do in semiauthoritarian environments. In addition, to be genuinely effective, democracy groups need to develop the means to monitor campaign and political finances and to advocate necessary reforms.

Elections in transition environments can provide significant new opportunities for citizen involvement in public affairs, for challenging old assumptions about political power, and for establishing new legal frameworks and new precedents for freedom of expression and association. Election monitoring, by both national and international groups, should be a means to this end. Democratic development programs must seek to help local democratic activists become continuing players with a stake in their country's future.

In the last decades of the twentieth century, democracy established itself as the world's dominant political ideal. Yet much of the world's population has yet to enjoy democratic rights, and the commitment of many ostensibly democratic countries remains open to question. To address that continuing challenge, the international community must maintain its commitment to genuinely universal democratic principles. As part of that commitment, more effective, rigorous, and principled election monitoring can make a more significant contribution to the global democratic cause.

Appendix

Elections and Election Monitoring in Newly Democratic and Semiauthoritarian Countries

Country or Territory	Freedom House Rating	Type of Election	Election Date	Election Date—Subsequent Round(s)	International Observers Present?	Selected Organizations	UN Involvement?	Domestic EMOs Present?	Observers' Assessment
Europe and the Former Soviet Union									
Albania	DEM	Parliamentary	June 24, 2001	July 8, 21, and 29 and August 19, 2001	Yes	OSCE		Yes	Positive
Albania		Parliamentary	June 29, 1997	July 6, 1997	Yes	OSCE		Yes	Mixed
Albania		Parliamentary	May 26, 1996	June 2, and 16, 1996	Yes	OSCE, EU	Declined observers	Yes	Negative
Albania		Parliamentary	July 26, 1992		Yes	CoE	TA	Yes	
Armenia	DEM	Parliamentary	May 30, 1999		Yes	OSCE	TA	Yes	Mixed
Armenia		Presidential	March 16, 1998	May 30, 1998	Yes	OSCE	TA, declined observers	Yes/No	Negative
Armenia		Presidential	September 22, 1996		Yes	OSCE	Declined observers	Yes/No	Negative
Armenia		Legislative	July 5, 1995	July 19, 1995	Yes	OSCE, UN	C&S		Negative
Armenia		Presidential	September 1, 1991		No?				Negative
Bosnia	P	Presidential and parliamentary	October 5, 2002		Yes	OSCE, CoE, EP		Yes	Positive
Bosnia		Parliamentary	November 11, 2000		Yes	CoE		Yes	
Bosnia		President	September 12–13, 1998		Yes	OSCE, CoE		Yes	Mixed
Bosnia		Presidential and parliamentary	September 14, 1996		Yes	OSCE, CoE		No	Mixed
Bulgaria	DEM	Parliamentary	June 17, 2001		Yes			Yes	
Bulgaria		Parliamentary	April 19, 1997		Yes	OSCE		Yes	Positive
Bulgaria		Presidential	O:tober 27, 1996	November 3, 1996	Yes	OSCE		Yes	Positive
Bulgaria		Parliamentary	December 18, 1994		Yes			Yes	
Bulgaria		Presidential	January 12, 1992	January 19, 1992	Yes			Yes	
Bulgaria		Parliamentary	October 13, 1991		Yes	OSCE, CoE		Yes	
Bulgaria		Presidential	June 10, 1990		Yes	CoE		Yes	

(continued)

311

Appendix *Continued*

Country or Territory	Freedom House Rating	Type of Election	Election Date	Election Date—Subsequent Round(s)	International Observers Present?	Selected Organizations	UN Involvement?	Domestic EMOs Present?	Observers' Assessment
Croatia	DEM	Presidential	January 24, 2000	February 7, 2000	Yes	OSCE		Yes	Positive
Croatia		Parliamentary	January 2–3, 2000		Yes	OSCE		Yes	Positive
Croatia		Parliamentary (chamber of counties)	June 15, 1997		Yes	OSCE		Yes/No	Negative
Croatia		General elections	April 17, 1997		Yes	OSCE, CoE	Yes	Yes/No	Mixed
Croatia		Parliamentary	October 29, 1995		Yes	Japan, OSCE			
Croatia		Presidential and parliamentary	August 2, 1992		Yes	Council of Europe			
Czech Republic	DEM	Parliamentary	June 14–15, 2002		Yes	OSCE		No	Positive
Czech Republic		Parliamentary	June 19–20, 1998		Yes	OSCE		No	Positive
Czech Republic		Parliamentary	May 31–June 1, 1996		Yes				Positive
Czechoslovakia		Parliamentary	June 5–6, 1992		Yes	NDI			Positive
Czechoslovakia		Parliamentary	June 8–9, 1990		Yes	CoE, NDI			Positive
Estonia	DEM	Parliamentary	March 7, 1999		Yes	OSCE		Yes	Positive
Estonia		Parliamentary	March 5, 1995		Yes	OSCE		Yes	Positive
Estonia		Presidential and parliamentary	September 20, 1992		Yes	OSCE, CoE			Positive
Georgia	DEM	Presidential	April 9, 2000		Yes	OSCE		Yes	Mixed
Georgia		Parliamentary	October 30, 1999	November 14, 1999	Yes	OSCE		Yes	Negative
Georgia		Presidential	November 5, 1995		Yes	OSCE, EU			Mixed
Georgia		Presidential	October 11, 1992		Yes	NDI, OSCE			Positive
Georgia		Presidential	May 26, 1991		No				
Hungary	DEM	Parliamentary	April 7, 2002	April 21, 2002	Yes	OSCE		No	
Hungary		Parliamentary	May 10, 1998	May 24, 1998	Yes	OSCE		No	Positive
Hungary		Parliamentary	May 8, 1994		Yes	OSCE	Declined observers	No	
Hungary		Parliamentary	March 25, 1990	April 8, 1990	Yes	CoE		No?	
Kyrgyz Republic	DEM	Presidential	October 29, 2000		Yes	OSCE		Yes	Negative
Kyrgyz Republic		Parliamentary	February 20, 2000	March 12, 2000	Yes	OSCE		Yes	Negative

Country	DEM	Type	Date		Monitored	Organizations	TA, C and S	Party only?	Mixed?
Kyrgyz Republic		Presidential	December 24, 1995		Yes	OSCE, UN			
Kyrgyz Republic		Parliamentary	February 5, 1995		Yes	UN, OSCE, EU			
Latvia	DEM	Parliamentary	October 5, 2002		Yes	OSCE, CoE	F&R		
Latvia		Parliamentary and referundum	October 3, 1998		Yes	OSCE		No	Positive
Latvia		Parliamentary	September 30-October 1, 1995		Yes	OSCE			Positive
Latvia		Parliamentary	June 5-6, 1993		Yes	OSCE, CoE			Positive
Lithuania	DEM	Parliamentary	October 8, 2000		No				
Lithuania		Presidential	December 21, 1997	January 4, 1998	Yes	OSCE		No	Positive
Lithuania		Parliamentary	October 20, 1996	November 10, 1996	Yes	OSCE			Positive
Lithuania		Presidential	February 15, 1993		No?				
Lithuania		Parliamentary	October 25, 1992	November 15, 1992	Yes	OSCE, CoE			
Macedonia	DEM	Parliamentary	September 15, 2002		Yes	OSCE, CoE		Yes	Mixed
Macedonia		Presidential	October 31, 1999	November 14 and December 5, 1999	Yes	OSCE, CoE			Positive
Macedonia		Parliamentary	October 18, 1998	November 1, 1998	Yes	OSCE, CoE	F&R		Positive
Macedonia		Presidential and parliamentary	October 16, 1994	October 30, 1994	Yes	OSCE, CoE			Positive
Moldova	DEM	Parliamentary	February 25, 2001		Yes	OSCE, CoE		Yes	Positive
Moldova		Parliamentary	March 22, 1998		Yes	OSCE, CoE		Yes	Positive
Moldova		Presidential	November 17, 1996	December 1, 1996	Yes	OSCE	Declined observers		Positive
Moldova		Parliamentary	February 27, 1994		Yes	UN, OSCE	F&R		
Moldova		Presidential	June 15, 1905		Yes	OSCE			
Poland	DEM	Presidential	October 8, 2000		No				
Poland		Parliamentary	September 21, 1997		No				
Poland		Presidential	November 5, 1995	November 19, 1995	No				
Poland		Parliamentary	October 1, 1991		Yes	OSCE, CoE			
Romania	DEM	Presidential	November 26, 2000	December 10, 2000	Yes	OSCE		Restricted	Positive
Romania		Presidential	November 3, 1996	November 17, 1996	Yes	OSCE		Restricted	Positive
Romania		Parliamentary	October 1, 1992		Yes	UN		Restricted	
Romania		Presidential	September 1, 1992		Yes	OSCE, CoE	F&R	Restricted	
Romania		Presidential	May 20, 1990		Yes	CoE, NDI	F&R		
Russia	DEM	Presidential	March 26, 2000		Yes	OSCE, CoE	TA	Yes	Positive

Country or Territory	Freedom House Rating	Type of Election	Election Date	Election Date—Subsequent Round(s)	International Observers Present?	Selected Organizations	UN Involvement?	Domestic EMOs Present?	Observers' Assessment
Russia		Parliamentary	December 19, 1999		Yes	OSCE, CoE, EP		Yes	Positive
Russia		Presidential	June 16, 1996	July 3, 1996	Yes	OSCE			Positive
Russia		Parliamentary and referundum	December 12, 1993		Yes	OSCE, CoE	F&R		Positive
Slovakia	DEM	Parliamentary	20–21-Sep-02		Yes	OSCE		Yes	Positive
Slovakia		Presidential	May 15, 1999	May 29, 1999	Yes	OSCE		Yes	Positive
Slovakia		Parliamentary	25–26-Sep-98		Yes	OSCE, CoE, EP		Restricted	Positive
Slovenia		Presidential	November 10, 2002		No				
Slovenia		Presidential	October 15, 2000		No				
Slovenia		Parliamentary	November 23, 1997		No				
Slovenia		Presidential	November 10, 1996		Yes				
Slovenia		Presidential	December 6, 1992		Yes	OSCE, CoE			
Ukraine	DEM	Presidential	March 31, 2002		Yes	CoE		Yes	Mixed
Ukraine		Presidential	October 31, 1999	November 14, 1999	Yes	OSCE, CoE		No	Negative
Ukraine		Parliamentary	March 29, 1998		Yes	OSCE, CoE		Yes	Negative
Ukraine		Presidential	June 26, 1994		Yes	OSCE, CoE	F&R	Yes	
Ukraine		Parliamentary	March 1, 1994		Yes	OSCE, CoE	F&R	Yes	
Montenegro	DEM	Parliamentary	October 20, 2002		Yes			Yes	
Montenegro		Parliamentary	April 22, 2001		Yes	OSCE, CoE		Yes	Positive
Serbia	DEM	Presidential	September 29, 2002		Yes			Yes	
Serbia		Parliamentary	December 23, 2000		Yes	OSCE, CoE		Yes	Positive
Azerbaijan	AR	Parliamentary	November 5, 2000	January 7, 2001	Yes	OSCE		Yes	Positive
Azerbaijan		Presidential	October 11, 1998		Yes	OSCE	Declined observers	Yes	Negative
Azerbaijan		Parliamentary and referundum	November 12, 1995		Yes	OSCE	C&S	Yes	Negative
Azerbaijan		Presidential	October 3, 1993		Yes				
Azerbaijan		Presidential	June 7, 1992		No		Declined observers		Negative

Country		Election	Date	Invited	IO	Other	Report	Assessment
Belarus	AR	Presidential	September 9, 2001	Yes (limited)			Yes	Negative
Belarus		Parliamentary	October 15, 2000	Yes	OSCE		Yes	Negative
Belarus		Parliamentary	November 29, 1995; December 10, 1995	Yes	OSCE			Negative
Belarus		Parliamentary	May 14, 1995; May 28, 1995	Yes	Norwegian Helsinki Commission			
Belarus	AR	Presidential	June 23, 1994	Yes (limited)	Yes	Declined observers		
German Democratic Republic	AR		March 18, 1990	Yes	Yes	CoE, NDI		
Kazakhstan	AR	Parliamentary	October 10, 1999; October 24, 1999	Yes	OSCE		Yes	Negative
Kazakhstan		Senatorial	September 17, 1999	Yes	OSCE			Mixed
Kazakhstan		Presidential	January 10, 1999	Yes	OSCE		Yes	Negative
Kazakhstan		Parliamentary	March 7, 1994	Yes	OSCE, OSCE PA, NDI			Negative
Tajikistan	RDP	Parliamentary	February 27, 2000; March 12, 2000	Yes	OSCE, UN	Yes	Yes	Negative
Tajikistan		Presidential	November 6, 1999	No	UN			
Tajikistan		Presidential	November 19, 1992					
Uzbekistan	AR	Presidential	January 9, 2000	Yes	OSCE		Yes	Negative
Uzbekistan		Parliamentary	December 5, 1999; December 15, 1999	Yes	OSCE	F&R		Negative
Uzbekistan		Parliamentary	December 25, 1994	Yes	UN			
Uzbekistan		Presidential	December 29, 1991	No				
Yugoslavia-Federal	AR	Presidential	September 24, 2000	No (barred)	OSCE		Yes/No	Negative
Yugoslavia-Federal		Parliamentary	November 3, 1996	No				
Montenegro	AR	Parliamentary	May 31, 1998	Yes	OSCE		Yes	Positive
Montenegro		Presidential	October 5, 1997; October 19, 1997	Yes	OSCE, EU		Yes	Positive
Serbia	AR	Presidential	December 7, 1997; December 21, 1997	Yes	OSCE	Yes	No	Negative
Serbia		Presidential (Rerun)	September 21, 1997; October 5, 1997	Yes	OSCE		No	Negative
Serbia		Presidential and parliamentary	December 20, 1992	Yes	OSCE		No	Negative

(continued)

315

Country or Territory	Freedom House Rating	Type of Election	Election Date	Election Date—Subsequent Round(s)	International Observers Present?	Selected Organizations	UN Involvement?	Domestic EMOs Present?	Observers' Assessment
Asia-Pacific									
Bangladesh	DEM	Parliamentary	October 1, 2001		Yes			Yes	Positive
Bangladesh		Parliamentary	June 12, 1996		Yes		TA	Yes	Positive
Bangladesh		Parliamentary	February 15, 1996		Yes			Yes	
Bangladesh		Parliamentary	February 27, 1991		Yes			Yes	Positive
East Timor	P	Presidential	April 14, 2002		Yes	EU		Yes	Positive
Fiji	DEM	Parliamentary	August 25, 2001	September 1, 2001	Yes	Commonwealth			
Fiji		Parliamentary	May 8, 1999	May 15, 1999	No				
Fiji		Parliamentary	February 18, 1994	February 25, 1994	No				
Fiji		Parliamentary	May 31, 1992		No				
Indonesia	DEM	Legislative	June 7, 1999		Yes	NDI, ANFREL, EU	Yes	Yes	Positive
Mongolia	DEM	Presidential	May 20, 2001		Yes?				
Mongolia		Parliamentary	July 2, 2000		Yes	IRI		Yes	Positive
Mongolia		Presidential	May 18, 1997		No				
Mongolia		Parliamentary	June 30, 1996		No				
Mongolia		Presidential	June 6, 1993		Yes	IFES			
Mongolia		Parliamentary	June 28, 1992		Yes	IFES, OSCE			
Nepal	DEM	Parliamentary	May 3, 1999	May 17, 1999	Yes		Yes	Yes	
Nepal		Parliamentary	November 15, 1994		Yes			Yes	
Papua New Guinea	DEM	Parliamentary	June 15, 2002		No				
Papua New Guinea		Parliamentary	June 14, 1997	June 28, 1997	Yes	Commonwealth			
Sri Lanka	DEM	Parliamentary	December 5, 2001		Yes	EU, Commonwealth		Yes	
Sri Lanka		Parliamentary	October 10, 2000		Yes	Commonwealth (staff)		Yes	Positive
Sri Lanka		Presidential	December 21, 1999		Yes			Yes	
Sri Lanka		Parliamentary	August 16, 1994		Yes			Yes	
Sri Lanka		Presidential	November 9, 1994		Yes			Yes	

Country		Election Type	Date						
Taiwan	DEM	Legislative	December 1, 2001		Yes				
Taiwan		Presidential	March 18, 2000		Yes				
Taiwan		Legislative	December 5, 1998		No?				
Taiwan		Presidential	March 23, 1996		Yes				
Thailand	DEM	Legislative (House)	January 6, 2001	January 29, 2001	Yes	Yes	ANFREL	Yes	
Thailand		Legislative	November 16, 1996		Yes	Yes			
Thailand		Legislative	September 13, 1992		No?	Yes			
Cambodia	RDP	Legislative	July 26, 1998		Yes	Yes		Yes	Negative
Cambodia	RDP	Legislative	May 23–28, 1993		Yes	Yes		Yes	Positive
Hong Kong	#	Legislative	September 10, 2000		Yes	Yes			
Hong Kong		Legislative	May 24, 1998		Yes	Yes			
Malaysia	RDP	Parliamentary	November 28–29, 1999		Yes	Yes			
Malaysia		Parliamentary	April 24–25, 1995		No?				
Malaysia		Parliamentary	February 4, 1994		No?				
Malaysia		Parliamentary	October 21, 1990		Yes		Commonwealth		
Pakistan	AR	Parliamentary	October 10, 2002		Yes	Yes	Commonwealth	TA, declined observers	Negative
Pakistan		Parliamentary	February 3, 1997		Yes	Yes	Commonwealth, NDI		
Pakistan		Parliamentary	October 6, 1993		Yes		NDI		
Pakistan		Parliamentary	October 24, 1990		Yes				
Sub-Saharan Africa									
Benin	DEM	Presidential	March 4, 2001	March 22, 2001	TA	Yes	GERDDES		Mixed
Benin		Legislative	March 30, 1999		Yes	Yes			
Benin		Presidential	March 3, 1999		Yes	Yes	NDI		
Benin		Presidential	March 18, 1996		Yes		NDI	Declined observers	
Benin		Legislative	March 28, 1995		Yes		UN	C&S	
Benin		Legislative	June 10, 1991	June 24, 1991	Yes		UN	UNDP C&S	
Central African Republic	DEM	Presidential	September 19, 1999	October 10, 1999	No?				
Central African Rep		Parliamentary	November 22, 1998	December 13, 1998	No?		UN	F&R	Yes
Central African Rep		Parliamentary	August 22, 1993	September 19, 1993	Yes				

(continued)

317

Country or Territory	Freedom House Rating	Type of Election	Election Date	Election Date—Subsequent Round(s)	International Observers Present?	Selected Organizations	UN Involvement?	Domestic EMOs Present?	Observers' Assessment
Central African Rep (results annulled)		Presidential	October 25, 1992		Yes	UN	C&S		Negative
Ghana	DEM	Presidential and legislative	December 7, 2000	December 28, 2000	Yes			Yes	
Ghana		Presidential and legislative	December 7, 1996		Yes	NDI	TA, F&R	Yes?	Mixed
Ghana		Legislative	December 29, 1992		Yes		UN offered C&S		
Ghana		Presidential	November 3, 1992		Yes	Commonwealth, OAU, TCC	UN offered C&S		
Guinea-Bissau	DEM	Presidential and parliamentary	November 28, 1999	January 16, 2000	Yes (TA)		TA		
Guinea-Bissau		Presidential and parliamentary	July 3, 1994	August 7, 1994	Yes	UN	TA, C&S		
Liberia	DEM	Presidential and legislative	July 19, 1997		Yes	Carter Center	TA, verification	Yes	Mixed
Madagascar	DEM	Presidential	December 16, 2001		Yes	EU			
Madagascar		Parliamentary	May 17, 1998		No?			Yes	
Madagascar		Presidential	November 3, 1996	December 29, 1996	Yes	UN	F&R		
Madagascar		Parliamentary	June 16, 1993		Yes	UN	TA, F&R		
Madagascar		Presidential	November 25, 1992	February 9, 1993	Yes	UN	TA, F&R		
Malawi	DEM	Presidential and parliamentary	June 15, 1999		Yes	SADC PF		Yes	
Malawi		Presidential and parliamentary	May 17, 1994		Yes	Commonwealth	TA, C&S		Positive
Mali	DEM	Presidential	April 28, 2002	May 12, 2002	Yes?			Yes	
Mali		Presidential	May 11, 1997		Yes				
Mali		Parliamentary	April 13, 1997	July 3 and 20, 1997	Yes		TA, C&S		Negative (results annulled)

Mali		Presidential and parliamentary	April 12, 1992	April 26, 1992	Yes	UN, OAU	TA, F&R		
Mali	DEM	Parliamentary	February 23, 1992	March 9, 1992	Yes				
Mozambique		Presidential and parliamentary	December 3–5, 1999		Yes	Commonwealth, TCC	TA		Positive
Mozambique		Presidential and parliamentary	October 27–29, 1994		Yes	EU	TA, Verification		Positive
Namibia	DEM	Presidential and parliamentary	November 30–December 1, 1999		Yes		Limited TA		
Namibia		Presidential and parliamentary	December 7–8, 1994		Yes	Commonwealth	C&S		Positive
Namibia		Constituent Assembly	November 7–11, 1999		Yes		UNTAG	Yes	
Niger	DEM	Presidential	October 17, 1999	November 24, 1999	Yes		No		Positive
Niger		Presidential	July 7–8, 1996	July 28, 1996	Yes	NDI	TA, Limited logistics, declined observers	Yes	
Niger		Legislative	January 12, 1995		Yes?		TA		
Niger		Presidential	February 27, 1993	March 27, 1993	Yes	UN	C&S		Positive
Niger		Legislative	February 14, 1993		Yes	UN	C&S		Positive
Nigeria	DEM	Presidential	February 27, 1999		Yes	UN, NDI, TCC	TA, C&S	Yes	Positive
Nigeria		Parliamentary	February 20, 1999		Yes	UN, NDI, TCC	TA, C&S	Yes	
Nigeria		Presidential	June 12, 1993		Yes	UK			Mixed
Sierra Leone	DEM	Presidential and legislative	May 14, 2002		Yes	EU, Commonwealth, TCC	UNDP TA, security	Yes	Positive
Sierra Leone		Presidential and legislative	February 26–27, 1996	March 15, 1996	Yes	Commonwealth	TA, C&S		Mixed
South Africa	DEM	Parliamentary	June 2, 1999		Yes	Commonwealth	TA, C&S		
South Africa		Parliamentary	April 26–19, 1994		Yes	Commonwealth	Verification		
Togo	DEM	Parliamentary	October 27, 2002		Yes	EU			
Togo		Parliamentary	March 21, 1999	April 4, 1999	No		Declined observers		Negative

(continued)

Country or Territory	Freedom House Rating	Type of Election	Election Date	Election Date—Subsequent Round(s)	International Observers Present?	Selected Organizations	UN Involvement?	Domestic EMOs Present?	Observers' Assessment
Togo		Presidential	June 21, 1998		Yes (TA)		TA, declined observers	Yes	Negative
Togo		Parliamentary	February 6, 1994	February 20, 1994	Yes	GERDDES			
Togo		Presidential	August 25, 1993		Yes	UN	TA, F&R		
Angola	AR	Presidential	September 1, 1992		Yes	UN	TA		
Burundi	AR	Presidential and legislative	June 1, 1993		Yes	UN	TA, C&S		
Cameroon	RDP	Legislative	June 30, 2002		Yes (TA)		TA	Yes	
Cameroon		Presidential	October 12, 1997		Yes	Commonwealth			Negative
Cameroon		Legislative	May 17, 1997		Yes	Commonwealth			Negative
Cameroon		Presidential	October 11, 1992		Yes	NDI		No	Negative
Cameroon		Legislative	March 1, 1992		Yes	UN	F&R	Yes	
Chad	RDP	Presidential	May 20, 2001		Yes (TA)	UN	TA	Yes	
Chad		Presidential	June 2, 1996	July 3, 1996	Yes	UN	C&S	Yes	Positive
Congo (Brazzaville)	AR	Legislative	May 26, 2002	June 23, 2002	No				
Congo (Brazzaville)		Presidential	March 10, 2002		Yes	EU	C&S		
Congo (Brazzaville)		Legislative	May 1, 1993	June 6, 1993	Yes	UN	F&R		
Congo (Brazzaville)		Presidential	August 1, 1992		Yes	UN			
Cote d'Ivoire	AR	Legislative	December 10, 2000		Yes (TA)		UN ceased coordination role		
Cote d'Ivoire		Legislative	November 26, 1995		Yes	UN	C&S		
Cote d'Ivoire		Presidential	October 22, 1995		Yes	UN	C&S		
Ethiopia	AR	Parliamentary	May 14, 2000	August 31, 2000	No			Yes	
Ethiopia		Parliamentary	May 7, 1995		Yes		UNDP TA	Yes	Positive
Ethiopia		Parliamentary	June 5, 1994		Yes	UN	TA, C&S		
Gabon	AR	Presidential	December 6, 1998		Yes	GERDDES			
Gabon		Presidential	December 1, 1993		Yes	UN	TA, F&R		
Gambia	AR	Presidential	October 18, 2001		Yes	Commonwealth			Positive

Country		Type of election	Date	Date (runoff)	Requested	International observers	Assistance	Domestic	Assessment
Gambia		Legislative	January 2, 1997		Yes (TA)	UN	Yes		Negative
Gambia		Presidential	September 26, 1996		Yes (TA)	UN	TA, declined observers		
Gambia	AR	Presidential and legislative	April 29, 1992		No?				
Guinea		Legislative	June 30, 2002		No?				
Guinea	AR	Presidential	December 14, 1998		TA		TA, declined observers	Yes	Mixed
Guinea		Legislative	June 11, 1995		Yes	UN	F&R		
Guinea		Presidential	December 19, 1993		Yes	IRI, AAI, UN	TA, F&R		Negative
Kenya	AR	Presidential and parliamentary	December 27, 2002		Yes	Commonwealth, EU, TCC	Yes—UNDP	Yes	Positive
Kenya		Presidential and parliamentary	December 29, 1997		Yes			Yes	Negative
Kenya		Presidential and parliamentary	December 29, 1992		Yes	Commonwealth, IRI	C&S	Yes	Negative
Lesotho	RDP	Parliamentary	May 25, 2002		Yes	UN, SADC PF	TA		
Lesotho		Parliamentary	May 23, 1998		Yes	Commonwealth	TA		
Lesotho		Parliamentary	March 28, 1993		Yes	Commonwealth	C&S		
Senegal	RDP	Legislative	April 29, 2001		Yes		F&R		
Senegal		Presidential	February 27, 2000	March 19, 2000	Yes	GERDDES	F&R	Yes	Positive
Senegal		Legislative	May 9, 1993	May 25, 1993	Yes	NDI	F&R		
Senegal		Presidential	February 21, 1993		Yes	NDI			
Tanzania	RDP	Presidential and parliamentary	October 29, 2000		Yes	Commonwealth	C&S	Yes	Mixed
Tanzania		Presidential and parliamentary	October 22 and 29, 1995	November 19, 1995	Yes	Commonwealth			Negative
Tanzania		Presidential	October 28, 1990		No?				
Uganda	AR	Parliamentary	June 27, 1996		Yes	UN	TA, F&R, C&S		Positive
Uganda		Presidential	May 9, 1996		Yes	UN, Commonwealth	TA, F&R, C&S	Yes	
Zambia	AR	Presidential and parliamentary	December 27, 2001		Yes			Yes	Negative
Zambia		Presidential and parliamentary	November 18, 1996		Yes		F&R	Yes	Negative

(continued)

Country or Territory	Freedom House Rating	Type of Election	Election Date	Election Date—Subsequent Round(s)	International Observers Present?	Selected Organizations	UN Involvement?	Domestic EMOs Present?	Observers' Assessment
Zambia		Presidential and parliamentary	October 31, 1991		Yes			Yes	Positive
Zimbabwe	RDP	Presidential	March 9-10, 2002		Yes			Yes	Negative
Zimbabwe		Parliamentary	June 24-25, 2000		Yes			Yes	Negative
Zimbabwe		Presidential	March 16-17, 1996		No?				
Zimbabwe		Presidential and parliamentary	March 28-30, 1990		No?				
Latin America and the Caribbean									
Bolivia	DEM	Presidential and legislative	June 30, 2002		Yes	OAS			
Bolivia		Legislative	June 1, 1997		Yes	OAS			
Brazil	DEM	Presidential and legislative	October 6, 2002	October 27, 2002	No?				
Brazil		Presidential and legislative	October 4, 1998	October 25 and 30, 1998	Yes	OAS, UN	TA		
Brazil		Presidential and legislative	October 3, 1994		Yes (TA)	UN	TA		
Colombia	DEM	Presidential	May 26, 2002		Yes	OAS			
Colombia		Legislative	March 10, 2002		No?				
Colombia		Presidential	May 31, 1998	June 21, 1998	No?				
Colombia		Legislative	March 8, 1998		No?				
Colombia		Legislative	October 26, 1997		Yes	OAS	TA		
Colombia		Presidential	May 29, 1994	June 19, 1994	Yes	OAS			
Dominican Republic	DEM	Legislative	May 16, 2002		Yes	OAS			Mixed
Dominican Republic		Presidential	May 16, 2000		Yes	OAS			
Dominican Republic		Legislative	May 6, 2000		Yes	OAS			
Dominican Republic		Legislative	May 16, 1998		Yes	OAS			

							Declined observers	No; restricted	
Dominican Republic		Presidential	May 16, 1996	June 30, 1996	Yes	OAS			Positive
Dominican Republic		Presidential	May 16, 1994		Yes	OAS			
Dominican Republic		Presidential	May 16, 1990		Yes	OAS			Negative
Ecuador	DEM	Presidential and legislative	October 20, 2002		Yes	OAS			
Ecuador		Presidential and legislative	May 31, 1998	July 16, 1998	Yes	OAS			
Ecuador		Presidential and legislative	May 19, 1996	July 7, 1996	Yes	OAS			
Ecuador		Presidential and legislative	May 17, 1992	July 5, 1992	No				
El Salvador	DEM	Legislative	March 12, 2000		Yes	OAS			
El Salvador		Presidential (canceled)	March 7, 1999		Yes	OAS	TA		
El Salvador		Legislative	March 16, 1997		Yes	OAS	TA		
El Salvador		Presidential	March 20, 1994	April 24, 1994	Yes	UN, OAS	TA and verification		
El Salvador		Legislative	March 10, 1991		Yes	OAS			
Guatemala	DEM	Presidential and legislative	November 7, 1999	December 26, 1999	Yes	OAS			
Guatemala		Presidential and legislative	November 12, 1995	January 7, 1996	Yes	OAS	No		
Guatemala		Presidential	November 16, 1990	January 6, 1991	Yes	OAS	No		
Guyana	DEM	Legislative	March 19, 2001		Yes	OAS, Commonwealth, TCC		Yes	Positive
Guyana		Legislative	December 15, 1997		Yes	OAS, Commonwealth	TA	Yes	Positive
Guyana		Legislative	October 5, 1992		Yes	OAS		Yes	Positive
Haiti	DEM	Presidential	November 26, 2000		Yes	OAS	TA		
Haiti		Legislative	May 21, 2000	July 9 and 30, 2000	Yes	OAS			
Haiti		Legislative	April 6, 1997		Yes	OAS			
Haiti		Presidential	December 17, 1995	January 7, 1996	Yes	OAS	TA		
Haiti		Legislative	June 25 and August 15, 1995	September 17, 1995	Yes	OAS	TA		

(continued)

Country or Territory	Freedom House Rating	Type of Election	Election Date	Election Date— Subsequent Round(s)	International Observers Present?	Selected Organizations	UN Involvement?	Domestic EMOs Present?	Observers' Assessment
Haiti		Presidential and legislative	December 16, 1990	January 17–21, 1991	Yes	OAS	TA and verification		
Honduras	DEM	Presidential and legislative	November 23, 2001		Yes	OAS			
Honduras		Presidential and legislative	November 30, 1997		Yes	OAS	TA		
Honduras		Presidential and legislative	November 28, 1993		Yes	OAS			
Jamaica	DEM	Parliamentary	October 16, 2002		Yes	TCC			
Jamaica		Parliamentary	December 18, 1997		Yes	TCC			
Jamaica		Parliamentary	March 30, 1993		No				
Nicaragua	DEM	Presidential and legislative	November 4, 2001		Yes	OAS		Yes	Positive
Nicaragua		Presidential and legislative	October 20, 1996		Yes	OAS		Yes	
Nicaragua		Presidential and legislative	February 25, 1990		Yes	OAS	TA and verification	No	
Panama	DEM	Presidential and legislative	May 2, 1999		Yes	OAS		Yes	Positive
Panama		Presidential and legislative	May 8, 1994		Yes	OAS	TA	Yes	Positive
Panama		Legislative	January 27, 1991		Yes	OAS			
Panama		Presidential and legislative	May 7, 1989		Yes	OAS			Negative
Paraguay	DEM	Vice presidential	August 13, 2000		Yes	OAS			
Paraguay		Presidential and legislative	May 10, 1998	October 5, 1998	Yes	OAS	Yes	Yes	Positive
Paraguay		Presidential and legislative	May 9, 1993		Yes	OAS	TA, F&R	Yes	Positive

Country		Election type	Date			Organization			Assessment
Paraguay		Constitutional Convention	December 1, 1991		Yes	OAS		Yes	
Paraguay		Presidential and legislative	May 1, 1989		Yes	NDI		Yes	
Trinidad & Tobago	DEM	Parliamentary	October 7, 2002		No				Positive
Trinidad & Tobago		Parliamentary	December 11, 2000		Yes	Commonwealth			
Trinidad & Tobago		Parliamentary	November 6, 1995		No				
Trinidad & Tobago		Parliamentary	December 16, 1991		No				
Venezuela	DEM	Presidential and legislative	May 28, 2000	July 30, 2000	Yes	OAS		Yes	Positive
Venezuela		Presidential	December 6, 1998		Yes	OAS		Yes	
Venezuela		Legislative	November 8, 1998		Yes	OAS		Yes	
Venezuela		Presidential and legislative	December 5, 1993		Yes	OAS			
Mexico	RDP	Presidential and legislative	July 2, 2000		Yes	NDI (media monitoring)		Yes	Positive
Mexico		Legislative	July 6, 1997		Yes			Yes	
Mexico		Presidential and legislative	August 21, 1994		Yes		TA, support to EMOs	Yes	Mixed
Peru	AR	Presidential and legislative	April 8, 2001	June 3, 2001	Yes	OAS		Yes	Positive
Peru		Presidential and legislative	April 9, 2000	May 28, 2000	Yes	OAS		Yes	Negative
Peru		Presidential and legislative	April 9, 1995		Yes	OAS	TA	Yes	
Peru		Constituent congress	November 22, 1992		Yes	OAS	TA		
Middle East and North Africa									
Algeria	AR	Presidential	May 31, 2002		No			No	
Algeria		Presidential	April 15, 1999		No				
Algeria		Legislative	June 5, 1997		Yes	OAU, Arab League	C&S		
Algeria		Presidential	November 16, 1995		Yes		F&R		Negative

(continued)

325

Country or Territory	Freedom House Rating	Type of Election	Election Date	Election Date—Subsequent Round(s)	International Observers Present?	Selected Organizations	UN Involvement?	Domestic EMOs Present?	Observers' Assessment
Algeria		Legislative	January 1, 1992		No				
West Bank and Gaza (Palestine)		Presidential and legislative	January 20, 1996	Positive	Yes		No	Yes	
Yemen	RDP	Parliamentary	March 15, 2001		TA				
Yemen		Presidential	September 23, 1999		Yes	NDI		Yes	
Yemen		Parliamentary	April 27, 1997		Yes		UNDP	Yes	
Yemen		Parliamentary	April 27, 1993		Yes		TA, F&R	Yes	Positive

Note: For summary information on these topics, see table 3.2.

Not from Freedom House Rankings

Abbreviations

Organizations: AAI, African American Institute; ANFREL, Asian Network for Free Elections; CoE, Council of Europe/Council of Europe Parliamentary Assembly; EP, European Parliament; EU, European Union. GERDDES, Study and Research Group on Democracy and Economic and Social Development; IRI, International Republican Institute; NDI, National Democratic Institute for International Affairs. OAS, Organization of American States; OSCE, Organization for Security and Cooperation in Europe; TCC, the Carter Center.

Types of assistance: C&S, Coordination and Support; F&R, Follow and Report; TA, Technical Assistance.

Freedom House country rankings: AR, Authoritarian; DEM, Democratic; P, Protectorate; RDP, Restricted Democratic Practices.

Criteria for Inclusion: Democratic Transition or International Observers since 1989; Rated DEM, RDP, or AR by Freedom House; National (or Territory-Wide) Elections; Countries with > 600,000 population; Elections under Universal Suffrage (except Hong Kong, where only part of legislature elected by universal suffrage). Elections on same date or with more than one round deemed same election.

Sources: United Nations Web site; OSCE/ODIHR Web site; OSCE/ODIHR statements and reports; OAS Electoral Calendar; OAS Electoral Missions, 1990–2000; IFES electionguide.org Web site; NDI statements and reports; Carter Center reports; Commonwealth election reports; Center on Democratic Performance, Binghamton University, Election Results Archive; author inquiries and interviews.

Notes

1　The Emergence of Election Monitoring

1. Jimmy Carter, interview by Bob Edwards, *Morning Edition,* National Public Radio, January 9, 2001.

2. Between November 7 and December 12, 2000, elections took place in Egypt (Phase 3 of parliamentary elections on November 8), Slovakia (referendum, November 11), Bosnia (November 11), Haiti (November 26), Romania (November 26 and December 10), Ghana (December 7 and 28), and Côte d'Ivoire (December 10). Elections were held in Serbia on December 23.

3. Mark Mitchell, "Weakened US Presidency May Be Dangerous for Asia," *Far Eastern Economic Review,* November 16, 2000.

4. Jill Lawless, "World Intrigued by Election Deadlock," *Associated Press,* November 10, 2000.

5. Nicole Winfield, "New Fla. Election Said 'Reasonable,'" *Associated Press,* November 10, 2000.

6. Mitchell, "Weakened US Presidency May Be Dangerous for Asia."

7. Carter Center's Council of Freely Elected Heads of Government and National Democratic Institute for International Affairs (NDI), *1990 Elections in the Dominican Republic: Report of an Observer Delegation* (Washington, D.C.: Council of Freely Elected Heads of Government and NDI, 1990), 20; also quoted in NDI and the Council of Freely Elected Heads of Government, *The 1996 Presidential Election in the Dominican Republic* (Washington, D.C.: NDI and Carter Center, 1996), 6.

8. U.S. Civil Rights Commission, *Voting Irregularities in Florida during the 2000 Presidential Election* (Washington, D.C.: U.S. Civil Rights Commission, June 2001), Executive Summary.

9. U.S. Civil Rights Commission, *Voting Irregularities in Florida.* Many developing countries have significantly better technologies for balloting and counting. For example, Brazil uses touch-screen machines throughout the country; see Larry Rohter, "Brazil Sets Example in Computerizing Its National Elections," *New York Times,* October 30, 2002.

10. Florida Statutes, title IX, chap. 101, sections 101.151, 101.191. The ballot had a fold down the middle with Bush's name appearing first, on the left side, third-party

candidate Pat Buchanan appearing second, on the right side, and Gore appearing third, back on the left. The places for voters to punch were located down the middle of the ballot. Some voters intending to vote for Gore inadvertently cast ballots for Buchanan because it was not obvious that they had to punch the third spot rather than the second. Although the courts declined to order reballoting as the remedy, the ballot arrangement also violated the law. Florida's election law required that the names of candidates appear in one column with a place to the right for voters to mark their choice. The law also called for listing the candidates in the order their parties finished in the last state election for governor. This meant that the major parties' candidates should have appeared first, without a minor party candidate being listed in between.

11. Samuel Huntington, *The Third Wave* (Norman: University of Oklahoma Press, 1991).

12. United Nations Development Program, *Human Development Report 2002: Deepening Democracy in a Fragmented World* (New York: Oxford University Press, 2002), 1, 10.

13. Even as international consensus has emerged on the importance and legitimacy of international efforts to promote democracy in other countries, few international documents or commentators make much of a distinction between promoting democracy as a universal value and democracy promotion as an internationally accepted development activity. Although "democracy promotion" used to refer to promotion of the idea of democracy in foreign policy, multilateral declarations, and political rhetoric, democracy promotion today refers as well to actual engagement and assistance—advice, technical assistance, money, moral support—that outsiders provide to countries, institutions, and organizations. Such concrete foreign aid and technical assistance might better be termed "democracy assistance" to deemphasize any connotation of proselytizing. Both are adequate rubrics for the broad range of international advice, engagement, and financial assistance for building and encouraging democratic institutions, organizations, and values abroad.

14. Thomas Carothers, *Aiding Democracy Abroad: The Learning Curve* (Washington, D.C.: Carnegie Endowment for International Peace, 1999), 11, 64. Though some have interpreted the book as a broadside on democracy-assistance providers and programs, Carothers actually takes pains to emphasize his support for the general effort to promote democracy abroad.

15. In his work since, Carothers has focused on high policy—for example, criticizing the "transition paradigm" that serves as the implicit intellectual framework of U.S. democracy-assistance programs or considering the lack of consistency in the U.S. commitment to democracy in various regions of the world. See Thomas Carothers, "The End of the Transition Paradigm," *Journal of Democracy* 13, no. 1 (2002): 5–21.

16. "The problem of establishing such criteria" for democracy programs, Carothers argues, "lies in trying to make objective what is inherently subjective." Carothers, *Aiding Democracy Abroad,* 282.

17. Jimmy Carter, interview with the author, July 16, 2003.

2   The Expansion of Democracy and Democracy Promotion

1. Amartya Sen, "Democracy as a Universal Value," *Journal of Democracy* 10, no. 3 (July 1999): 3.

2. Wilson committed the United States to World War I "for the ultimate peace of the world and for the liberation of its peoples . . . for the rights of nations great and small and the privilege of men everywhere to choose their way of life." Woodrow Wilson, "Address Recommending the Declaration of a State of War" (speech, April 2, 1917); Tony Smith, *The United States and the Worldwide Struggle for Democracy in the Twentieth Century* (Princeton, N.J.: Princeton University Press, 1994), 3.

3. Abraham Lincoln, "Speech at Independence Hall, Philadelphia, February 22, 1861," in *Abraham Lincoln: Speeches and Writings, 1859–1865,* ed. Don D. Fehrenbacher (New York: Library of America, 1989), quoted in Gideon Rose, "Democracy Promotion and American Foreign Policy," *International Security* 25, no. 3 (2000): 186–203; Jimmy Carter (speech, May 2, 1977), quoted in Tony Smith, *The United States and the Worldwide Struggle for Democracy in the Twentieth Century* (Princeton, N.J.: Princeton University Press, 1994), 239; Ronald Reagan, "We Will Be a City upon a Hill" (speech to Conservative Political Action Conference, January 25, 1974); Reagan, "Speech to Republican National Convention" (August 19, 1976); Reagan, "America's Purpose in the World" (speech to Conservative Political Action Conference, March 17, 1978).

4. *The Universal Declaration of Human Rights,* UN General Assembly Resolution 217A (III) UN Doc. A/810 (1948), arts. 19-21, 29; *Charter of the Organization of American States* (1948), art. 2; *Statute of the Council of Europe* (1949), Preamble; UN General Assembly, *Declaration on the Granting of Independence to Colonial Countries and Peoples,* Resolution 1514 (XV) (December 14, 1960), art. 2.

5. UN General Assembly, *Enhancing the Effectiveness of the Principle of Periodic and Genuine Elections,* Resolution 43/157 (December 8, 1988); Conference on Security and Cooperation in Europe, *The Document of the 1990 Copenhagen Meeting of the Conference on the Human Dimension* (Copenhagen, June 29, 1990); Organization of American States, *Santiago Commitment to Democracy and the Renewal of the Inter-American System,* General Assembly Resolution 1080 (Santiago, 1991); *The Harare Commonwealth Declaration* (declaration issued by Commonwealth heads of government, Harare, Zimbabwe, 1991), art. 9; UN Human Rights Commission, *Promotion of the Right to Democracy,* Resolution 1999/57 (The reference to a "right to democracy" in the title of the resolution was controversial; a Cuban effort to delete the term was defeated by a vote of 28 to 12 with 13 abstentions); Roland Rich, "Bringing Democracy into International Law," *Journal of Democracy* 12, no. 3 (July 2001): 24–25. Regarding a "democratic entitlement," see Gregory H. Fox, "The Right to Political Participation in International Law," in *Democratic Governance and International Law,* ed. Gregory H. Fox and Brad R. Roth (Cambridge: Cambridge University Press, 2001); Thomas Frank, "The Emerging Right to Democratic Governance," *American Journal of International Law* 86 (January 1992): 46–91; and Henry J. Steiner, "Political Participation as a Human Right," *Harvard Human Rights Year Book,* 1 (1988).

6. UN General Assembly, *United Nations Millennium Declaration,* Resolution 55/2 (September 8, 2000), sec. V, arts. 24–25; Organization of American States General Assembly, *Inter-American Democratic Charter* (resolution, Lima, September 11, 2001); The New Partnership for Africa's Development, *Declaration on Democracy, Political, Economic and Corporate Governance* (Durban, South Africa, July 7, 2002), paragraphs 4, 7.

7. See Sen, "Democracy as a Universal Value," 5. Sen argues that universal consent is not necessary for a value to be universal. "Rather, the claim of a universal value is that people anywhere may have reason to see it as valuable" (p. 12).

8. World Conference on Human Rights, Vienna Declaration and Programme of Action, A/CONF.157/23 (Vienna, June 14–15, 1993), art. 8; Final Warsaw Declaration: Toward a Community of Democracies (Warsaw, June 27, 2000); Mark Malloch Brown, "Foreword," in United Nations Development Program, *Human Development Report 2002: Deepening Democracy in a Fragmented World* (New York: Oxford University Press, 2002); Bureau of Democracy, Human Rights, and Labor, U.S. Department of State, "Democracy," www.state.gov/g/drl/democ/.

9. Final Warsaw Declaration; Final Communiqué of the Community of Democracies Convening Group, Organization of American States Meeting of Regional and Multilateral Organizations on Promoting and Defending Democracy, February 21, 2001, par. 5. The Clinton administration was deeply involved in initiating the Community of Democracies process and convening the meeting in Warsaw. The ten convening countries were Chile, the Czech Republic, India, Mali, Mexico, Poland, Portugal, South Africa, South Korea, and the United States. For the second biannual meeting of the Community of Democracies in Seoul in November 2002, the Bush administration moved the process forward by ensuring that some countries with a more debatable commitment to democracy were invited only as observers.

10. UN Millennium Declaration, sec. V, arts. 24–25.

11. Ronald Reagan, "Evil Empire Speech" (speech to the House of Commons, June 8, 1982).

12. The relationship between the U.S. political parties and the party institutes (IRI and NDI) is unofficial, and Congress has made NED funding contingent on separation between each party's national committee and its party institute. On its Web site, IRI curiously calls itself a "nonpartisan organization" and avers that "IRI is not part of the Republican Party of the United States" without further comment on its relationship with the party; www.iri.org and www.iri.org/about.asp.

13. The United States provided $9.4 billion in foreign aid in 2000, including $8.0 billion in bilateral aid and $1.4 billion through multilateral organizations. Carol Lancaster, *Transforming Foreign Aid: Unites States Assistance in the 21st Century* (Washington, D.C.: Institute for International Economics, 2000), 10–11. The estimate of $700 million of U.S. funding for democracy and governance programs in 2000 is a typical one. For example, Thomas Carothers, *The Clinton Record on Democracy Promotion,* Working Paper 16 (Washington, D.C.: Carnegie Endowment for International Peace, 2000), 4.

14. "Independent Auditor's Report," *National Endowment for Democracy 2000 Annual Report,* 3, available at www.ned.org/publications/00annual/pdf/AuditorsReport .pdf. For fiscal 2005, the administration proposed a substantial increase in funding for NED.

15. Thomas Melia of NDI coined this phrase during the 1990s.

16. Bill Clinton, "A New Democratic Lays Out His Plan: A New Covenant for American Security," *Harvard International Review* 14, no. 4 (1992): 26 (article adapted from speech at Georgetown University, December 12, 1991); Anthony Lake, assistant to the president for national security affairs, "From Containment to Enlargement" (speech at Nitze School of Advanced International Studies, Johns Hopkins University, Washington, September 21, 1993); Clinton, *A National Security Strategy of Engagement and Enlargement* (Washington, D.C.: White House, 1996); Strobe Talbott, "Democracy and the National Interest," *Foreign Affairs* 75, no. 6 (1996): 47–63.

17. Carothers, *Clinton Record on Democracy Promotion,* 5.

18. George W. Bush, "Presidential Debate at Wake Forest University" (answer in

presidential debate, October 11, 2000); William Drozdiak, "Bush Plan Worries Europeans: Removing U.S. Troops From Balkans Is Seen as Divisive," *Washington Post,* October 24, 2000.

19. Colin Powell, "Speech at the Republican Convention" (July 30, 2000).

20. Roger Winter, assistant administrator for democracy, conflict, and humanitarian assistance, U.S. Agency for International Development (USAID) (testimony to Senate Appropriations Committee Subcommittee on Foreign Operations, March 6, 2002); George W. Bush, "Remarks by the President at United Nations Financing for Development Conference" (Monterrey, Mexico, March 22, 2002); USAID, "Millennium Challenge Account Update, Fact Sheet" (June 3, 2002); cf. George W. Bush, "Remarks by the President on Global Development" (speech at Inter-American Development Bank, Washington, March 14, 2002). Bush signed the law establishing the Millennium Challenge Corporation (MCC) on January 23, 2004. The adminstration's plan is to increase core foreign assistance by 50 percent over three years, resulting in a $5 billion annual increase by fiscal 2006. The MCC has proposed indicators for assessing whether countries meet the three requirements for Millennium Challenge Account assistance. To meet the eligibility test for "governing justly," countries must score well on several democracy "indicators," as measured in part by Freedom House's annual survey of respect for political rights and civil liberties. See Jennifer Windsor, "Democracy and Development: The Evolution of U.S. Foreign Assistance Policy," *Fletcher Forum of World Affairs* 27, no. 2 (summer–fall 2003): 145.

21. For example, John Shattuck, assistant secretary of state for democracy, human rights, and labor (testimony to U.S. House of Representatives Committee on International Relations, September 17, 1997); Center for Democracy and Governance, USAID, *User's Guide* (Washington, D.C.: USAID, 2000), 2; Center for Democracy and Governance, USAID, *Democracy and Governance: A Conceptual Framework* (Washington, D.C.: USAID, 1998) , 5. Elections are only one category of what Thomas Carothers has called the "democracy template." He lists state institutions and civil society as the others. Carothers, *Aiding Democracy Abroad: The Learning Curve* (Washington, D.C.: Carnegie Endowment for International Peace, 1999), 86–94.

22. Center for Democracy and Governance, *User's Guide,* 2.

23. The Ebert Foundation was founded in in 1925 and reestablished in 1947, the Adenauer Foundation was founded in 1956, and the Naumann Foundation was founded in 1958. Other publicly supported party-affiliated foundations are the Hanns Seidel Foundation (Christian Social Union) and the Heinrich Boll Foundation (Greens). Regarding the amount of funding for the German political party foundations, see Konrad Adenauer Stiftung Web site, www1.kas.de/stiftung/englisch/intro.html (annual budget of 200 million marks or approximately $118 million); Freidrich Ebert Stiftung Web site, www.fes.de/intro_en.html (€110 million or more than $125 million in 2002); Michael Pinto-Duschinsky, "Parties and Candidates: Political Foundations," Administration and Cost of Elections Project, www.aceproject.org/main/ english/pc/pcd01b05.htm (citing a 1996 report by the Naumann Foundation); Carothers, *Aiding Democracy Abroad,* 141 (putting the annual budget of the Adenauer Stiftung at $130 million). See also Larry Diamond, "Promoting Democracy in the 1990s: Actors, Instruments, and Issues," in *Democracy's Victory and Crisis,* ed. Axel Hadenius (Cambridge: Cambridge University Press, 1997), 314–15.

24. Sarah E. Mendelson, "Democracy Assistance and Political Transition in Russia," *International Security* 25, no. 4 (spring 2001): 74. Mendelson sees Western democracy

NGOs as transnational "advocacy networks" as described by Margaret Keck and Kathryn Sikkink; see Keck and Sikkink, *Activists Beyond Borders: Advocacy Networks in International Politics* (Ithaca, N.Y.: Cornell University Press, 1998). Democracy NGOs, like other transnational civil society movements, constitute what Ann Florini has called a "third force" of international democracy promotion. Ann M. Florini, ed., *The Third Force: The Rise of Transnational Civil Society* (Tokyo and Washington: Japan Center for International Exchange and the Carnegie Endowment for International Peace, 2000).

3   Elections and Election Monitoring

1. UN secretary general Kofi Annan, "Closing Remarks to the Ministerial" (Warsaw, June 27, 2000).

2. Fareed Zakaria, *The Future of Freedom: Illiberal Democracy at Home and Abroad* (New York: Norton, 2003), 17.

3. Zakaria, *Future of Freedom,* 18.

4. Jack Snyder, *From Voting to Violence: Democratization and Nationalist Conflict* (New York: Norton, 2000), 16.

5. Amy Chua, *World on Fire: How Exporting Free Market Democracy Breeds Ethnic Hatred and Global Instability* (New York: Doubleday, 2003), 194.

6. Samuel Huntington, *The Third Wave* (Norman: University of Oklahoma Press, 1991), 9.

7. *The Universal Declaration of Human Rights,* art. 21(3); UN General Assembly, *International Covenant on Civil and Political Rights,* Resolution 2200A (XXI), UN Doc. A/6316 (December 16, 1966), art. 25.

8. "American Convention on Human Rights" (signed at San José, Costa Rica, November 22, 1969; entered into force July 18, 1978), art. 23(1)(b) ("Every citizen shall enjoy the following rights and opportunities . . . to vote and to be elected in genuine periodic elections, which shall be by universal and equal suffrage and by secret ballot that guarantees the free expression of the will of the voters"); Conference on Security and Cooperation in Europe, *The Document of the 1990 Copenhagen Meeting of the Conference on the Human Dimension of the CSCE* (Copenhagen, June 29, 1990), arts. 5–7 ("The will of the people, freely and fairly expressed through periodic and genuine elections, is the basis of the authority and legitimacy of all government"), art. 6; Council of Europe, *Protocol (No. 1) to the European Convention for the Protection of Human Rights and Fundamental Freedoms,* (Paris, 1952), art. 3 (in which the parties "undertake to hold free elections at reasonable intervals by secret ballot"); Organization of African Unity, *The African Charter on Human and People's Rights,* OAU Doc. CAB/LEG/67/3 rev. 5 (Banjul, Gambia, June 27, 1981), art. 13; Inter-Parliamentary Council, *Declaration on Criteria for Free and Fair Elections,* 154th Session (Paris, March 26, 1994), art. 1. Organization of African Unity, *The African Charter for Popular Participation in Development and Transformation* (Arusha, 1990), art. 10 ("Popular participation is the fundamental right of the people to fully and effectively participate in the determination of the decisions which affect their lives"); African Union, *The Durban Declaration in Tribute to the Organization of African Unity on the Occasion of the Launching of the African Union* (Durban, South Africa, July 11, 2002), art. 10 (calling for Africa to be "governed

on the basis of democracy and by governments emanating from the will of the people expressed through transparent, free and fair elections"); Organization of American States, *American Declaration of the Rights and Duties of Man,* General Assembly Resolution 30, art. 20 (elections "shall be honest, periodic and free"); UN Human Rights Commission, *Promoting and Consolidating Democracy,* Resolution 2000/47, par. 1(d)(ii).

9. Elizabeth Spiro Clark, "Why Elections Matter," *Washington Quarterly* (summer 2000) 32.

10. Adrian Karatnycky, "The 1998 Freedom House Survey: The Decline of Illiberal Democracy," *Journal of Democracy* 10, no. 1 (January 1999): 112–25.

11. Generally, the plural "elections" is preferable if the reference is to parliamentary or legislative contests (because there is more than one contest to be decided) or if there is more than one body being chosen (as when presidential and legislative elections or parliamentary and local elections are held simultaneously).

12. Subclassification is possible, for example, "back-sliding" elections as a subcategory of consolidating elections in which a country holds elections to "disguise a deteriorating democratic process" while it appears to be failing to hold on to democratic gains or "managed transition" elections as a subcategory of transitional elections, where existing power holders hold elections as a part of a managed reform process. See International Institute for Democracy and Electoral Assistance (International IDEA), *The Future of International Electoral Observation: Lessons Learned and Recommendations* (Stockholm: International IDEA, 1999), 4; National Democratic Institute for International Affairs (NDI), "Lessons Learned and Challenges Facing International Election Monitoring" (paper prepared by Patrick Merloe, April 1999).

13. Commonwealth Heads of Government, "Declaration" (Kuala Lumpur, 1989), cited in Amanda Sives, "Adding Value to the Commonwealth Democracy Programme: ACPSU Submission to the High Level Review Group" (evaluation paper, Institute for Commonwealth Studies, London, n.d.), 3; Organization on Security and Cooperation in Europe, *Document of the Copenhagen Meeting of the Conference on the Human Dimension of the CSCE* (Copenhagen, June 29, 1990), art. 8. The article adds, "They will also endeavor to facilitate similar access for election proceedings held below the national level"; "Israeli-Palestinian Interim Agreement on the West Bank and Gaza Strip" Annex II, Protocol Concerning Elections (Washington, September 28, 1995), art. V, sections 2, 3 and 11 and appendix 2, part A; Commission of the European Communities, "Communication from the Commission on EU Election Assistance and Observation" (report, Brussels, April 11, 2000), 3.

14. For example, George M. Houser, American Committee on Africa (letter, March 4, 1980), http://richardknight.homestead.com/files/zimletmarch80.htm; American Committee on Africa, "America Observers Report Intimidation in Rhodesian Elections" (press release, New York, February 20, 1980), http://richardknight.homestead.com/files/zimintimidation.htm.

15. See Larry Garber, *Guidelines for International Election Observing* (Washington, D.C.: International Human Rights Law Group, 1984), annex I, 94–96, citing, for example, British Parliamentary Human Rights Group, *The Election in El Salvador in March 1982* (London: British Parliamentary Human Rights Group, 1982); The Disarm Education Fund, *Eyewitness Report on the Salvadoran Elections* (New York: Disarm Education Fund, 1982); Freedom House, *Report of the Freedom House Mission to Observe the Election in El Salvador, March 28, 1982* (Washington, D.C.: Freedom House, 1982);

Robert L. Wenman, member of Parliament, Canada, *Report on the El Salvadoran Elections and Central America* (Ottawa: Parliament of Canada, 1982).

16. There is no single acronym or abbreviation for nonpartisan domestic election monitoring organizations that is universally used. A 1995 publication of NDI and the National Citizens Movement for Free Elections (NAMFREL) in the Philippines suggested the abbreviation "EMO" for an election-monitoring organization. NDI and NAMFREL, *Making Every Vote Count: Domestic Election Monitoring in Asia,* (Washington, D.C.: NDI, 1996), 3. The book was translated into the Indonesian language, and the term became part of the lexicon in Indonesia for transitional elections in 1999. It has also been used in other Asian countries. It has not become a commonly recognized acronym outside the region, but neither has any other acronym or shorthand term for nonpartisan domestic election monitoring organizations.

17. International IDEA, *Future of International Electoral Observation,* 3.

18. International IDEA, *Code of Conduct: Ethical and Professional Observation of Elections* (Stockholm: International IDEA, 1997), 8.

19. "Usually the distinction [between observation and monitoring] is made by the length of the period during which the election is being watched. Observation, then, is restricted to the actual election day(s) and (part of) the counting of the votes during the day(s) afterwards. Monitoring covers a much longer period and includes the months prior to the actual election day(s)." D. Foeken and T. Dietz, "Of Ethnicity, Manipulation and Observation: the 1992 and 1997 Elections in Kenya," in *Election Observation and Democratization in Africa,* ed. Jon Abbink and Gerti Hesseling (New York: St. Martin's Press, 2000), 136.

20. For example, Krishna Kumar, ed., *Postconflict Elections, Democratization & International Assistance* (Boulder, Colo.: Lynne Reinner, 1998); Michael W. Doyle, Ian Johnstone, and Robert C. Orr, ed., *Keeping the Peace: Multidimensional UN Operations in Cambodia and El Salvador* (Cambridge: Cambridge University Press, 1997); Janet E. Heininger, *Peacekeeping in Transition: The United Nations in Cambodia* (New York: Twentieth Century Fund Press, 1994); NDI, *Nation Building: The U.N. and Namibia* (Washington, D.C.: NDI, 1990).

21. The country ratings are from Freedom House, *Democracy's Century: A Survey of Global Political Change in the 21st Century* (n.d.), available at www.freedomhouse.org. The database includes only countries that have populations of more than 600,000. The data cover all countries rated as "democratic" by Freedom House that held their first multiparty elections after 1989. All these countries would probably be considered Third Wave democracies. The database also includes all elections in countries rated as "authoritarian" or as "restricting democratic practices" that have had at least one election witnessed by international observers. The data do not include Third Wave democracies, however, that made transitions before 1989, or states that have never allowed international observers. Beginning with the first competitive election or the first election subject to international observation, whichever comes first, the data include all national elections in the selected countries. I consider elections for different national offices held on the same date (for example, presidential and legislative elections) to be one election but count them as separate elections if they are held on different dates. The data do not count runoff elections or re-polling as separate elections. Yugoslavia (Serbia and Montenegro) is counted in both categories, but the republics of Serbia and Montenegro are not counted as seperate countries even though the database includes elections in these republics.

In addition to national elections in sovereign countries, the study includes elections in the Hong Kong Special Administrative Region of China, in the West Bank and Gaza, and in the republics of Serbia and Montenegro, which are in a federation. Each of these jurisdictions operates for purposes of elections more like an independent country than a more typical subnational entity. Bosnia and Herzegovina is included as a democracy even though, as of 2000, Freedom House rated it a "protectorate." Freedom House rated the Federal Republic of Yugoslavia as "authoritarian" as of 2000, but because of the dramatic transition in Yugoslavia in September 2000, I have considered it a democracy in categorizing all elections in Yugoslavia, Serbia, or Montenegro since then.

22. Hrair Balian, "Ten Years of International Election Assistance and Observation" (article, OSCE Office of Democratic Institutions and Human Rights, Warsaw, 2001), 4.

23. A coalition of 20 national organizations, including People for the American Way, the NAACP, and the American Civil Liberties Union, monitored the 2002 Florida election. The Center for Democracy, a nongovernmental election monitoring organization, contracted with Miami-Dade officials to provide observers. Tatsha Robertson, "Outside Monitors to Keep Eye on Florida Votes," *Boston Globe,* November 5, 2002. The OSCE's Office for Democratic Institutions and Human Rights (ODIHR) also sent a team of monitoring experts. OSCE/ODIHR, *United States of America, General Elections, 5 November 2002, Implementation of Election Reforms* (Warsaw: OSCE, 2003).

4   From Nongovernmental to Intergovernmental Organizations: Actors in International Election Monitoring

1. UN General Assembly Resolution 174 (II) (November 21, 1947).

2. *Human Rights Questions Including Alternative Approaches for Improving the Effective Enjoyment of Human Rights and Fundamental Freedoms: Enhancing the Effectiveness of the Principle of Periodic and Genuine Elections,* Report of the Secretary General, A/46/609 (November 19, 1991), para. 12.

3. UN Security Council Resolution 435 (September 29, 1978), para. 3.

4. Larry Garber and Clark Gibson, "Review of United Nations Electoral Assistance, 1992–93" (report, United Nations Development Program, Project INT/91/033, August 18, 1993), 19; Marjorie Ann Browne, *United Nations Peacekeeping: Issues for Congress* (Washington, D.C.: Congressional Research Service, updated February 23, 2001), 7; UN General Assembly Resolution 44/10 (October 23, 1989).

5. UN General Assembly Resolution 45/2 (October 10, 1990).

6. UN General Assembly Resolution 43/157 (December 8, 1988). See, generally, Nigel White, "The United Nations and Democracy Assistance: Developing Practice within a Constitutional Framework," in *Democracy Assistance: International Co-Operation for Democratization,* ed. Peter Burnell (Portland, Ore.: Frank Cass, 2000), 67–89.

7. UN General Assembly Resolution 46/137 (December 17, 1991).

8. UN General Assembly Resolution 46/137 (December 17, 1991), sec. 4.

9. UN General Assembly Resolution 47/138 (December 18, 1992).

10. For example, UN General Assembly Resolution 56/159 (December 19, 2001); UN General Assembly Resolution 54/173 (December 17, 1999).

11. Electoral Assistance Division, Department of Political Affairs, United Nations, www.un.org/Depts/dpa/ead/website9.htm; Report of the Secretary General, *Enhancing*

the Effectiveness of the Principle of Periodic and Genuine Elections, A/56/344 (October 19, 2001), para. 27.

12. International Institute for Democracy and Electoral Assistance (International IDEA), *Democracy and Global Co-operation at the United Nations* (Stockholm: International IDEA, 2000), 6.

13. UN General Assembly Resolution 46/137 (1992); Electoral Assistance Division, Department of Political Affairs, United Nations, www.un.org/Depts/dpa/ead/ead-home.htm.

14. "Note of Guidance for UNDPA and UNDP on Electoral Assistance," January 2001, reprinted in the Report of the Secretary General, *Enhancing the Effectiveness of the Principle of Periodic and Genuine Elections,* A/56/344, annex II (October 19, 2001), 2–3.

15. UN General Assembly Resolution 56/159 (December 19, 2001), para. 3, 6, 11, 12.

16. Report of the Secretary General, *Enhancing the Effectiveness of the Principle of Periodic and Genuine Elections* (2001), para. 30.

17. Report of the Secretary General, *Enhancing the Effectiveness of the Principle of Periodic and Genuine Elections* (2001), para. 30.

18. Report of the Secretary General, *Enhancing the Effectiveness of the Principle of Periodic and Genuine Elections* (2001), para. 40, 43–48.

19. Ibid., para. 34.

20. UN General Assembly Resolution 58/280 (July 25, 2001).

21. Commission of the European Communities, "Communication on EU Election Assistance and Observation" (report, Brussels, April 11, 2000), 3.

22. Council of Europe, *Vienna Declaration* (declaration of heads of state and government of member states of Council of Europe, October 9, 1993).

23. Amanda Sives, "Adding Value to the Commonwealth Democracy Programme: A CPSU Submission to the High Level Review Group" (evaluation paper, Institute of Commonwealth Studies, London, n.d.), 3.

24. Organization for Security and Cooperation in Europe (OSCE), Office for Democratic Institutions and Human Rights (ODIHR), "Election Observation," www.osce.org/odihr/elections/.

25. Hrair Balian, "Ten Years of International Election Assistance and Observation" (article, OSCE/Office of Democratic Institutions and Human Rights, Warsaw, 2001), 3–4.

26. OSCE, "Observation of the Parliamentary Elections Held in the Republic of Albania, May 26 and June 2, 1996" (postelection statement, Tirana, Albania, n.d.), 3–7.

27. Commission of the European Communities, "Communication on EU Election Assistance," 3.

28. International IDEA, "Mission Statement" (June 15, 1999), www.idea.int/institute/1-03.html.

29. International IDEA, "Mission Statement."

30. International IDEA, *The Future of International Electoral Observation: Lessons Learned and Recommendations* (Stockholm: International IDEA, 1999), 12. In addition to offering a neutral forum for developing professional standards and learning lessons, International IDEA has also carried out its own "capacity-building" programs. It offers technical assistance, including assistance to domestic election-monitoring organizations.

31. The International Foundation for Election Systems was founded in 1987, at the urging of USAID, to provide professional advice and technical assistance to electoral

authorities in new and emerging democracies. Initially focused on election planning and administration, the foundation has since expanded its programs into the areas of rule of law, governance, and civil society.

32. International Foundation for Election Systems, "New Initiatives: Description of Services," www.ifes.org//new_initiatives/new_initiatives.htm.

5   Jimmy Carter and the Popularization of International Election Observation

1. Jimmy Carter, "Nobel Lecture" (Oslo, December 10, 2002).

2. Gunnar Berge, "Nobel Award Ceremony Address" (Oslo, December 10, 2002).

3. Jimmy Carter, interview with the author, July 16, 2003.

4. Douglas Brinkley, *The Unfinished Presidency: Jimmy Carter's Journey Beyond the White House* (New York: Viking, 1998), 228–30.

5. Jimmy Carter, interview with the author, July 16, 2003; Jimmy Carter, "Free Elections Are Only the Beginning," *Foreign Service Journal,* February 2001.

6. National Republican Institute for International Affairs and National Democratic Institute for International Affairs (NRI/NDI), *The May 7, 1989 Panamanian Elections: International Delegation Report* (Washington, D.C.: NRI/NDI, 1989), 10–11; Brinkley, *Unfinished Presidency,* 278–80.

7. Carter, "Free Elections Are Only the Beginning"; Jimmy Carter, *Talking Peace* (New York: Dutton Childrens' Books, 1993, 1995), 132; NRI/NDI, *The May 7, 1989 Panamanian Elections* (Washington, D.C.: NRI/NDI, 1989), 55–57; Communicado de la Conferencia Episcopal Panama, May 8, 1989, reprinted in NRI/NDI, *Panama Report,* appendix 10, p. 90.

8. Carter, "Free Elections Are Only the Beginning"; Carter, *Talking Peace,* 132–33.

9. Election Tribunal, Decreto 58 (May 10, 1989), reprinted in NRI/NDI, *Panama Report,* appendix 18, p. 116; NRI/NDI, *Panama Report,* 59.

10. E. J. Dionne Jr., "Carter Begins to Shed Negative Public Image," *New York Times,* May 18, 1989; *New Republic,* May 1989, cited in Brinkley, *Unfinished Presidency,* 287.

11. Brinkley, *Unfinished Presidency,* 288.

12. Council of Freely Elected Heads of Government, *Observing Nicaragua's Elections, 1989–1990* (Atlanta: Carter Center, 1990), 15, appendix 3, p. 45, and appendix 4, pp. 46–48. Since his presidency, President Carter had maintained good relations with Daniel Ortega and the Sandinista government. In August 1989, just before the invitation to observe the elections was issued, a Carter representative attended a celebration of the tenth anniversary of the Sandinista revolution in Managua.

13. Jimmy Carter, interview with the author, July 16, 2003. Indeed, polls conducted for the Sandinista government by prominent American pollster Stanley Greenberg showed Ortega with a considerable lead, and a *Washington Post*/ABC News poll five days before the election showed Ortega winning comfortably. Brinkley, *Unfinished Presidency,* 303 (saying that Carter predicted a Sandinista victory to reporters on February 7, 1990); Robert A. Pastor, *Not Condemned to Repetition: The United States and Nicaragua, Second Edition* (Boulder, Colo.: Westview Press, 2002), 255; Robert Kagan, *A Twilight Struggle: American Power and Nicaragua, 1977–1990* (New York: Free Press, 1996), 706. Although he had seen conflicting polls and carefully avoided any pub-

lic predictions, Carter also had guessed that the Sandinistas would prevail; Jimmy Carter, interview with the author, July 16, 2003.

14. Pastor, *Not Condemned to Repetition,* 232, 251; Robert A. Pastor, "Comment: Mediating Elections," *Journal of Democracy* 9, no. 1 (January 1998); Robert A. Pastor, "Nicaragua's Choice: The Making of a Free Election," *Journal of Democracy* 1, no. 3 (summer 1990).

15. Brinkley, *Unfinished Presidency,* 298; Pastor, *Not Condemned to Repetition,* 237, 239, 241–45.

16. Council of Freely Elected, *Nicaragua Report,* 17–18; Brinkley, *Unfinished Presidency,* 298, 301. Pastor, *Not Condemned to Repetition,* 241–44, 254 Regarding the Esquipulas agreement, see James D. Rudolph, ed., *Nicaragua: A Country Study* (Washington, D.C.: Library of Congress, 1994), 47–48.

17. Brinkley, *Unfinished Presidency,* 298–303; Kagan, *Twilight Struggle,* 706.

18. Council of Freely Elected, *Nicaragua Report;* Brinkley, *Unfinished Presidency,* 303. Latin American leaders on the delegation included George Price, prime minister of Belize; Rafael Caldera, former president of Venezuela; Daniel Oduber, former president of Costa Rica; Raúl Alfonsín, former president of Argentina; Alfonso Lopez Michelsen, former president of Colombia; and Rodrigo Carazo Odio, former president of Costa Rica. U.S. senators who participated included John Danforth (Republican, Mo.), Christopher Dodd (Democrat, Conn.), Patrick Leahy (Democrat, Vt.), Clairborne Pell (Republican, R.I.), and Larry Pressler (Republican, S.D.). House members were Douglas Bereuter (Republican, Neb.), David Bonior (Democrat, Mich.), Elton Gallegly (Republican, Calif.), Ben Jones (Democrat, Ga.), Bill Richardson (Democrat, N.M.) and Olympia Snowe (Republican, Maine). Dan Evans, former U.S. senator and Washington governor, cochaired the U.S. group. The group also included former first lady Rosalyn Carter; Bruce Babbitt, former governor of Arizona; Mike O'Connell, former governor of Nevada; and John Whitehead, former deputy secretary of state. About 1,500 foreign journalists were also present in the country.

19. Pastor, *Not Condemned to Repetition,* 238, 240–41, 249–52. The OAS hired PVT experts Glenn Cowan and Larry Garber of NDI to advise on the design and implementation of a parallel vote tabulation. See chapter 13 for further discussion of quick counts and PVTs.

20. Brinkley, *Unfinished Presidency,* 306–7; Pastor, *Not Condemned to Repetition,* 262; Council of Freely Elected, *Nicaragua Report,* 25.

21. Brinkley, *Unfinished Presidency,* 307, 311; Carter, *Talking Peace,* 137.

22. Brinkley, *Unfinished Presidency,* 309.

23. Carter Center's Council of Freely Elected Heads of Government and the National Democratic Institute for International Affairs (NDI), *1990 Elections in the Dominican Republic: Report of an Observer Delegation* (Washington, D.C.: Council of Freely Elected Heads of Government and NDI, 1990); NDI and Council of Freely Elected Heads of Government, *The 1996 Presidential Election in the Dominican Republic* (Washington, D.C.: NDI and Carter Center, 1996), 5.

24. Jimmy Carter to Dr. Froilan J. R. Tavares, Electoral Board chair, letter, June 13, 1990, quoted in Brinkley, *Unfinished Presidency,* 312; Council of Freely Elected Heads of Government and NDI, *1990 Elections in the Dominican Republic,* 20.

25. Carter, *Talking Peace,* 142.

26. The Commonwealth Secretariat, the Organization of African Unity (OAU), and several governmental and private organizations also sent observers. For the OAU, the Zam-

bian elections marked the organization's first foray into election observation in a sovereign African country. (On the NDI—Carter Center support for domestic monitors, see chapter 11.) A consortium of international donors, including Japan, the United States, and several European countries, funded these efforts. The Carter Center—NDI project received direct support from the governments or international aid agencies of Denmark, Finland, Germany, the Netherlands, Norway, Sweden, and the United States and coordinated support given directly to Zambian monitoring groups by Canada and the United Kingdom.

27. NDI and Carter Center, *The October 31, 1991, Elections in Zambia* (Washington, D.C.: NDI, 1992), 11–12, and appendix 4.

28. Eric Bjornlund, Michael Bratton, and Clark Gibson, "Observing Multiparty Elections in Africa: Lessons from Zambia," *African Affairs* 91 (1992): 425; *Times of Zambia,* October 24 and 25, 1991, reprinted NDI and Carter Center, *Elections in Zambia,* appendix 14, p. 141.

29. Carter had left Atlanta for Zambia without yet learning about the logistical breakdown. He only learned of the problem when he asked about the seals in a meeting with domestic monitoring groups after his arrival in Lusaka shortly before election day. None of them appeared to be familiar with the seals; some suggested that the election commission had misled the former president about their intentions to use the seals. Only then, in front of a couple dozen Zambians and Americans, did one of Carter's own staffers step in to tell him about the mistake. Carter was furious.

30. Benjamin Mibenge, foreign minister and United National Independence Party campaign chair, Paper, October 1991, reprinted in NDI—Carter Center, *Elections in Zambia,* appendix 17, p. 159; NDI—Carter Center, *Elections in Zambia,* 49.

31. NDI—Carter Center, *Elections in Zambia,* 50. In response, President Carter undertook to forgo announcing any PVT results until consulting with the election commission and the contending political parties. Jimmy Carter to Mathew Nglube, letter, October 30, 1991, reprinted in NDI—Carter Center, *Elections in Zambia,* appendix 18, p. 164.

32. National Address of President Kenneth Kaunda (October 30, 1991), reprinted in NDI—Carter Center, *Elections in Zambia,* appendix 16, p. 149.

33. Carter Center, "Elections Monitored by the Carter Center," December 2002, www.cartercenter.org/documents/nondatabase/electionstats.pdf. Beginning in 1997, Carter Center teams observed village elections in China on nine different occasions, and the center has hosted observers from China to U.S. elections. The center's willingness to take seriously these fundamentally constrained local elections in China, despite that country's poor human rights record and rejection of multiparty democracy, is consistent with Carter's long-standing belief in the value of international engagement.

34. Jimmy Carter, interview with the author, July 16, 2003. Sonn later became the South African ambassador to the United States.

35. Carter Center, "Elections Monitored by the Carter Center."

36. Marc Lacey, "Kenya's Ruling Party Is Defeated after 39 Years," *New York Times,* December 30, 2002.

6   Toward "Free and Fair" Elections?

1. Kondwane Chirambo, "SADC Must Establish Election Observation Criteria," *Elections 2000,* June 13, 2000; www.sardc.net/sd/elections2000/ namibia_sadc.html.

2. *Universal Declaration of Human Rights,* art. 21(3) (". . . periodic and genuine elections which shall be by universal and equal suffrage and shall be held by secret vote or by equivalent free voting procedures"); International Covenant on Civil and Political Rights, art. 21(3) ("genuine periodic elections which shall be by universal and equal suffrage and shall be held by secret ballot . . ."); *American Declaration of the Rights and Duties of Man,* art. XX ("Every person having legal capacity is entitled . . . to take part in popular elections, which shall be by secret ballot . . ."); *American Convention on Human Rights,* art. 23 (". . . genuine periodic elections, which shall be by universal and equal suffrage and by secret ballot"); Conference on Security and Cooperation in Europe, *Document of the Copenhagen Meeting of the Conference on the Human Dimension of the CSCE* (Copenhagen, June 29, 1990), art. 5.1 (". . . by secret ballot or by equivalent free voting procedure"), art. 7.3 ("universal and equal suffrage"); *Protocol (No. 1) to the European Convention for the Protection of Human Rights and Fundamental Freedoms,* art. 3 ("secret ballot"); Inter-Parliamentary Council, *Declaration on Criteria for Free and Fair Elections* (154th Session, Paris, March 26, 1994; www.ipu.org/cnl-e/154-free.htm), art. 1 (". . . universal, equal and secret suffrage").

3. *Convention on the Elimination of All Forms of Racial Discrimination,* General Assembly Resolution 2106 (XX) (December 21, 1965), art. 5 ("States Parties undertake . . . to guarantee the right of everyone, without distinction as to race, color, or national or ethnic origin, to equality before the law, notably in the enjoyment of the following rights: . . . (c) Political rights, in particular the right to participate in elections—to vote and to stand for election—on the basis of universal and equal suffrage, to take part in the Government as well as in the conduct of public affairs at any level and to have equal access to public service"); *Convention on the Elimination of All Forms of Discrimination against Women,* General Assembly Resolution 34/180 (December 18, 1979), art. 7 ("States Parties shall take all appropriate measures to eliminate discrimination against women in the political and public life of the country and, in particular, shall ensure to women, on equal terms with men, the right: (a) To vote in all elections and public referenda and to be eligible for election to all publicly elected bodies").

4. *International Covenant on Civil and Political Rights,* arts. 19–21. Art. 19 provides for the "right to hold opinions without interference" and "right to freedom of expression . . . includ[ing] freedom to seek, receive and impart information and ideas of all kinds, regardless of frontiers, either orally, in writing or in print" subject only to restrictions "provided by law and . . . necessary: (a) for respect of the rights or reputations of others; (b) for the protection of national security or of public order or of public health or morals."

5. Henry L. Stimson and McGeorge Bundy, *On Active Service in Peace and War* (New York: Harper & Brothers, 1948), 115. Stimson and Bundy wrote, "Within a week of his arrival [in Nicaragua in 1927], Stimson had succeeded in restoring general peace. He had also pledged the United States to a fair and free election, and only the redemption of this pledge could mark a real ending point of his efforts. After his return to the United States, he did much work in preparation for the 1928 elections, and was in constant touch with the officer who supervised, his friend General Frank McCoy. . . . McCoy organized an election of complete probity in which a full and secret suffrage was maintained. . . . Thus, the United States at some expense and with considerable effort succeeded in this one war in substituting ballots for bullets."

6. UN General Assembly Resolution 944 (X) (1955), cited in Rupert Emerson, *From Empire to Nation: The Rise to Self-Assertion of Asian and African Peoples* (Boston: Beacon Press, 1960), 323.

7. UN Security Council Resolution 435 (September 29, 1978); emphasis added.

8. *Document of the Copenhagen Meeting of the Conference on the Human Dimension of the CSCE,* arts. 6, 7.

9. Inter-Parliamentary Council, *Declaration on Criteria for Free and Fair Elections.* Representatives of 112 of the Inter-Parliamentary Union's 129 member parliaments were present and adopted the declaration unanimously.

10. Jørgen Elklit and Palle Svensson, "What Makes Elections Free and Fair?" *Journal of Democracy* 8, no. 3 (July 1997): 35; emphasis in original.

11. Stefan Mair, "International Election Observation: One Form of Democratization Assistance" (report, Stiftung Wissenschaft und Politik, Research Institute for International Politics and Security, Bonn, April/July 1994), 34.

12. For example, Mair, "International Election Observation," 34 ("The English-speaking world increasingly uses the metaphor of the level playing-field, on which the political parties compete, for the fairness of an election"); Patrick Merloe, "Electoral Campaigns and Pre-Election Issues: The 'Level Playing Field' and Democratic Elections" (paper presented at African Election Administrators' Colloquium, Zimbabwe, November 1994), reprinted in National Democratic Institute for International Affairs (NDI), *Democratic Elections: Human Rights, Public Confidence and Fair Competition* (Washington, D.C.: NDI, 1997); NDI, "Lessons Learned and Challenges Facing International Election Monitoring" (paper prepared by Patrick Merloe, April 1999) ("Political contestants must, in fact, be given a fair chance of reaching the voters and winning their support—that is, a reasonably 'level playing field'").

13. Organization for Security and Cooperation in Europe (OSCE), Office for Democratic Institutions and Human Rights (ODIHR), *The ODIHR Election Observation Handbook,* 4th ed. (Warsaw: OSCE/ODIHR, 1999), 4. The *ODIHR Handbook* continues, "But at a minimum it [the principle of fairness] should ensure the voter's exposure to basic information about all the contestants."

14. Elklit and Svensson, "What Makes Elections Free and Fair?" 37.

15. Theodor Hanf, Maria R. Macchiaverna, Bernard Owen, and Julian Santamaria, *Observing Democratic Elections: A European Approach* (Frieburg, Germany: Arnold Bergstraesser Institut, 1995), 17. Cf. Mair, "International Election Observation," 34 ("general, equal, secret and free").

16. Hanf et al., *Observing Democratic Elections,* 17–18.

17. Norwegian Helsinki Committee, *Election Observation: An Introduction to the Methodology and Organization* (Oslo: Norwegian Helsinki Committee, 2000), sec. 2; www.nhc.no/engelsk/reports/election/electionmanual.html. Norwegian Helsinki Committee, *Manual for Election Observation* (Oslo: Norwegian Helsinki Committee, 1996), sec. 2.

18. OSCE, *ODIHR Election Observation Handbook,* 4–5.

19. Anders Erikson, ed., *Handbook for European Union Election Observation Missions* (Stockholm: Swedish International Development Cooperation Agency, 2002), 12. (These criteria are not directly comparable to those offered by the Bergstraesser Institute, the Norwegian Helsinki Committee, and ODIHR.)

20. NDI, "Lessons Learned and Challenges Facing International Election Monitoring."

21. O. van Cranenburgh, "Democratization in Africa: the Role of Election Observation," in *Election Observation and Democratization in Africa,* ed. Jon Abbink and Gerti Hesseling (London: Macmillan, and New York: St. Martin's Press, 2000), 30.

22. Cited in D. Foeken and T. Dietz, "Of Ethnicity, Manipulation and Observation:

The 1992 and 1997 Elections in Kenya," in *Election Observation and Democratization in Africa,* ed. Abbink and Hesseling, 140.

23. Amanda Sives, "Adding Value to the Commonwealth Democracy Programme: A CPSU Submission to the High Level Review Group" (evaluation paper, Institute of Commonwealth Studies, London, n.d.), 4.

24. European Union Observation Unit, "Statement by European Union Special Representative, Glenys Kinnock MEP" (postelection statement, Phnom Penh, July 29, 1998), 1; reprinted in NDI, *The July 26, 1998 Cambodian National Assembly Elections* (Washington, D.C.: NDI, 1999) appendix S.

25. Committee on Development and Cooperation, European Parliament, January 9, 2001, quoted in *Handbook for European Union Election Observation Missions,* ed. Erikson , 3.

26. An NDI delegation apparently last assessed elections as "free and fair" in Czechoslovakia and Hungary in 1990. "Statement by the International Observer Delegation to the Czech and Slovak Federative Republic Elections" (post-election statement, Prague, June 10, 1990), 1 ("We believe that these elections have been free and fair and that the international community should respect and support the results"); "Final Statement: International Delegation to Hungary's Parliamentary Elections" (postelection statement, Budapest, March 26, 1990), 2 ("If the tabulation and the second round of elections are conducted in a similar manner as what we expect, then Hungary's new government will receive the internal and international legitimacy that derives from a free and fair election"). There was no NDI policy on whether to use the free and fair phrase and each delegation or mission was semiautonomous, but there was a general aversion to its use among the senior staff.

27. Senator Alan Ferguson, "Transcript of Delegation Press Conference," June 29, 2000, in Parliament of the Commonwealth of Australia, *The Parliamentary Elections in Zimbabwe, 24–25 June 2000: Report of the Australian Parliamentary Observer Delegation* (Canberra, October 2000), appendix C, 72; emphasis added. Ironically, Ferguson went on to contradict himself by averring, "It is not for us, as international observers to make that judgement" but rather is a question only for the "Zimbabwean people themselves." The Election Commissions' Forum of the Southern African Development Community (SADC) concluded that those elections in Zimbabwe indeed "reflect[ed] the *will of the people*"; Kondwane Chirambo, " Zimbabweans Expressed Their Will, says SADC Parliamentarians, Commissions," *Elections 2000,* South African Development Community Web site; www.sardc.net/sd/elections2000/zimbabwe/zim_expressed.html; emphasis added.

28. Sives, "Adding Value to the Commonwealth Democracy Programme," 4; emphasis added.

29. James Rupert, "Nigeria Confirms Vote Result," *Washington Post,* March 2, 1999; emphasis added; Commission of the European Communities, "Communication on EU Election Assistance and Observation" (report, Brussels, April 11, 2000), 30.

30. International Republican Institute (IRI), *Mongolian Parliament Election Observation Mission Report, July 2, 2000,* (Washington, D.C.: IRI, 2000), 4; emphasis added.

31. Erikson, ed., *Handbook for European Union Election Observation Missions,* 3–4.

32. Mair, "International Election Observation," 35.

33. Elizabeth Spiro Clark, "Why Elections Matter," *Washington Quarterly* (Summer 2000), 38.

34. OSCE/ODIHR, OSCE Parliamentary Assembly, Council of Europe, and Euro-

pean Parliament, International Election Observation Mission, "Republic of Montenegro, Federal Republic of Yugoslavia, Early Parliamentary Elections, October 20, 2002: Statement of Preliminary Findings and Conclusions" (postelection statement, Podgorica, Montenegro: October 21, 2002), 1.

35. OSCE/ODIHR, OSCE Parliamentary Assembly, Council of Europe and European Parliament, International Election Observation Mission, "2002 Elections to the Verkhovna Rada of Ukraine, Statement of Preliminary Findings and Conclusions" (postelection statement, Kyiv, April 1, 2002), 2.

36. NDI, International Observer Delegation to the Pakistan National Elections, "Preliminary Statement" (postelection statement, Karachi, October 26, 1990), reprinted in NDI, *The October 1990 Elections in Pakistan* (Washington, D.C.: NDI, 1991), appendix 9, 159.

37. Mair, "International Election Observation," 35.

38. Cited in D. Foeken and T. Dietz, "Of Ethnicity, Manipulation and Observation: The 1992 and 1997 Elections in Kenya," in *Election Observation and Democratization in Africa,* ed. Abbink and Hesseling, 137.

39. OSCE/ODIHR Election Observation Mission—Armenia Extraordinary Presidential Election, "Preliminary Statement by the Election Observation Mission to the Extraordinary Presidential Election Second Round—30 March 1998" (postelection statement, Yerevan, April 1, 1998).

40. IRI and NDI, "Cambodian Elections: Balloting, Counting Observed Thus Far Appear to Be Significant Steps in Democratic Direction" (press release, Phnom Penh, July 28, 1998). Mair endorses this focus on a judgment about whether an election was "a step forward or backward." Mair, "International Election Observation," 36.

41. Elklit and Svensson, "What Makes Elections Free and Fair?" 39.

42. Elklit and Svensson, "What Makes Elections Free and Fair?" 43.

43. Krishna Kumar and Marina Ottaway, "General Conclusions and Priorities for Policy Research," in *Post-Conflict Elections, Democratization & International Assistance,* ed. Krishna Kumar (Boulder, Colo.: Lynne Reinner, 1998), 233.

44. See Thomas Carothers, "The Observers Observed," *Journal of Democracy,* 8, no. 3 (July 1997): 25 (observing that many election observers argue that developing countries should not be held to universal standards); NDI, *The 1989 Paraguayan Elections: Foundation for Democratic Change* (Washington, D.C.: NDI, 1989), 43. Also see Hugh McCullum and Kondwane Chirambo, "OAU Observers to Watch Zimbabwe Election Process Carefully," *Elections 2000* (June 22, 2000); www.sardc.net/sd/elections 2000/zimbabwe/zim_oau.html.

45. Patrick Merloe, "Zimbabwe: Democracy on the Line" (statement before the U.S. House of Representatives Committee on International Relations, Subcommittee on Africa, June 13, 2000).

46. "Statement of the NDI International Delegation to Mexico's July 2, 2000, Elections" (postelection statement, Mexico City, July 3, 2000), 1.

47. "Statement of the NDI Pre-Election Delegation to Armenia" (preelection statement, Yerevan, Armenia, November 23, 2002), 2.

48. European Commission, *Communication on EU Election Assistance and Observation,* 5.

49. "Note of Guidance for UNDPA and UNDP on Electoral Assistance," January 2001, reprinted in the Report of the Secretary General, *Enhancing the Effectiveness of the Principle of Periodic and Genuine Elections,* A/56/344, annex II (October 19, 2001), 2.

50. Reginald Austin, "The Challenge of Election Observation: The Zimbabwean Experience," *International IDEA News,* Stockholm, June 2002; www.idea.int/newsletters/2002_06/opinion.htm.

51. O. van Cranenburgh, "Election Observation: Policies of the Netherlands Government 1992–7," in *Election Observation and Democratization in Africa,* ed. Abbink and Hesseling, 271–72.

52. Sue Nelson, "Integrity in International Observation," *Administration and Cost of Elections (ACE)* (New York: International Foundation for Election Systems, UN Department of Economic and Social Affairs, and International Institute for Democracy and Electoral Assistance, 2001).

53. OSCE, *ODIHR Election Observation Handbook,* 5.

54. International Institute for Democracy and Electoral Assistance (International IDEA), *The Future of International Electoral Observation: Lessons Learned and Recommendations* (Stockholm: International IDEA, 1999), 7, 9.

55. Mair, "International Election Observation," 14.

56. European Commission, *Communication on EU Election Assistance and Observation,* 17.

57. Council of the European Union, *Guidelines—EU Policy on Electoral Observation,* Council Decision 9262/98 (1998), sections 6 and 7.

58. International IDEA, *Future of International Electoral Observation,* 7.

59. European Commission, *Communication on EU Election Assistance and Observation,* 17; Erikson, ed., *Handbook for European Union Election Observation Missions,* 17.

60. International IDEA, *Future of International Electoral Observation,* 7.

61. Hanf et al., *Observing Democratic Elections,* 9–11; Norwegian Helsinki Committee, *Manual for Election Observation,* sec. 3.2 (the wording is very similar).

62. "Note of Guidance for UNDPA and UNDP on Electoral Assistance," 2.

63. Hanf et al., *Observing Democratic Elections,* 9–11. Norwegian Helsinki Committee, *Manual for Election Observation,* March 1996, section 3.2 (the wording is very similar).

64. NDI, "Memo to International Community Regarding Whether to Send International Observers to Elections in Indonesia" (memorandum, March 1999).

65. Hanf et al., *Observing Democratic Elections,* 9–11.

66. NDI and IRI, "Statement by the Pre-Election Assessment Mission" (postelection statement, Phnom Penh, Cambodia, July 14, 1998), reprinted in NDI, *July 26, 1998 Cambodian National Assembly Elections,* appendix D, 1–2. Although their decision to send observers under the circumstances was defensible, NDI and IRI ultimately failed to communicate effectively their concerns about the process in Cambodia to the international community.

67. Austin, "Challenge of Election Observation: The Zimbabwean Experience."

7   The Scope and Methodology of International Election Observation

1. "Undemocratic Elections" (editorial), *New York Times,* June 27, 1999.

2. Thomas Carothers, *Aiding Democracy Abroad: The Learning Curve* (Washington, D.C.: Carnegie Endowment for International Peace, 1999), 131.

3. Amanda Sives, "Adding Value to the Commonwealth Democracy Programme: A CPSU Submission to the High Level Review Group" (evaluation paper, Institute of Commonwealth Studies, London, n.d.), 3.

4. "Undemocratic Elections," *New York Times.*

5. Council of Freely Elected Heads of Government and National Democratic Institute for International Affairs (NDI) Election Observation Mission, "Post-Election Statement" (Port-au-Prince, Haiti, December 17, 1990), reprinted as appendix 10a in Council of Freely Elected Heads of Government and NDI, *The 1990 Elections in Haiti* (Washington, D.C.: NDI, 1991), 95.

6. Conference for Security and Cooperation in Europe, *Budapest Document 1994: Towards a Genuine Partnership in a New Era* (Budapest: December 5–6, 1994), par. 12; Organization for Security and Cooperation in Europe (OSCE), *The ODIHR Election Observation Handbook,* 4th ed. (Warsaw: OSCE Office for Democratic Institutions and Human Rights, 1999), 1.

7. Stefan Mair, "International Election Observation: One Form of Democratization Assistance" (report, Stiftung Wissenschaft und Politik, Research Institute for International Politics and Security, Bonn, April/July, 1994), 19, citing Jennifer McCoy, Larry Garber, and Robert Pastor, "Pollwatching and Peacemaking," *Journal of Democracy* 2, no. 4 (fall 1991); Eric Bjornlund, Michael Bratton, and Clark Gibson, "Observing Multiparty Elections in Africa: Lessons from Zambia," *African Affairs* 9 (1992): 405–31; Bengt Save-Soderbergh, "Wachsamkeit von Anfang an," *Der Uberblick* (1993): 24–26.

8. International Institute for Democracy and Electoral Assistance (International IDEA), *Code of Conduct: Ethical and Professional Observation of Elections* (Stockholm: International IDEA, 1997), 11, 19.

9. Commission of the European Communities, "Communication on EU Election Assistance and Observation" (report, Brussels, April 11, 2000), 6. The European Union *Handbook* uses essentially similar language: "An election is not a one-day event, and . . . therefore any meaningful assessment of the election process must be based on the process in its entirety." Anders Erikson, ed., *Handbook for European Union Election Observation Missions* (Stockholm: Swedish International Development Cooperation Agency, 2002), 110.

10. NDI, "Lessons Learned and Challenges Facing International Election Monitoring" (paper prepared by Patrick Merloe, April 1999).

11. Larry Garber, *Guidelines for International Election Observing* (Washington, D.C.: International Human Rights Law Group, 1984); cf. Theodor Hanf, Maria R. Macchiaverna, Bernard Owen, and Julian Santamaria, *Observing Democratic Elections: A European Approach* (Frieburg, Germany: Arnold Bergstraesser Institut, 1995), 13–15. In a footnote, Hanf and his coauthors suggest the possibility of "formalizing the status of observers in a special convention"; p. 13, n. 11; International IDEA, *Code of Conduct: Ethical and Professional Observation of Elections* (Stockholm: International IDEA, 1997); OSCE, *ODIHR Election Observation Handbook,* 6; Erikson, *Handbook for European Union Election Observation Missions,* 18–20; Council of the European Union, *Guidelines—EU Policy on Electoral Observation,* Council Decision 9262/98 (1998).

12. OSCE, *ODIHR Election Observation Handbook,* 6; Erikson, *Handbook for European Union Election Observation Missions,* 19.

13. OSCE, *ODIHR Election Observation Handbook,* 6; Erikson, *Handbook for European Union Election Observation Missions,* 19.

14. International Republican Institute, *Nicaragua Election Observation Report, November 4, 2001* (Washington, D.C.: International Republican Institute, 2002), 4.

15. Ron Gould, assistant chief electoral officer, Elections Canada, "Toward Free and Fair Elections—The Role of International Observers" (unpublished paper, 1994), 1.

16. J. Abbink, "The Organization and Observation of Elections in Federal Ethiopia: Retrospect and Prospect," in *Election Observation and Democratization in Africa,* ed. Jon Abbink and Gerti Hesseling (New York: St. Martin's Press, 2000), 169.

17. Conference on Security and Cooperation in Europe, *Document of the Copenhagen Meeting of the Conference on the Human Dimension of the CSCE* (Copenhagen, June 29, 1990), art. 8.

18. Sam Dillon and Julia Preston, "Old Ways Die Hard in Mexican Election Despite the Pledges," *New York Times,* May 9, 2000.

19. International IDEA, *Code of Conduct,* 11.

20. International IDEA, *The Future of International Electoral Observation: Lessons Learned and Recommendations* (Stockholm: International IDEA, 1999), 3. See also W. van Binsbergen and J. Abbink, "International Election Observation: A Discussion on Policy and Practice," in *Election Observation and Democratization in Africa,* ed. Abbink and Hesseling, 273.

21. O. van Cranenburgh, "Election Observation: Policies of the Netherlands Government 1992–7," in *Election Observation and Democratization in Africa,* ed. Abbink and Hesseling, 288.

22. Hanf et al., *Observing Democratic Elections,* 55.

23. International IDEA, *Code of Conduct,* sec. 27(ii)(a).

24. Hanf et al., *Observing Democratic Elections,* 55; Garber, *Guidelines for International Election Observing,* guideline VB(2), p. 33.

25. International IDEA, *Code of Conduct,* sections 19(iv), (v), (vii), (ix), and (xiii).

26. "Proposal for a Settlement of the Namibian Situation," S/12636 (April 10, 1978), para. 5; "Explanatory Statement by the Secretary-General regarding his Report Submitted pursuant to Paragraph 2 of Security Council Resolution 431 (1978) concerning the Situation in Namibia," S/12869 (September 29, 1978); emphasis added.

27. Hrair Balian, "Ten Years of International Election Assistance and Observation" (article, OSCE Office of Democratic Institutions and Human Rights, Warsaw, 2001), 3.

28. UN General Assembly, *Strengthening the Role of the United Nations in Enhancing the Effectiveness of the Principle of Periodic and Genuine Elections and the Promotion of Democratization,* Resolution 173, A/RES/54/173 (February 15, 2000), para. 6.

29. Horacio Boneo et al., "International IDEA Evaluation of the Impact of External Assistance on the Electoral Process in Nicaragua" (evaluation report, International IDEA, October 1997), 29.

30. D. Foeken and T. Dietz, "Of Ethnicity, Manipulation and Observation: The 1992 and 1997 Elections in Kenya," in *Election Observation and Democratization in Africa,* ed. Abbink and Hesseling, 137.

31. Erikson, *Handbook for European Union Election Observation Missions,* 109.

32. Sives, "Adding Value to the Commonwealth Democracy Programme," 3.

33. Boneo et al., "Impact of External Assistance on the Electoral Process in Nicaragua," 28.

34. For example, Mair argues that a plenary session with "sufficient time for a detailed discussion" is mandatory: "Before release, this final statement must be intensively discussed by a plenum of all observers." Mair, "International Election Observation," 37.

Van Binsbergen and Abbink worry about the process of arriving at a consensus statement: "Minority opinions within the team of observers are difficult to accommodate. There is great pressure toward unanimity, and there may also be pressure, to a lesser extent, towards a positive assessment." W. van Binsbergen and J. Abbink, "International Election Observation: A Discussion on Policy and Practice," in *Election Observation and Democratization in Africa,* ed. Abbink and Hesseling, 271–72.

35. Van Binsbergen and Abbink, "International Election Observation," 260.

36. J. Abbink, "The Organization and Observation of Elections in Federal Ethiopia: Retrospect and Prospect," in *Election Observation and Democratization in Africa,* ed. Abbink and Hesseling, 169.

37. OSCE/ODIHR Election Observation Mission—Armenia Extraordinary Presidential Election, "Preliminary Statement by the Election Observation Mission to the Extraordinary Presidential Election Second Round—30 March 1998" (Yerevan, postelection statement, April 1, 1998).

38. OSCE Office for Democratic Institutions and Human Rights (ODIHR), *Republic of Armenia Presidential Election, March 16 and 30, 1996: Final Report* (Warsaw: OSCE/ODIHR, April 9, 1998), 3.

39. Sarah E. Mendelson, "Democracy Assistance and Political Transition in Russia," *International Security,* 25, no. 4 (spring 2001): 101.

40. International Election Observation Mission, Russian Federation—Presidential Election, "Statement of Preliminary Findings & Conclusions" (postelection statement, Moscow, March 27, 2000), 1.

41. Robert Coalson, "OSCE Verdict on Elections Outstrips State Propaganda," *Moscow Times* (March 31, 2000).

42. Mendelson, "Democracy Assistance and Political Transition in Russia," 101.

43. OSCE/ODIHR, *Russian Federation Presidential Election 26 March 2000: Final Report* (Warsaw: OSCE/ODIHR, 2000), 5.

44. Erikson, *Handbook for European Union Election Observation Missions,* 111.

45. Jørgen Elklit and Palle Svensson, "What Makes Elections Free and Fair?" *Journal of Democracy* 8, no. 3 (July 1997): 35 38.

46. International IDEA, *Future of International Electoral Observation,* 12.

47. Melissa Estok, Neil Nevitte, and Glenn Cowan, *The Quick Count and Election Observation: An NDI Handbook for Civic Organizations and Political Parties* (Washington, D.C.: NDI, 2002), 84–99.

48. Estok, Nevitte, and Cowan, *Quick Count and Election Observation,* 81–83.

49. Garber, *Guidelines for International Election Observing,* 34.

50. NDI, "NDI International Observer Delegation to the May 16 Dominican Republic Elections: Preliminary Statement" (postelection statement, Santo Domingo, May 18, 1994), 4.

51. Carter Center and NDI, "Statement of the Carter Center/NDI Observer Delegation to the Nigerian 1999 Presidential Election, March 1, 1999" (postelection statement, Abuja, March 3, 1999), 3.

52. NDI, "NDI Election Observer Delegation Preliminary Statement," (postelection statement, Dakar, February 23, 1993), 3

53. NDI, "Preliminary Statement: NDI International Observer Delegation to the Pakistan National Elections October 8, 1993" (postelection statement, 1993), 3; reprinted in NDI, *The 1993 Elections in Pakistan* (Washington, D.C.: NDI, 1994).

54. NDI and Council of Freely Elected Heads of Government, "International Ob-

server Delegation to the June 30, 1996 Dominican Republic Presidential Election: Preliminary Statement" (postelection statement, Santo Domingo, July 1, 1996), 5.

55. International Republican Institute, "Parliamentary Elections in Mongolia" (postelection statement, Ulaan Baator, July 2, 2000).

56. Jimmy Carter, interview with the author, July 16, 2003.

57. International IDEA, *Future of International Electoral Observation,* 5.

58. Erikson, *Handbook for European Union Election Observation Missions,* 110.

59. Mair, "International Election Observation," 28.

60. NDI, "Lessons Learned and Challenges Facing International Election Monitoring."

61. United Nations Development Program (UNDP), *Transition to Democracy: Report on the UNDP Technical Assistance Programme for the 1999 Indonesian General Elections* (Jakarta: UNDP, 1999), 71–72. "By the sheer weight of information and services that it made available, the Centre became a sort of clearinghouse for ideas and people during the electoral process," concluded the UNDP report.

62. "Israeli—Palestinian Interim Agreement on the West Bank and Gaza Strip," annex II, Protocol Concerning Elections (Washington, September 28, 1995), art. V, sections 2, 3, and 11, and appendix 2, part A; author's notes, Coordination Meeting at European Commission, Brussels, October 18, 1995.

63. Boneo et al., "Impact of External Assistance on the Electoral Process in Nicaragua," 27.

8   Cambodia: Challenges to International Election Observation

1. Sam Rainsy, "A Call for International Standards in Cambodia" (speech to National Press Club, Washington, April 10, 2002).

2. *Agreement on a Comprehensive Political Settlement of the Cambodia Conflict* (Paris Peace Accord), October 23, 1991, annex 5, section 4.

3. United Nations, www.un.org/Depts/DPKO/Missions/untac.htm.

4. Michael Maley, "Reflections on the Electoral Process in Cambodia," in *Peace-keeping—Challenges for the Future,* ed. Hugh Smith (Canberra: Australian Defense Studies Center, 1993).

5. Janet E. Heininger, *Peacekeeping in Transition: The United Nations in Cambodia* (New York: Twentieth Century Fund Press, 1994), 118.

6. UN Security Council Resolution 880 (1993).

7. "Paris Peace Accord," annex ii, article 5, sections 1–3, and annex v, article 5.

8. See, for example, "Calling a Coup a Coup" (editorial), *Washington Post,* July 9, 1997.

9. Philip Gourevitch, "Pol Pot's Children," *New Yorker,* August 10, 1998, 48.

10. Ung Huot and Hun Sen to the UN secretary general, October 22, 1997. "Annex I to Letter Dated 27 October 1997 from the Secretary-General Addressed to the President of the Security Council," S/1997/998, December 22, 1997.

11. For example, "Communiqué: 'Friends of Cambodia' Meeting" (press release, Bangkok, June 20, 1998), available at www.deplu.go.id/english2/pr33-98.html ("The 'Friends' [of Cambodia] encouraged the Cambodian Government to promote actively a

climate conducive to the holding of *free, fair and credible elections*"; emphasis added); Alexander Downer, "Meeting between ASEAN and the 'Friends of Cambodia'" (press release, Australian Ministry of Foreign Affairs, November 23, 1997), available at www.dfat.gov.au/media/releases/foreign/1997/fa142_97.html ("We look now to the Cambodian Government to live up to its commitments to ensure *free, fair and credible elections*"; emphasis added); Sam Rainsy, interview with Australian Broadcasting Company, "Cambodia's Opposition Threatens to Boycott July Elections," April 4, 1998, available at www.abc.net.au/ra/asiapac/archive/1998/may/raap-1may1998-8.htm ("We want to have guarantees, that the election will be *free, fair and credible*"; emphasis added); Union of Cambodian Democrats, "Technical Advance Team (TAT) Report" (unpublished report, December 12, 1997), available at www.datagraphic.fr/ucd/pr07.htm ("The UCD team believes that the Hun Sen Government continues to use intimidation and political pressure to prevent the development of a competitive political environment necessary for *free fair and credible elections*"; emphasis added); and Ralph A. Boyce, Deputy Assistant Secretary for East Asian and Pacific Affairs, U.S. Department of State, "TestimonyBefore the House International Relations Committee, Subcommittee on Asia and the Pacific" (Washington, September 28, 1998) (emphasizing that elections must be "*credible*"; emphasis added).

12. James P. Rubin, spokesperson, U.S. Department of State (daily press briefing, Washington, July 23, 1998).

13. National Democratic Institute for International Affairs (NDI) and International Republican Institute (IRI), "Statement by the Pre-Election Assessment Mission" (preelection statement, Phnom Penh, July 14, 1998), reprinted in NDI, *The July 26, 1998 Cambodian National Assembly Elections* (Washington, D.C.: NDI, 1999), appendix D, pp. 1–2.

14. Special representative of the United Nations secretary general for human rights in Cambodia, "Monitoring of Intimidation and Violence: Report, 10–17 July 1998" (report, July 18, 1999), cited in NDI, *July 26, 1998 Cambodian National Assembly Elections,* 34.

15. Matt McKinney, "UN Report Sharply Criticizes Election Violence," *Cambodia Daily,* January 16, 2002, 1.

16. NDI and IRI, "Statement by the Pre-Election Assessment Mission," 1.

17. Asian Network for Free Elections—Forum-Asia, "Asian NGOs Monitor Cambodian Election; Express Concern on Pre-Election Situation," (press release, Phnom Penh, July 24, 1998), reprinted in NDI, *July 26, 1998 Cambodian National Assembly Elections,* appendix N.

18. Prendergast to Mehrotra (cable from UN New York to secretary general's special representative in Phnom Pehn, dated July 14, 1998).

19. NDI and IRI, *The Continuing Crisis in Cambodia: Obstacles to Democratic Elections* (Washington, D.C.: NDI, 1998), 11.

20. NDI and IRI, *Continuing Crisis in Cambodia,* 11.

21. Committee for Free and Far Elections in Cambodia, "Statement: Pre-Election Assessment" (Phnom Penh, July 24, 1998), 3, reprinted in NDI, *July 26, 1998 Cambodian National Assembly Elections,* appendix M.

22. United Nations Electoral Assistance Secretariat, "Statement of the Joint International Observer Group," (preelection statement, Phnom Penh, July 24, 1998), 3, reprinted in NDI, *July 26, 1998 Cambodian National Assembly Elections,* appendix O.

23. NDI, *July 26, 1998 Cambodian National Assembly Elections,* 38.

24. Commission of the European Communities, "Communication on EU Election Assistance and Observation" (report, Brussels, April 11, 2000), 7.

25. Human Rights Watch, "Cambodia: Aftermath of the Coup" (report, August 1, 1997), 6.

26. Volunteer Observers for the Cambodian Election (VOCE), "Press Release" (pre-election statement, Phnom Penh, n.d.), quoted in NDI, *July 26, 1998 Cambodian National Assembly Elections,* 24. VOCE included 28 individuals from Australia, Canada, the United States, and New Zealand.

27. MacAlister Brown, "Election Observers in Cambodia, 1998: What Can We Learn?" *Government and Opposition,* 1998, 84.

28. United Nations Electoral Assistance Secretariat, Joint International Observer Group, (press release, Phnom Penh, July 27, 1998), 2. Similarly, the VOCE group, which was co-led by Ambassador Kevin, categorically ruled out the existence of intimidation and urged foreign governments to "accept the results of this election without any qualification." VOCE, "Volunteer Observers of the Cambodian Election (VOCE) Finds the Election Free and Fair" (postelection statement, Phnom Penh, July 28, 1997), 2, reprinted in NDI, *July 26, 1998 Cambodian National Assembly Elections,* appendix R.

29. Rod Amis, "Election in Kampuchea, Part Three: BOTH Sides of The Coin," *G21;* www.g21.net/asia17.htm.

30. The quotation is from NDI and IRI, "Preliminary Statement of the IRI-NDI Delegation to the July 26, 1998 Elections in Cambodia" (postelection statement, Phnom Penh, July 28, 1998), reprinted in NDI, *July 26, 1998, Cambodian National Assembly Elections,* appendix E. On the EU's observation of the problems, see European Union Observation Unit, 1998 Election in Cambodia, "Statement by European Union Special Representative, Glenys Kinnock MEP" (postelection statement, Phnom Penh, July 29, 1998), hereafter "EU Statement," reprinted in NDI, *July 26, 1998 Cambodian National Assembly Elections,* appendix S.

31. For example, Nate Thayer and Rodney Tasker, "Unfree, Unfair," *Far Eastern Economic Review,* August 13, 1997, 16 ("Many western officials were in an equally back-slapping mood. Former U.S. congressman Stephen Solarz, head of the American observer team, on July 28 called the election the 'miracle on the Mekong' despite the fact that vote counting—on which many of the charges of fraud were focused—had still to be completed").

32. "EU Statement," 1.

33. NDI and IRI, *Restoring Democracy in Cambodia: The Difficult Road Ahead* (Washington, D.C.: NDI and IRI, 1997).

34. Kenneth Wollack, president, NDI, and Lorne Craner, president, IRI, cover letter to NDI-IRI report, February 4, 1998.

35. Stephen Solarz, "Cambodia: A Reasonably Fair Election," *Washington Post,* September 4, 1998.

36. Lorne W. Craner, president, IRI, "Testimony before the House International Relations Committee Subcommittee on East Asian and Pacific Affairs" (September 28, 1998), reprinted as "IRI: Cambodia's Elections 'among the Worst We Have Seen since 1993,'" *Phnom Penh Post,* October 16–29, 1998.

37. International Republican Institute, *Kingdom of Cambodia Parliamentary Elections, July 26, 1998: Observation Report* (Washington, D.C.: IRI, 1999), 16.

38. IRI and NDI, "Cambodian Elections: Balloting, Counting Observed Thus Far Appear to Be Significant Steps in Democratic Direction" (press release, Phnom Penh, July 28, 1998).

39. NDI and IRI, "Preliminary Statement of the IRI-NDI Delegation to the July 26, 1998 Elections in Cambodia" (July 28, 1998), 3.

40. Brown, "Election Observers in Cambodia," 84.

41. NDI, "Second Post-Election Statement on the Cambodian Election Process" (postelection statement, Phnom Penh and Washington, August 22, 1998), 1–2, reprinted in NDI, *July 26, 1998 Cambodian National Assembly Elections,* appendix D.

42. Communes in Cambodia are groups of villages, typically including only a few thousand residents. The idea for commune elections was discussed at the Paris peace negotiations in 1991 and emerged again after the 1993 elections, but no international advisers or diplomats working in Cambodia at the time of the 2002 elections could explain why the Cambodian government and the international community had focused exclusively on elections and decentralization at such a low level of government. Neither elections nor decentralization appear to have ever been considered for provincial or district governments or councils.

43. United Nations Development Program (UNDP), *Report on the Elections of the Commune Councils* (New York:UNDP, 2002), 20, para. 9.1.

44. The only changes were the replacement of ostensible FUNCINPEC representative Tea Chamrat, who had actually supported the CPP after the coup in 1997, with a genuine FUNCINPEC representative, Oung Kheng, and the addition of a member from the Sam Rainsy Party to replace the previous representative of the now-defunct Buddhist Liberal Democratic Party. The representative from the tiny Molinaka Party appointed in 1998 retained his position on the election commission even though the party no longer held a seat in the National Assembly.

45. UNDP, *Report on the Elections of the Commune Councils,* 9, para. 1.14 and table 1. This support came from twelve countries, the European Commission, and the UNDP 1998 Trust Fund.

46. Kingdom of Cambodia, Commune Election Law, arts. 148, 149, 152 (An unofficial translation of the name of the body in the law is the Coordination Committee of Associations and Nongovernmental Organizations for Observing the Elections). Committee for Free and Fair Elections, Committee for Free and Fair Elections, and Neutral, Impartial Committee for Free Elections, "Joint Memorandum of Understanding Relating to NGO Coordinating Committee" (Phnom Penh, February 21, 2001), reprinted in NDI, *The 2002 Cambodian Commune Elections* (Washington, D.C.: NDI, 2002), appendix R. NDI, *2002 Cambodian Commune Elections,* section 4. Pok Nanda, chair, Coordination Committee for NGO Electoral Observation, to Koul Panh Nha, executive director, COMFREL (letter regarding response to application for registration for electoral observation, unofficial translation, October 15, 2001), reprinted in NDI, *2002 Cambodian Commune Elections,* appendix T. UNDP, *Report on the Elections of the Commune Councils,* March 2002, 20, para. 9.3. The initially announced process for accreditation required each organization to get prior approval for its list of observers from the NGOCC and the election commission. Then individual observers would have to report in person to provincial electoral authorities to present photographs and photocopies of the identification cards in order to be issued accreditation cards. Given the serious problem of intimidation and the country's extreme poverty, these requirements were simply not feasible. In response to criticism, the election commission subsequently relaxed the process somewhat at the provincial level.

47. UNDP, *Report on the Elections of the Commune Councils,* 21, para. 10.2; special representative of the secretary general of the United Nations for human rights in Cambodia, "Commune Council Elections, 2002, January 2001–January 10, 2002: The Pre-

Campaign Period" (report, n.d.) (documenting fifteen murders or suspicious deaths through January 10), reprinted in NDI, *2002 Cambodian Commune Elections,* appendix U.

48. "Statement of Spokesman of Ministry of Interior" (Phnom Penh, February 6, 2002), reprinted in NDI, *2002 Cambodian Commune Elections,* appendix E.

49. UNDP, *Report on the Elections of the Commune Councils,* 9, para. 1.10–1.11.

50. UNDP, *Report on the Elections of the Commune Councils,* 22, para. 10.4.

51. Special representative of the secretary general of the United Nations for human rights in Cambodia, "Commune Council Elections," 2.

52. UNDP, *Report on the Elections of the Commune Councils,* 8, para. 1.7.

53. UNDP, *Report on the Elections of the Commune Councils,* 32, para. 17.7.

54. Lor Chandara and Jody McPhillips, "NEC Widely Criticized for Debate Blackout," *Cambodia Daily,* January 14, 2002, 9.

55. Lor Chandra and David Kihara, "NEC Reverses Decision on Roundtables," *Cambodia Daily,* January 24, 2002, 1.

56. UNDP, *Report on the Elections of the Commune Councils,* annex 7, sub-annex H, p. 61.

57. UNDP, *Report on the Elections of the Commune Councils,* 8, par. 1.5.

58. Kingdom of Cambodia, Commune Election Law, arts. 16 and 132.

59. "UN Agency Condemned for Lobbying Tactics," *Phnom Penh Post,* February 15–28, 2002, 6.

60. UNDP, *Report on the Elections of the Commune Councils,* 8, para. 1.1. Embassy of Japan, Phnom Penh, "Statement of the Japanese Election Observation Mission on Commune Council Elections in the Kingdom of Cambodia, February 3, 2002" (postelection statement, Phnom Penh, February 5, 2002), 1, reprinted in NDI, *2002 Cambodian Commune Elections,* appendix DD. "Cambodians Vote to End One Party Dominance Over Village Life," *Cambodia Daily,* January 31, 2002 (quoting IRI representative). Carlos Costa Neyes, EU Election Observation Mission, Cambodia Commune Elections 2002, "Preliminary Statement" (postelection statement, Phnom Penh, February 5, 2002), 1, reprinted in NDI, *2002 Cambodian Commune Elections,* appendix BB. Asian Network for Free Elections, "Final Statement on Cambodian Commune Council Elections" (postelection statement, Bangkok, February 15, 2002), 1, reprinted in NDI, *2002 Cambodian Commune Elections,* appendix AA. NDI, *2002 Cambodian Commune Elections,* section I (Introduction).

61. Sam Rainsy, "A Call for International Standards in Cambodia." Rainsy called for foreign aid to be withheld until the government meets international standards for justice, elections, and governance.

62. Ham Samnang, "Hun Sen: 'Long Noses' Must Study Before Criticizing Vote," *Cambodia Daily,* February 8, 2002, 16.

9   Host-Government Manipulation of Observers: Elections in Zimbabwe

1. Nelson Mandela, speech on receiving a special Carter-Menil Human Rights Award, Houston, 1992, cited in Erskine Childers and Brian Urquhart, *Renewing the United Nations System* (Uppsala, Sweden: Dag Hammarskjold Foundation, 1994), 105.

2. There are still exceptions, however. For elections in Malaysia in 1999, for ex-

ample, the government of Mahathir Mohamad neither permitted international observers nor accepted the legitimacy of domestic monitors without paying a significant international price, even after it jailed the popular and internationally respected Anwar Ibrahim and other opposition leaders and manipulated the process.

3. National Democratic Institute for International Affairs (NDI), "Statement of the National Democratic Institute (NDI) Pre-Election Delegation to Zimbabwe" (preelection statement, Harare, Zimbabwe, May 22, 2000), 2, 14.

4. The Electoral (Amendment) Regulations, no. 7 (2000), sec. 15B(i), cited in Commonwealth Secretariat, *The Parliamentary Elections in Zimbabwe, 24–25 June 2000: The Report of the Commonwealth Observer Group* (London: Commonwealth Secretariat, 2000), 9; see also, Parliament of the Commonwealth of Australia, *The Parliamentary Elections in Zimbabwe, 24–25 June 2000: Report of the Australian Parliamentary Observer Delegation* (Canberra: Commonwealth of Australia, 2000), 49. (The Electoral Supervisory Commission unsuccessfully challenged the new regulation in court.)

5. "Zimbabwe bars election monitors," BBC News, June 20, 2000; http://news .bbc.co.uk/1/hi/world/africa/799256.stm.

6. EU Election Observation Mission, *Elections in Zimbabwe on 24–25 June 2000: Report of the EU Election Observation Mission on the Parliamentary Elections* (Brussels: European Union, 2000), chap. 1.

7. "Zimbabwe Rejects African Observers," *BBC News,* June 19, 2000; http://news .bbc.co.uk/1/hi/world/africa/797124.stm.

8. Alex Duval Smith and Peter Fabricius, "Election Observers Are UK Spies, Says Zanu-PF," the (U.K.) *Independent,* June 20, 2000. "Zimbabwe Criticised over Election Tactics," *BBC News,* June 13, 2000; http://news.bbc.co.uk/1/hi/world/africa/ 789126.stm. "$100 Fee for Zimbabwe Monitors," *BBC News,* June 12, 2000; http://news .bbc.co.uk/1/hi/ world/africa/788087.stm.

9. "Zimbabwe Criticised over Election Tactics"; Peter Manikas, NDI, interview with the author, September 19, 2000.

10. "Zimbabwe Bars Election Monitors," *BBC News,* June 20, 2000; http://news.bbc .co.uk/1/hi/world/africa/799256.stm.

11. Pierre Schori, head of EU Election Observation Mission, "Interim Statement" (postelection statement, Harare, June 26, 2000), reprinted in to EU Election Observation Mission, *Elections in Zimbabwe on 24–25 June 2000,* annex A; Chris Patten, European commissioner responsible for external relations, and Poul Nielson, European commissioner responsible for development and humanitarian aid on Zimbabwe elections, speaking points for speech to European Parliament, speech/00/255, Strasbourg, July 4, 2000; *Elections in Zimbabwe on 24–25 June 2000: Report of the EU Election Observation Mission,* chap. 4.

12. Electoral (Amendment) Regulations, No. 8 of 2000, June 20, 2000, cited in Commonwealth Secretariat, *The Parliamentary Elections in Zimbabwe, 24–25 June 2000,* 10, 15, 28; chairman of the Election Directorate, "Circular" (June 23, 2000), reprinted in Commonwealth Secretariat, *Parliamentary Elections in Zimbabwe, 24–25 June 2000,* annex 8, 57 (agreeing to allow two monitors during the day and two at night with only one at a time allowed "inside the polling structure"); EU Election Observation Mission, *Elections in Zimbabwe on 24–25 June 2000;* Schori, "Interim Statement," reprinted in EU Election Observation Mission, *Elections in Zimbabwe on 24–25 June 2000,* annex A.

13. Organization of African Unity, "Interim Statement" (postelection statement, Harare, June 26, 2000); Nora Schimming-Chase and Moises Kamabaya, "Statement of

the SADC Parliamentary Forum Observer Delegation" (postelection statement, Harare, June 27, 2000). (They pronounced themselves "pleased and relieved that on the whole, voting has been orderly and peaceful.") Nora Schimming-Chase and Moises Kamabaya, "SADC Parliamentary Forum Observation Delegation Interim Statement" (preliminary postelection statement, Harare, June 25, 2000); Kondwane Chirambo, " Zimbabweans Expressed Their Will, says SADC Parliamentarians, Commissions," *Elections 2000,* SADC Web site, www.sardc.net/sd/elections2000/zimbabwe/zim_expressed.html; R. W. Johnson, "Commonwealth Monitors Accused of Whitewash," *Sunday Times,* July 2, 2000.

14. General Abdulsalami Abubakar, "Interim Statement by the Chairperson, Zimbabwe Parliamentary Election, Commonwealth Observer Group" (postelection statement, Harare, June 17, 2000), reprinted in Commonwealth Secretariat, *Parliamentary Elections in Zimbabwe, 24–25 June 2000,* annex 6, 53.

15. Johnson, "Commonwealth Monitors Accused of Whitewash"; Chirambo, " Zimbabweans Expressed Their Will."

16. "Delegation Statement" (postelection statement, Harare, June 29, 2000), reprinted in Parliament of Australia, *Parliamentary Elections in Zimbabwe,* appendix B, 68; Senator Alan Ferguson, Transcript of Delegation Press Conference, June 29, 2000, reprinted in Parliament of Australia, *Parliamentary Elections in Zimbabwe,* appendix C, 72.

17. EU Election Observation Mission, *Elections in Zimbabwe on 24–25 June 2000,* chap. 7.

18. "Anger over Zimbabwe Sanctions," *CNN.com,* February 19, 2002; "EU Observers Leave Zimbabwe," *CNN.com,* February 20, 2002; Council of the European Union, "Council Common Position of 18 February 2002 Concerning Restrictive Measures against Zimbabwe" (Brussels, February 18, 2002).

19. "Divisions Grow over Zimbabwe Poll," *BBC News,* March 14, 2002; http://news .bbc.co.uk/1/hi/world/africa/1871900.stm (reporting on OAU statement). D. K. Kadima, "African Election Observer and Monitoring Missions: Towards Best Practices and Common Standards" (conference paper, April 2003), 4 (quoting statement of South African delegation and reporting on statements of delegations from Kenya, Namibia, Tanzania and SADC). Rachel L. Swarns and Terence Neilan, "Mugabe Wins in Zimbabwe Vote, but Chorus of Criticism Grows," *New York Times,* March 13, 2002 (reporting on Nigerian statement). "Zimbabwe Poll Reaction Mixed," *CNN.com,* March 13, 2002 (reporting on Nigerian statement). Chris Alden and Philip Pank, "Zimbabwe," *Guardian Unlimited,* March 20, 2002 (reporting on Nigerian statement).

20. Rachel L. Swarns, "Officials Begin Counting Ballots in Zimbabwe," *New York Times,* March 12, 2002 (quoting Zimbabwe Election Support Network). Swarns and Neilan, "Mugabe Wins in Zimbabwe Vote" (quoting Zimbabwe Election Support Network). Kadima, "African Election Observer and Monitoring Missions," 4 (reporting on statements smaller domestic monitoring organizations). Dean Snyder and Jane Malone, "Church Leaders Decline to Endorse Zimbabwe Election Results," United Methodist News Service, March 14, 2002 (reporting on African church delegation). "Divisions Grow over Zimbabwe Poll," *BBC News* (reporting on statements of Norwegian and EU representatives). Western diplomats agreed. In Washington, U.S. secretary of state Colin Powell, citing "numerous, profound irregularities," said, "Mugabe can claim victory but not democratic legitimacy"; Swarns and Neilan, "Mugabe Wins in Zimbabwe Vote." Even before the elections in Zimbabwe in 2000 and 2002, some commentators had noted

the "paradox that the burgeoning number of international observers and monitors of elections in Africa are more inclined to endorse the results of a flawed, 'second hand' electoral process than their domestic African counterparts." Michael Cowen and Liisa Laakso, "Election Studies in Africa," *Journal of Modern African Studies* 8, no. 3 (1997): 736.

21. Commonwealth, "Preliminary Report of the Commonwealth Observer Group to the Presidential Election in Zimbabwe 9–10 March 2002" (postelection statement, Harare, March 14, 2002).

22. Duke G. Lefhoko and Elvy Mtafu, "Statement by the SADC Parliamentary Forum Election Observation Mission, Zimbabwe Presidential Elections 9–10 March 2002" (postelection statement, Harare, March 13, 2002). See Reginald Austin, "The Challenge of Election Observation: The Zimbabwean Experience," *International IDEA News,* Stockholm, June 2002; www.idea.int/newsletters/2002_06/opinion.htm.

23. Sunder Katwala and Mark Olive, "Zimbabwe and the Commonwealth," *Guardian Unlimited,* March 20, 2002; www.guardian.co.uk/theissues/article/ 0,6512,631253,00 .html. "Commonwealth Suspends Zimbabwe," *Guardian Unlimited,* March 19, 2002; www.guardian.co.uk/zimbabwe/article/0,2763,670191,00.html.

24. "G8 Africa Action Plan," July 7, 2002 (regarding pledge by African leaders). New Partnership for Africa's Development (NEPAD), "Declaration on Democracy, Political, Economic and Corporate Governance" (Durban, South Africa, July 7, 2002), para. 4, 7. Thabo Mbeki, "Launch of the African Union: Address by the Chairperson of the AU" (Durban, South Africa, July 9, 2002). Rachel L. Swarns, "African Leaders Drop Old Group for One That Has Power," *New York Times,* July 9, 2002. Rachel L. Swarns, "Role in Group Enhances Mbeki's Image," *New York Times,* July 10, 2002.

10   The Origins of Domestic Election Monitoring: NAMFREL and Its Successors

1. David Timberman, *A Changeless Land: Continuity and Change in Philippine Politics* (Manila: Bookmark, and Singapore: Institute of Southeast Asian Studies, 1991), 118. See also D. R. SarDesai, *Southeast Asia: Past and Present,* 3rd ed. (Boulder, Colo.: Westview Press, 1994), 197–98.

2. A different group with a very similar name, the National Movement for Free Elections, that was formed before the 1953 elections, also used the nickname NAMFREL. Some observers charged that this earlier NAMFREL funneled CIA funds to the presidential campaign of Ramon Magsaysay, who was elected president in 1953. Kaa Byington, *Bantay ng Bayan: Stories from the NAMFREL Crusade, 1984–1986* (Manila: Bookmark, 1988), 69; Raymond Bonner, *Waltzing with a Dictator: The Marcoses and the Making of American Policy* (New York: Random House, 1987), 40; David Wurfel, *Filipino Politics: Development and Decay* (Ithaca, N.Y.: Cornell University Press, 1988), 285.

3. National Democratic Institute for International Affairs (NDI), *Reforming the Philippine Electoral Process: Developments 1986–88* (Washington, D.C.: NDI, 1991), 45.

4. Byington, *NAMFREL Crusade,* 46–47.

5. Byington, *NAMFREL Crusade,* 60–61; Wurfel, *Filipino Politics,* 286.

6. Byington, *NAMFREL Crusade,* 66.

7. NDI, *Reforming the Philippine Electoral Process,* 47; NDI and National Citizens Movement for Free Elections (NAMFREL), *Making Every Vote Count: Nonpartisan Domestic Election Monitoring in Asia* (Washington, D.C.: NDI, 1996), 56; Carl H. Lande, "The Political Crisis," in *Crisis in the Philippines: The Marcos Era and Beyond,* ed. John Bresnan (Princeton, N.J.: Princeton University Press, 1986), 142.

8. NDI, *Reforming the Philippine Electoral Process,* 48.

9. Lewis M. Simons, *Worth Dying For* (New York: William Morrow, 1987), 247; Timberman, *Changeless Land,* 147.

10. NAMFREL, *The NAMFREL Report on the February 7, 1986, Philippine Presidential Elections* (Manila: National Citizens Movement for Free Elections, 1986), 74.

11. Simons, *Worth Dying For,* 247.

12. Wurfel, *Filipino Politics,* 299–300.

13. NAMFREL, *NAMFREL Report on the February 7, 1986, Philippine Presidential Elections,* 103. NDI, *Reforming the Philippines Electoral Process,* 48; Timberman, *Changeless Land,* 147. The official election results were based on 20.1 million votes counted, or 77 percent of registered voters, but the actual turnout was likely higher because these results appeared to significantly undercount ballots from areas with substantial opposition support and turnout in previous elections had been significantly higher. Timberman, *Changeless Land,* 147. One book reports that a CIA estimate leaked to the press claimed Aquino actually received 58 percent of the votes. Wurfel, *Filipino Politics,* 300.

14. NDI, *Reforming the Philippines Electoral Process,* 14.

15. NDI, *Reforming the Philippines Electoral Process,* 48.

16. NDI, *Reforming the Philippines Electoral Process,* 49–51.

17. NDI and NAMFREL, *Making Every Vote Count,* 59.

18. See, generally, NDI, *NDI Handbook: How Domestic Organizations Monitoring Elections, An A to Z Guide* (Washington, D.C.: NDI, 1995).

19. Seth Mydans, "Nurturing Democracy from the Grass Roots," *New York Times,* June 13, 1999.

20. Sergio Aguayo Quezada, "Electoral Observation and Democracy in Mexico," in *Electoral Observation and Democratic Transition in Latin America,* ed. Kevin J. Middlebrook (La Jolla, Calif.: Center for U.S.–Mexican Studies, University of California, San Diego, 1998); Sergio Aguayo, "A Mexican Milestone," *Journal of Democracy* 6, no. 2 (April 1995): 157–67.

21. See, generally, Neil Nevitte and Santiago A. Canton, "The Role of Domestic Observers," *Journal of Democracy* 8, no. 3 (July 1997): 53; NDI, *How Domestic Organizations Monitor Elections* (Washington, D.C.: NDI, 1995), 9; Larry Garber and Eric Bjornlund, eds., *The New Democratic Frontier: A Country-by-Country Review of Elections in Eastern and Central Europe* (Washington, D.C.: NDI, 1992).

22. NDI, *How Domestic Organizations Monitor Elections,* 11; NDI, *Promoting Participation in Yemen's 1993 Elections* (Washington, D.C.: NDI, 1994).

23. Conference on Security and Cooperation in Europe, *Document of the Copenhagen Meeting of the Conference on the Human Dimension of the CSCE* (Copenhagen, June 29, 1990), art. 8.

24. NDI, *Promoting Participation in Yemen's 1993 Elections,* 22–36, appendices 15–17.

25. U.S. Commission on Security and Cooperation in Europe, *Ukraine's Parliamentary Election, March 27 and April 10, 1994* (Washington, D.C.: U.S. Commission

on Security and Cooperation in Europe, April 1994); Organization for Security and Co-operation in Europe (OSCE) Office for Democratic Institutions and Human Rights (ODIHR) and Council of Europe Parliamentary Assembly, "International Election Observation Mission, Ukraine Presidential Election, 31 October 1999: Joint Preliminary Statement" (postelection statement, Kyiv, November 1, 1999), 2.

26. OSCE/ODIHR, *Final Report: Romanian Parliamentary and Presidential Elections, 3rd and 17th November 1996* (Warsaw: OSCE, 1996), 13; OSCE/ODIHR, "Romanian Parliamentary and Presidential Elections, 3rd November 1996" (postelection statement, Bucharest, n.d.); OSCE/ODIHR, Election Observation Mission to Slovakia 1999, "Preliminary Statement" (postelection statement, Bratislava, May 16, 1999), 3; OSCE/ODIHR, *The Slovak Republic Presidential Elections, 15 and 29 May 1999* (Warsaw: OSCE, 1999), 7, 20; OSCE/ODIHR, *Belarus Parliamentary Elections, 15 and 29 October 2000: Technical Assessment Mission Final Report* (Warsaw: OSCE, 2001), 16; OSCE/ODIHR, *Kyrgyz Republic Presidential Elections, 29 October 2000: OSCE/ODIHR Final Report* (Warsaw: OSCE, 2001), 16.

27. "Statement by Senator Paul Simon, Special Coordinator for Monitoring of the Croatian Presidential Elections," OSCE/ODIHR (postelection statement, Zagreb, June 16, 1997), par. 5; OSCE/ODIHR, Observation Delegation to the Croatian Presidential Elections 1997, "Statement: Presidential Election in the Republic of Croatia, 15 June 1997" (postelection statement, Zagreb, June 15, 1997), 3, 8–9; OSCE Election Observation Mission, "Presidential and Parliamentary Election, Republic of Serbia," (postelection statement, Belgrade, September 21, 1997), 3; OSCE/ODIHR, *Republic of Serbia, Parliamentary Election, September 21, 1997, and Presidential Election, September 21 and October 5, 1997* (Warsaw: OSCE, 1997), 8, 18; OSCE Technical Assessment Mission—Presidential Elections , Serbia, "Re-run of the Presidential Election, Republic of Serbia: Preliminary Statement," (postelection statement, Belgrade, December 7, 1997), 2; OSCE/ODIHR, *Republic of Serbia, Rerun of the Presidential Election, December 7 and December 21, 1997* (Warsaw: OSCE, 1997), 5; OSCE/ODIHR, *Republic of Armenia, Presidential Election, March 16 and 30, 1998: Final Report* (Warsaw: OSCE, 1998), 4.

28. OSCE/ODIHR, "Preliminary Statement by the Election Observation Mission to the Presidential Election of the Republic of Azerbaijan" (postelection statement, Baku, October 11, 1998), 6; OSCE/ODIHR, *Presidential Election in the Republic of Azerbaijan, 11 October 1998,* (Warsaw: OSCE, n.d.), 15; OSCE/ODIHR, *Republic of Azerbaijan Parliamentary Elections, 5 November 2000 & 7 January 2001: Final Report* (Warsaw: OSCE, 2001), 11.

29. "Statement of the National Democratic Institute (NDI) International Observer Delegation to Azerbaijan's November 5, 2000 Parliamentary Election" (postelection statement, Baku, November 7, 2000), 1.

30. OSCE Parliamentary Assembly, OSCE/ODIHR, Council of Europe, and European Parliament, "Election Observation Mission, Slovak Republic, September 1998: Joint Preliminary Statement," (postelection statement, Bratislava, September 27, 1998), 2, 3; OSCE/ODIHR, *The Slovak Republic Parliamentary Elections: 25 and 26 September 1998* (Warsaw: OSCE, n.d.), 4, 11, 27.

31. OSCE/ODIHR, *The Republic of Kazakhstan, Presidential Election, 10 January 1999: Assessment Mission* (Warsaw: OSCE, 1999), 18; OSCE Election Observation Mission to Kazakhstan, "10 October 1999, Election of Deputies to the Majilis of the Parliament: Preliminary Statement," (postelection statement, Almaty, October 11, 1999), 2.

32. OSCE/ODIHR, *Kyrgyz Republic Presidential Elections, 29 October 2000: OSCE/ODIHR Final Report* (Warsaw: OSCE, 2001), 11; OSCE/ODIHR, *Election Obser-*

vation Mission Kyrgyz Republic Presidential Elections, 29 October 2000, (Warsaw: OSCE, 2001, 1; Hrair Balian, "Ten Years of International Election Assistance and Observation" (article, OSCE Office of Democracy and International Human Rights, Warsaw, 2001), 9.

33. OSCE/ODIHR, *Republic of Belarus Presidential Election, 9 September 2001, OSCE/ODIHR Limited Election Observation Mission Final Report* (revised) (Warsaw: OSCE, 2001), section 10. Presidential Directive No. 8, cited in Ben Nighthorse Campbell, chair, U.S. Commission on Security and Cooperation in Europe, "Democracy Under Siege in Belarus" (statement, May 10, 2001), available at www.usis.minsk.by/html/nighthorse_siege.html; Josiah B. Rosenblatt, Charge d'Affaires, U.S. Mission to OSCE, "Statement on Belarus" (statement, Vienna, May 24, 2001), available at www.usis.minsk.by/html/rosenblatt_amg.html.

34. NDI, *Promoting Participation in Yemen's 1993 Elections,* 22–36, appendices 15–17.

35. Jimmy Carter and others to Vladimir Meciar, premier, Slovak Republic (letter, September 22, 1998).

36. "Israeli—Palestinian Interim Agreement on the West Bank and Gaza Strip," annex II, Protocol Concerning Elections (Washington, September 28, 1995), art. V, sec. 11, and appendix 2, part B; Palestinian Election Law, 1995, art. 103, sec. 1; Peter Hatch, ODIHR representative, "Romanian Local Elections, 2nd and 16th June 1996" (report, n.d.), 24; OSCE/ODIHR, *Republic of Croatia Extraordinary Presidential Elections, 24 January and 7 February 2000: Final Report* (Warsaw: OSCE, May 31, 2000), 14.

37. Author's notes, Coordination Meeting at European Commission, Brussels, October 18, 1995.

38. "Human Rights Questions Including Alternative Approaches for Improving the Effective Enjoyment of Human Rights and Fundamental Freedoms: Enhancing the Effectiveness of the Principle of Periodic and Genuine Elections," Report of the Secretary General, A/49/675 (November 17, 1994), paragraphs 26–28 (regarding UN support for domestic election monitors in Mexico); "Support by the United Nations System of the Efforts of Governments to Promote and Consolidate New or Restored Democracies," Report of the Secretary General, A/52/513 (October 21, 1997), para. 21 (regarding UN support for domestic election monitoring); Administration and Cost of Elections Project, "National Election Observation," www.aceproject.org/main/english/ei/eig03.htm; Commission of the European Communities, "Communication on EU Election Assistance and Observation" (report, Brussels, April 11, 2000), 15–16; Amanda Sives, "Adding Value to the Commonwealth Democracy Programme: A CPSU Submission to the High Level Review Group" (evaluation paper, Institute of Commonwealth Studies, London, n.d.), 5.

39. Gerard Stoudman, remarks at International Conference on Election Monitoring, Organization for Security and Cooperation in Europe, Warsaw, May 29, 2001 (author's notes).

11 Domestic Election Monitoring as an End and a Means

1. International Institute for Democracy and Electoral Assistance (International IDEA), *Lessons Learnt from International Observation* (Stockholm: International IDEA, 1995) 9.

2. Robert A. Pastor, "Comment: Mediating Elections," *Journal of Democracy* 9, no. 1 (January 1998): 158.

3. National Democratic Institute for International Affairs (NDI), *Asia Monitoring Network Conference: Cambodian Election Monitoring Organizations, Lessons Learned and Future Directions* (Washington, D.C.: NDI, 1999), 15. See also Feroz Hassan, "Recruitment," in *Good Practice Guidelines for Commonwealth Domestic Observer Groups,* ed. Amanda Sives (London: Commonwealth Policy Studies Unit, 2002).

4. "Sample Pledge," in *Good Practice Guidelines for Commonwealth Domestic Observer Groups,* ed. Sives, 94.

5. NDI and National Citizens Movement for Free Elections (NAMFREL), *Making Every Vote Count: Domestic Election Monitoring in Asia* (Washington, D.C.: NDI, 1996), 66.

6. R. van Dijk, "Secret Worlds, Democratization and Election Observation in Malawi," in *Election Observation and Democratization in Africa,* ed. Jon Abbink and Gerti Hesseling (New York: St. Martin's Press, 2000), 205.

7. Stefan Mair, "International Election Observation: One Form of Democratization Assistance" (report, Stiftung Wissenschaft und Politik, Research Institute for International Politics and Security, Bonn, April/July, 1994), 13.

8. Hrair Balian, "Ten Years of International Election Assistance and Observation" (article, OSCE Office of Democracy and International Human Rights, Warsaw, 2001), 4.

9. Anders Erikson, ed., *Handbook for European Union Election Observation Missions* (Stockholm: Swedish International Development Cooperation Agency, 2002), 47.

10. Mair, "International Election Observation," 29–30.

11. Balian, "Ten Years of International Election Assistance and Observation," 9.

12. Erikson, *Handbook for European Union Election Observation Missions,* 47. See also Mair, *International Election Observation,* 19.

13. Hassan, "Recruitment."

14. See Eric Bjornlund, Michael Bratton, and Clark Gibson, "Observing Multiparty Elections in Africa: Lessons from Zambia," *African Affairs* 91 (1992): 405–31; and NDI, *The October 31, 1991 National Elections in Zambia* (Washington, D.C.: NDI, 1992).

15. See Bjornlund, Bratton, and Gibson, "Observing Multiparty Elections in Africa"; and Bard Anders Andreasson, Gisela Giesler, and Arne Tostensen, *Setting a Standard for Africa? Lessons from the 1991 Zambian Elections* (Oslo: Fantoft-Bergen, Christian Michelsen Institute, 1992), 76.

16. Roger Cohen, "Who Really Brought Down Milosevic?" *New York Times Magazine,* November 26, 2000, 44.

17. Thomas Carothers, *Ousting Foreign Strongmen: Lessons from Serbia,* Policy Brief (Washington, D.C.: Carnegie Endowment for International Peace, 2001), 4.

18. Wimal Fernando, quoted in NDI and NAMFREL, *Making Every Vote Count,* 26.

19. Cohen, "Who Really Brought Down Milosevic?" 148.

12   Foreign Support for Domestic Election Monitoring in Indonesia: Missed Opportunities and Unintended Consequences

1. United Nations Development Program (UNDP), *Transition to Democracy: Report on the UNDP Technical Assistance Programme for the 1999 Indonesian General Elections* (Jakarta: UNDP, 1999) (hereafter *UNDP Indonesia Report*), 17.

2. National Democratic Institute for International Affairs, "The May 29, 1997 Parliamentary Elections in Indonesia: A Background Paper" (unpublished paper, May 23, 1997), 9.

3. "Citizens Organize Themselves," *Inside Indonesia,* July–September 1997.

4. These groups included the prominent environmental group WAHLI (Wahana Lingkungan Hidup Indonesia or Indonesian Forum for the Environment), NGO forum YAPPIKA (Yayasan Penguatan Partisipasi, Inisiatif dan Kemitraan Masyarakat Indonesia), the independent labor organization SBSI (Serikat Buruh Sejahtera Indonesia, or Indonesian Prosperous Trade Union), and the newly formed JAMPPI (Jaringan Masyarakat Pemantau Pemilu Indonesia or Community Network of Indonesian Election Monitors).

5. *UNDP Indonesia Report,* 67.

6. *UNDP Indonesia Report,* exhibit 6.5, 70.

7. *UNDP Indonesia Report,* exhibit 6.5, 70.

8. "UNFREL's Press Release," June 7, 1999; Agence France-Presse, June 18; *UNDP Indonesia Report,* exhibit. 6.5, 70.

9. "UNDP to Assist Three Poll Watch Networks," *Jakarta Post,* March 2, 1999, 2.

10. "Poll Watchdogs 'Lacking Coordination,'" *Jakarta Post,* March 17, 1999, 2.

11. "Setting Aside $2.5 for Citizens' Way to Democracy," *Jakarta Post,* March 25, 1999; "24 organizations Receive UNDP Funds for Elections," *Jakarta Post,* April 9, 1999.

12. *UNDP Indonesia Report,* exhibit 2.2, 18; cf. "Donor Collaboration," *UNDP Website for the 1999 Indonesian Parliamentary Election,* June 18, 1999; www.un.or.id/ge/.

13. Edith Hartanto, "Election Monitoring Has Become a Commodity," *Jakarta Post,* April 18, 1999.

14. *UNDP Indonesia Report,* 67. See also UNDP Presentation, June 12, 1999; www.undp.or.id/statements/presentations/19990612_undp_indonesia.pdf, slide 15.

15. U.S. Agency for International Development, Grant 497-G-00-99-00014-00, 6; Letter of Agreement between the Asia Foundation and KIPP (n.d.).

16. John Gwyn Morgan, head of EU Observer Unit / EU executive coordinator, "Indonesian Elections: 7 June 1999" (postelection statement, Jakarta, n.d.), 1; "EU Preparing US $7.6 Million Package for RI," Antara News Agency, March 30, 1999.

17. Commission of the European Communities, "Communication on EU Election Assistance and Observation" (report, Brussels, April 11, 2000), 10.

18. Calculated from data provided in *UNDP Indonesia Report,* exhibit 2.2, 18.

19. *UNDP Indonesia Report,* 19.

20. *UNDP Indonesia Report,* 67.

21. Interview with Rectors' Forum staff, Medan, Institute Sains dan Teknologie Pardede, June 14, 1999.

22. Lina Widjaya, University Network for Free Election-Depok (letter, March 17, 1999), 3.

23. *UNDP Indonesia Report,* 66–67.

24. *UNDP Indonesia Report,* 66.

25. *UNDP Indonesia Report,* 71; National Democratic Institute for International Affairs, "UNDP Election Facilitation Center for the Indonesian Election: June 1999 Final Report" (report to UNDP, June 11, 1999), appendix 5.

26. Morgan, head of EU Observer Unit, "Indonesian Elections: 7 June 1999," 4.

27. Peter Symonds, "Indonesian Elections: An Overwhelming Vote against the Ruling Golkar Party," World Socialist Web site, June 12, 1999; "Stop Whingeing and Welcome Democracy, Australia Tells Indonesians," *Agence France Press,* June 11, 1999.

28. Keith B. Richburg, "Long-Dominant Party Faces Defeat In Indonesian Vote," *Washington Post,* Wednesday, June 9, 1999.

29. "Megawati Sets Up Early Lead, But Golkar Still There," Australian Broadcasting Corporation News, June 8, 1999; www.abc.net.au/ra/asiapac/archive/1999/jun/raap-8jun1999-4.htm.

30. T. Mulya Lubis, "Open Letter to President Jimmy Carter," University Network for Free and Fair Elections (delivered on June 9, 1999).

31. Seth Mydans, "Delays in Vote Count Have Indonesians Worried about Cheating," *New York Times,* June 10, 1999.

13   Verifying the Vote Count: Quick Counts, Parallel Tabulations, and Exit Polls in Macedonia and Indonesia

1. Tom Stoppard, *Jumpers* (New York: Grove Press, 1972).

2. Jimmy Carter, interview with the author, July 16, 2003.

3. Larry Garber and Glenn Cowan, "The Virtues of Parallel Vote Tabulations," *Journal of Democracy* 4, no. 2 (April 1993): 95–96.

4. Even though experts from the National Democratic Institute for International Affairs (NDI) invented and named PVTs, NDI itself used the term "quick count" in its handbook. Melissa Estok, Neil Nevitte, and Glenn Cowan, *The Quick Count and Election Observation: An NDI Handbook for Civic Organizations and Political Parties* (Washington, D.C.: NDI, 2002).

5. Michael Dobbs, "U.S. Advice Guided Milosevic Opposition," *Washington Post,* December 11, 2000, A1.

6. Sarah E. Mendelson, "Democracy Assistance and Political Transition in Russia," *International Security* 25, no. 4 (spring 2001): 85.

7. Glenn Cowan and Larry Garber advised the Organization of American States on the design and implementation of the parallel vote tabulation.

8. International Republican Institute (IRI), "IRI Sponsored First-Ever Exit Poll in Macedonia Shows SDSM Coalition Leading" (press release, September 16, 2002).

9. Election Law of Macedonia, Official Gazette of the Republic of Macedonia, no. 42/2002, published June 25, 2002, art. 3(2) (unofficial translation by International Foundation for Election Systems).

10. IRI, "Statement: Observation Mission to the 2002 Macedonia Parliamentary Elections" (election statement, September 16, 2002).

11. Williams and Associates, "Exit Poll Analysis: Republic of Macedonia 2002 Parliamentary Elections" (report posted on IRI Web site, November 2002), 4; available at www.iri.org/pdfs/MK_Exit_Poll.pdf. To use the official results to validate the effectiveness of an exit poll, quick count or PVT is arguably circular, because it implicitly presumes that the official results were reported accurately, which is exactly what the verification exercise is intended to determine. If there were significant manipulation of the actual tabulation, it would not track a well-executed exit poll or PVT. In the absence of

any external reason to doubt the official results, the exit poll or PVT results and the actual results can be mutually reinforcing.

12. Jimmy Carter, interview with the author, July 16, 2003.

13. Jimmy Carter, interview with the author, July 16, 2003.

14. "Indonesian Election Results at 0045 GMT," Reuters, June 8, 1999.

15. "Indonesian Election Results at 1715 GMT," Reuters, June 10, 1999.

16. Seth Mydans, "Delays in Vote Count Have Indonesians Worried About Cheating," *New York Times,* June 10, 1999.

17. Hank Valentino, "Joint Operations Media Center Opening Remarks" (May 18, 1999).

18. Ravi Rajan, "Statement by Mr. Ravi Rajan, UNDP Resident Representative, on the Occasion of the Official Opening of the Joint Operations and Media Center" (May 18, 1999).

19. Agence France-Presse, "Initial Indonesian Poll Results to Arrive within Hours," June 4, 1999

20. "Media Center's $80 Million [*sic*] Counting System," *Jakarta Post,* June 9, 1999.

21. "Indonesian Military Calls for Patience as Vote Count Drags On," *CNN.com,* June 9, 1999.

22. Lindsay Murdoch, "Golkar Votes Grow as Count Slows," *Sydney Morning Herald,* June 10, 1999; Raphael Pura and Richard Borsuk, "Indonesia's Election Chief Says Final Tally Could Take 2 Weeks," *Wall Street Journal,* June 11, 1999.

23. Garber and Cowan, "Virtues of Parallel Vote Tabulations," 99. In Indonesia, following NAMFREL's terminology, the comprehensive independent tabulation was known as the "quick count" and the sample-based verification conducted by NDI and the Rectors' Forum was known as the "PVT." This was anomalous, given that a comprehensive tabulation invariably would be slower than one based on samples. In other countries, the term "quick count" has referred to any independent vote tabulation used to collect information quickly in order to project the outcome of elections (or, at times, for the purposed verification after the fact as well), even when based on statistical sampling.

Concepción's first trip before the 1999 elections was at the invitation of NDI, which is ironic given NDI's disagreement with his subsequent advice. In January, before the PVT debate was fully joined, NDI also brought NAMFREL's executive director, Telibert Laoc, to Indonesia to advise Indonesian monitoring groups. The UNDP declined to fund a proposed, major NAMFREL international monitoring program in Indonesia, but NAMFREL did have a presence in Indonesia for the elections.

24. In 1999, Indonesia had twenty-seven provinces, including East Timor. In January 1999, the government agreed to hold a referendum in East Timor on independence, which took place on August 30. Although East Timor was still part of Indonesia at the time of the elections in June, there was relatively little interest in national elections in the province as many were looking ahead to the referendum.

25. In addition to only collecting results from sample locations, PVT organizers chose to collect and analyze data only for the fifteen parties they judged to have any significant amount of support. They were correct that the other parties would not garner significant numbers of votes, but it was actually these very small parties that complained the loudest after the election and that irresponsibly used their positions on the election commission to hold up the final certification of the results. The PVT, for all its technical success, could not specifically address the results for, or claims of fraud by, any of the parties beyond the fifteen for which it had collected results.

26. The PVT's designers actually used villages (or their urban equivalents), rather than polling stations, as the main sample unit because information about the number and location of polling stations would not be available until just before election day. In contrast, information about population and location of villages was available. First, they weighted villages according to population. Thus, a village ten times larger in population than another would be ten times as likely to be selected for the PVT sample. Then, they used a second round of random sampling to select polling stations within this random selection of villages. The vote count at these randomly selected, representative locations would provide the raw data for the PVT. This process of double random sampling ensured that every voter had an equal chance of being included in the sample.

27. The "confidence interval" was 95 percent. That is, one could be 95 percent certain that the actual results would be within 1.5 percentage points either way of the results found by the survey.

28. Originally, the Rectors' Forum intended to gather data first at the provincial level, using computers in 310 districts nationwide, and then to pass along the data electronically to a national data center. When the donor community declined to fund the Rectors' Forum's request for the elaborate, costly infrastructure of computers and communication equipment necessary for a district-based collection system, Rectors' Forum adjusted its plans to have all results come directly to a national call-in center.

29. Rectors' Forum press release, June 10, 1999.

30. See, for example, Agence France-Presse, "Latest Indonesian Election Vote Count," June 10, 1999; Reuters, "Indonesian Election Results at 1715 GMT," June 10, 1999.

31. Similarly, it did not matter to the outcome of the 2000 U.S. presidential race that Al Gore outpolled George W. Bush nationally, because a U.S. presidential election is actually fifty-one separate, mostly winner-take-all elections in each of the states and the District of Columbia. This principle—that national aggregate vote tallies are not decisive—is even more true for legislative elections, as in Indonesia. The aggregate number of votes nationally for Democrats and Republicans running for Congress tells nothing about how many seats each party has won.

32. Rectors' Forum press release, June 18, 1999.

33. "Poll Watchers Dispatched to Observe Data Entry," *Jakarta Post,* June 12, 1999.

34. NDI–Carter Center Post-Election Statement (July 15, 1999), 2. The report acknowledged that there were "undoubtedly some examples of localized manipulation of the counting and tabulation," but it concluded that such manipulation could not have altered the results of any races without being detected.

35. These included the international community's JOMC, the election commission's own separate "bank system," the Rectors' Forum PVT, the tabulation of the state news agency Antara, and the Independent Election Monitoring Committee (KIPP). Not all those sources had tabulated results for all provinces; KIPP had collected meaningful comprehensive results only for Jakarta. As is discussed above, each of these independent tabulations drew its data from tabulations done at different levels of election administration.

36. NDI–Carter Center Post-Election Statement (July 15, 1999), 2. The statement also discounted the possibility of large numbers of "ghost" polling stations (i.e., polling stations that never existed in reality but which were allegedly added to the tabulation), although it criticized deficiencies in the distribution of ballot papers and called for the authorities to investigate discrepancies with respect to the number of ballots used in provincial tabulations.

14 Toward More Meaningful International Election Monitoring

1. Kofi Annan, "Closing Remarks to the Ministerial" (speech to Community of Democracies, Warsaw, June 27, 2000), 2.

2. United Nations Development Program, *Human Development Report 2002: Deepening Democracy in a Fragmented World* (New York: Oxford University Press, 2002), 10.

Index

Italic *t* following page numbers indicates tables.